“JUST AS IN THE TIME OF THE APOSTLES”

"JUST AS IN THE TIME OF THE APOSTLES"

USES OF HISTORY IN THE RADICAL REFORMATION

GEOFFREY DIPPLE

National Library of Canada Cataloguing in Publication

Dipple, Geoffrey Luke, 1960-
"Just as in the time of the Apostles": uses of history in the Radical Reformation / Geoffrey Dipple.

Includes bibliographical references and index.
ISBN 1-894710-58-4

1. Reformation. 2. Church history--Primitive and early church, ca. 30-600--Historiography. I. Title.

BR307.D56 2005 270.6 C2005-905204-X

"Just as in the time of the Apostles"

33 Kent Avenue
Kitchener, Ontario, N2G 3R2
www.pandorapress.com

International Standard Book Number: 1-894710-58-4
Printed in Canada on acid-free paper.
Cover and book design by Clifford Snyder

The cover illustration is a woodcut found in the 1531 edition of the Froschauer Bible, printed in Zurich. It was coloured by persons unknown. Courtesy of Conrad Grebel University College, rare book collection.

10 09 08 07 06 05 12 11 10 9 8 7 6 5 4 3 2 1

Geschichte treiben heißt Brücken zwischen
Vergangenheit und Gegenwart schlagen
und beide Ufer beobachten und
an beiden tätig werden.

Bernhard Schlink, Der Vorleser

TABLE OF CONTENTS

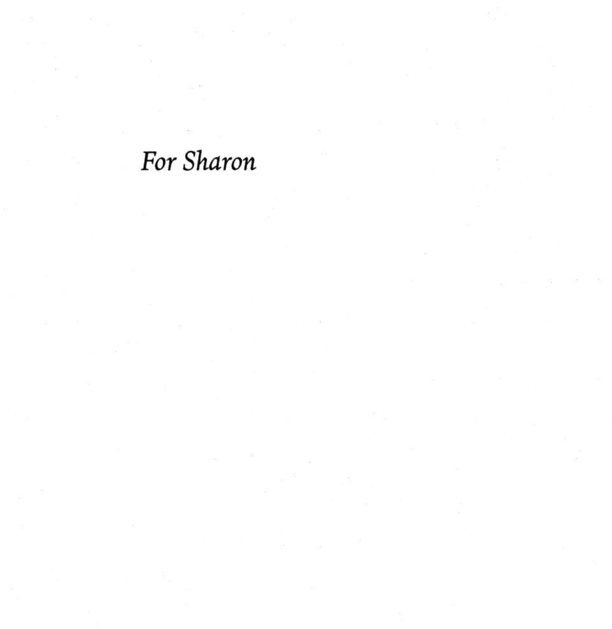

For Sharon

ACKNOWLEDGEMENTS

Research for this project was supported in part through grants from the Augustana Research and Artist Fund. Much of that research would have been considerably more difficult without the assistance of staff members at Mikkelsen Library at Augustana College and the Kaiser-Ramaker Library at the North American Baptist Seminary in Sioux Falls. Special thanks are due to Becky Folkerts in the interlibrary loan department at the Mikkelsen Library for her tireless efforts in obtaining sources not readily available in South Dakota. Further research was conducted at the Centre for Reformation and Renaissance Studies, Victoria University in the University of Toronto and at the Mennonite Historical Library in Goshen Indiana. I am indebted to numerous individuals at both of those institutions.

Much of the material contained in this study first saw the light of day as conference papers presented at the Anabaptist Colloquium, the Sixteenth Century Studies Conference and St. Andrews University. Discussions of the papers at all three venues were invaluable for the further development of my thought on this topic. James Stayer, John Roth and Arnold Snyder all read drafts of this work at various stages of its completion and shared their responses to it with me. I am grateful for their comments and the book is much better as a result of their input than it would have been without it. Thanks are also due to Ray and Judy Lindberg for helping to keep me rooted in the reality of here and now as I tried to write history about people writing history. Finally, this project would never have been completed without the constant support of Sharon Judd, my partner in every sense of the term. This book is dedicated to her.

ABBREVIATIONS

Allen *Opus epistularum Des. Erasmi Roterodami*. 11 vols. Allen, P.S.; Allen, H.M.; and Garrod, H.W. eds. Oxford: Clarendon Press, 1906-1958.

ARG *Archiv für Reformationsgeschichte*

Barge Barge, Hermann. *Andreas Bodenstein von Karlstadt*, vol. 1: *Karlstadt und die Anfänge der Reformation*. Leipzig: Friedrich Brandstetter, 1905. Vol. 2: *Karlstadt als Vorkämpfer des laienchristlichen Puritanismus*. Leipzig: Friedrich Brandstetter, 1905.

Baylor, *Revelation and Revolution*
Baylor, Michael. ed. and trans. *Revelation and Revolution: Basic Writings of Thomas Müntzer*. Bethlehem, PA: Lehigh University Press, 1993.

CS *Corpus Schwenckfeldianorum*. 19 vols. Hatranft, Chester D.; Johnson, Elmer E.S.; and Schultz, Selina Gerhard; eds. Leipzig & Pennsburg, 1907-1961.

CWMS Verduin, Leonard. trans. and Wenger, John C. ed. *The Complete Writings of Menno Simons c. 1496-1561*. Scottdale, PA: Herald Press, 1956.

Franck, *Chronica*
Franck, Sebastian. *Chronica, Zeitbuch unnd Geschichtsbibel*. Ulm, 1536; photoreprint ed., Darmstadt: Wissenschaftliche Buchgesellschaft, 1969.

Franck, *Werke*

Franck, Sebastian. *Sämtliche Werke*, Vol. 1: *Frühe Schriften*. Krauer, Peter Klaus. ed. Berlin: Peter Lang, 1993.

Köhler Köhler, Hans-Joachim; et al. *Early Modern Pamphlets: Sixteenth-Century German and Latin 1501-1530*. Leiden: IDC, 1980ff.

Kolb Philips, Dietrich. *Enchiridion or Handbook of the Christian Doctrine and Religion compiled (by the grace of God) from the Holy Scriptures for the benefit of all lovers of the Truth*. Kolb, A.B. trans. Berne: Light and Hope, 1958.

Laube Laube, Adolf; Schneider, Annerose; and Weiß, Ulman. eds. *Flugschriften vom Bauernkrieg zum Täuferreich (1526-1535)*. 2 vols. Berlin: Akademie Verlag, 1992.

LB *Desiderii Erasmi Roterdami opera omnia*. Leclerc, Jean. ed. 10 vols. Leiden, 1703-1706; reprint ed. 1961-1962.

MQR *Mennonite Quarterly Review*

MSB *Thomas Müntzer. Schriften und Briefe: Kritische Gesamtausgabe*. Gütersloh: Gütersloher Verlagshaus Gerd Mohn, 1968.

Matheson, *Collected Works*

Matheson, Peter. ed. and trans. *The Collected Works of Thomas Müntzer*. Edinburgh: T&T Clark, 1988.

***QGT* 6** *Hans Denck: Schriften*. 3 vols. Baring, Georg and Fellmann, Walter. eds. *Quellen zur Geschichte der Täufer*, vol. 6. Gütersloh: C. Bertelsmann Verlag, 1955-1960.

***QGT* 7** Krebs, Manfred; Rott, Hans Georg. eds. *Quellen zur Geschichte der Täufer*. Vol. 7: *Elsaß, 1. Teil: Stadt Straßburg 1522-1532*. Gütersloh: Gerd Mohn, 1959.

***QGT* 9** Hubmaier, Balthasar. *Schriften*. Westin, Gunnar and Bergsten, Torsten. eds. *Quellen zur Geschichte der Täufer*, vol. 9. Gütersloh: Gütersloher Verlagshaus Gerd Mohn, 1962.

QGT 12 Friedmann, Robert. ed. *Glaubenszeugnisse oberdeutscher Taufgesinnter II. Quellen zur Geschichte der Täufer*. Vol. 12. Gütersloh: Gerd Mohn, 1967.

QGTS 1 Muralt, Leonhard von and Schmid, Walter. eds. *Quellen zur Geschichte der Täufer in der Schweiz*. Vol. 1: *Zurich*. Zurich: S. Hirzel Verlag, 1952.

QGTS 2 Fast, Heinold. ed. *Quellen zur Geschichte der Täufer in der Schweiz*, Vol. 2: *Ostschweiz*. Zurich: Theologischer Verlag, 1973.

SAW Williams, George H. and Mergal, Angel M. eds and trans. *Spiritualist and Anabaptist Writers: Documents Illustrative of the Radical Reformation*. Philadelphia: Westminster Press, 1957.

SBR *Die Schriften Bernhard Rothmanns*. Stupperich, Robert. ed. Münster: Aschendorffsche Verlagsbuchhandlung, 1970.

SCJ *Sixteenth Century Journal*

TRE *Theologische Realenzyklopädie*. Berlin and New York: Walter de Gruyter, 2001.

WA *D. Martin Luthers Werke: Kritische Gesamtausgabe*. 63 vols. Weimar: Böhlau, 1883-1983.

WABr *D. Martin Luthers Werke: Kritische Gesamtausgabe: Briefwechsel*. 18 vols. Weimar: Böhlau, 1930-1985.

WDP Dyck, Cornelius J.; Keeney, William E.; and Beachy, Alvin J. eds. and trans. *The Writings of Dirk Philips, 1504-1568*. Scottdale, PA and Waterloo, ON: Herald Press, 1992.

WPM Klassen, William, Klaassen, Walter, eds and trans. *The Writings of Pilgram Marpeck*. Scottdale, PA and Kitchener, ON: Herald Press, 1978.

ZKG *Zeitschrift für Kirchengeschichte*

ZW *Huldrych Zwingli sämtliche Werke*. Egli, Emil; Finsler, Georg; Köhler, Walther; Farner, Oscar; Blanke, Fritz; Muralt, Leonard von; Künzli, Edwin; and Pfister, Rudolph. eds. Leipzig: Hensius, 1911-1935

INTRODUCTION

For it is certain that a single monk must err if he stands against the opinion of all Christendom. Otherwise Christendom itself would have erred for more than a thousand years.[1]

This statement, ascribed to Charles V, sums up succinctly the challenge faced by would-be religious reformers of the sixteenth century. If the traditional church was the false church as they claimed, where had the true church been – the one with whom Christ had promised to remain throughout the ages – for much of Christian history? This challenge threw the Reformers back onto arguments from history to justify their reforming programmes, thereby reinforcing the established veneration of tradition and suspicion of novelty central to the medieval and Renaissance thought world. Not surprisingly, then, history was "a vital, omnipresent force" during the Reformation, as Irena Backus has claimed.[2]

Appeals to history were no less important in the agendas of Reformation radicals than they were in the programmes of their counterparts in the magisterial Reformation. Discussion of the nature and place of historical visions in the Radical Reformation has been dominated for the last half century by the interpretation of Franklin H. Littell. Littell regarded historical reflection as a crucial component of the enterprises of Reformation radicals. The radicals, he argued, shared in the general primitivism of the age. However, in their uncompromising desire to restore and follow the model of the primitive church of the apostles in their own chruches they went beyond their counterparts among the Renaissance humanists and the magisterial Reformers. Of the groups in the Radical Reformation, the Anabaptists in particular were committed to a thoroughgoing restitution of the primitive church which distinguishesd their vision from the reforming agendas of many of their contemporaries.[3]

The present study revisits some of the central assumptions and conclusions of Littell's thesis. In doing so, it focuses both on the details of historical visions formulated by radical Reformers, and on the uses to which those visions were put. It looks, then, not only at the content of those visions, but also at the role they played in the reforming plans of the groups and individuals involved. In the process it attempts to answer some fundamental questions about the historical reflection of the Reformation radicals and its relationship to the supposed primitivism of the age.

- Was there a common perception of ecclesiastical history among the Reformation radicals? If so, was it distinct from the historical reflection of the humanists and magisterial Reformers as Littell claims?
- Did different groups use the past in different ways during the age of reform?
- Were there variations in the visions and uses of the past between different groups in the Radical Reformation?
- What relationships existed between the formulation of historical visions and the interaction between different reforming parties?

To answer these questions we will remain attentive to subtle variations and changes in the historical visions involved. The views of history we examine here will not be treated as static visions, but as evolving perceptions that interacted with the lived experiences of the individuals who reconstructed them.

Franklin Littell identified the thought of the Renaissance humanists and the magisterial Reformers as two sources of primitivist thinking underlying the Radical Reformation's approach to ecclesiastical history. Chapter one of this study will look at historical references in the writings of representatives of these two groups. With their calls for the return to the sources of the classical world and primitive church, the humanists are natural candidates for promoters of the age's primitivist mood. When discussing the humanists Littell focused his attention especially on Erasmus,[4] and the thought of the "prince of the humanists" is a valuable starting point for an assessment of the primitivism of the age. Erasmus frequently made comments suggesting that he believed that the church had deteriorated from an earlier, pristine state. However, the extent to which these statements indicate that he identified a past age of the church as its golden age, as Littell's language about primitivism would suggest, is questionable. Recent studies of Erasmus' thought indicate that his understanding of the church's history was more nuanced than simply a direct comparison of the contemporary institution with an idealized vision of its origins. Also at issue is the question of the relationship between Erasmus' perception of ecclesiastical history and his criticism of contemporary abuses in the church, especially those he associated with scholasticism. Recent research suggests that in Erasmus' thought the primitive church served more as a mirror to reflect contemporary problems than as a model dictating the details of a reform agenda.[5]

Erasmus was hardly the only humanist reformer to develop a vision of ecclesiastical history. Not surprisingly, this was a common tactic among humanist critics of abuses in the church. Many of these visions took as important starting points statements of Erasmus, and they often paralleled his vision in important ways. However, these common elements also allowed room for distinctive emphases and developments in the historical visions of individual humanists. These variations on a common theme began to take on increasing importance after the humanists began choosing sides over the Luther issue. The common humanist historical vision allowed sufficient flexibility that its adherents could still return to the fold of the church, although this move often accompanied a softening of some of the criticisms of the contemporary church, or it could be used as a springboard into the abyss of more radical opposition to the church. These trends are evident in the writings of two of the more prominent German humanists and writers of history: Beatus Rhenanus and Ulrich von Hutten. Like Erasmus, both men developed sophisticated schemes of ecclesiastical history as backdrops to their criticisms of scholasticism and other contemporary abuses in the church. But faced with a split in Christendom, they chose different paths: Rhenanus returned to the church while Hutten threw in his lot with the Reformers and ultimately the enterprise of Franz von Sickingen. In both cases, however, historical research and argumentation appear as important auxiliaries in the further development of their reforming visions. They also serve as a useful barometer in assessing the response of humanist reformers to the Luther issue.

Noting the relationship between historical reflection and the creation of a Protestant identity, Bruce Gordon has commented:

> All issues of reform, whether medieval or early modern, hinged on a historical argument whose logic held that through the course of human history the church had repeatedly fallen away from the intentions of its founder and was in need of correction.

Gordon continues that while pre-Reformation reform movements looked to a restoration of the church through a reaffirmation of existing laws and institutions the Reformers, initially at least, discarded this approach. Instead, they looked to the Bible as the source of their history and identity.[6] However, despite the Reformation's radical rejection of tradition implied in the appeal to *sola scriptura*, we see even in the early writings of the Reformers serious reflection on the history of the post-apostolic church. As is the case with humanist reformers, those historical reflections are tightly woven into the fabric of their reforming programmes and agendas. In that sense the Reformers shared in the primitivism identified by Littell as an important characteristic of the age, and the approach of the magisterial Reformers was not fundamentally different from that of the humanist reformers. Interestingly, this observation is as accurate for the vision of Ulrich Zwingli, whose reforming thought is recognized as growing out of the Christian Renaissance of the Erasmian humanist tradition, as for that of Luther, whose reform is thought to have originated in a completely different thought world. Rather than simply setting the primitive church over against the contemporary, as their rhetoric would imply, both turned to Christian history to justify and deepen criticisms of specific abuses and teachings in the church, and to circumvent traditional authority structures defending those teachings and traditions. As we will see, this strategy was highly adaptable, and as their criticisms of the church around them became more radical, the Reformers looked further back into its history for the sources of the abuses they opposed and for the fall of the institutional church which those abuses manifested.

According to Littell's thesis, historical reflection among the Reformation radicals developed from a different starting point and took on different contours than did historical reflection among the humanists and magisterial Reformers. Their more thoroughgoing primitivism implied that the apostolic church became a normative model for their reforming visions in a way that it wasn't for their more "respectable" contemporaries. Although he posited a general distinction between the magisterial and the radical Reformations, Littell did not regard the latter as a unified phenomenon with a homogeneous historical vision. Instead, he treated the historical utterances of the various groups and individuals in the Radical Reformation as variations on a common theme.[7]

Distinctions within the Radical Reformation have long been understood in terms of the different typologies of religious movements derived from the sociology of religion. Particularly important have been Max Weber's distinction between church and sect types of religious movements, and especially Ernst Troeltsch's differentiation between sect and spiritualist types. According to Troeltsch, the roots for both the sect and spiritualist types were laid alongside those of the church type in the age of primitive Christianity. The sectarian tradition, and Troeltsch claims to be using the term in a non-pejorative sense, with its closed, voluntary membership and tightly knit organization, stood in opposition to the dominant church type throughout the Middle Ages. The coming of the Reformation witnessed the continued vitality of the sect type, and Anabaptism, with its emphasis on believers' baptism as the basis for the establishment of a gathered church, qualifies as the first manifestation of Protestant sectarianism. Troeltsch further distinguished between sectarians and Spiritualists in the Radical Reformation. These he described as two fundamentally distinct movements, "... separate streams, which only mingle their waters now and again, but which historically vary greatly in their sources and their development." In contrast to the essentially corporate orientation of the sect type, the Spiritualists were fundamentally individualistic.[8]

The characteristics identified with these sociological types have had a significant impact on how historians have understood the approach to history by their adherents. According to Troeltsch, the sectarians' vision of themselves as a community ruled by Christ led to an emphasis on the law of Christ, external organization and ceremonies, and an identification with the church of the Gospel and of primitive Christianity.[9] By way of contrast, he described the Spiritualists as the "highest and noblest" expression of Protestant mysticism. Defining mysticism as "... the insistence upon a direct inward and present religious experience," he maintained that the mystics, and along with them the Spiritualists, were independent of and took for granted the historical and objective forms of religious life: worship, ritual, myth and dogma. As a result, Spiritualists were intensely individualistic, and religious organizations existed for them merely as "intimate circles for edification" not embodiments of the true church. A mere means of stimulation for the Spiritualists, the historic element in religion was often swept away in a movement that tended to become "nonhistorical, formless, and purely individualistic."[10] Troeltsch's types, and his characterizations of them, have carried over into a long and rich tradition of interpreting the Radical Reformation. Included in that tradition is Littell's distinction between the historical visions of the Anabaptists and the Spiritualists.[11]

Troeltsch's characterizations have not gone unchallenged. Historians have paid serious attention to the criticism of his contemporary rival, Karl Holl, that Troeltsch's ideal types do more to obscure the historical relations between groups in the Radical Reformation than they illuminate them.[12] Prominent among criticisms of Troeltsch's categories is Walter Klaassen's challenge to the very existence of a distinct Spiritualist movement in the Reformation. Klaassen describes spiritualism not as a grouping in the Reformation, but as an underlying principle opposing the externalization of religion, which appears in varying degrees of intensity throughout the Reformation, especially in its non-Lutheran manifestations. As a result, he argues, there was no independent movement called "Spiritualism."[13] Although Klaassen's critique has not carried the day, it has encouraged a more cautious approach to reliance on "cut and dried" ideal types in the study of Reformation radicals. Increasingly focus has been placed on the historic groups of radicals rather than ideal types. This approach has recently been undertaken most comprehensively in the work of the Anabaptist historian James Stayer. Stayer distinguishes between proto-Anabaptist Zurich radicals and anti-Lutheran Saxon radicals. Although allowing for significant interactions between these two groups, and for important blurring of the lines separating them, Stayer's characterizations retain many of the old distinctions between Anabaptists and Spiritualists.[14]

Most prominent among the early Saxon radicals were Andreas Bodenstein von Karlstadt and Thomas Müntzer, and their reflections on history and the history of the church are the subject of chapter two in this study. Traditionally their reforming activity and thought has been treated as a variation on the spiritualist type. Expanding on Troeltsch's model, George H. Williams characterized them as revolutionary Spiritualists and Heinold Fast as *Schwärmer*. These variations on Troeltsch indicate a recognition that the basic characteristics of the spiritualist type did not exactly fit these individuals, that both took seriously at some level the structures of church and society.[15] Karlstadt and Müntzer provide interesting opportunities to examine not only the assumed distinctions between the Anabaptist and Spiritualist visions of history, but also those thought to distinguish the magisterial from the radical Reformers. Their attempts at local reform of the church, particularly Karlstadt's activities in Orlamünde and Müntzer's in Allstedt, betray a willingness to jettison ecclesiastical institutions and traditions in an attempt to restore the primitive church with a zeal unparalleled among the magisterial Reformers. And yet, the evolution of their historical visions suggests that they began with the same starting point as the magisterial Reformers. Furthermore, their perceptions of the primitive church suggest that distinctions between Saxon and Swiss traditions of religious radicals, with some overtones of the distinction between sectarianism and spiritualism, are not without merit when trying to understand the historical visions of Reformation radicals.

According to Littell, the primitivism of the Reformation era reached its fullest development and most consistent application among the Anabaptists, especially those he designated as "Anabaptists proper." This group, which he characterized as those who "gathered and disciplined a 'True Church' upon the apostolic pattern," were synonymous with the Evangelical Anabaptists claimed by Mennonite scholars as their spiritual ancestors: the Swiss Brethren, Hutterites, Marpeckites and Dutch Mennonites.[16] Subsequent scholarship has challenged the restriction of the title Anabaptist to only those traditionally identified as "Evangelical Anabaptists" or "Anabaptists Proper," and scholars have argued for the inclusion of other rebaptizers among the ranks of the Anabaptists. Among the least contentious of the new inductees is Balthasar Hubmaier. Traditionally kept at arms length from the Evangelical Anabaptists largely because of his views on the Sword, Hubmaier has in recent years been rehabilitated to the point where he is now appealed to as an authoritative voice in early Anabaptist theology.[17] Similarly, the recognition of the distinctive characteristics and development of south German and Austrian Anabaptism has highlighted the importance of Hans Hut and his followers for subsequent developments in Anabaptism. In the process, it has recognized the significance of apocalypticism in the early phases of south German and Austrian Anabaptism, and has accepted more direct ties to the Saxon radicals, especially Müntzer, in this tradition. However, while revisionist scholarship has challenged assumptions about who was and who was not an Anabaptist, it has tended to accept Littell's claim that Anabaptists were distinguished by their New Testament primitivism.[18] An important task of the present study is to test that claim. Chapter three lays the groundwork for this analysis by revisiting the central elements of Littell's thesis about Anabaptist primitivism and criticisms of it.

Implicit in Littell's thesis is the assumption that from the beginnings of the Anabaptist movement there was a connection between primitivism and a separatist ecclesiology. Interestingly, among the Anabaptist traditions which survived the sixteenth century, all of which qualify as "Evangelical Anabaptists," the group with the clearest separatist ecclesiology, the Swiss Brethren, had the least developed historical vision with the fewest characteristics of the Anabaptist view of church history as defined by Littell. The fullest and clearest statement of that historical vision appears instead in *The Great Chronicle* of the Hutterites, a group traditionally treated as a subsidiary and somewhat eccentric variation on the main Anabaptist story. Reminiscent of the Hutterite version of the history of Christianity, and indebted to it on a number of details, is the vision presented in the *Martyrs Mirror*, the mid seventeenth-century culmination of the Mennonite martyrological tradition. Chapter three will also look at these examples of the Anabaptist historical vision as defined by Littell.

Equally interesting is the fact that among the early Anabaptists a distinctive vision of ecclesiastical history appears in only an embryonic form, and cases in which it is more fully elaborated appear in some of the least expected places. For example, Balthasar Hubmaier, who attempted to establish an Anabaptist version of a magisterial Reformation in Waldshut and later Nicolsburg, provides one of the most detailed variants. But even in Hubmaier's case, that vision was not spelled out *in toto* at the beginning of his reforming activity. Rather he developed it as he responded to specific challenges and concerns in his reforming activity, especially in the midst of controversy and polemical exchanges. With Hubmaier and the other early Anabaptists it appears that a particular vision of the past was not a determining feature of their reforming visions from the outset. Rather, like the Saxon radicals, they produced a distinctive vision of ecclesiastical history from an initial dissatisfaction with the status of the contemporary church and on the basis of the belief that the primitive church was a model to be emulated at some level. The development of detailed and sophisticated visions of ecclesiastical history among those usually regarded as Evangelical Anabaptists is the subject of chapter four.

According to traditional assumptions about historical thinking in the Radical Reformation, at the opposite end of the continuum from the Evangelical Anabaptists stood the Spiritualists. Ever since Ernst Troeltsch took over the designation from Alfred Hegler and expanded its definition, the Spiritualists have been categorized as nonhistorical. However, the identification of a distinct Spiritualist movement in the Radical Reformation and the question of its relationship to Anabaptism remain matters of debate. Despite recent criticisms of it, I believe there are good reasons to retain the category "Spiritualist" to designate a distinct group in the Radical Reformation. However, there are also solid reasons to reassess some of its central characteristics. This applies especially to Troeltsch's assumptions about spiritualism and its relationship to history. One of the great ironies in historical writing about the Radical Reformation is the fact that its most comprehensive historical vision was produced by a "programmatic Spiritualist": Sebastian Franck's *Chronica, Zeitbuch und Geschichtsbibel* encompasses three distinct chronicles covering a variety of human activities from creation to the author's own day and is widely recognized as one of the most influential historical writings of the Radical Reformation. In the words of Rufus Jones, Franck was "the chronicler of the world's spiritual development."[19] By way of contrast, the other arch-Spiritualist of the early Reformation, Caspar Schwenckfeld, appears to have been comparatively unconcerned with the events of human history. Like all reformers of the age, he makes scattered references to the history of the church throughout his writings, but provides no overarching scheme to interpret human history and only rarely refers to its value in understanding divine providence or the human condition. The differences between the visions of Franck and Schwenckfeld raise interesting questions about the relationship between Spiritualism and historical visions: Can we posit a relationship between them? And if there exists a Spiritualist vision of church history, how does it relate to the Anabaptist vision? Chapter five attempts to answer these questions through a study of the writings of Franck and Schwenckfeld.

If the Evangelical Anabaptists and Spiritualists occupy opposite ends of a continuum as Walter Klaassen has suggested, between them are a number of groups and individuals who do not fit neatly into either category. Among these are a group of Reformers usually referred to as the Spiritualist Anabaptists or Spiritualizers: Hans Denck, Ludwig Hätzer, Jacob Kautz, Johannes Bünderlin and Christian Entfelder. While all of these men were at some point active participants in the Anabaptist movement, they all later either repudiated their earlier activity in favour of a more spiritualist vision or espoused reform programmes which included strongly spiritualist elements. Also defying the definitions derived from Troeltsch's sociology of religion were large segments of the Melchiorite Anabaptist movement. Regarded by some as a crucial figure in north German and Dutch Anabaptism, Melchior Hoffman is still excluded by other scholars from the ranks of the Anabaptists.[20] Other elements of the Melchiorite movement, most notably the Anabaptist regime in Münster, appear even more difficult to include among the Anabaptists. And yet some of these groups and individuals developed some of the most elaborate historical visions of the Radical Reformation. Here again, as with the early Anabaptists and the Spiritualists, it is difficult to speak of one distinct Spiritualist Anabaptist or Melchiorite vision of the church's past. These visions, which will be explored in chapter six, provide us with some interesting perspectives not only into the relationship between these Reformers and others in the Radical Reformation, but also into the ways in which historical visions were constructed in the Reformation and the roles they played in reforming agendas.

The variety of historical visions developed by Reformation radicals points to the adaptability and importance of these historical conceptions in defending reforming plans. Closer attention to their development suggests as well the importance of the interaction of these historical visions in that development. As we will see, the formulation of detailed accounts of the church's past tends to cluster around specific points where different reforming traditions came into direct and vigorous contact with one another. Probably the most obvious of these occurrences came in Strasbourg at the beginning of the 1530s. It was in Strasbourg that Pilgram Marpeck developed one of the most consistent and detailed historical visions of the first-generation Anabaptists, Sebastian Franck published his *Chronica*, and Johannes Bünderlin and Christian Entfelder grounded their developing critiques of Anabaptism in elaborate schemes of salvation history. Such a confluence of ideas leads to the suspicion that the confrontation between reforming traditions, and the dialogue this confrontation produced, was an important catalyst for revisiting Christian history and for the elaboration of detailed and comprehensive historical visions. That suspicion is confirmed by the subsequent development of historical visions among the Hutterites and Mennonites. In both cases visions of the Christian past were fleshed out in the context of responding to ongoing challenges to the movements in question. Ultimately, these developments led to the establishment of a fairly consistent and uniform Anabaptist vision of church history as portrayed in *The Hutterite Chronicle* and the *Martyrs Mirror*.

Studies of Anabaptist history have in recent years begun to focus less on the early "heroic" years of the movement and more on its subsequent generations. This trend has reinforced a growing recognition of the limitations of the polygenesis model of Anabaptist beginnings which posits the initial development of three distinct Anabaptist groups, the Swiss, south German/Austrian, and north German/Dutch, to explain the subsequent development of the movement. Both revisionist exponents of the polygenesis model and its post-revisionist critics now recognize the importance of interaction between Anabaptist groups after their disparate beginnings.[21] The formulation of a shared vision of the church's past out of a common, vague primitivism was an important part of the creation of the common ground shared by different branches of the Anabaptist movement. But the formulation of that vision was a long and at times arduous process which often involved instances of conflict and exclusion as well as reconciliation and inclusion. In fact, formulated histories of the church were crucial elements in the formation of Anabaptist confessional identities which served as both bridges between the Anabaptist groups as well as barriers between different groups of Anabaptists and between Anabaptists and others in the Radical Reformation. The importance of conflict and dialogue in the formation of Radical Reformation historical visions, and the role of those visions in Anabaptist confessionalist strategies of the later sixteenth and seventeenth centuries will be addressed in chapter seven.

Notes

1 Cited in Glanmore Williams, *Reformation Views of Church History* (Richmond, VA: John Knox Press, 1970), 8.

2 Irena Backus, *Historical Method and Confessional Identity in the Era of the Reformation (1378-1615)* (Leiden and Boston: E.J. Brill, 2003), 390.

3 Franklin H. Littell, *The Origins of Sectarian Protestantism: A Study of the Anabaptist View of the Church* (New York: MacMillan, 1964), xvii, 46-57, 61-64, 77, 79.

4 Ibid., 50-51.

5 Irena Backus, "Erasmus and the Spirituality of the Early Church," in Hilmar Pabel, ed., *Erasmus' Vision of the Church* (Kirksville, MO: Sixteenth Century Journal Publishers, 1995): 95-114; István Bejczy, *Erasmus and the Middle Ages: the Historical Consciousness of a Christian Humanist* (Leiden: E.J. Brill, 2001).

6 Bruce Gordon, "The Changing Face of Protestant History and Identity in the Sixteenth Century," in *Protestant History and Identity in Sixteenth-Century Europe*, vol. 1: *The Medieval Inheritance* (Aldershot: Scolar Press, 1996), 3.

7 Littell, *Origins of Sectarian Protestantism*, 47-48, 64, 79.

8 Ernst Troeltsch, *The Social Teachings of the Christian Churches*, 2 vols., translated by Olive Wyon (London: George Allen and Unwin, 1931), I: 328-82; II: 691-807, especially 694-706, 729-53.

9 Ibid., I: 334; II: 742-43.

10 Ibid., II: 729-53.

11 For an overview of the Troeltsch's impact on subsequent historical writing on Reformation radicals, see Guy Herschberger, ed. *The Recovery of the Anabaptist Vision. A Sixtieth Anniversary Tribute to Harold S. Bender* (Scottdale, PA: Herald Press, 1957), 5, 57-58, 332; James Stayer, "The Anabaptists," in Steven Ozment, ed. *Reformation Europe: A*

Guide to Research (St. Louis: Center for Reformation Research, 1982), 135-36; idem, "Saxon Radicalism and Swiss Anabaptism: The Return of the Repressed," *MQR* 67 (1993), 7; idem, "The Radical Reformation," in Thomas A. Brady, Jr., Heiko A. Oberman and James D. Tracy, eds. *Handbook of European History, 1400 - 1600: Late Middle Ages, Renaissance and Reformation*, vol. 2: *Visions, Programmes and Outcomes* (Grand Rapids, MI: Eerdmans, 1996), 249. Troeltsch's broader influence on Reformation studies is evident in Roland Bainton, *The Reformation of the Sixteenth Century* (Boston: Beacon Press, 1952), 123-40; A.G. Dickens, *Reformation and Society in Sixteenth-Century Europe* (London: Thames and Hudson, 1966), 125-50; G.R. Elton, *Reformation Europe, 1517-1559* (London: Fontana, 1963), 86-103; DeLamar Jensen, *Reformation Europe: Age of Reform and Revolution* (Toronto: D.C. Heath, 1992), 118-120. For Littell's distinction between the historical visions of Anabaptists and Spiritualists, see *Origins of Sectarian Protestantism*, 21-24, 57, 77.

12 Karl Holl, "Luther und die Schwärmer," *Gesammelte Aufsätze zur Kirchengeschichte*, vol. 1: *Luther* (Tübingen: J.C.B. Mohr [Paul Siebeck], 1927), 424-25; James M. Stayer, "'Luther und die Schwärmer,' Karl Holl und das abenteuerliche Leben eines Textes," in Norbert Fischer and Marion Kobelt-Groch, eds. *Aussenseiter zwischen Mittelalter und Neuzeit: Festschrift für Hans-Jürgen Goertz* (Leiden: E.J. Brill, 1997), 281-83.

13 Walter Klaassen, "Spiritualization in the Reformation," *MQR* 37 (1963): 67-77.

14 See Stayer, "Saxon Radicalism and Swiss Anabaptism," 5-30 and "The Radical Reformation," 249-82.

15 Troeltsch, II: 754-56; George H. Williams, *The Radical Reformation*, 3rd ed., (Kirksville, MO: Sixteenth Century Journal Publishers, 1992), 1298-99; idem., *SAW*, 32-33; Heinold Fast, *Der linke Flügel der Reformation: Glaubenszeugnisse der Täufer, Spiritualisten, Schwärmer und Antitrinitarier* (Bremen: Carl Schünemann Verlag, 1962), xii-xiii, xxvii-xxxi.

16 Littell, *Origins of Sectarian Protestantism*, xvii, 36-48. On Littell's debt to the Mennonite category of Evangelical Anabaptism, see James Stayer, *Anabaptists and the Sword*, 2nd ed. (Lawrence, KS: Coronado Press, 1976), 8-9.

17 An excellent example of Hubmaier's rehabilitation is Arnold Snyder's essay "Beyond Polygenesis: Recovering the Unity and Diversity of Anabaptist Theology," in H. Wayne Pipkin, ed. *Essays in Anabaptist Theology* (Elkhart, IN: Institute of Mennonite Studies, 1994): 1-33, see especially pp. 12-16.

18 See, for example, Stayer, *The German Peasants' War and Anabaptist Community of Goods* (Kingston and Montreal: McGill-Queen's University Press, 1991), 95-99, 104-5; idem, "Radical Reformation," 255; Hans-Jürgen Goertz, "'A common future conversation': A revisionist interpretation of the September 1524 Grebel letters to Thomas Müntzer," in Werner O. Packull and Geoffrey L. Dipple, eds., *Radical Reformation Studies: Essays Presented to James M. Stayer* (Aldershot: Ashgate Publishing, 1999), 84.

19 Rufus M. Jones, *Spiritual Reformers in the 16th and 17th Centuries* (MacMillan, 1914; reprint ed., Boston: Beacon Press, 1959), 51.

20 A recent attempt to exclude Hoffman from the ranks of true Anabaptists has been Abraham Friesen's *Erasmus, the Anabaptists, and the Great Commission* (Grand Rapids,MI: Eerdmans, 1998).

21 The clearest statement of the polygenesis model remains James M. Stayer, Werner O. Packull and Klaus Deppermann, "From Monogenesis to Polygenesis: The Historical Discussion of Anabaptist Origins," *MQR* 49 (1975): 83-121. For the recognition of the limitations of the polygenesis model, see Snyder, "Beyond Polygenesis," 1-33 and Stayer, "Review Essay: Anabaptist History and Theology," *MQR* 70 (1996): 473-82.

CHAPTER 1

HUMANISTS AND REFORMERS ON THE FALL OF THE CHURCH

For, because histories describe nothing other than God's work—that is grace and wrath—which one must believe, as if they stood in the Bible, they should be written with the greatest diligence, faithfulness, and truth.

Martin Luther, Preface to the *Historia Galeatii Capellae* (1538)[1]

Among the weapons employed by Lorenzo Valla in his attack on *The Donation of Constantine* and on the papal authority it was used to justify, was the tactic of juxtaposing the contemporary institution of the papacy with the popes of the primitive church:

> But the supreme Pontiffs of our time, who abound in wealth and pleasure, strive, it appears, to be wicked and foolish just as much as the early Popes strove to be wise and holy; they try to outdo with every kind of infamy the brilliant glory of their predecessors. Can anyone who deserves to be called a Christian tolerate this calamity?[2]

Valla was not alone in his use of this tactic. In the later Middle Ages and Renaissance, reformers of all stripes looked to the church of the past, and especially the primitive church, as a standard against which to measure contemporary abuses. The potency of appeals by would-be reformers to the distant past of the church was matched by the versatility of these appeals. As we will see, this tactic served well both moderate reformers and their more radical counterparts even after the Luther issue had divided the church and western Christendom. Given the frequency with which the primitive church and ecclesiastical history were invoked, we are faced with the question of what role these appeals played in the reforming visions of early modern Europe. Were they comprehensive normative standards driving the agendas of a variety of religious reformers? Or were they *ex post facto* legitimations of already established reforming agendas? Or were they something in between, visions which were determined by reforming programmes, but entities that took on lives of their own as they became established elements of reforming traditions?

Ecclesiastical History and Church Reform in the Later Middle Ages

Historical writing on the later Middle Ages commonly assumes that the crisis of the late medieval church included the perception that the church had fallen from an original, pristine state. Gordon Leff, a prominent historian of the late medieval church, has described the development of a new historical-critical attitude toward the church as "one of the most striking developments of the later Middle Ages," and the ideal of an apostolic church as "the great new ecclesiological fact" of the age. According to his argument, in this period the perception of discontinuity between the apostolic church and the post-apostolic church became "the main source of anti-papalism and/or opposition to ecclesiastical power." The strength of the ideal of the apostolic church as an alternative ecclesiological model is evident in its adaptability. According to Leff, it developed as a subversive force in two distinct traditions. One version, a dissident force within the church associated especially with the Franciscan Spirituals, combined Franciscan teaching on apostolic poverty with the eschatological expectation of Joachimite prophecy. The other, Waldensian formulation of the apostolic ideal lacked the apocalyptic overtones of its Franciscan counterpart but explicitly identified the Donation of Constantine as the moment when the church abandoned its apostolic simplicity. Leff traced the influence of Waldensian tenets on the English Lollards and the Hussites and suggested that as a common attitude, although not as a specific program, the apostolic ideal can be found among most of the radical thinkers of the age, including Dante, Marsilius of Padua, William of Occam, Dietrich of Niem, John Wyclif and Jan Hus.[3]

Leff's thesis has been challenged and in important ways modified, but not entirely discarded, by Scott Hendrix. Hendrix places Leff's observations in a larger context both temporally and ecclesiologically. He indicates that the apostolic ideal was not a novelty in the later Middle Ages, but that it was a crucial component of reforming movements throughout much of the church's history. The novelty was, rather, the crisis atmosphere in which the ideal was used as a stick to beat the contemporary church, especially the upper reaches of its hierarchy. Furthermore, within the context of that crisis reformers and critics of the institutional church did not discard the apostolic ideal, but they did supplement it with other ecclesiological models. The result was "a much more complex ecclesiological landscape than had hitherto existed."[4] Despite differences of detail, the conclusions of Leff and Hendrix support Franklin Littell's suggestion that a general primitivism marked the historical thinking of the late medieval and early modern period. Certainly, by the end of the fifteenth century even orthodox preachers were conveying a general pessimism about the state of the church. And when they measured the contemporary church against the church of the past, it was found to be wanting.[5]

Ecclesiastical History in the Reforming Visions of Renaissance Humanists

However, a more immediate backdrop for historical visions of the Reformation and Radical Reformation was provided by the reforming agendas of the Renaissance humanists. These visions included a healthy dose of primitivism as defined by Littell. When applied to ecclesiastical concerns, and more specifically ecclesiology, the humanist principle of returning to the original sources of Christianity could be a potent weapon against the ecclesiastical hierarchy. Lorenzo Valla's *The Falsely-Believed and Forged Donation of Constantine* indicates clearly the continued vitality of the ideal of the primitive church as a reforming tool in the hands of the humanists. However, the humanist vision of ecclesiastical history was much more complex than a simple appeal to the model of the apostolic church. While it is difficult to identify one vision of ecclesiastical history as representative of all humanists, certain elements of a common vision do exist. Not surprisingly, many of those elements were laid out by Erasmus of Rotterdam.

Studies of Erasmus' Christian humanism have often noted the importance of historical reflection and historical arguments in his vision for the reform of the church. In addition, they have emphasized that in Erasmus' writings there is no formal treatment of history as an independent subject of investigation, but that Erasmus' statements about history, which are comments primarily about church history, are essentially extensions of his reforming plans.[6] Peter Bietenholz has suggested that Erasmus' reflections on the history of the Church are more notable for his departure from the conventions of historical periodization of his day than his adherence to them, although, in the end, "they proved too convenient to be completely disposed of."[7] Erasmus did provide a clear schematization of church history in an oft quoted passage from the *Method of True Theology* of 1518. Here he identifies five *tempora*: the first two antedate the Incarnation; the third is that of Christ, the apostles and evangelists; the fourth the age of the established church, which witnessed the growth of its secular power, wealth and the promulgation of new law; and finally a fifth age of outright degeneration. However, Erasmus concludes by warning against the dangers of such periodization and moves on to other matters.[8] But this was not an isolated remark and Erasmus' infrequent references to the history of the church suggest a sense of deterioration from its pristine state. Already in the 1516 Basel edition of Jerome's works, he compared the wealth and temporal authority of the contemporary clergy with apostolic poverty and simplicity:

> For there is a very great difference between that original and primitive church of Christ and this church of our time. In those days, bereft of every advantage of this world, she was strong with the strength of Christ alone, and she flourished all the more gloriously thereby the further she kept from worldly advantages. Then gradually wealth came to her, and the favour of princes now Christian also came to her. Finally property came to her, power came to her. Whether or not this is in accord with the philosophy of Christ I leave to the judgement of others.[9]

If one draws together Erasmus' statements from throughout his writings, one is able to piece together a comprehensive vision of the history of the Christian church. As has been noted, this institution and its history is at the centre of Erasmus' understanding of, and concern with, the past. In the broad sweep of world history the most important event in Erasmus' eyes was the Incarnation, and as a result his historical vision can be characterized as Christocentric.[10] History since the Incarnation was further divided into four periods by Erasmus: two during the ancient age, the apostolic and patristic; and two during the medieval age, the monastic and the scholastic. Despite his emphasis on the importance of the Incarnation and his perception of the church's decline, Erasmus identified none of these ages as absolutely normative for the reform of the contemporary church.[11] Even the church of the apostolic period, which stood apart from the others because it received the gospel, the very basis of Erasmus' *Philosophia Christi*, provided only a limited model for reform. The early Christians had shunned literary education and, therefore, were able to fulfill only one half Erasmus' goal of synthesizing *pietas* and *eloquentia* as the basis for the reform of church and society. In the apostolic period Christ did not establish a golden age of the church, but he laid the basis for its subsequent development.[12]

At first glance, the patristic period seems an even better candidate for the golden age of the church. It witnessed the integration of the gospel and classical learning central to Erasmus' vision of reform, and its religious life appeared relatively uncorrupted. But here, too, the church served as a model for reform only in a qualified sense. The literary culture of classical Rome was already in decline when taken up by the church fathers and the religious life of the patristic age was marred by the personal ambitions of some of its intellectual and religious leaders. The heresies which afflicted the church in the fourth and fifth centuries led Erasmus to distinguish between old antiquity and middle antiquity. The former was the age of the fathers Irenaeus, Origen and Tertullian, in Erasmus' eyes, following closely on the heels of the apostolic period. The latter, the age of Basil, Chrysostum, Augustine, Ambrose and Jerome, witnessed the increasingly rigid definition of doctrine and the growth of the church hierarchy's control of religious life. The need for clear doctrinal definitions and ecclesiastical control was itself a response to the challenges of the heretics, but amounted, nonetheless, to the first step in the process of religious decline.[13] Erasmus described this process most clearly in the preface to his 1523 edition of the works of Hilary:

> Once faith was more a matter of a way of life than a profession of articles. Soon necessity inspired the imposition of articles, but these were few, and apostolic in their moderation. ... Articles increased, but sincerity decreased: contention boiled over, charity grew cold. The teachings of Christ, which in former times were not touched by the clash of words, began to depend on the support of philosophy: this was the first step of the Church on the downward path. There was an increase of wealth and an accretion of power.[14]

In the medieval age both the cultural and religious decline which were apparent in the ancient age continued. The conversion of Constantine amounted to a double-edged sword. It occasioned the victory of Christianity after years of persecution, but it also opened the doors to a mixture of spiritual and worldly concerns in the church. However, in

Erasmus' mind the decline of the church had more to do with cultural than political developments. And here his primary concern was with the increasing encroachment of philosophy on religion, a process he saw closely associated with Augustine as the transitional figure between the patristic and monastic periods and the "father and fountainhead" of scholastic theology.[15] During the monastic period the greatest factor in the church's decline was continuing cultural deterioration. Erasmus lamented the decline of literature, "reduced to a few sophistic niceties, ... to be found only in certain summary compilers and makers of excerpts, whose impudence stood in inverse proportion to their knowledge." This state of affairs arose from the increasing temporal authority of the bishops and the delegation of their teaching office to "a certain class, who today claim charity and religion as their private trademark."[16] By the seventh century universal cultural decline had set in. However, Erasmus continued to laud the efforts of the monks to maintain classical literary culture until the twelfth century, despite the fact that the times and many of their contemporaries worked against them. Slower and less serious was the moral and religious decline during the monastic period. Erasmus regarded the founding of monastic orders and rules as a sign that religious passion had cooled, but, nonetheless, maintained respect for the founders of a number of the great religious orders.[17]

While Erasmus saw in no age of the church's history a comprehensive model for the reform of the church, he did see in the scholastic period a clearly defined anti-model.[18] During this age the deterioration of letters which began during the patristic period reached its lowest stage. The detrimental effects of this development on theology is a consistent theme throughout Erasmus' writings. Already in the 1490s he was questioning the activity of the "modern" theologians in his correspondence.[19] This criticism became more explicit in the *Handbook of a Christian Soldier* where he compared the methods of the ancient with the modern theologians, characterizing the latter as merely cunning debate and shows of ingenuity. He sums up his criticism:

> I have heard tell of some individuals who were so pleased with these petty human commentaries that they despised the interpretations of the ancient Fathers as if they were dreams, and such was their confidence in Scotus that without ever having read the scriptures they thought they were accomplished theologians.[20]

Frequently he juxtaposes the sophistic subtleties of scholastics over against the writings of the fathers:

> It is worth their while for Clement, Irenaeus, Polycarp, Origen, Arnobius to fall out of use, that in their stead the world might read Occam, Durandus, Capreolus, Lyra, Burgensis, and even poorer stuff than that.[21]

The point is probably made most forcefully in *The Antibarbarians*, a work which has been described as the manifesto of Erasmus' Christian humanism:

> They do not quote Basil, Origen, Chrysostum, and men like them, or if they do it is with contempt, censoriously; but when they jingle those names of theirs, Holy Doctors, Irrefragable Doctors, Most Subtle Doctors, Seraphic Doctors, they think they are announcing something which should take precedence over even the majesty of the Gospel.[22]

Furthermore, the deterioration of humane letters affected not only theology, but all fields of learning. For example, Erasmus denounces Gratian and the development of later medieval legal traditions. It also undermined morality and religion, and it lies at the basis of the abuses in church and society criticized by Erasmus, especially in *Praise of Folly*.[23]

It is often noted that in his criticism of scholasticism the primary objects of Erasmus' ire are the successors of the great medieval scholastics, not the renowned doctors themselves. Especially in his later writings, after the battle lines were drawn over the Luther issue, Erasmus clarified this fact.

> I do not think that the works of Thomas or Scotus should be rejected in their entirety. They wrote for their own age, and they

> passed on to us much that was drawn from the books of the ancient Fathers and examined with some discrimination. But I do not approve of the rudeness of those who ascribe so much to this kind of author that they believe they have an obligation to clamour against good literature happily springing up again everywhere.[24]

Margaret Mann Phillips has suggested that Erasmus admired Thomas, "as far as he could admire a 'modern' theologian without Greek."[25] Among Erasmus' statements censured by the University of Paris was the claim that the energy of the Gospel had cooled in the last 400 years. The theologians of the Sorbonne claimed this amounted to an implicit denial of the sanctity and erudition of luminaries such as Bernard, Peter Lombard, Thomas and Bonaventure.[26] Erasmus' response restates his consistent position on the assessment of scholastic and patristic theology:

> Indeed, I judge them all to be good men; but it is one thing to be a good man, another to be inspired by the vigour of the Gospel. However, of these Bernard appears most eager in mood, but how much he languishes, if you would compare him with Cyprian, with Jerome, etc. ...[27]

In spite of these qualifications, Erasmus remained consistently critical of scholasticism and the great scholastic doctors, including Thomas Aquinas.[28]

The emerging Reformation, with its hardening of lines between reformers and traditionalists in the church, did affect Erasmus' perceptions of reform and ecclesiastical history. Throughout his writings Erasmus consistently defended the value of tradition in the formulation of Christian doctrine. This stance was further reinforced by the radical position of the Reformers, their rejection of that tradition and their seemingly whimsical appeal to the primitive church and its practices to justify their reforming agendas. As a result, in his later writings Erasmus began moderating his criticisms of the abuses which had crept into the church's traditions.[29] Given his assessment of the value of tradition and of the church, it is no surprise that Erasmus in no way identified with opposition to the medieval church, even during the scholastic period. In fact, in his denunciations of the Reformation he often associated Luther with late medieval heretics like Peter Waldo, Jan Hus and especially John Wyclif.[30] Erasmus' return to the church under pressure from the radicalism of the Reformation led to a modification, but a not a major rethinking, of his historical vision. Consistently throughout his writings he alludes to an historical deterioration of the church which is especially apparent when comparing contemporary abuses to the simplicity of the primitive church. However, these allusions did not involve the identification of a past golden age of the church—for Erasmus no period in the church's history was normative as a model for reform. The heyday of scholasticism often appeared as the age in which the church's deterioration was most advanced, but even here Erasmus was sometimes circumspect in his treatment of the greatest scholastic doctors.

The connection between reforming vision and historical reflection apparent in Erasmus' thought can also be observed in the writings of other northern humanists. The split in the ranks of the humanists occasioned by the Reformation has long been noted.[31] Interestingly, as humanists were forced to decide between joining the Reformation or rejoining the ranks of the Roman church, they found historical visions similar to that espoused by Erasmus easily adaptable to their decisions. This fact is clear in the thought of two prominent German humanists: Beatus Rhenanus and Ulrich von Hutten. Both men developed detailed visions of history which initially paralleled each other, but gradually diverged as the Reformation forced them to choose between religious camps.[32]

Beatus Rhenanus' views on the history of Christianity are laid out especially clearly in his edition of the writings of the church father Tertullian. His comments there indicate that he shared Erasmus' opposition to scholasticism and his opinions on the teachings of the fathers. With these elements of Erasmus' reforming vision he also shared the general outlines of his historical vision.[33] Rhenanus regarded Tertullian's description of the practices of the early church as a viable model for reform, but the primitive church did not amount to a model in its entirety. Rhenanus also had a dynamic sense of the church's development and an appreciation for its post-apostolic tradition. Like Erasmus, he bemoaned the baneful effects of philosophy on theology, and he interpreted Tertullian as an early opponent of the introduction of philosophical methods and categories into theology. Nonetheless, formal theology and the clarification of doctrine were the necessary consequences of the challenges posed to the church by early medieval heresies. Rhenanus saw the process of deterioration resulting from the integration of theology and philosophy as a gradual one. Although he provides few details about the history of the church between the age of Augustine and the twelfth century, his comments suggest that he believed patristic theology lasted on into the early Middle Ages and that he regarded Peter Lombard as the transitional figure from patristic to scholastic theology.[34]

Rhenanus provides more detail when he reaches the twelfth century and the age of scholasticism. This age witnessed the establishment of a complete academical theological system, and with it a disruptive formalization of Christian thought:

> Soon since the number of doctors were increasing, laws of promotion and the number of years [of study] were established, and it was ratified that those discussing divine matters not only should follow the accepted statements of the school but should use the vocabulary and formulas of speech developed in that school, ... And such is the beginning of the reign of the theologians. Moreover, who can say that the ancients spoke as these speak, who divert all the philosophy of Aristotle, unlearnedly changed, into their theology.[35]

Initially Rhenanus sympathized with the goals of the Lutheran Reformation, and his historical vision was easily adapted to accommodate that sympathy. Later in his life, Tertullian had become an adherent of the Montanist heresy. Rhenanus regarded Tertullian's later condemnation as a clear indication of the baneful effects of the infiltration of philosophy into theology and the sharpening definitions of dogma. And he regarded his own attempts to rehabilitate Tertullian as striking a blow at the contemporary papacy. Within this context, Luther's patriotic appeals to

Germans to stand against the abuses of the Italian papacy found a willing reception by Rhenanus, and he undertook his own investigations into the historical abuses of the papacy. He edited an edition of Marsilius of Padua's *Defensor Pacis* as a supplement to Hutten's more famous edition of Valla's exposure of the Donation of Constantine. But gradually, as the Reformation became more radical Rhenanus' relations with the Reformers cooled, and in 1525 he broke with them. This break is reflected in his 1539 edition of Tertullian's *Opera*. Rhenanus' hostility to scholasticism undergoes no fundamental change, but there is a new emphasis on moderation and a call for concord in this work. The value of post-apostolic ecclesiastical tradition is stressed even more than in earlier editions and the criticism of the papacy is moderated.[36]

While Rhenanus' vision of ecclesiastical history allowed him to criticize crucial aspects of the contemporary church, but ultimately remain faithful to it, Ulrich von Hutten employed a similar vision as a springboard to an even more radical and comprehensive attack on the religious establishment of his day. Although he sees in Hutten's statements on this matter his debt and proximity to the vision of Erasmus, Hajo Holborn argues that Hutten's polemics lack any sophisticated understanding of theological argument or subtlety.[37] Hutten first reflected on the issue in the midst of the Reuchlin affair, the drawn out conflict between 1506 and 1520 over the religious and cultural value of Jewish books which pitted the humanist and Hebraist Johannes Reuchlin and a group of humanist supporters against Johannes Pfefferkorn and his backers among the Dominicans at the University of Cologne. Although Pfefferkorn's campaign against Jewish literature was motivated more by anti-Semitism than anti-humanism, Hutten more than anyone else perceived this event as the climactic showdown between humanism and scholasticism.[38] The foundation for Hutten's historical vision is laid in the works he wrote between 1515 and 1518: the introductions to *Nemo* and *Reuchlin's Triumph* and his contributions to *The Letters of Obscure Men*. These comments, then, stem from the period before Hutten took seriously the activity of Luther and his attack on Rome.[39] In the introduction to *Nemo* Hutten observes, much as Erasmus does in *The Antibarbarians*, that in recent years secular studies have declined and with them theology. This deplorable state of affairs has resulted from the departure from the old theology (ancient authors) and has resulted in a clouding of the true cult of God by "the most pestilential of superstitions."[40] This point is made more explicitly in part II of *The Letters of Obscure Men*. Here Hutten denounces the "Impoverished, obscure and useless theology of the last few centuries" which has turned from "the old, learned theology developed from the true light of Scripture." Hutten goes on to compare this "new" theology with the return to the ancients and a more useful theology by the humanists. Chief among the signs of this revival are Erasmus' editions of the New Testament and the works of Jerome.[41]

Already in the language employed, it is clear that Hutten has radicalized the position of Erasmus. Where Erasmus showed at least some tact in dealing with the greatest of medieval theologians, Hutten dismisses all scholastics out of hand. Their theology consists of nothing but "disputing, arguing and throwing out useless questions." In fact, Erasmus' edition of the New Testament is of more use "than twenty thousand Scotists or Thomists disputing *de ente et essentia* for one hundred years." Indeed, when referring to the Cologne theologians, he calls them philosophers, that is Sophists, not theologians.[42] In the introduction to *Reuchlin's Triumph*, he labels the theologians Turks, "by whom true studies have perished, letters been trampled, and divine theology reduced to useless loquacity, unadulterated jests, silly trifles."[43]

Hutten cannot be overly faulted for his sharpening of the criticism of scholastics. As we have seen, Erasmus' statements before 1523 did leave the definition vague of those responsible for the perversion of theology, and with it the church. Hutten was firmly convinced that his own condemnation of the scholastics was in full accord with Erasmus' program. His sharpened tone did, however, set the stage for the receptivity to the writings of Luther after Hutten stopped seeing in him merely a participant in yet another monkish squabble.

The shift in Hutten's role from that of a critic of the scholastics to an enemy of the papacy and the church of Rome generally is intimately linked to his changing opinion of Luther and his activities. Hutten did not derive his anti-papal stance from Luther, but rather saw in Luther's anti-papalism the expression of a kindred spirit. In his correspondence from the middle of 1518 Hutten rejoiced that the monks were still at each other's throats.[44] However, at the same time he was turning his pen against the papacy. In a letter dated 3 August 1518 he indicates that he has begun work on *Vadiscus*.[45] This worked linked humanistically-oriented criticism of scholasticism with his campaign to restore German freedoms and reawaken German honour. This campaign also involved historical reflection because Hutten was convinced that German freedoms and honour had been eroded by the gradual papal usurpation of imperial power and authority throughout most of the Middle Ages.[46]

The developing criticisms of Rome in the thought of Luther and Hutten converged the following year. Holborn suggests that the point of crystalization was Luther's anti-papal stance at the Leipzig disputation.[47] Hutten's correspondence from the autumn of 1519 indicates a gradual reassessment of Luther.[48] Early in the new year, Hutten began corresponding with Phillip Melanchthon and at this time extended Franz von Sickingen's offer of protection to Luther.[49] Finally, in May and June of that year Hutten began corresponding directly with Luther.[50] However, Hutten's own criticism of Rome continued on the political basis established earlier. In March 1520 he sent to Ferdinand of Austria a document from the eleventh-century conflict between Henry IV and Pope Gregory VII.[51] And in late May Hutten sent to the printer a collection of documents from the Great Schism. In the preface to this work he indicated in slightly veiled terms his support for Luther.[52] Later in the year he produced several pamphlets indicating the fruit of his research into the history of imperial-papal relations. In these works the contest is fought out in terms of power politics and legal manipulation, but scholasticism, as the perversion of the Gospel and Truth, continues to hold its place in the papal armoury.[53]

Church History in the Thought of the Magisterial Reformers

Luther's "Reformation breakthrough" has traditionally been portrayed as something divorced from the Renaissance; his was a monastic discovery distinct from the intellectual world of the humanists.[54] And with that distinctive vision, it has been assumed, went a different perception of history. John Headley has cautioned against the simple identification of a conception of the fall of the church in the thought of Luther. Luther's emphasis on the action of the Word and the hidden hand of God in history led to a stress on the constant restoration of the church from above rather than its horizontal development in history. Consequently, in Luther's writings one encounters references to repeated apostasies rather than the notion of a single loss of a pristine age of the church—the latter pattern of historical development Headley associates with the vision of the humanists—and this continual apostasy is integral to church history. For Luther, then, no period in church history is absolutely normative. Nonetheless, he continued to be influenced by the practice of periodizing history. And although he dismissed the idea of an absolute norm of a pristine age of the church, Luther did allow for tentative norms for the organization of the institutional church, and for degeneration or decline from these tentative norms.[55]

However, Luther's vision of ecclesiastical history appears not to have been as unique as Headley suggests. Like Erasmus, Luther recognized positive attributes from past ages of the church, but regarded none of those ages as normative *in toto* as the model for the reform of the church. Not surprisingly, Luther saw the apostolic age as a felicitous time for the church, and he regarded the apostolic church as a model for specific ecclesiastical reforms.[56] Similarly, Luther employed the church of the patristic age as a model by which to judge the contemporary church; as we will see, this was a particularly effective tactic in his attack on scholasticism. But even the church of the fathers had its limits. Like Erasmus, Luther traced these shortcomings to a decline in the quality of classical literary culture, and with it a deterioration of theology.

Furthermore, like the prince of the humanists he saw the revival of languages and theology as the great accomplishment of his own age. Luther made these points most clearly and forcefully in 1524:

> And since the time that the languages declined, nothing of importance has taken place in Christendom, but many abominations have occurred because of the ignorance of languages. Now, however, since the languages have returned, they bring with them so much light, and are doing such great things that the whole world is astonished and forced to admit that we now posses the Gospel in almost as pure and undefiled a fashion as the apostles did. And it has returned in its original purity, indeed, it is now purer than at the time of Jerome or Augustine.[57]

Luther's criticism of scholasticism, especially in his early writings, suggests that if he was not influenced by the reform program of the humanists, he was certainly depicting his own activity as amenable to it. For the purposes of the present study, it is important to emphasize that long before his identification of the papacy as the Antichrist, Luther's chief academic concern was with the reform of theology and the purging from it of Aristotelian accretions of the last 300 to 400 years.[58] In a letter to Johannes Lang dated 18 May 1517, Luther reported on the advance of "our theology and St. Augustine" and the parallel decline of Aristotle at Wittenberg.[59] In August or early September of that year he wrote a "Disputation against Scholastic Theology."[60]

That Luther saw this reform of theology as occurring within the context of the activities of the humanists is suggested by his comments in a letter to Staupitz dated 31 March 1518:

> [My opponents] excite hatred against me from the scholastic doctors. Because I prefer the fathers and the Bible to them...[61]

As Luther continues, his proximity to the Erasmian position becomes clear:

> I read the scholastics with judgement, not with closed eyes (as is their wont)... I do not disdain all of them, but I do not commend all. ... If it was permitted to Scotus and Gabriel and

> others of that ilk to dissent from St. Thomas, and, on the other hand, it is permissible for the Thomists to contradict the whole world, until there are so many sects among the scholastics, so many heads, indeed so many hairs on those heads, why do they not permit me the same against them, the same right that they appropriate to themselves against themselves?[62]

In a letter to Jodocus Trutvetter dated 9 May, Luther widened his scope, suggesting that a reform not only of scholastic theology, but also of canon law, philosophy and logic was essential to the reform of the church.[63] In June Luther published the second edition of the *German Theology*, in the introduction to which he complains:

> But God's anger, incurred through our sin, has rendered us unworthy to see or hear the [true theology], for it is clear that for a long time such matters have not been dealt with in the universities, so that not only has the Word lain under a bench, but is nearly destroyed by dust and moths.[64]

At about the same time Luther continued his open denunciation of the scholastics in *Resolutions on the Merit of Disputing Indulgences*, and shortly thereafter in his response to Prierias identified this perversion of true theology as having occurred in the last 300 years.[65]

Ulrich Bubenheimer has suggested that Luther first overstepped the boundaries of humanist criticism of the church when he began to include papal primacy as part of the deterioration of the church in the last 400 years, during the conflict with Eck leading up to the Leipzig disputation.[66] Shortly thereafter Luther began to identify the papacy with the Antichrist. On 13 March 1519 he wrote to Staupitz:

> I don't know whether the pope is the Antichrist himself or his apostle, so much is Christ (i.e. the Truth) corrupted and crucified by him in the decretals.[67]

The temporal convergence of the rise of scholasticism and the promulgation of canon law was not lost on Luther, and it is likely that his identification of the papacy with the Antichrist derives in part from it.

John Headley has noted the importance of Luther's concern with the rise of papal primacy leading up to the Leipzig Disputation as an impetus for his historical studies.[68] In thesis 13 of those prepared for debate at Leipzig Luther argued that the primacy of Rome was based solely on papal decrees from the last 400 years, and he insisted that claims that it rested on divine foundations from the beginning of the church contradicted authentic histories from the last 1100 years, Holy Scripture and the decisions of the Council of Nicea. Luther had access to the decisions of Nicea through his reading of Eusebius and he discovered that at the Council Rome was not assigned universal dominion, but only the authority to supervise churches in Italy and in the vicinity of Rome. Insofar as the Council recognized any form of preeminence, this was accorded to Antioch and Jerusalem.[69] This discovery had significant implications for Luther's reform suggestions. For example, he combined this image of the primitive church hierarchy with statements from the writings of Jerome and Cyprian, to argue that in the primitive church bishops were chosen by popular election and then confirmed in their offices by other bishops. In *The Address to the Christian Nobility* he took up this description of the episcopal office as a model for the reform of the church hierarchy in the German lands.[70]

In his preparation for the Leipzig debate, Luther realized that while papal primacy had only been a fact in the preceding 400 years, the struggle to establish that primacy had raged for at least 1100 years. This perception was reinforced during the course of the debate, and it led Luther to backdate the establishment of papal preeminence to the Byzantine emperor Constantine IV's grant of formal honour to Rome at the end of the seventh century.[71] This was not Luther's last statement on the subject, however, and later in his life he identified the establishment of papal primacy at 606 CE and the emperor Phokas' murder of Pope Maurice and conferral of the papal office on Boniface III.[72]

In the meantime, however, even after he looked to the late seventh century for the source of papal primacy, Luther continued to focus attention on the preceding 400 years as the time in which ecclesiastical corruption came to full fruition. In *On the Power of the Papacy* he attributed the expansion of canon law, by which the Gospel was suppressed, to the pontificates of Gregory IX, Boniface VIII and Clement V, hence within the last 400 years.[73] Luther came to the logical conclusion of this line of reasoning, that canon law and scholastic theology were the primary methods used by the Antichrist in the suppression of the church, in his *Commentaries on the Psalms*, written between 1519 and 1521. His commentary on the twenty-second Psalm states this clearly:

> And from these two wells of the abyss came the ravaging locusts to that land, the professors of that twin faculty, law and theology. For the wisdom of these is directed by the papal tyrant, they sit in all dioceses. Indeed, they occupy the consistories of law and the seats of theology in the temples, and both teach nothing of Christ, but everything of the pope and Aristotle and oppress the miserable people.[74]

This position is reflected in Luther's subsequent writings from 1520 and 1521. In *The Babylonian Captivity of the Church* he again claims that the perversion of theology in the preceding 300 years by the scholastics has played a crucial role in the extension of papal authority.[75] The universities, as the primary perverters of theology, appear as important allies of the papacy in Luther's response to Ambrosius Catharinus.[76]

Especially in the early years of the Reformation Luther's vision of ecclesiastical history does not appear as sharply demarcated from that of the humanists as has often been suggested. The assumption that humanists held to a pattern of historical development which saw a golden age of the church in the past and a single cataclysmic fall from that event cannot be maintained in light of the historical visions we have seen outlined in the writings of both Erasmus and Beatus Rhenanus. In that sense, Headley's description of the tentative norms of past ages of the church in the thought of Luther seems applicable in some measure to the historical vision of the Christian Renaissance as well. Furthermore, Luther's concern with the rise of scholasticism as a primary culprit in both the perversion of the gospel truth and the establishment of papal authority highlights his proximity to the position of the humanists. The events leading up to the Leipzig Disputation indicate further that historical research was an important element in his criticism of the established church and that as that criticism deepened, he searched further back in history for the origins of contemporary abuses. But in the end Luther's reform agenda dictated the historical vision rather than the historical vision dictating his reform agenda, and historical arguments remained in a secondary position supporting theological positions and arguments.[77]

A similar interaction of reform program and historical vision is evident in the thought of Ulrich Zwingli. The importance of Zwingli's statements on the fall of the church have been downplayed by his interpreters as was also the case for Luther. Gottfried Locher has argued that, as it is filled with change and innovation, ecclesiastical history has for Zwingli only a relative worth when compared with the standard of Scripture.[78] As with Erasmus and Luther, it is difficult to speak of a clear-cut concept of the fall of the church in Zwingli's early writings. Nonetheless, a fairly clear perception of the church's deterioration can be gleaned from them. Zwingli's statements on this matter provide insights into two important issues of current Zwingli interpretation: the point at which he came to his Reformation breakthrough and the importance of Luther for this transformation. In addition Zwingli, who was much more consciously an adherent of the Christian Renaissance than Luther and educated in the *via antiqua*, not the *via moderna* like Luther, provides an interesting contrast to the Wittenberger.

Recent Zwingli research has established the importance of Erasmian humanism for his early reforming activity. It is now generally accepted that until 1522 Zwingli saw his own activity as part of the greater Christian Renaissance carried on by the humanists.[79] In a letter to Erasmus, written while Zwingli was still at Glarus, he addressed the prince of the humanists as *philosopho et theologo maximo* and expressed the optimism that "the holy literature, delivered by him [Erasmus] from barbarity and sophisms, would grow into a more perfect age."[80] A letter of 6 December 1518 from Beatus Rhenanus to Zwingli indicates that the early liturgical reforms in Zurich were carried out in the spirit of the Christian Renaissance. Rhenanus bemoans the corruption of the liturgy by priests deceived by the doctrines of the sophists. Over against this perversion, Rhenanus praises the reforms of Zwingli:

> ... nor does it escape my notice that you and your fellows present to the people the purest philosophy of Christ from the sources themselves, not corrupted by the Scotist and Gabrielist interpretations, but expounded genuinely and purely from Augustine, Ambrose, Cyprian, Jerome.[81]

That Zwingli himself came to identify the rise of scholasticism with the degeneration of the church is suggested by the report of one of his conservative critics in Zurich, Konrad Hofmann. In late 1521 Hofmann complained that Zwingli had preached against all theologians who had written or taught in the last 380 years, including among them Bonaventure, Albertus Magnus, Scotus and Thomas.[82] Zwingli apparently also claimed that the Gospel had been "suppressed, concealed, or not preached, or not preached correctly."[83] It is important who Zwingli blamed for the perversion of theology. Educated in the *via antiqua*, his earliest criticism of modern theologians was directed at the *moderni* or *terministi*. However, likely under the influence of the Reuchlin affair Zwingli expanded the scope of his criticism to include all scholastics.[84]

The point at which Zwingli came to his Reformation breakthrough continues to be a matter of dispute among historians. Arthur Rich has suggested that already in early 1521 Zwingli had identified the papacy as the Antichrist.[85] Wilhelm Neuser has successfully countered Rich's claims and argues instead that Zwingli's criticism of Rome from 1519 to 1522 occurred in an Erasmian context.[86] Nonetheless, he sees the breakthrough as having occurred by Lent 1522 and regards Hofmann's comments on Zwingli's preaching in late 1521 as indicating that Zwingli was by then presenting a developed critique of Catholic authority.[87] James Stayer suggests as the turning point Zwingli's resolution of the competing claims to authority of Scripture and the papacy, which is first clearly expressed in Zwingli's writings of late August and early September 1522: *Defence called Archeteles* and *On Clarity and Certainty of the Force of God's Word*.[88]

Zwingli's statements on the papacy and the fall of the church suggest that he was grappling with the issue of authority throughout 1522, but that he first resolved it in August of that year. In his discussion of the Lenten fast, *On Choice and Liberty Respecting Food*, Zwingli takes his first step toward the rejection of ecclesiastical authority by suggesting that the obligatory fast is of diabolical inspiration, and he identifies it with Paul's warning in 1 Timothy 4 against those who in the last days will enjoin abstinence from foods created by God to be received in thanksgiving.[89] In *A Friendly Request and Exhortation to the Confederates*, written in July, he compares the contradictory statements of church councils on the issue of clerical celibacy, and here again he suggests that demonic influence is behind the later restriction of Christian freedom.[90] In *Archeteles* Zwingli first turns his attention to the papacy, and although he does not identify this institution with the Antichrist outright, he does call into question papal supremacy and infallibility.[91] More importantly, in this work Zwingli first openly dates the degeneration of the church to a period prior to the rise of scholasticism. He suggests that abuses, among which he includes clerical celibacy, obligatory fasts, works righteousness and the entire system of penance, have been increasing for one thousand years.[92] Zwingli does not provide specific details of the reason for his choice of 500 CE as the beginning of the fall, but his criticism of papal supremacy and clerical luxury suggest a link to the ascendancy of Rome. While Zwingli does not return to this theme in his subsequent writings of 1522 and 1523, he does deepen his criticism of the papacy and openly identifies it with the Antichrist.[93]

At the same time, Zwingli continued his attacks on scholasticism in these works. The place of scholasticism in the more general degeneration of the church is not as clearly spelled out in Zwingli's works as it is in Luther's. However, Zwingli's references suggest that he adopted much the same stance as Luther. In his Lenten tract Zwingli ridicules the role of Thomas Aquinas in deciding details of the fast, "as if a mendicant has the authority to promulgate a law for all Christian people."[94] Later in the same work he provides a lengthy exposition on the role of Aristotle in the introduction of works theology.[95] The link between scholasticism and canon law, which is implied here and which figures so prominently in Luther's thought, is more fully developed in the *Archeteles*. Here Zwingli identifies Thomas and Scotus and the jurists Bartolus and Baldus as those responsible for perverting the Gospel.[96] Shortly thereafter he blames scholasticism and its worship of Aristotle for the host of evils that have arisen in Christendom.[97]

Zwingli's criticism of the papacy in the *Archeteles* lacks the apocalyptic shrillness of Luther's writings. But his perception that abuses held the upper hand in the church for a thousand years indicates that on the critical issue of the locus of authority he had moved beyond the Erasmian position. In the continued perception of the role of scholasticism in the deterioration of the church, and especially the intimate connection between it and canon law, one can see Zwingli's agreement with Luther, if not his debt to him. The groundwork for the adoption of this position was laid by Zwingli's adherence to the program of the Christian Renaissance. In this case the humanist context which joined the two Reformers, rather than the conflicting scholastic traditions in which Luther and Zwingli were trained, is of central importance. Furthermore, like Luther, as he moved beyond the humanist criticism of contemporary abuses in the church Zwingli looked further into its past for the sources of the church's degeneration. That this process was common among early Reformers is suggested by the developing reforming vision of the south German Franciscan turned Reformer and pamphleteer Johann Eberlin von Günzburg.

Eberlin's career as a Reformer provides an interesting variation on those studied already. Like Zwingli, he came to Luther's writings within the context of the Christian Renaissance. However, he came to this movement much later than the Zurich reformer, was never as completely immersed in it, and made a more rapid move to the camp of the Reformers. Unlike Zwingli, Eberlin did commit himself to the Lutheran reform movement and claimed to be an adherent of the cause of Wittenberg until his death.

The evolution of Eberlin's reforming vision is best traced in his best-known publication, *The Fifteen Confederates*, a collection of distinct but related *Flugschriften* published in 1521 which addressed topical reforming issues. In *The Second Confederate*, Eberlin claims that God has allowed Christendom to be engulfed in darkness for the past 200 years:

> Do not be concerned that some teachers, such as Thomas and the likes, have placed much stock in this and other Roman or human ordinances, for they lived in the tangible darkness with which God has veiled Christendom for two hundred years, and I believe that such teachers, who perhaps are with God in heaven, take compassion on us that we have been led astray by their errors, and diligently implore God for our illumination ...[98]

That Eberlin's criticism stems from the humanist attempt to purify theology by a return to the fathers is made clear in the next Confederate:

> Note here that from frequent reading of the holy Bible and its ancient commentators, such as Origen, Chrysostum, Jerome, Augustine, etc., arises proper sentiment and devotion.[99]

However, there are a number of problems in assessing the exact nature of his criticism. The claim that darkness has shrouded Christendom for 200 years would apparently not include Thomas, or for that matter Scotus who died in 1308. Elsewhere in his writings, Eberlin betrays a good sense of the history of the medieval church and it is unlikely that he would have mistaken the dates of Thomas' activity. It is tempting to see in Eberlin's statements a criticism of the *via moderna* or Erasmus' more moderate criticism of the "compilers." However, we have no clear indication of Eberlin's scholastic training and the south German humanists with whom Eberlin likely had contact prior to his career as a Reformer included Beatus Rhenanus and Zwingli, both of whom early rejected the *via antiqua* along with the *via moderna*.[100]

Eberlin's choice of 200 years for the duration of the perversion of theology and the mildness with which he treats Thomas may have been a tactical consideration. Wilhelm Lucke has argued convincingly that the constituent elements of *The Fifteen Confederates* were written in an order different from that in which they appear in the finished version of the work. The first tracts to be written were numbers seven, two, three and four. Although strongly critical of ecclesiastical abuses, they were written from an orthodox position.[101] Throughout this group of Confederates one frequently encounters the language of Erasmus' works and of Luther's *Address to the Christian Nobility*. Two of the recent interpreters of Eberlin's works, Gottfried Geiger and Günther Heger, have argued that Eberlin derived specific *gravamina* from Luther's pamphlet, but that at this stage in his career Eberlin's thought is primarily Erasmian.[102] I have suggested elsewhere that Eberlin looked initially to a humanist inspired reform movement within the Franciscan order. He therefore avoided the theological subtleties of Erasmus' and Luther's works and instead mined these for a catalogue of ecclesiastical abuses.[103] This may explain the ambivalence of his position on Thomas, who should come under censure as a scholastic but could not be rejected out of hand as a prominent doctor of the church and member of a mendicant order.

Eberlin's conciliatory stance evaporates in the next group of Confederates—numbers one, five, six, eight, nine, thirteen and fourteen, written according to Lucke during or shortly after the conflict that culminated in Eberlin's departure or expulsion from the Franciscan order.[104] In *The Fifth Confederate* he demands that preaching be based on "the pure fountain of the Bible and the old, holy teachers, not on the pits, poisons and pools of the new preaching books which have appeared in the last three hundred years."[105] *The Eighth Confederate* is even more pointed in its criticism, contrasting the true Christian teaching, which dominated the church for more than a thousand years, with scholastic theology which has only been dreamed up in the last three hundred.[106]

The radicalization of Eberlin's position stems not only from his own experiences among the south German Franciscans, but also from a deeper immersion in the writings of those who had moved beyond Erasmus' criticism of ecclesiastical abuses. The thought of Luther and Hutten in particular plays an increasingly important role in this group of Confederates.[107] Eberlin did, however, continue to regard all calls for the reform of the church as a unity. *The First Confederate* draws a direct line from Reuchlin, through Erasmus and the German humanists, to Luther and Hutten.[108] In *The Eighth Confederate* Erasmus, Luther and Hutten are identified as the chief representatives of the new learning, and *The Thirteenth Confederate* adds to this list the names of Karlstadt and Melanchthon.[109] The expansion of this list to include the names of more Reformers indicates clearly the direction in which Eberlin's thought was developing. However, Erasmus remained a prominent representative of the calls for reform according to Eberlin, and the sixth and fourteenth Confederates consist of translations of the *Praise of Folly* with commentaries by Eberlin. The only historical event that Eberlin associates with the fall or deterioration of the church is the rise of scholastic theology. However, he does imply that this is only the latest stage in a process that began with the ascendancy of Rome, which he depicts in the apocalyptic terms employed by Luther. In *The Fifth Confederate* Eberlin begins to identify the Roman church as a synagogue of Satan.[110] At the same time he suggests that the mendicant orders are responsible for much of the perversion of the Gospel.[111] Their exact role in this process becomes clear in *The Eighth Confederate*:

> As soon as the pope and his court noted that the begging monks were inclined—out of self interest—to all that would further

> their own honour and interests ... they entered into a pact with the begging monks, and they set them up as blood hounds throughout the world ...[112]

The consequence of this was that "the universities were forcibly occupied by the friars as were all pulpits and confessionals," the independence of the bishops and parish priests was broken and the scales tipped in favour of the pope in his bid for power over the emperor.[113] In this way Eberlin places the mendicants, and with them scholastic theology, at the centre of the papal victory instituting the final stage of the church's depravity. At the same time he successfully integrates the political vision of Hutten with the theological vision of Luther. The evolution of Eberlin's historical vision provides a useful barometer for charting the radicalization of his thought as he moved from a demand for reform of the church within the Franciscan order to humanist-inspired criticism of contemporary abuses and finally to more complete identification with the Wittenberg reform movement.

The cases examined here indicate that the historical visions of sixteenth century reformers were not static concepts directing reforming agendas from the outset. Instead they evolved as reforming agendas developed. In many cases one can discern a common trend in the relationship between reforming and historical visions. As reformers became more alienated from the established church, they tended to search further back into church history for the moment when the true church was lost. While the apostolic age was regarded by all reform-minded individuals examined here as a glorious period in church history, none of them saw in it a complete model for the reform of the contemporary church. Criticism of contemporary abuses in the church, not the revival of an apostolic ecclesiology, was the starting point for Reformation assessments of ecclesiastical history.

CHAPTER 1

Notes

1 *WA* 50:385.

2 Lorenzo Valla, *The Profession of the Religious and the principal arguments from The Falsely-Believed and Forged Donation of Constantine*, trans. and ed. by Olga Zorzi Pugliese (Toronto: Centre for Reformation and Renaissance Studies, 1985), 71.

3 Gordon Leff, "The Apostolic Ideal in Later Medieval Ecclesiology," *Journal of Theological Studies*, n.s. 18 (1967), 58-82; idem, "The Making of the Myth of a True Church in the Later Middle Ages," *The Journal of Medieval and Renaissance Studies* 1 (1971), 1-15.

4 Scott H. Hendrix, "In Quest of the *Vera Ecclesia*: The Crisis of Late Medieval Ecclesiology," *Viator* 7 (1976), 347-78.

5 See E. Jane Dempsey Douglass, *Justification in Late Medieval Preaching: A Study of John Geiler of Keisersberg*, 2nd ed. (Leiden: E.J. Brill, 1989), 94-100.

6 For a good summary of studies into Erasmus' perception and use of history, see István Bejczy, *Erasmus and the Middle Ages: The Historical Consciousness of a Christian Humanist* (Leiden: E.J. Brill, 2001), xii.

7 Peter Bietenholz, *History and Biography in the Work of Erasmus of Rotterdam* (Geneva: Librarie Droz, 1966), 29-30.

8 *LB*, 5: 86-88.

9 *Collected Works of Erasmus*, vol. 61: *Patristic Scholarship: The Edition of St. Jerome*, ed., trans., and ann. by James F. Brady and John C. Olin (Toronto: University of Toronto Press, 1992), 153.

10 Bejczy, xii-xiii.

11 Ibid., 18-19, 41, 192.

12 Ibid., 18-24.

13 Ibid., 24-32. See also Irena Backus, "Erasmus and the Spirituality of the Early Church," in Hilmar Pabel, ed. *Erasmus' Vision of the Church* (Kirksville, MO: Sixteenth Century Journal Publishers, 1995), 102-3, 110-11. Jan den Boeft, "Erasmus and the Church Fathers," in Irena Backus, ed., *The Reception of the Church Fathers in the West: From the Carolingians to the Maurists* (Leiden: E.J. Brill, 2001), 2:537-72, describes Erasmus' treatment of the church fathers as much less critical than Bejczy does.

14 *Collected Works of Erasmus*, vol., 9: *The Correspondence of Erasmus: Letters 1252 to 1355, 1522 to 1523*, trans., by R.A.B. Mynors, ann. J.M. Estes (Toronto: University of Toronto Press, 1989), 257 (= Allen, 5:180-81)

15 Bejczy, 29-31, 36-38.

16 *Collected Works of Erasmus*, vol. 3: *The Correspondence of Erasmus: Letters 298 to 445, 1514 to 1516*, trans. by R.A.B. Mynors and D.F.S. Thompson, ann. by J.K. McConica (Toronto: University of Toronto Press, 1976), 257 (= Allen, 2:213).

17 Bejczy, 10-12, 33-61.

18 Ibid., 192.

19 *Collected Works of Erasmus*, vol. 1: *The Correspondence of Erasmus: Letters 1 to 141, 1484 to 1500*, trans., by R.A.B. Mynors and D.F.S. Thompson, ann. by W.K. Ferguson (Toronto: University of Toronto Press, 1974), 135-38, 202-6 (= Allen, 1:190-93, 245-49).

20 *Collected Works of Erasmus*, vol. 66: *Spiritualia: Enchiridion/De Contemptu Mundi/de Vidua Christiana*, ed. by John W. O'Malley (Toronto: University of Toronto Press, 1988), 34-35, 69-71 (= *LB*, 5:8, 29-30).

21 *Collected Works of Erasmus*, 3:258 (= Allen, 2:214).

22 *Collected Works of Erasmus*, vol. 23: *Literary and Educational Writings*, vol. 1: *Antibarbari/ Parabolae*, trans. and ann. by Margaret Mann Phillips (Toronto: University of Toronto Press, 1978), 67 (= *LB* 10:1716). On the identification of this work as the manifesto of Christian humanism, see Bejczy, 8-9.

23 Bejczy, 62-103.

24 *Collected Works of Erasmus*, 9:274 (= Allen, 5:192).

25 *Collected Works of Erasmus*, 23:67, n.6.

26 *LB*, 9:910.

27 Ibid., 911.

28 For a detailed analysis of Erasmus' treatment of Thomas, see Bejczy, 86-93.

29 Ibid., 161-64, 170-82.

30 Ibid., 85.

31 For example, see Bernd Moeller, "The German Humanists and the Beginnings of the Reformation," in *Imperial Cities and the Reformation*, ed. and trans., by H.C. Erik Middlefort and Mark U. Edwards (Durham, NC: Labyrinth Press, 1982), 19-38.

32 For the details of the historical visions of Rhenanus and Hutten, see John F. D'Amico, "Ulrich von Hutten and Beatus Rhenanus as Medieval Historians and Religious Propagandists in the Early Reformation," in Paul Grendler, ed. *Roman and German Humanism, 1450-1550* (Aldershot: Variorum, 1993), XII:1-33.

33 John D'Amico, "Beatus Rhenanus, Tertullian and the Reformation: A Humanist's Critique of Scholasticism," *ARG* 71 (1980), 38-40, 47-48. D'Amico suggests that the details of the historical vision laid out in Erasmus' 1523 edition of the writings of Hilary may have been borrowed from Rhenanus' Tertullian edition.

34 Ibid., 42-45, 47, 56-57. The general outlines of this historical vision were shared as well by Cornelius Agrippa. See Charles G. Nauert, *Agrippa and the Crisis of Renaissance Thought* (Urbana, IL: University of Illinois Press, 1965), 157-93.

35 *Opera Q.F.S. Tertullian* as quoted in D'Amico, "Rhenanus, Tertullian and the Reformation," 43, see also 45-56.

36 D'Amico, "Rhenanus, Tertullian and the Reformation," 38, 41-43, 57-60.

37 Hajo Holborn, *Ulrich von Hutten* (Göttingen: Vandanhoeck & Ruprecht, 1968), 54.

38 James Overfield, *Humanism and Scholasticism in Late Medieval Germany* (Princeton: Princeton University Press, 1984), 297.

39 On the dating of these works and the beginning of Hutten's attack on Rome, see Holborn, 50, 56, 103.

40 *Ulrich von Hutten, Opera*, 7 vols., ed. by E. Böcking (Leipzig: B.G. Teubner, 1859-1869; reprint ed., Aalen and Osnabrück: Otto Zeller, 1963-1966), vol. 1, 182.

41 Böcking, 6:264-65.

42 Ibid., 265.

43 Böcking 1:237.

44 Ibid., 167, 216.

45 Ibid., 302.

46 Holborn, 113; Böcking, 4:145-268.

47 Holborn, 107.

48 Ibid., 106; see Böcking, 1:302, 313.

49 Böcking, 1:320-21, 324-25.

50 Holborn, 112.

51 Ibid., 110-11; see Böcking, 1:325-34.

52 Holborn, 112; see Böcking, 1:371-83.

53 See especially, "Clag und vormanung gegen übermässigen unchristlichen gewalt des Bapsts zü Rom," Böcking, 3: 473-526 and "Anzöig, wie allwegen sich die Römischen Bischöf, oder Bäpst gegen den teütschen Kayßern gehalten haben," Böcking, 5: 363-95. On the importance of historical research into papal-imperial relations in the thought of Hutten and the German humanists, see D'Amico, "Hutten and Rhenanus," 1-33 and Kurt Stadtwald, *Roman Popes and German Patriots: Antipapalism in the Politics of the German Humanists from Gregor Heimburg to Martin Luther* (Geneva: Librarie Droz, 1996), especially 92-103.

54 Moeller, "German Humanists and the Beginnings of the Reformation," 23.

55 John M. Headley, *Luther's View of Church History* (New Haven and London: Yale University Press, 1963), 104, 156-81.

56 For example, in *The Babylonian Captivity of the Church* he holds up the apostolic mass as a model for contemporary reform of the mass. See *WA* 6:523-24. Luther also suggested at one point reforming the clergy on the basis of Paul's description of the offices of the apostolic church. See my "Luther, Emser and the Development of Reformation Anticlericalism," *ARG* 87 (1996), 38-56.

57 *WA* 15:39. On Luther's attitude toward and use of the writings of the church fathers, see Manfred Schulze, "Martin Luther and the Church Fathers," in Backus, ed., *Reception of the Church Fathers in the West*, 2:573-626.

58 See Scott H. Hendrix, *Luther and the Papacy: Stages in a Reformation Conflict* (Philadelphia: Fortress Press, 1981), 37, 167-68.

59 *WABr* 1:99.

60 *WA* 1:221.

61 *WABr* 1:160.

62 Ibid.

63 Ibid., 170.

64 Ibid., 379.

65 *WA* 1:613, 620, 677.

66 Ulrich Bubenheimer, *Thomas Müntzer: Herkunft und Bildung* (Leiden: E.J. Brill, 1989), 188; see *WA* 2:161. On the relationship between Luther's anti-papal polemics and those of the humanists, see Stadtwald, *Roman Popes and German Patriots*, 179-203.

67 *WABr* 1:359-60.

68 Headley, 162-63.

69 *WA* 2:226, 238, 285; Headley, 164-65; Schulze, 597-600.

70 *WA* 2:227-32, 423; *WA* 6:407-8; Headley, 166-67, 172-74.

71 *WA* 2:225, 227, 287; Headley, 164, 182, 192.

72 Headley, 192-93.

73 *WA* 2:226.

74 Ibid., 5:649-50. See also pages 281 and 644.

75 Ibid., 6:509, 571.

76 Ibid., 7:739; 8:460,473-74.

77 On Luther's use of historical arguments, see Headley, 178-79.

78 Gottfried Locher, "Das Geschichtsbild Huldrych Zwinglis," *Theologische Zeitschrift* 9 (1953), 294.

79 See James M. Stayer, "Zwingli and the 'viri multi et excellentes': The Christian Renaissance's repudiation of the *Neoterici* and the Beginnings of Reformed Protestantism," in E.J. Furcha and H. Wayne Pipkin, eds. *Prophet, Pastor, Protestant: The Work of Huldrych Zwingli after Five Hundred Years* (Allison Park, PA: Pickwick Publications, 1984), 138, 142-44; J.F. Gerhard Goeters, "Zwinglis Werdegang als

Erasmianer," in Martin Greschat and J.F.G. Goeters, eds., *Reformation und Humanismus. Robert Stupperich zum 65. Geburtstag* (Witten: Luther-Verlag, 1969), 265-71; Wilhelm H. Neuser, *Die reformatorische Wende bei Zwingli* (Neukirchen: Nuekirchener Verlag, 1977), 38-59, 101-47.

80 *ZW* 7:36.

81 Ibid., 115. On Zwingli's knowledge of patristic writings and their place in his thought, see Irena Backus, "Ulrich Zwingli, Martin Bucer and the Church Fathers," in Backus, ed., *Reception of the Church Fathers in the West*, 2:627-60.

82 Stayer, "Zwingli and the 'viri multi et excellentes," 153, n. 55. See also 145-46.

83 Ibid., 154, n. 70.

84 Ibid., 140.

85 Arthur Rich, *Die Anfänge der Theologie Huldrych Zwinglis* (Zurich, 1949), 91.

86 Neuser, 50, 76, 104, 107-8.

87 Ibid., 101, 146-47.

88 Stayer, "Zwingli and the 'viri multi et excellentes,'" 138-39.

89 *ZW* 1:95.

90 Ibid., 234.

91 Ibid., 317.

92 Ibid., 282.

93 Ibid., 2:27, 50, 67, 71, 104, 108, 111 (*Analysis and Reasons for the Concluding Statements*); Ibid., 3:888, 895, 907 (*Commentary about True and False Religion*).

94 Ibid., 1:109.

95 Ibid., 126-27.

96 Ibid., 303-4.

97 Ibid., 322.

98 Ludwig Enders, ed., *Johann Eberlin von Günzburg, Ausgewählte Schriften*, vol. 1 (Halle: Max Niemeyer, 1896), 22.

99 Ibid., 29.

100 Wilhelm Lucke, "Die Entstehung der '15 Bundesgenossen' des Johann Eberlin von Günzburg," (Phil. Diss., Halle, 1902), 10-18; Curt Wulkau, "Das kirchliche Idea des Johann Eberlin von Günzburg," (Phil. Diss., Halle-Wittenberg, 1922), 11; Gottfried Geiger, "Die reformatorischen Initia Johann Eberlins von Günzburg nach seinen Flugschriften," in Horst Rabe, et al., eds., *Festgabe für Ernst Walter Zeeden zum 60. Geburtstag am 14. Mai 1976* (Münster: Aschendorffsche Verlagsbuchhandlung, 1976), 180.

101 Lucke, 33-48; Geiger, 181-82, suggests some modification of Lucke's dating of these works.

102 Geiger, 191-93; Günther Heger, *Johann Eberlin von Günzburg und seine Vorstellungen über eine Reform in Reich und Kirche* (Berlin: Duncker und Humblot, 1985), 20.

103 Geoffrey Dipple, *Antifraternalism and Anticlericalism in the German Reformation: Johann Eberlin von Günzburg and the Campaign against the Friars* (Aldershot: Scolar Press, 1996), 37-59. Geiger, 186-87, suggests that *The Fifteen Confederates* are not so much concerned with developing theological issues as with providing a catalogue of ecclesiastical abuses.

104 Lucke, 49-94.

105 Enders, 1:51.

106 Ibid., 86.

107 Max Radlkofer, *Johann Eberlin von Günzburg und sein Vetter Hans Jakob Wehe von Leipheim* (Nördlingen: Verlag der C.H. Beck'schen Buchhandlung, 1887), 17-18; Hans-Herbert

Ahrens, "Die religiosen, nationalen und sozialen Gedanken Johann Eberlins von Günzburg mit besonderer Berücksichtigung seiner anonymen Flugschriften," (Phil. Diss., Hamburg, 1939), 22-24, 33-40; Lucke, 72, 95-97; Geiger, 183, 191. Geiger, 189-90, suggests as the source of Eberlin's historical vision Philip Melanchthon's *Didymi Faventini adversus Thomam Placentinum pro Martino Luthero theologo ratio* which identifies the perversion of true teaching and the appearance of the Antichrist with events in the preceding three hundred to four hundred years. However, given the prevalence of these dates in references to the fall of the church by humanists and Reformers, identifying the specific source of Eberlin's vision, if there was a specific source, seems impossible.

108 Enders, 1:3-4.

109 Ibid., 86, 148.

110 Ibid., 85.

111 Ibid., 49.

112 Ibid., 82.

113 Ibid., 81-82.

CHAPTER 2

THE SAXON RADICALS AND THE PRIMITIVE CHURCH

Hegesippus, a trustworthy historian and pupil of the apostles, states explicitly in the fifth book of Memoirs as does Eusebius in the fourth book about the Christian Churches, that the holy bride of Christ remained a virgin until after the death of the followers of the apostles, but from that moment on became an immoral adulteress.

Thomas Müntzer, *German Church Service Book*[1]

On the surface, historical reflection among Reformation radicals appears to be on a different order than that of the humanists and magisterial Reformers. The starting point for the latter was criticism of the contemporary church, especially scholasticism. As their criticisms become more radical, the Reformers looked further back into history for the sources of the abuses they saw around them. By way of contrast, the most common reference among the radicals was to the apostolic or the primitive church. This trend has been observed by historians of the Reformation. According to Franklin H. Littell, a "common dream of the Early Church" united those on the left wing of the Reformation.[2] This observation raises several questions about the nature of historical reflection in the Radical Reformation and its relationship to historical thinking among the magisterial Reformers and the humanists. Was this appeal to the primitive church the result of a different starting point in the historical visions of the radicals or was it the consequence of developments we have seen at work among the magisterial Reformers? What characteristics of the apostolic church appealed to the radicals, and what do these tell us about their reforming visions, and their relationships to each other and to the magisterial Reformers and humanists? A fruitful place to begin looking for answers to these questions are the writings of the Saxon Radicals, Andreas Bodenstein von Karlstadt and Thomas Müntzer.

As is well known, Martin Luther was fond of lumping together Karlstadt and Müntzer in less than flattering terms. By labelling both men *Schwärmer*, Enthusiasts, he drew an implicit connection between their spiritualism and their social and political radicalism. Luther's comments cast a long shadow over subsequent treatments of these two men, and since the sixteenth century their names have often been joined together. Defenders of Karlstadt's honour have challenged this identification, usually by playing down his spiritualism in favour of his biblicism and minimizing the significance of his interaction with Müntzer.[3]

More recently, though, the connections between the two men have been reemphasized. The primary impetus for this revision has come from Müntzer studies, and in particular from attempts to cast Müntzer as less of a fanatic. Recent research has been especially fruitful in reestablishing the connections between Karlstadt and Müntzer between 1517/18, when the latter went to Wittenberg to study the new theology, and their break in 1524 over Müntzer's invitation to Karlstadt and his congregation at Orlamünde to join the eternal covenant. The results of this research suggest that the connections between these two men were more extensive and closer than previously thought and that their influence on each other was significant. As a result, Müntzer's character has been rehabilitated along with Karlstadt's. While the spiritualist impulses of their theologies have not been denied by most interpreters, closer attention has been paid to humanist elements in their thought, and they have been regarded as representatives of more "respectable" reforming traditions. At the same time the gulf between their social visions has been narrowed. Müntzer's theology is regarded less as inherently revolutionary and Karlstadt is no longer treated as a categorical pacifist.[4]

Traditional characterizations of Karlstadt and Müntzer as Spiritualists have tended to divert attention from their understanding of, and appeals to, history. Ernst Troeltsch's suggestion that focus on the immediacy of the Spirit crowded out historical concerns among the Spiritualists continues to influence research into the thought of Müntzer and Karlstadt. However, recent reassessments of their connections to humanism suggest that the place of historical reflection in the thought of these two men must also be seen differently. Of the two, Karlstadt's humanist credentials are most firmly established and widely recognized. And yet, his statements about the history of the church are less extensive, and have received much less attention than Müntzer's.

Karlstadt—From Humanist to Reformer, 1517–1520

Given what we know both about the development of Karlstadt's thought and about the development of historical visions in the reform programmes of humanists and magisterial Reformers, Karlstadt's earliest statements on the history of the church provide us with no surprises. In fact, they appear to be a textbook case of the interaction of historical reflection and religious radicalization, particularly in their relationship to Karlstadt's wrestling with the question of ecclesiastical and religious authority. The starting point for his comments comes with his early activity as member of the humanist reforming movement in Wittenberg. 1517 is now regarded as a crucial year in Karlstadt's intellectual and spiritual development as he went from being a scholastic/humanist reformer to a strictly humanist reformer. At this point his comments on the history of the church, not surprisingly, single out scholasticism as a danger for ecclesiastical tradition, but otherwise he remains respectful of that tradition.[5] Karlstadt held firmly to the essentials of that position through the next two years. He retained his respect for the church fathers and the papacy, and he continued to believe in the essential harmony between Scripture, ecclesiastical tradition—with the exception of scholasticism—and the liturgy of the church.[6] Even at the Leipzig Disputation he appears to have held to a generally humanist vision of ecclesiastical history. There he claimed that Aristotle had dominated theology for the preceding 400 years, not without a loss of souls and with a setting aside of the Spirit and the light of the Gospel.[7]

But, it seems, Leipzig and then especially the events of early 1520 occasioned a reassessment of ecclesiastical history. In this reassessment we see a continued interaction of Karlstadt's developing historical vision and his wrestling with the nature and locus of religious authority. Already in 1518 he had asserted the superior authority of Scripture to that of the pope, councils and the church. Subsequent events were to sharpen the conflict between these competing loci of authority in his mind. Also in 1518 he had begun to abandon his earlier concilliarist position. In *On Which Books are Canonical* of 1520, he sharpened his criticism of councils and suggested that historical evidence indicated that popes could err, although he thought the foundations of the papacy were still solid and he still hoped for the possibility of a reformed papacy. But with the publication of the papal bull *Exsurge Domine* in Wittenberg, his position on spiritual authority, and with it his view of ecclesiastical history, became more radical. In his *Ten Disputation Theses* he denounced the errors of the Council of Meaux (845-46), especially the claim that canon law was binding on Christians in spiritual matters. With this claim went a rejection of much of the authority of canon law and the beginning of the elevation of Scripture to a *ius divinum* governing the church. At this point Karlstadt's treatment of the papacy was still more cautious. In these theses he traced the origin of papal errors to the pontificate of Alexander IV (1254-61), likely because of the pontiff's proclamation that the laity were prohibited from disputing about theological matters. The importance of context in the evolution of Karlstadt's thought is highlighted by the implications of his new assertion: if all popes after Alexander were anathema, Leo X's excommunication of Luther, and with him Karlstadt, was invalid.[8] At roughly the same time, in his *Tract on the Supreme Virtue of Gelassenheit*, he underlined his rejection of the authorities arrayed against the Wittenberg reform movement by identifying them with Annas, Caiaphas, the scribes and hypocrites.[9] The end result was a stinging historically-rooted criticism of the ecclesiastical hierarchy and canon law. Particularly the attack on the papacy dovetailed well with his earlier criticism of scholasticism, suggesting a serious deterioration of the church between 300 and 400 years previously. All of this suggests the development of an historical vision closely parallel to Luther's.[10]

Karlstadt—The Wittenberg Movement and Orlamünde, 1520–1524

Karlstadt's subsequent radicalization involved continued reflection on history, as is evident in the development of his thought in Wittenberg and then subsequently in Orlamünde. In the background to his statements about the history of the church looms the constant question of authority and the right by which he is challenging the structures of ecclesiastical authority and centuries of ecclesiastical practice. But also clear is the fact that Karlstadt's actual scrutiny of the historical record was usually occasioned by specific reform issues. These specific issues, and the historical investigation they encouraged, flowed together to produce a comprehensive vision of the historical decline of the church. But the evolution of that vision indicates the primacy of lived experience in dictating its outlines. The starting point remained the humanist attack on scholasticism and the assertion that the church had been in decline for the preceding 400 years. However, as Karlstadt's reforming vision evolved, the dates associated with the church's decline quickly changed.

Indications are that even as he moved to a more radical vision of reform during 1521, Karlstadt at first attempted to incorporate his demands into his established perception of ecclesiastical history. During the fall of that year, Karlstadt wrestled at length with the question of vows and their legitimacy, largely as an extension of the more concrete issues of monastic reform and the legitimacy of clerical celibacy. In the process, he began looking to the historical roots of contemporary abuses and, initially at least, these reinforced his view that the church had fallen in the last few centuries. Calistus II's firm enforcement of clerical celibacy in the twelfth century stood out as a further indication of deterioration during that time. Karlstadt was able to claim, therefore, that for 400 years the pope and his forebears had lain under the ban, anathemas and curses of God. He later claimed that Innocent III (1198-1216) should have been severely punished for his use of vows in promoting the crusades, and that other popes deserved punishment for their treatments of pilgrimages undertaken as the result of a vow.[11] A 1521 report of the Wittenberg University Committee, likely authored by Karlstadt, pushed back the date of the church's fall 100 years with the claim that until 500 years previously cloisters and *Stiftungen* had been Christian schools.[12] Soon after that, though, Karlstadt's views changed drastically. As part of the attack on what he regarded as the idolatry of medieval Christendom, he suggested that a key element in the church's decline appeared in the seventh century when Gregory the Great declared sacred images the "books of the laity." According to Karlstadt, nothing but carnal perversion of the Christian message arose from this statement.[13] In February 1522 he denounced the moves of Alexander III (1159-1181) against the Waldensians as a clear instance of the ecclesiastical hierarchy keeping the word from the laity.[14]

Parallel to this developing criticism of the established church, Karlstadt began to clarify the contours of an apostolic counter model. William McNiel has commented that Karlstadt used the humanist *ad fontes* principle to good effect in his developing criticism of the church.[15] It appears that at this time he scoured the fathers and other sources from primitive Christianity in an attempt to establish the nature of the apostolic church. For example, in his denunciation of the idolatry of sacred images he refers to a Bishop of Epiphanus who in the late fourth century removed a cloth from a church because it had an image of a saint or the crucified Christ painted on it.[16] However, Karlstadt was not aiming at a straightforward identification of the apostolic church with the true church, although in his mind the apostolic church did go a long way in identifying the essential characteristics of the true church. Instead he claimed that the kingdom of God has existed through all ages, and had been persecuted from Abel to Moses, the prophets, Christ and the apostles down to the present age.[17] Unfortunately, Karlstadt failed to elaborate extensively on the general outlines of the history of that persecuted church throughout the ages or on the soteriological importance of that history.

The nature of the true, spiritual church and the place of the apostolic church in its definition becomes clearer if we look at some of the specific reforms Karlstadt envisioned and/or implemented. Particularly valuable are his ideas for the clerical office and liturgical reforms, especially his treatment of baptism and the Lord's Supper. In his attempted reforms of the clerical office both in Wittenberg and Orlamünde culminating in Karlstadt's self-identification as Brother Andreas, the importance of the model of the apostolic church is immediately apparent. He repeatedly defines clerical offices and status, including strictures against clerical marriage, on the basis of Titus 1 and 1 Timothy 3. The existing ecclesiastical hierarchy is to be discarded and replaced by the establishment of a body of roughly equal clergy, distinguished in their status only on the basis of office. But the defining feature of the apostolic church insofar as Karlstadt holds it as normative here is the clear presence of the Spirit in it. This feature is confirmed by the demand, and apparently in Orlamünde the practice, of casting lots to confirm the calling of clergy, as well as his allowance for the possibility of direct inspiration among the parishioners on the basis of 1 Corinthians 11:4-5 and 14:1-2.[18] But the apostolic church was not the exclusive model for Karlstadt's vision, as his frequent citation of the Old Testament indicates. His discussion of vows, which is a crucial stepping stone in his thinking about reforming the clerical office, is primarily an exposition of Numbers 30, and elsewhere the casting of lots to determine the divine will is justified with reference to the activities of Joshua.[19]

This is no less clear in Karlstadt's treatment of liturgical reforms, the consideration of which in Wittenberg occasioned significant historical reflection. In the report of the University Committee to Frederick the

Wise, the Elector was informed that until the time of Cyprian the mass had been received in both elements by the laity and that the current abuses of it could be laid at the feet of popes Damasus, Gelasius, Celestine and Gregory.[20] Other writings related to the Wittenberg reforms contain repeated calls to return to the practices of the primitive church.[21] Further indications are that Karlstadt made a serious attempt to institute some of the practices of the primitive church in both Wittenberg and Orlamünde. He translated the Psalms so his parishioners could sing and understand them, he allowed for sermon interruptions to demand clarifications or to challenge statements of the preacher on the basis of I Corinthians 14:26-31, and he reformed the celebration of baptism and the Lord's Supper to conform to what he regarded as apostolic practice.[22] Particularly intriguing from the present perspective is that he preached daily on the book of Acts, suggesting that he was expounding a model for emulation. But before turning Karlstadt into a proto-Anabaptist New Testament restitutionist, it is important to acknowledge the role Old Testament models played in his thinking. Liturgical reform in Wittenberg was supplemented by a focus on social concerns in the Wittenberg ordinance which derived from Deuteronnomic ideas of social justice and renewal, and Karlstadt's tactical suggestions for the implementation of reform measures further highlight the amalgam of Old and New Testament models in his thinking. While his warnings against the dangers of tarrying for the weak hold up as models the activities of Peter and Paul, the means and authority for implementing reforms look to Old Testament examples of communal or royal activity.[23] Once again, Karlstadt is pointing to a wider vision of the church than just the apostolic.

The nature of the church to be emulated is further clarified in Karlstadt's sacramental theology. Despite his repeated calls for adherence to the apostolic practices in celebrating the sacraments, Karlstadt placed increasing emphasis on the spiritual reality behind those practices. Especially in Orlamünde, he began to reject the term sacrament and to treat the associated rite or ceremony as merely an external sign. The visible sacrament was no longer a medium for the communication of grace, but rather an indication of the grace already received. This thinking was given concrete expression in Karlstadt's likely suspension of infant baptism in fall 1523 and in his reforms of the Eucharist.[24]

Clearly, Karlstadt's vision for the reform of the church at Wittenberg after Luther's disappearance and at Orlamünde looked to the model of the apostolic church in ways unparalleled in the thought of the magisterial Reformers. According to his vision, wherever possible the practices and structures of the primitive church were to be revived. But this vision of the apostolic church did not determine his reforming vision from the outset of his activities as a reformer. Instead, it was a consequence of the radicalization of his thought as a result of the intransigence of the ecclesiastical authorities in the face of demands for reform and as a result of his increasing emphasis on the authority of Scripture as the source of religious truth. His search for true Christian traditions untainted by human teachings forced him to look further back into the history of the church. The apostolic church, as described in Scripture, became increasingly the model for ecclesiastical, and to a certain degree social, reform. But Karlstadt did not aim at a simple restoration of the structures and practices of the primitive church. The primary characteristic of that church was that it was Spirit-filled; other attributes derived their value as an extension from their proximity to the presence of the Holy Spirit. Karlstadt, then, is correctly labelled as a Spiritualist, and his vision of history did not make the apostolic church normative for reform of the church *in toto*.

Müntzer—From Humanist to Reformer, 1517–1519

Thomas Müntzer's forays into history, especially ecclesiastical history, have attracted more attention than Karlstadt's. Traditionally, though, this aspect of his thought has been treated largely as an extension of his apocalypticism. Rather than an independent and influential aspect of his theology, history has been regarded as a tool he employed in the service of his eschatological musings: history is first and foremost a means of reading the signs of the times. In that sense, in the eyes of some interpreters, historical reflection played an important role in turning Müntzer from a mystic into a revolutionary.[25] More recently an interpretive tradition has grown up which treats his historical vision as not necessarily divorced from his apocalypticism, but as a more independent element of his thought with a more significant role in determining its overall contours.[26] The most radical statement of this line of interpretation has come from the pen of Abraham Friesen. According to Friesen, historical research played a crucial role in the development of Müntzer's reforming vision. He portrays Müntzer's thought as an amalgam of mystical theology from Tauler with a vision of ecclesiastical history derived from Eusebius and Augustine's reflections on the end times. Within this melange, the view of ecclesiastical history is of prime importance: "Eusebius provided the paradigm or context for Müntzer's thinking." Although nowhere systematically developed, a model of the apostolic church is a central theme in his reforming thought. The conclusions Friesen draws from these assertions are surprising. Friesen claims that like the "Evangelical Anabaptists" Müntzer was a thorough-going critic of the Constantinian church and, even more surprisingly, he was not a Spiritualist, or even a revolutionary Spiritualist, but "... a man obsessed with reestablishing the Apostolic Church he had seen described by Eusebius and confirmed in the book of Acts."[27]

Recent research has highlighted Müntzer's connections to the Wittenberg reform movement. Within this context, his initial statements about the history of the church, too, contain no surprises. During the Easter season (April 24 to 26) of 1519, he preached three sermons in the town of Jüterbog. The details of these sermons have come down to us through a report to the episcopal authorities of the region written by one of Müntzer's opponents there, a local Franciscan named Bernhard Dappen. Dappen's report claims that Müntzer denounced central elements of the medieval church in his sermons: he attacked the hierarchical structure of ecclesiastical authority, emphasizing the authority of councils and the episcopacy against that of the papacy and of the parochial clergy against that of the episcopacy; he bemoaned the neglect of pastoral duties by the bishops of his day; and he railed against scholastic theology, especially as embodied in the teachings of Thomas and Bonaventure. At the conclusion of this catalogue of abuses, Dappen reported that Müntzer had claimed, alluding to Mark 4:21, that the Gospel had lain under a bench for the preceding 400 years.[28]

Most interpreters of Müntzer's thought have seen in this reference a dating of the "fall" of the church, and a variety of different "abuses" have been identified as bearing primary responsibility for that fall.[29] However a careful reading of the passage suggests that such speculation may be misplaced. Dappen's statement, coming at the end of the list of abuses, reads as follows: "Likewise, he said, not once but repeatedly, that for more than 400 years the holy Gospel had lain under a bench ..."[30] Müntzer's repeated references to the fall of the church would indicate, then, that many, or even all, of the abuses he identified contributed to that fall.

More contentious have been discussions of possible intellectual influences on Müntzer reflected in this statement. On the basis of the similarity of the language employed, Friesen has argued that Müntzer's dating of the fall of the church reflects Luther's statements in the preface to *The German Theology*.[31] However, as we have seen, Luther's position on this matter was hardly original or unique. Bubenheimer, by way of contrast, argues that during Müntzer's stay in Wittenberg, theology there was a complex mixture that allowed for no clear distinction between the thought of Erasmus and that of Luther. Furthermore, he suggests that when Müntzer arrived in Jüterbog he was portraying himself as a humanist, and his reference to the fall of the church reflected the position of both Luther and the humanists.[32] Closely related to the question of Müntzer's intellectual debts is that of the independence and radicalism of his vision. In other words, are there any clues in Müntzer's historical vision in 1519 that point to his later radicalism? Various aspects of Müntzer's criticism of the contemporary church, from his conciliarism to the vehemence of his criticism of the bishops, have been held up as evidence of his independence and radicalism.[33] A particularly interesting line of investigation on this issue has been pointed out by Ulrich

Bubenheimer's claim that Müntzer developed a critique of ecclesiastical authority distinct from that of his contemporaries at Wittenberg. According to Bubenheimer, Müntzer did not criticize the structure of the ecclesiastical hierarchy *per se*, but rather its lines of authority. His claim that members of the hierarchy, specifically the pope and bishops, hold their authority at the pleasure of their charges amounted to a democratization of the existing ecclesiastical structure.[34] Nonetheless, Luther's support for Müntzer in Jüterbog – Luther wrote to the Jüterbog Franciscans in defence of Müntzer's activities – and subsequent recommendation of him for a post in Zwickau suggests that his contemporaries saw nothing radical or untoward in the Jüterbog sermons.[35]

Müntzer—Zwickau and Prague, 1520–1522

Müntzer's next clear statement about the history of the church indicates that his perspective had changed drastically. Two years after his Jüterbog sermons, in the so-called *Prague Manifesto*, he wrote:

> I have read here and there in the history of the early fathers, and find that the immaculate, virginal church, after the death of the pupils of the apostles, soon became a whore because of the seductive priests. For the priests have always wanted to sit up at the top, as Hegesippus and Eusebius plainly testify, and others too.[36]

As we will see, this vision of the post-apostolic fall of the church remained constant in his subsequent references to ecclesiastical history. Most interpreters of Müntzer's writings see in this statement some sort of "primitivist ecclesiology" integral to the radicalization of his reforming vision. That is, it is assumed that as Müntzer broke with the humanists and Wittenberg Reformers, the apostolic church became a central feature in his thought, providing a model for the reform, or the basis for criticism, of the contemporary church.[37] This line of interpretation is developed most fully by Friesen, who sees Müntzer formulating a comprehensive and normative vision of the apostolic church as the result of intense historical research already at the time of the Leipzig Disputation. By the time he arrived in Zwickau, in May 1520, then, the essentials of Müntzer's independent reforming vision were already hammered out. According to Friesen, the central feature of the apostolic church for Müntzer was the presence of the Holy Spirit. The consequence of its presence, however, was that the apostolic church manifested its gifts: a life in conformity with the teachings of Christ, dreams, visions and prophecy.[38]

There is much to commend in Friesen's interpretation. However, some of its details are in need of revision. Recent studies have indicated that Müntzer's historical research was a much more drawn out process, likely lasting from his period of study in Wittenberg to his stay in Zwickau from May 1520 to April 1521 or even to his brief sojourn in Prague from June to November 1521.[39] As we will see, this had significant implications for the role played by historical reflection in his thought. Rather than a set, formative principle firmly in place from the beginning of his activity, his vision of ecclesiastical history was an evolving organism responding to the challenges he faced. Naturally, as it evolved some of its details changed—certain crucial elements at its heart remained consistent, but it was initially neither as uniform nor as comprehensive as Friesen claims.

As Friesen notes, the distinguishing feature of the apostolic church in Müntzer's thought is the presence of the Spirit.[40] The church's perversion is traced to the clergy, who live without the Spirit and, consequently, fail to open themselves to the "living Word," ongoing revelation, and the "order of things."[41] Because of this defection by the clergy, church councils concentrated on child's play, ceremonies and externals, and they neglected the essence of Christianity, the ongoing speaking of the Spirit and experienced faith. As a result the wheat and tares became mingled and the true church was subverted. The crucial issue, then, is the presence of the Spirit; other characteristics of the apostolic church – the separation of the wheat and tares, signs, visions and the continued revelation – are the fruits of its presence.[42]

To this point, Friesen's interpretation seems to hold. It seems quite clear that Müntzer had established the essential pneumatological character of the apostolic church through his reading of Tauler and Eusebius prior to his arrival in Zwickau, although Karlstadt was likely more influential in this process than was Luther as Friesen claims.[43] However, what is not so clear is the extent to which his vision of ecclesiastical history was a "finished product" at that time. A number of historians regard Müntzer's conflict with the humanist reformer of Zwickau, Egranus, as playing a crucial role in the radicalization of his reforming vision.[44] Surviving evidence indicates that a central issue of contention in this conflict was the necessity of the continued presence of the Spirit in the post-apostolic church.[45] It seems likely that Müntzer's vision of the apostolic church and the conflict in which he was embroiled developed in a symbiotic relationship.

Other evidence from this period of Müntzer's life suggests such a relationship. In his annotations on the writings of the church fathers Cyprian and Tertullian, dating likely from his time in Zwickau or Prague, we see indications of Müntzer scouring the historical record for the fate of the "Spirit-filled" church. Yet, in the process he also further clarifies the nature of that church. Measured against his basic criterion, the presence of the Spirit, more and more traditions of the church begin to fall. Because of the defection of the clergy, all but the four apostolic councils of the church have opposed the "ancient faith," and are to be regarded as satanic. Even the church fathers come under careful scrutiny, and Müntzer criticizes Tertullian, Gregory and Chrysostom because they show no signs of experiencing the ongoing revelation. In a clear sign that he had broken with the humanist reform program, Müntzer later derides Tertullian for his reliance on Scripture alone and not the Spirit.[46]

Perhaps the best example of the interaction of historical research and reforming agenda appears in a letter Müntzer wrote to Phillip Melanchthon in March 1522 commenting on the nature and pace of reforms undertaken in Wittenberg to that date. Müntzer opens the letter by voicing his support for what the Wittenberg Reformers have undertaken, and he is especially laudatory about their teachings: "Your theology I embrace with all my heart for it has snatched many souls from the snares of the hunters."[47] But then his tone becomes more critical and, among other things, he chastises the Wittenbergers for their failure to reform the idolatrous, papal mass according to the "plumb line" of the apostolic rite.[48] On the surface, these comments seem to suggest that the apostolic church is normative *in toto* for Müntzer's vision, and this passage is an important source for Friesen's understanding of Müntzer's vision of the apostolic church.[49] However, a careful examination of the letter as a whole indicates that Müntzer is continuing to draw further conclusions about the nature of the apostolic church from his basic definition of the "Spirit-filled" community, and then confirming them with the scriptural record. His comments here and elsewhere in the letter indicate that he was interested not so much in imitating a normative vision of the apostolic church as in avoiding openly idolatrous practices which led the people away from the true faith. Müntzer's particular concern with the celebration of the mass in Wittenberg was that communicants were not being questioned about the content of their faith prior to communing. Ernst Koch has argued that Müntzer's treatment of the sacraments here parallels his treatment of the external word of Scripture elsewhere: they are intended to serve as a means to an inner spiritual change in the believer.[50] Criticisms of the Wittenbergers elsewhere in the letter confirm Koch's suspicions. Despite his opening praise for the Wittenbergers' teachings, Müntzer voices his concern that they are worshipping a "dumb god," that is, like the Catholic clergy, they are not holding themselves open to the speech of the Spirit. As a result, they remain ignorant of the "living word," and they fail to distinguish the elect from the reprobate and consequently will not recognize the coming church. He concludes by referring to the Wittenbergers as "delicate biblical scholars" and then promises to back up his assertions from Scripture, from the order of creation, from experience and from the clear word of God.[51] This letter, then, forms an important bridge between Müntzer's conflict with Egranus and his later break with the Wittenbergers, indicating the primacy of questions about the Spirit in both conflicts.

Müntzer's offer to justify his claims with reference to, among other things, the order of creation points to another level on which he read history. Repeatedly in *The Prague Manifesto*, he denounced the clergy for their refusal to open themselves to the living word and the "order of nature" or "order of creation."[52] His annotations on Tertullian indicate that that order can be discerned, among other places, in the record of human history.[53] Bubenheimer has elucidated the importance of the *ordo rerum,* or order of things, as a fundamental element in Müntzer's theology. A rhetorical principle derived from Quintillian, it played a determinative role in his approach not only to Scripture, but also to all hermeneutical questions writ large. For our purposes, the important matter is how this method is applied to history. Stated simply, it emphasizes the importance of parallels between distinct historical ages and events. The lessons extracted from one historical age can aid in illuminating another, provided, however, that one understands the over-arching scheme of history.[54]

For Müntzer, the over-arching historical scheme from creation to the impending apocalypse was that shared by many of his contemporaries.[55] More illuminating for our purposes is his treatment of parallels between parts of that history. Despite his references to the writings of early Christian historians, Müntzer's most important historical source remained the Bible. Correspondence with his followers in 1521 suggests he was encouraging them to draw parallels between events in the present church and its history in both testaments.[56] The "church" of the Old Testament was, then, potentially normative for his reform vision just as the church of the New Testament was. This goes a long way to explain the vehemence with which he attacked Egranus and the "Erasmians" as new Marcionites for their slighting of the Old Testament's authority.[57]

The specific historical parallels drawn by Müntzer reveal a loose integration of three different ages of the church's history: the "church" of the Old Testament, especially of the prophets; the apostolic church; and the coming church. But these parallels are scattered throughout his writings and are not developed into a clear, comprehensive vision, further suggesting that his historical outlook was still evolving. Certainly, there is no evidence of a clearly formulated view of a normative apostolic church even in the letter to Melanchthon, despite its reference to the "apostolic plumb line." Rather, it is invoked only where deemed necessary to justify specific claims.[58] In the *Prague Manifesto*, Müntzer's allusions to historical parallels focus more on the "church" of the Old Testament prophets than the apostolic church. He introduces the theme of the historical fall of the church with the claim that the clergy have taught the people to pray to Baal, and at the conclusion of the work he refers to his own activity as occurring in the spirit of Elijah and then indicates his willingness to suffer for the truth like Jeremiah.[59] In his growing crescendo of diatribes against the clergy contained in this work, Müntzer characterizes them with a whole series of references to Old Testament types of the false priest or false prophet. They are the scribes with false pens described in Jeremiah 8:8, false prophets described in Jeremiah 23:18 and those who have stolen the "word" from Jeremiah 23:30. He also identifies the clergy with the worthless or false shepherds mentioned in Zechariah 11:17 and Ezekial 34:2,4,8, the shunned priest of Hosea 4:6 and those for whom the book is sealed and who lack the key of David of Isaiah 22:22 and 29:11.[60] Insofar as he relies on the New Testament to illuminate the contemporary state of affairs, Müntzer is less forthcoming. To drive home his point that the true preacher must be open to ongoing revelation in dreams and visions, he alludes to the apostolic church, but not to its practice and organization; instead he points his readers to Paul's discussion of the gifts of the Spirit contained in 1 Corinthians 14.[61] Further New Testament citations appear, not surprisingly, in Müntzer's denunciation of the clergy, but here the references are not so much to historical descriptions of the apostolic church as to prophetic warnings about the appearance of false prophets and false apostles. The clergy are characterized as children of the devil alluded to in John 8 or those who lack the key of David or who have stolen the key to the book as prophesied in Revelation 3:7 and Luke 11:52.[62]

There are two matters of note in Müntzer's vision of the church as outlined here. First of all, the apostolic church is hardly uniquely normative; in fact, more historical parallels are drawn to the "church" of the prophets than to that of the apostles. Abraham Friesen has argued that for Müntzer the apostolic church was normative, although he allows as well that Müntzer thought that the Old Testament prophets, too, had attempted to establish the true church.[63] It is clear, however, that in the *Prague Manifesto* the "church" of the prophets was more than just an afterthought. Furthermore, at this point in the development of his thought, Müntzer looked to the "Spirit-filled" church of Pentecost insofar as he held the apostolic church as normative at all. In the second place, Müntzer's reforming vision is not deduced exclusively *a priori* from a normative model of the apostolic church. Instead, working on the basis of a definition of the primitive church as a Spirit-filled congregation, he fleshes out the further details from the historical record as specific issues confront him.

Müntzer—Reform in Allstedt, 1523–1524

Shortly before Easter 1523 Müntzer received a pastorate in the town of Allstedt where he attempted to realize his reforming vision on a local level. His focus on the apostolic church as primarily a Spirit-filled congregation helps us to understand an apparent anomaly in some of the liturgical reforms he implemented. A number of Müntzer scholars have commented with surprise on the conservatism of these reforms.[64] In fact, statements contained in them seem on the surface to contradict his claims about the deterioration of the church. In his preface to *The Evangelical German Mass*, he goes so far as to praise the Latin liturgy which accompanied the original introduction of Christianity to Germany. He then suggests that the liturgy is capable of a progressive evolution, that is, one can actually improve on the received liturgy.[65] As Wolfgang Ullmann has noted, these comments seem to seriously qualify any sense that Müntzer at this time held to a consistent theory of the fall of the church.[66] And yet, Müntzer's vision of the demise of the primitive church is no less clearly or forcefully formulated in his liturgical writings than it is elsewhere. Here too, citing Eusebius and Hegesippus, he repeats his statements from the *Prague Manifesto* about the perversion of the apostolic church.[67] He also appeals to apostolic practice as described in both scriptural and extra-scriptural sources to justify his reforms.[68]

The normative character of the apostolic church is, then, not straightforward. Again, Müntzer himself provides clues to understanding this matter. In a letter written to Frederick the Wise in October 1523, he justifies his reforms by claiming they are intended in the first instance as a way to build up the faith of the people, and he cites Paul's admonitions in Ephesians 5:19 and I Corinthians 14:19.[69] The same theme is developed more fully and completely in *The Order and Explanation of the German Church Service*:

> O! What blind ignorant men we are to vaunt ourselves as the only Christians in outward ostentation, quarrelling madly among ourselves more like beasts than men! Surely every servant of the word of God has the authority to teach the people of his parish a pattern of worship using Psalms and songs of praise from the Bible readings to edify them. As Paul says so clearly in Ephesians 5: "You should ," he says, "be filled with the holy spirit, and greet one another with Psalms and songs of praise and spiritual hymns and tunes, singing and playing before the Lord and giving thanks at all times for one another." I Corinthians 14 says the same.[70]

The crucial issue for Müntzer, then, remains not the exact form of the outward rite, but that the congregation be "Spirit-filled." In his justification for his continued reliance on "papist" forms in the reform of the liturgy, Müntzer further clarifies matters. He describes his reformed liturgies as provisional, and encourages their further adaptation to fit local circumstances. The reformed liturgy is in Müntzer's mind primarily an instrument to wean the people away from papal idolatry. In other words, it is a pedagogic device whose structure can be adapted to allow for its greatest effectiveness.[71]

The intentions of Müntzer's liturgical reforms and their significance for his vision of the apostolic church are further clarified if we look at his sacramental theology. In his discussion of the reform of the Lord's Supper in *The Order and Explanation*, he hints at the basics of his sacramental theology, describing the sacrament as symbolic, as a sign pointing to a deeper spiritual truth. This definition of the sacraments is taken up and further developed in his treatment of baptism in two related pamphlets of late 1523 or early 1524: *Protestation or Proposition* and *On Counterfeit Faith*.[72] In these works, especially in the former, Müntzer outlines the process of the deterioration of the apostolic church and the role the perversion of baptism played in this process. The practice of baptizing infants rather than adults capable of making an informed commitment to the faith, he claims, has led the church to lay its foundations on sandy ground. Later Müntzer integrates this thesis into a more general assessment of the church's fall. It becomes part and parcel of a fall associated with developing ceremonialism, much of which was derived from pagan sources, and with growing dogmatism and sectarianism.[73] Yet, despite the prominent role that the perversion of apostolic baptism plays in the deterioration of the church, Müntzer does not call for a return to the apostolic practice. The issue for him is not so much the correct practice as it is the contemporary superstitious trust in holy symbols rather than the inward reality. The rite is merely symbolic of an inner suffering and transformation; the water of baptism is a metaphor for the working of the Spirit in the believer's soul. In and of itself, then, water baptism is merely a meaningless rite. To bolster this claim, Müntzer reaches back to the earliest days of Christianity, pointing out that in no place does Scripture indicate that Mary and the apostles were ever baptized with water.[74]

In these two pamphlets, then, Müntzer further clarifies his spiritualist conceptions of both the sacraments and the church, but in the process he continues to bolster his argument with appeals to apostolic practice. It should be clear, however, that this appeal is not a straightforward matter of taking up the model of the apostolic church as normative for his reforming vision. Friesen claims that at this point in his reforming career Müntzer looked to the establishment of a new apostolic church built on the twin pillars of separation and sanctification.[75] However, the envisioned new apostolic church was hardly that of the Anabaptists, as is evidenced by Müntzer's frequent references to parallels between it and the "church" of the Old Testament. His clearest identification of the new apostolic church is reference to it as the daughter of Zion, thereby bridging both testaments through an allusion to Zechariah 9:9 and Matthew 21:4. Its current situation had been foretold not only in 2 Timothy 3:1, but also in Zechariah 9:9, Isaiah 5, Jeremiah 2 and Psalm 79. In his defence of the church of the elect, Müntzer's situation parallels not only that of Christ before Pilate, but also those of Jeremiah and Ezekiel before the false prophets, and like the Old Testament prophets it is his duty to chastise the chosen people.[76] His opponents are the Scribes, Pharisees, false prophets and false apostles described or predicted in a variety of Old and New Testament passages.[77]

Müntzer—Sermon to the Princes and Final Pamphlets, 1524–1525

On 13 July, 1524 Müntzer preached his famous sermon before the Saxon princes in the electoral castle in Allstedt. Subsequently published as *Interpretation of the Second Chapter of Daniel*, this work has been a lightning rod for interpretations of Müntzer's historical vision. At the centre of this work is Müntzer's exegesis of Daniel 2, with its description of Nebuchadnezzar's dream and the vision of the world monarchies. Not surprisingly this text, with its explicit attention to the flow of profane history and its sharpened eschatology, has excited considerable attention and spawned ongoing speculation about Müntzer's reading of history. In particular, it has been a perennial favourite for those who see apocalyptic themes as predominant in Müntzer's historical vision.[78] However, as several interpreters of Müntzer's writings have indicated, his exegesis of Daniel is on the whole remarkably traditional. Furthermore, Rolf Dismer has suggested correctly that in this work Müntzer does not so much take over a historical scheme from Daniel as he inserts the prophet's vision of the five world empires into his own established historical vision. According to this interpretation, the five world empires are intended to highlight the proximity of the end times, but otherwise they are of secondary importance in Müntzer's perception of history.[79]

In fact, Müntzer's statements about the history of the church in *The Sermon to the Princes* provide us with no immediate surprises. He continues to bemoan the "wretched ruinous condition" of the contemporary church. This state of affairs has resulted from its perversion shortly after the death of the apostles' pupils, and here again he goes back to the descriptions of that event in the writings of Eusebius and Hegesippus.[80] This experience was, however, not without precedent, and Müntzer continues to draw clear parallels between the history of the present age and that of the church in biblical times:

> There can, however, be no doubt that Christ, the Son of God, and his apostles and his holy prophets before him, founded a pure and true Christianity, and cast the pure wheat into the field, that is, planted the precious word of God in the hearts of the elect, as we read in Mt. 12, Mark 4, Luke 8 and Ezek. 36.[81]

Here more than previously he emphasizes the relationship between the experiences of the present church and those of the "church" of the Old Testament prophets. In fact, the circumstances currently faced by the church directly parallel those confronting Isaiah, Jeremiah, Ezekiel and others, "When the whole congregation of God's elect had become completely caught up in idolatrous ways."[82] Elsewhere he casts the current state of affairs as similar to the Babylonian Captivity or to the "dangerous last days" predicted in both the Old and New Testaments by the prophets, Christ and the apostles.[83] Naturally, in these circumstances Müntzer portrays his opponents as the enemies of the Gospel and God's people from these parallel ages in the church's history: the priests of Baal, false prophets and false apostles. As is often noted, he also casts himself in the role of a new Daniel, prepared to advise the Saxon princes on the progress of the Reformation.[84]

In the *Sermon to the Princes*, then, Müntzer's use of history remains consistent with that of his earlier writings, but his reliance on such an apocalyptically charged text as Daniel 2 and his use of Old Testament parallels raise the question of whether his vision of ecclesiastical history is modified in any substantive way in this work. Was the coming church beginning to supplant the historical church in his vision? Or, was the Old Testament church of the prophets edging out the church of the New

Testament? On the surface at least both suggestions seem possible. Müntzer appears to anticipate a radical disjuncture in history, especially in his suggestion that in its previous incarnations the true church had failed because it relied for its foundation on the stone described in both Daniel 2 and Isaiah 28:16 as still too small.[85] Despite this reference, however, Müntzer does not focus on the novelty of the present age. On one occasion he advises the Saxon princes to follow the examples of the "biblical fathers," and elsewhere he identifies as the goal of the current Reformation the return of the church to its origins.[86]

This emphasis on continuity raises the question of the nature of the model provided by the church of past ages. Much has been made about Müntzer's identification of himself as the new Daniel in this work. However, the extent to which his perception of the nature of the church has changed is debatable. Wolfgang Ullmann has suggested that to be understood in its context, this work must be read as a defence of the Allstedt liturgical reforms.[87] Yet the model of the biblical church presented here at first glance looks notably different from that appealed to in the liturgical reforms. Müntzer calls to mind much more often the people of Israel as the model for the church than he does the congregation of the apostles. When he calls on the princes to follow the examples of the Biblical fathers, more often the examples held up are those drawn from the Old Testament, and more frequently than not they are examples of how Old Testament rulers dealt with the godless. The princes are exhorted to adopt the zeal of King Jehu. They should drive out the godless as the Israelites expelled the Canaanites from the Holy Land. The obstinate among the godless should be killed like the priests of Baal.[88] The nature of this advice provides some insight into the roots of Müntzer's apparent change of heart. The change of perspective relates more to the nature of this writing and its intended audience than to a development in Müntzer's thinking about the history of the church. As advice to the princes about political aspects of the Reformation, it was natural to draw more on lessons from the Old Testament church than from the New, but this in no way indicates that the New Testament model had lost any of its force for him.[89]

While many of the examples provided by the "biblical fathers" in *The Sermon to the Princes* were drawn from the Old Testament, this in no way means that the New Testament had receded from view. This fact is most clearly evident in Müntzer's subsequent writings. In fact, in *The Manifest Exposé of False Faith* and *The Highly Provoked Vindication or Refutation*, both of which were written in early autumn 1524, parallels between the existing church and that of Christ and the apostles actually return to the forefront. Müntzer continues to regard his own age as that described in the apocalyptic prophecies of both testaments.[90] He also continues to portray his opponents as the archetypical opponents of the Gospel and of God's people from both ages.[91] But when he turns to the characterization of his own activity, the parallels are drawn primarily to the New Testament. The Old Testament model is still present, particularly when he portrays himself as a new prophet with the spirit of Elijah.[92] However, his most extended and developed metaphors identify his cause with that of John the Baptist or draw direct parallels between his situation and that of Christ's conflict with the Jewish religious establishment.[93]

Aside from these parallels, Müntzer provides little further detail about the church's history and the nature of the "new apostolic church," but what evidence is available suggests little change in his vision of the true church of the elect. A note discussing the sacrament of baptism, penned in Müntzer's hand and dated August 1524, suggests that he was toying with the idea of raising the age of catechumens to the age of discernment.[94] The following spring, his followers in the community of Ehrich wrote to Müntzer indicating that they were involved in a reform of the local church on an apostolic model; their discussion of the disposal of ecclesiastical property, celebration of the Eucharist and reform of the liturgy indicate an attempt to approximate the apostolic model as closely as possible.[95] And in the *Exposé of False Faith* Müntzer appears to be advocating the establishment of a separated church, in which the chaff will be winnowed from the wheat on what he perceives to be the apostolic model.[96]

Statements such as these have led Friesen to claim that Müntzer adhered to the normative model of the apostolic church to the end, to the extent that he labels the *Highly Provoked Vindication* the culmination of Müntzer's attempt to understand church history.[97] But in the end the crucial issue in Müntzer's identification of the true church remains the presence of the Spirit; all other characteristics are secondary to it.[98] The spirit-filled church of all ages, not the specific pattern of the apostolic church, is the model for the "new apostolic church" of the elect. These conclusions have implications both for how we assess Müntzer's perception of the history of the church and how we characterize his reforming vision more generally. Historical reflection does play a crucial role in the development of Müntzer's thought, but not as a fixed principle driving all aspects of his reforming vision. In 1519 he had already developed a normative vision of the apostolic church as a pnuematological community, but its other characteristics were developed over time. However, this reflection on the history of the church and commitment to a normative vision of the apostolic church in no way disqualifies Müntzer as a Spiritualist. The church he wanted restored was in fact the church of the Spirit.

History and Political Activism

Traditionally a sharp line of demarcation between Karlstadt and Müntzer has been drawn based on the latter's involvement with the Peasants' War. Müntzer's "revolutionary" activity has been sharply contrasted with Karlstadt's assumed political quietism. If we can believe the account contained in the *Acta Jenensia*, this differentiation goes back to Karlstadt himself who, in his meeting with Luther at the Black Bear, claimed to have nothing to do with the "murdering and rebellious spirit at Allstedt."[99] However, more recent treatments have begun to erode some of the force of this claim. Müntzer is being treated less and less like a theologian of revolution and Karlstadt is looking increasingly less like a categorical pacifist.[100]

Despite these revisions, however, there is no denying Karlstadt's rebuff of Müntzer's invitation to join the elect band in Allstedt or Müntzer's subsequent involvement in the Peasants' War. Studies of Müntzer's political involvement and radicalization have long dealt at least implicitly with the thorny question of the relationship between his theology and his social activism. It has long been assumed that there was a direct connection between these two aspects of Müntzer's life, although there has been little agreement on the exact nature of that relationship. More recently, however, that connection was been challenged. Increasingly, interpreters see Müntzer's decision to reach for the sword as more circumstantial than systematic.[101] The present study looks to cast light on this theme through an investigation of the historical models drawn on by Müntzer in his discussions of secular authority. To what extent does he develop a vision of secular history to complement that of ecclesiastical history and what role does that vision play in the process of his political radicalization?

An important starting point in answering these questions is James Stayer's oft quoted observation: "About the Sword and about tyrants, Müntzer had a teaching, but about rulers and government, only an attitude."[102] When focusing on the place of historical reflection in Müntzer's teachings and attitudes, particularly useful is Eike Wolgast's study of his teaching on authority and justified resistance to it. Wolgast argues that Müntzer's opinions about the legitimacy of authority and justifiable resistance to illegitimate authority are closely tied up with his exegesis of several crucial biblical texts: the touchstone of Reformation discussions of the legitimacy of secular authority, Romans 13; Mary's exclamation at the annunciation that the mighty have been cast down and the lowly raised up, contained in Luke 1:52; the apocalyptic prophecy in Daniel 7:27 that the kingdom and dominion will be given to the people; the description of the founding of the ancient Hebrew monarchy in 1 Samuel 8:7-18; and God's claim in Hosea 13:11 that He gave the Israelites kings in His anger, and had taken them away in His wrath. Wolgast argues further that in his exegesis of these texts, Müntzer's concern with rights of resistance remains secondary to his soteriological concerns and that before 1525 his discussion of right of resistance is dominated by that exegesis.[103] However, as Michael Baylor has argued, any discussion which treats Müntzer's thought as an extension of his hermeneutics begs the question of the presuppositions with which he approached the text of Scripture.[104]

Müntzer's criticism of tyranny and the unjust exercise of authority grew out of his attacks on the ecclesiastical hierarchy, and it is with his statements about ecclesiastical structure and authority that we must begin our investigation. There is little doubt either that democratic structures figure prominently in Müntzer's early reforming vision of the ecclesiastical hierarchy or that they are directly related to his historical interests and research. In Jüterbog he had held up as an ideal a more democratized ecclesiastical hierarchy, although at that time he said nothing about the relationship between the congregation and the local clergy.[105] His subsequent research, however, led him quickly to redress this omission. In the *Prague Manifesto* he challenged clerical authority with a direct application of Daniel 7:27.[106] That this changed perspective was closely related to his historical research is clearly indicated by his comments on Tertullian. There he notes that the congregational choice of the pastor was crucial in keeping the apostolic church free from the wiles of the Antichrist or the domination of the godless.[107] On the basis of this perspective he makes occasional references at this time to the papacy in conjunction with the archetypes of tyranny: Nimrod and Herod.[108] Yet, at this point at least, he makes no moves to apply this critique to secular authority.[109]

As has been noted, Müntzer's activity in Allstedt, at least prior to the *Sermon to the Princes*, was focused primarily on the matters associated with reform of the church, especially his liturgical reforms. As a result his writings from this time, especially the pamphlets *On Counterfeit Faith* and *Protestation*, are usually regarded as primarily religious works. However, as Peter Matheson has pointed out, the *Protestation* at least must be read in conjunction with Müntzer's interaction with secular authorities, particularly as this is revealed in his letters to Frederick the Wise and Count Ernst of Mansfield, of September and October 1523.[110] These two letters, along with that written to the brethren in Stolberg in July 1523, show us the beginnings of Müntzer's active political involvement as he sought to defend adherents of his cause from neighbouring Catholic territories.

The *Letter to the Brethren at Stolberg*, which Müntzer published and which should be treated as an encyclical, seems to stand in sharp contrast to his other pamphlets of this period, and a number of historians have seen in it evidence of Müntzer's increasing politicization.[111] Both here and in the letters to Frederick and Ernst of Mansfield Müntzer openly abuses those he regards as tyrants. For example, he upbraids the Catholic count for persecuting his followers and threatens to attack him in print if he does not desist from these activities.[112] Noteworthy is Michael Baylor's observation that in the letter to Stolberg Müntzer more clearly identifies the opponents of the Gospel as the parsons *and* the tyrants than he does in the *Prague Manifesto*.[113] Also noteworthy is his willingness in the letter to Frederick the Wise to turn Daniel 7, with its threat to transfer authority to the people, against such tyrants.[114]

Such diatribes do not mean that Müntzer had rejected the legitimacy of secular authority, or even of established secular authorities. He hints instead at the possibility of a truly Christian government and by implication at least appeals for help from such a government.[115] Furthermore, as Wolgast notes, despite his appeal to Daniel 7, Müntzer at this point treats the oppression of the pious from a primarily soteriological perspective.[116] This is especially clear in his allusions to the historical founding of the ancient Hebrew monarchy. When he cites 1 Samuel 8 and Hosea 13:11 in the letter to Stolberg, Müntzer does not take the opportunity to launch into a critique of the institution of monarchy, but focuses instead on the role of tyrants in awakening spiritual poverty among the elect.[117] According to Wolgast, at this point Müntzer's thought on justifiable resistance to constituted authority is in a transitional stage: he has begun to use Daniel 7 to balance his exegesis of Romans 13, but does not yet provide details of the opposition between these two visions.[118] At this point, then, Müntzer indicates that he has a vague sense about the rule of the elect in an apocalyptic context and that he has begun the most rudimentary of historical parallels between political situations based on the Old Testament.

Müntzer's allusions to the authority and responsibility of secular government are fleshed out more fully in *The Sermon to the Princes*. As an exegesis of Daniel 2 with its vision of the progression of world monarchies, and as an appeal to the Saxon princes to defend and support the Reformation at Allstedt, this sermon naturally deals explicitly with political concerns. Here Müntzer's exegesis of Romans 13 assigns wide-ranging responsibilities to secular authorities, to the point of using violence in the promotion of the cause of the Gospel, [119] but the activities of the princes remain under an apocalyptic cloud. Müntzer holds up the threat contained in Daniel 7 that power will be given to the people and closes the sermon with the claim, bolstered by Matthew 28:18, that God will soon take government into His own hands.[120]

Müntzer's appeal to the princes and its place in his reforming vision is further clarified by the parallels he draws between the situation facing the Saxon princes and similar occasions from the history of God's people. The most obvious parallel at the centre of this work places Müntzer advising the princes in the role of Daniel advising Nebuchadnezzer against the wiles of the Babylonian soothsayers (the Wittenberg Reformers). In addition to this example, he draws a number of other parallels to events of the Old Testament. He calls on the princes to follow the models of the kings Josiah and Jehu and form a covenant with the people to stand firm against God's enemies. Elsewhere he appeals to the injunctions to destroy the priests of Baal or the Canaanites to justify his claims that the opponents of the Gospel must be exterminated.[121] Müntzer's appeals to the Old Testament, then, take the form not of a reference to a normative model, but an appeal to a parallel example to justify specific tactical choices. His political references remain distinct from the eventual rule of the saints.[122] However, also apparent in the *Sermon to the Princes* is a new emphasis on the importance of political history in reading the apocalyptic timetable. Tyranny here begins to appear as an important sign of the times. It was no accident that Christ was born at the time of Octavian when wickedness had reached a climax, and Caesar Augustus appears here as the prototype for the godless tyrant.[123]

Given the failure of Müntzer's appeal in the *Sermon to the Princes*, it comes as no surprise that his subsequent writings and correspondence chart the further politicization and radicalization of his thought. However, they chronicle as well his reluctant alienation from established authority. Evidence from the first half of 1524 suggests that Müntzer only reluctantly gave up on the Saxon princes as agents of reform. Correspondence between the council of Allstedt and the electoral court from June suggests that Müntzer's understanding of Romans 13 had not changed significantly.[124] Müntzer's statements here may appear to stand in sharp contrast to the violence of his attacks on tyrants the following month in his letters to the people of Sangerhausen and to Hans Zeiss. However, the discrepancies soon disappear when one looks at the context of the latter statements and distinguishes between his treatment of the legitimate rulers of Saxony and the Catholic tyrants who oppose the spread of the Gospel in neighbouring territories. In the letters to Zeiss, Müntzer continues to hold up for the Saxon princes the models of kings Jehu and Josiah.[125] These models provide valuable insights into understanding the league which Müntzer founded in Allstedt at the time. Maron suggests that this league was to form the nucleus for the revived church.[126] More convincing, given the use of Old Testament models, are interpretations of the league which emphasize its conservative, defensive nature.[127] Wolgast has called attention to the development of the league from an emergency, defensive institution to an active instrument of apocalyptic vengeance.[128] In early summer 1524 it was clearly of the former variety, and Müntzer goes no further than to warn Zeiss on that occasion that power will be taken from the tyrants and given to the people.[129]

Müntzer's assessment of the secular authorities changed drastically, however, as a result of events at the end of July and beginning of August, especially his interrogation at Weimar and the subsequent closing of his printing press. These events were crucial in his realization that the Saxon princes were not the divinely appointed agents of Reformation and his developing perception that the local authorities in Allstedt had sold him out. Immediately after the summons to Weimar, in a letter to the Elector he compared his own hearing to Christ's appearance before Annas and claimed that God was turning His attention from the godless rulers to the people. His sense of betrayal by the princes is even more clearly voiced in the new warning that the promises of Joshua 11:20 that the godless will be exterminated will not be fulfilled in the person of Frederick.[130]

Müntzer's rejection of the Saxon princes, and with them established secular authority, becomes increasingly evident in his last two published works: *A Manifest Exposé* and *A Highly Provoked Vindication*. Together, they chronicle his rejection of established political authority as tyrannical and unchristian. In the *Exposé* tyranny becomes the defining feature of all secular authority. The current political authorities are compared to Herod and their rule matches up to his at the time of Christ.[131] Herod now becomes the model for secular authority. Müntzer brings together 1 Samuel 8 and Hosea 13 to claim that monarchy was established as a result of the fall and as an expression of divine anger. This produces a new reading of Romans 13, with an emphasis now on verse 3 yielding the conclusion that the rulers are nothing more than hangmen and jailers.[132] Furthermore, tyranny begins to play an even more important role in Müntzer's reading of the apocalyptic timetable. It heralds the birth of the new age and Müntzer casts himself as a new John the Baptist in the cosmic drama about to unfold. Earlier he had made allusion to the fact that some day the saints would rule the earth. Now he is beginning to tie this claim to a critique of secular authority. Part and parcel of the restoration of the order of creation in the last age will be an end to coercive secular authority, and in his role as John he is announcing this transition. The mighty will soon be cast down and the lowly will be raised up—Mary, Zecheriah and Elizabeth will supplant Herod, Annas and Caiaphas.[133] Beyond this development, however, he also makes an important tactical adjustment—in the transitional phase to the establishment of the reign of Christ monarchy has abdicated its role.

Müntzer's further radicalization is already apparent in the opening lines of *A Highly Provoked Vindication* with its address to the one true prince, Jesus. As has often been noted, Müntzer is here parodying the salutation in Luther's letter to the princes.[134] The further significance of this parody becomes clearer as one looks at the historical models Müntzer utilizes to justify his claims. As has often been noted, he here expands his justification for popular sovereignty, arguing that the sword and the execution of justice belong ultimately in the hands of the community. Such claims are buttressed with the expected apocalyptic texts: Daniel 7:27, Revelation 6:15ff. That this amounts as well to a final rejection of monarchical authority as it exists is clear in Müntzer's historical allusions: he claims that Christ alone deserves the title of prince, largely because earthly kings have from the beginning of the world abused their power. Their very institution is an indication of the rejection of God's sovereignty as indicated in 1 Samuel 8:7. It comes as no surprise, then, that they consistently violate the strictures laid down for them in Deuteronomy 17:18ff. Consequently they stand under God's curse (Isaiah 10:1) and must be watched over by the whole community. This historical critique yields a drastically new reading of Romans 13:1 and its call for obedience to the established authorities, whose legitimacy is now tied directly to their adherence to divine commands.[135]

The fullest development of Müntzer's teaching on popular sovereignty occurred, not surprisingly, in the context of the Peasants' War. There we see him adopting a number of postures which appear to put into practice his teaching that political authority and the exercise of justice belong ultimately in the hands of the community. These activities raise the question of Müntzer's understanding of his actions. Was he instituting the structures of the kingdom of the end of times? Or was he merely looking to structures to usher in that kingdom? His correspondence from this period of his life indicates that the latter was the case. It suggests as well that his political radicalization grew out of his failure to enlist the regents as agents of his reforming program. Not surprisingly, he continues to cast contemporary figures as counterparts to historical types, especially from the Old Testament. Frequently he denounces the established secular rulers as tyrants, in some cases identifying the Saxon princes with Nimrod the archetypical Old Testament tyrant and elsewhere claiming the rulers should be equated with Pharaoh or Canaanite kings whose hearts God had hardened.[136] Relying on Daniel 7 and with it Hosea 13, he demands that they be cast down.[137] With the end to legitimate princely authority, Müntzer began looking for an alternative model for secular authority in the history of Israel prior to the establishment of the monarchy in 1 Samuel 8. Particularly applicable were the circumstances surrounding the conquest of Canaan, and Müntzer began to draw parallels between contemporary affairs and those of the ancient Hebrews. Wavering allies, for example the community at Langensalza, appeared as the back-sliding kings Saul and Agag, and Müntzer began dispensing justice like Joshua and signing his letters as Thomas Müntzer with the sword of Gideon.[138] While many of Müntzer's criticisms of existing authorities are made in a clearly apocalyptic context, there is no indication that his identification with pre-monarchical Israel was to serve as a structure for the kingdom of Christ or the restored apostolic church. He continues to refer to the coming kingdom of Christ and the letter from the community of Ehrich mentioned above suggests that the apostolic church remained the goal of the restoration. The Israelites in Canaan served instead as a model for the means to reach that goal.

Conclusion

Despite differences of detail, Müntzer and Karlstadt shared a common vision of the apostolic church as a Spirit-filled community, and they held that community up as a model for reform of the church of their own age. Both men also adopted this "primitivist ecclesiology" only after their reforming activities were well underway. Like the Reformers of the magisterial Reformation, they began their historical research in an attempt to identify the source of specific abuses in the church of their own day. Initially they associated these abuses with the rise of scholasticism. This led them, as it did the humanists and magisterial Reformers, to the perception that the church had fallen in the preceding 400 years. However, as their spiritualism pushed them to a more radical rejection of ecclesiastical tradition—increasingly they saw elements of that tradition acting as fetters on the free working of the Spirit—they moved beyond, and became critical of, the humanist reform movement and its vision of ecclesiastical history. This process is clearest in Müntzer's break with Egranus in Zwickau. Soon this spiritualism also led to a break with the magisterial Reformers as is evident in Müntzer's criticism of the Wittenbergers' worship of a "dumb god" and Karlstadt's developing critique of the Reformers' sacramental theology.

As Karlstadt and Müntzer moved beyond the reform programmes of their contemporaries, they looked further into the past for a model of the church unsoiled by the abuses they saw around them. Ultimately, they came to a vision of the apostolic church as the purest example of the "Spirit-filled" community on earth, and they looked to the restoration of that community. However, this appeal to the apostolic church did not make them "restitutionists" in the sense that this term has been used to describe the program of the "Evangelical Anabaptists." For Karlstadt and Müntzer the apostolic church was not an exclusive model for the reform of the church. Rather, it was only one example, although a very important example, of attempts to realize on earth the church of the Spirit. As a result, both Karlstadt and Müntzer could appeal to examples from the Old Testament "church," as well as its counterpart in the New Testament, to justify their reforming agendas and activities. In the end, they would draw different lessons on specific issues from the history of the church. However, these differences stemmed not so much from competing visions of the church's history as they did from different questions and concerns they took to their shared vision of the church of the Spirit through the ages.

As we will see, others in the Radical Reformation shared Karlstadt's and Müntzer's belief that the apostolic church should serve as a model for the reform of the contemporary church. However, they did not all agree on the nature and central characteristics of that church. How differing conceptions of the primitive church interacted provides valuable insights into the role of historical reflection in both holding together and distinguishing those on the Left Wing of the Reformation.

NOTES

1 Matheson, *Collected Works*, 166-67 (=*MSB*, 161-62).

2 Franklin H. Littell, *The Origins of Sectarian Protestantism: A Study of the Anabaptist View of the Church* (New York: MacMillan, 1964), 47.

3 For example, see Barge I: 40 and II: 14-17, 114-17; Ronald J. Sider, *Andreas Bodenstein von Karlstadt: The Development of His Thought 1517-1525* (Leiden: E.J. Brill, 1974), 25-30, 112-22, 259-77; idem., trans., *Karlstadt's Battle With Luther: Documents in a Liberal-Radical Debate* (Philadelphia: Fortress Press, 1978), 36; idem., "Andreas Bodenstein von Karlstadt: Between Liberal and Radical," in Hans-Jürgen Goertz, ed. *Profiles of Radical Reformers. Biographical Sketches from Paracelsus to Thomas Müntzer* (Kitchener, ON: Herald Press, 1982), 51-52; Calvin A. Pater, *Karlstadt as the Father of the Baptist Movements* (Toronto: University of Toronto Press, 1984), 15-24. This line of interpretation has at times spilled over into Müntzer studies, for example, see Carl Hinrichs, *Luther und Müntzer: Ihre Auseinandersetzung über Obrigkeit und Widerstandsrecht* (Berlin: Walter de Gruyter and Co., 1952), 89.

4 On recent revisions in the treatment of Karlstadt and Müntzer, see especially, Ulrich Bubenheimer, *Thomas Müntzer: Herkunft und Bildung* (Leiden: E.J. Brill, 1989); William McNiel, "Andreas von Karlstadt and Thomas Müntzer: Relatives in Theology and Reformation," (Ph.D. diss., Queen's University, 1999), esp. 208-10; James M. Stayer, "The Radical Reformation," in Thomas A. Brady, Jr., Heiko A. Oberman and James D. Tracy, eds. *Handbook of European History, 1400-1600: Late Middle Ages, Renaissance and Reformation*, vol. 2: *Visions, Programs and Outcomes* (Grand Rapids, MI: Eerdmans, 1996), 251-54.

5 William McNiel, "Andreas von Karlstadt as a Humanist Theologian," in Werner Packull and Geoffrey Dipple, eds. *Radical Reformation Studies. Essays Presented to James M. Stayer* (Aldershot: Ashgate, 1999).

6 Sider, *Karlstadt: Development of his Thought*, 56-57.

7 Barge I: 156.

8 See McNiel, "Karlstadt and Müntzer," 51-52; Barge I: 235; Pater, 49-50.

9 E. J. Furcha, ed. and trans., *The Essential Carlstadt: Fifteen Tracts by Andreas Bodenstein (Carlstadt) from Karlstadt* (Waterloo, ON and Scottdale, PA: Herald Press, 1995), 28, 31.

10 Ulrich Bubenheimer, *Consonantia Theologiae et Iurisprudentiae: Andreas Bodenstein von Karlstadt als Theologe und Jurist zwischen Scholastik und Reformation* (Tübingen: J.C.B. Mohr (Paul Siebeck), 1977), 171-75, notes both Karlstadt's inconsistency in dating the beginnings of papal perversion at this time and his disagreement with Luther on this issue. While focusing his attention on the pontificate of Alexander IV in the *Ten Disputation Theses*, in *Von Bepstlicher heylickeit*, also from 1520, he takes issue with a decretal of Innocent III (1198-1216). Bubenheimer concludes that to this point Karlstadt had not yet undertaken an independent investigation of history.

11 McNiel, "Karlstadt and Müntzer," 52-53; Pater, 49; Furcha, *Essential Carlstadt*, 77, 93. Furcha suggests that the reference to 400 years may include criticism of the Cluniac reforms and the Investiture Controversy. See *Essential Carlstadt*, 77, n. 26.

12 Barge I: 344.

13 McNiel, "Karlstadt and Müntzer," 53; Pater, 49; Bubenheimer, *Consonantia Theologiae et Iurisprudentiae*, 174-75; Furcha, *Essential Carlstadt*, 106-7. On Karlstadt's iconoclasm, see J. Travis Moger, "Pamphlets, Preaching and Politics: The Image Controversy in Reformation Wittenberg, Zürich and Strasbourg," *MQR* 75 (2001), 329-35.

14 James Preus, *Carlstadt's* Ordinaciones *and Luther's Liberty: A Study of the Wittenberg Movement 1521-22* (Cambridge MA: Harvard University Press, 1974), 50.

15 McNiel, "Karlstadt and Müntzer," 71.

16 Furcha, *Essential Carlstadt*, 109.

17 Preus, 15-16.

18 Karlstadt referred to apostolic precedent in both Acts 1:15 and 26. See Pater, 20, 74-78; George H. Williams, *The Radical Reformation*, 3rd ed. (Kirksville, MO: Sixteenth Century Journal Publishers, 1992), 117; Furcha, *Essential Carlstadt*, 178-79.

19 Furcha, *Essential Carlstadt*, 52, 225. See Sider, *Karlstadt: Development of his Thought*, 108-9 on Karlstadt's increasing application of Old Testament texts to the church after 1520.

20 Barge I: 344.

21 Barge I: 292-93, 368; Preus, 18; Furcha, *Essential Carlstadt*, 43, 46. Karlstadt continued to make such demands into the time of the Eucharistic controversy. See Barge II, 164, 173-74.

22 Sider, "Karlstadt," 51; Pater, 67, 112; Erich Hertzsch, ed., *Karlstadt's Flugschriften aus den Jahren 1523-1525*, vol. 1 (Halle (Saale): Max Niemeyer Verlag, 1956), xiv.

23 Williams, *Radical Reformation*, 116; Furcha, *Essential Carlstadt*, 252-58, 101-28; Carter Lindberg, ed. and trans., "Karlstadt's *Dialogue* on the Lord's Supper," *MQR* 53 (1979), 37.

24 Sider, *Karlstadt*, 291-99. See especially Karlstadt's *Dialogue*, Lindberg, 39-77; Furcha, *Essential Carlstadt*, 270-316; Hertzsch II: 5-49, and *Regarding the Sabbath and Statuatory Holy Days*, Furcha, *Essential Carlstadt*, 318-38; Hertzsch I: 21-47.

25 There has been a long tradition of interpretation which identifies Müntzer's apocalyptic reading of history with Joachimism. See Wilhelm Zimmermann, *Der große deutsche Bauernkrieg* (Berlin: Dietz Verlag, 1953), 160-77; Hans Hillerbrand, *A Fellowship of Discontent* (New York: Harper and Row, 1967), 28-29; Richard Bailey, "The Sixteenth Century's Apocalyptic Heritage and Thomas Müntzer," *MQR* 57 (1983), 27-44; Kee Ryun Kim, *Das Reich Gottes in der Theologie Thomas Müntzers* (Frankfurt: Peter Lang, 1994), 92-93, 99, 104-5. More recently the tendency has been to play down Müntzer's possible parallels to Joachim, but to retain the primacy of apocalypticism and subsume his historical vision under it. See, for example, Eric Gritsch, *Reformer Without a Church: Thomas Muentzer* (Philadelphia: Fortress Press, 1967), 16, 86-89, 103, 107-8, 191, 195; idem., *Thomas Müntzer: A Tragedy of Errors* (Minneapolis: Fortress Press, 1989), 30, 39, 116; Norman Cohn, *The Pursuit of the Millenium*, 2nd ed. (New York: Harper Torchbooks, 1961), 252-53; Andrew W. Drummond, "The Divine and Mortal Worlds of Thomas Müntzer," *ARG* (1980), 99-112; Gottfried Maron, "Thomas Müntzer als Theologe des Gerichts," in Abraham Friesen and Hans-Jürgen Goertz, eds., *Thomas Müntzer: Wege der Forschung* (Darmstadt: Wissenschaftliche Buchgesellschaft, 1978), 339-82; Richard Schwarz, *Die apokalyptische Theologie Thomas Müntzers und der Taboriten* (Tübingen: J.C.B. Mohr, 1977), 5-6, 12, 70; Manfred Bensing, *Thomas Müntzer und der Thüringer Aufstand 1525* (Berlin: VEB Deutscher Verlag der Wissenschaft, 1966), 45-46, 61; Tom Scott, *Thomas Müntzer: Theology and Revolution in the German Reformation* (New York: St. Martin's Press, 1989), xviii, 182-83. The most consistent criticism of treating apocalypticism as the dominant motif in Müntzer's thought has come from Hans-Jürgen Goertz. See especially *Innere und äussere Ordnung in der Theologie Thomas Müntzers* (Leiden: E.J. Brill, 1967), 148 and "Zu Thomas Müntzers Geistverständnis," in Siegfried Bräuer and Helmar Junghans, eds., *Der Theologe Thomas Müntzer: Untersuchungen zu seiner Entwicklung und Lehre* (Göttingen: Vandenhoeck and Ruprecht, 1989), 95.

26 The groundwork for this approach was laid by Walter Elliger, *Thomas Müntzer: Leben und Werk* 3rd ed. (Göttingen: Vandenhoeck and Ruprecht, 1976), especially 2-3, 202, 460-62, and significantly extended by the work of Rolf Dismer, "Geschichte, Glaube und Revolution: Zur Schriftauslegung Thomas Müntzers," (Ph.D. diss., Hamburg,

1974), see especially ii, 4-6. Recently this approach has been receiving more widespread endorsement. See Michael Baylor, "Theology and Politics in the Thought of Thomas Müntzer: The Case of the Elect," *ARG* 79 (1988), 81-102; Joachim Rogge, "Müntzers und Luthers Verständnis von der Reformation der Kirche," in Christoph Demke, ed., *Thomas Müntzer: Anfragen an Theologie und Kirche* (Berlin: Evangelische Verlagsanstalt, 1977), esp. 8-12; Günter Vogler, *Thomas Müntzer* (Berlin: Dietz Verlag, 1989), 272-73; Gerhard Brendler, *Thomas Müntzer: Geist und Faust* (Berlin: VEB Verlag der Wissenschaft, 1989), 47-48.

27 Abraham Friesen, *Thomas Muentzer, A Destroyer of the Godless* (Berkeley and Los Angeles: University of California Press, 1990), 40, 112, 168-70.

28 Matheson, *Collected Works*, 449-50 (=*MSB*, 562-63).

29 Friesen, *Muentzer*, 4; Scott, *Müntzer*, 10-11; and Vogler, *Müntzer*, 49-50 connect the date of the church's fall to the bishops' neglect of their pastoral duties. Bubenheimer, *Herkunft und Bildung*, 188-89; Matheson, *Collected Works*, 499, n. 14; McNiel, "Karlstadt and Müntzer," 51; and my own "Humanists, Reformers and Anabaptists on Scholasticism and the Fall of the Church," *MQR* 68 (1994), 470-71 focus instead on the criticism of scholasticism. Brendler, *Geist und Faust*, 43 relates this statement to a general perception of decline and refuses to isolate any specific factor in the church's deterioration.

30 Matheson, *Collected Works*, 450 (=*MSB*, 563).

31 Friesen, *Muentzer*, 33-36.

32 This argument is developed most fully by Bubenheimer, *Müntzer: Herkunft und Bildung*, 152-54 and 186-89. A number of other scholars have since endorsed Bubenheimer's interpretation, see also Gritsch, *Tragedy of Errors*, 9-10; Vogler, *Müntzer*, 49-52; Matheson, *Collected Works*, 450, n. 18; and Helmar Junghans, "Thomas Müntzer als Wittenberger Theologe," in Bräuer and Junghans, eds., *Der Theologe Thomas Müntzer*, 264-71. Wolfgang Ullmann, "Die Geschichtsverständnis Thomas Müntzers," in Demke, ed., *Thomas Müntzer: Anfragen an Theologie und Kirche*, 46-47, emphasizes more the autonomy of Müntzer's historical vision at this point.

33 Junghans, "Wittenberger Theologe," 27; Siegfried Bräuer, "Thomas Müntzers Kirchenverständnis vor seiner Allstedter Zeit," in Bräuer and Junghans, eds., *Der Theologe Thomas Müntzer*, 106-7; Bubenheimer, *Müntzer: Herkunft und Bildung*, 188-89.

34 Bubenheimer, *Herkunft und Bildung*, pp. 188-91.

35 Goertz, *Innere und äußere Ordnung*, 21-22; Gritsch, *Tragedy of Errors*, 11-12, 18. For Luther's support for Müntzer in Jüterbog and Zwickau, see *WABr* 1: 387-93.

36 This passage is cited from the longer German version of the *Manifesto*, Matheson, *Collected Works*, 370 (= *MSB*, 503-4, Baylor, *Revelation and Revolution*, 59). See also, Matheson, 360, 377 (= *MSB*, 494, 509-10).

37 Matheson, *Collected Works*, 355, has applied the term "primitivist ecclesiology" to Müntzer's statement. Others agree with the sentiment even if they don't employ the term. See Bräuer, "Kirchenverständnis," 111; AnneMarie Lohmann, *Zur geistigen Entwicklung Thomas Müntzers* (Leipzig and Berlin: B.G. Teubner, 1931; reprint ed., Hildesheim: Verlag Dr. H.A. Gerstenberg, 1972), 27; Junghans, "Wittenberger Theologe," 264; Rogge, "Verständnis," 10; Ullmann, "Geschichtsverständnis," 47; Dismar, 54-56. Those emphasizing the primacy of apocalypticism in Müntzer's thought, especially those who see in it a reflection of Joachimite themes, instead look beyond the apostolic church to the spiritual church of the third age, for example Bailey, "Heritage," 35-37. Goertz, "Geistverständnis," 93-94 and *Thomas Müntzer: Apocalyptic Mystic and Revolutionary*, translated by Jocelyn Jaquiery and edited by Peter Matheson (Edinburgh: T & T Clark, 1993), 82-83, and following him, Scott, *Müntzer*, 36-38, argue convincingly that in this work Müntzer's apocalypticism is in the service of his pneumatological arguments.

38 Friesen, *Muentzer*, 6-7, 33-52, 73-99, 100-120.

39 Bubenheimer, *Herkunft und Bildung*, 203-5; see also Bräuer, "Kirchenverständnis," 113; Ullmann, "Geschichtsverständnis," 49-50.

40 The primacy of the pneumatological community in Müntzer's vision of the primitive church in *The Prague Manifesto* has been recognized by a number of scholars. See Lohmann, 24-27; Goertz, "Geistverständnis," 88-89; Vogler, *Müntzer*, 107.

41 Matheson, *Collected Works*, 362-68 (= *MSB*, 495-501; Baylor, *Revelation and Revolution*, 53-57).

42 Matheson, *Collected Works*, 368, 370 (= *MSB*, 501, 504; Baylor, *Revelation and Revolution*, 57, 59). Goertz, "Geistverständnis," 88, has highlighted this point well, arguing that the *Prague Manifesto* revolves around the "pneumatological starting point of Christian existence." By way of contrast, Maron, "Gericht," 342-43, emphasizes more the consequences of the Spirit's presence, the separation of the wheat and tares. However, as Michael Baylor, *Revelation and Revolution*, 57, has indicated, the mingling of wheat and tares is itself a consequence of the failure to heed the "living word." See also Matheson, *Collected Works*, 355

43 See Bubenheimer, *Müntzer: Herkunft und Bildung*, 180-85; James Stayer, "Thomas Müntzer in 1989: A Review Article," *SCJ* 21 (1990), 660. The importance of historical research for the development of Müntzer's thought at this time has been recognized by a number of historians, see Bräuer, "Kirchenverständnis," 107; Gritsch, *Reformer Without a Church*, 13-16; Vogler, *Müntzer*, 58-61; Scott, *Müntzer*, 12-13; Williams, *Radical Reformation*, 122.

44 Bubenheimer, *Müntzer: Herkunft und Bildung*, 216-29. Others, too, note the importance of Müntzer's experiences in Zwickau for his growing independence from the humanists and from Wittenberg. See Goertz, *Innere und äußere Ordnung*, 25, 27-34, 51-52; Baylor, *Revelation and Revolution*, 14; Bräuer, "Kirchenverständnis," 117-18.

45 In his letter to Nicholas Hausmann, Müntzer had denounced Egranus for allegedly claiming that the Spirit had been present only in the apostolic church. See Matheson, *Collected Works*, 34 (= *MSB*, 372). See also Egranus' disparaging comments about "your spirit" in his letter to Müntzer of February 1521, Matheson, *Collected Works*, 28-29 (=*MSB*, 367-68). Theses 21 and 22 of the Propositions attributed to Egranus picked up again on this theme. See Matheson, *Collected Works*, 382 (= *MSB*, 515). Goertz, "Geistverständnis," 89, argues that in these theses the argument from the Spirit appears but is not central. However, its appearance at the end of the list points to its growing importance in Müntzer's thought. On the value of these propositions for recovering the arguments of Egranus, see Goertz, *Apocalyptic Mystic*, 61.

46 Matheson, *Collected Works*, 409-11, 418, 427. For the dating of Müntzer's annotations on Cyprian and Tertullian see Bubenheimer, *Müntzer: Herkunft und Bildung*, 203-4 and Bräuer, "Kirchenverständnis," 113.

47 Matheson, *Collected Works*, 43 (=*MSB*, 380; Baylor, *Revelation and Revolution*, 155).

48 Ibid., 45 (= *MSB*, 381; Baylor, *Revelation and Revolution*, 156).

49 Friesen, *Muentzer*, 124-30, 169-70. Although he does not concentrate on the normative nature of the apostolic church in his detailed analysis of the letter (pp. 124-30), it plays an important role in the subsequent discussion of the normative nature of the apostolic church.

50 Ernst Koch, "Das Sacramentsverständnis Thomas Müntzers," in Bräuer and Junghans, 133.

51 Matheson, *Collected Works*, 43-46 (= *MSB*, 379-82; Baylor, *Revelation and Revolution*, 155-57). Siegfried Bräuer, "Kirchenverständnis," 111-12, argues that in the final analysis Müntzer's criticism of the Wittenbergers is based on their failure to accept ongoing revelation.

52 Matheson, *Collected Works*, 357, 359, 360, 363, 370, 372, 377 (= *MSB*, 491, 492, 494, 496, 504, 505-6, 510; Baylor, *Revelation and Revolution*, 53-54, 59). Baylor's translation of *Ordnung* as "proper liturgy" is problematic in this context.

53 Matheson, *Collected Works*, 412-17, 419-20, 422-24.

54 See Bubenheimer, *Müntzer: Herkunft und Bildung*, 210-16, 224-26. Bubenheimer's conclusions have been applauded by a number of Müntzer scholars, for example see Scott, *Müntzer*, 9-10; Vogler, *Müntzer*, 104; Goertz, *Apocalyptic Mystic*, 47; Stayer, "Müntzer in 1989," 659. Stayer, "Reeling History Backwards: The Anabaptists as a Key to Understanding Thomas Müntzer more Conservatively," Meiji University International Exchange Programs Guest Lecture Series, No. 9 (1995), (Center for International Programs, Meiji University: 1996), 20, has suggested that Friesen's findings provide a good indication that the *ordo* is revealed through history for Müntzer. As the following should suggest, with some important qualifications I endorse this assessment.

55 See Daryl Reid, "Luther, Müntzer and the Last Days: Eschatological Hope, Apocalyptic Expectations," *MQR* 68 (1995), 53-74.

56 The clearest evidence comes, in fact, from a letter written by one of his adherents in Zwickau to Müntzer shortly after his departure from the city. In July 1521, Hans Sommerschuh wrote to Müntzer that the persecution of his followers was paralleled by that suffered by the prophets and by Christ. Matheson, *Collected Works*, 39 (= *MSB*, 375-76). The issue may also have cropped up in the conflict with Egranus. The third thesis attributed to him asserts that Israel did not have the grace of Christ, see Matheson, *Collected Works*, 380 (=*MSB*, 513).

57 Sermon fragments from 1520 indicate that Müntzer was discussing the relationship between the testaments openly in Zwickau and a letter from Agricola to Müntzer, dated February 1521, suggests that at that point the question was recognized beyond the city's walls as a central issue in the conflict with Egranus. See Matheson, *Collected Works*, 29-31, 381-82 (= *MSB*, 368-69, 514). For the relationship between the order of things and the proper assessment of the authority of the Old Testament, see the annotations on Tertullian, Matheson, *Collected Works*, 412-13.

58 Matheson, *Collected Works*, 43-46 (= *MSB*, 379-82; Baylor, *Revelation and Revolution*, 155-57).

59 Matheson, *Collected Works*, 360, 370-71 (= *MSB*, 494, 503-4; Baylor, *Revelation and Revolution*, 59).

60 Matheson *Collected Works*, 357-58, 363-65, 367 (= *MSB*, 492, 496-500; Baylor, *Revelation and Revolution*, 54-56).

61 Matheson, *Collected Works*, 359 (= *MSB*, 493).

62 Matheson, *Collected Works*, 364-65, 368 (= *MSB*, 497-98, 501; Baylor, *Revelation and Revolution*, 54-55, 57)

63 Friesen, *Muentzer*, 169-70.

64 Robert Friedmann, "Thomas Müntzer's Relation to Anabaptism," *MQR* 31 (1957), 77, went so far as to claim they deviated "from Catholicism in degree not in substance,"and Harold Bender, "The Zwickau Prophets, Thomas Müntzer and the Anabaptists," *MQR* 27 (1953), 6, has suggested that they agree with Luther's reforming vision.

65 Matheson, *Collected Works*, 166-68 (= *MSB*, 161-62). On Müntzer's liturgical reforms, see Brendler, *Geist und Faust*, 92-98.

66 Ullmann, "Geschichtsverständnis," 47.

67 Matheson, *Collected Works*, 166-68 (= *MSB*, 161-62).

68 Ibid., 170, 174 (= *MSB*, 208, 211-12).

69 Ibid., 68-69 (= *MSB*, 211-12; Baylor, *Revelation and Revolution*, 163).

70 Ibid., 177 (= *MSB*, 213-14; Baylor, *Revelation and Revolution*, 91).

71 Ibid., 172, 180-82 (= *MSB*, 163-65, 209-10). For more detailed analysis of Müntzer's intentions in the liturgical reforms, see Bräuer, "Kirchenverständnis," 142-45; Goertz, *Innere und äußere Ordnung*, 77 and *Apocalyptic Mystic*, 101; Karl Honemeyer, "Thomas

Müntzers Allstedter Gottesdienst als Symbol und Bestandteil der Volksreformation," in Friesen and Goertz, 218-19; Koch, "Sakramentsverständnis," 134-35; Lohmann, 40-43; Mario Josipovic and William McNiel, "Thomas Müntzer as 'Disturber of the Godless:' A Reassessment of his Revolutionary Nature," *MQR* 70 (1996), 431-47; Matheson, *Collected Works*, 162-65; Schwarz, *Apokalyptische Theologie*, 32-34.

72 Matheson, *Collected Works*, 174-76 (= *MSB*, 211-13; Baylor, *Revelation and Revolution*, 89-91). On the dating of these two works and the relationship between them, and between them and the liturgical reforms, see Matheson, *Collected Works*, 164, 183-84.

73 This vision of the church's fall is developed most fully in *Protestation or Proposition*, see Matheson, *Collected Works*, 191-95 (= *MSB*, 228-31; Baylor, *Revelation and Revolution*, 66-68), but is also touched on in *On Counterfeit Faith*. See Matheson, *Collected Works*, 219 (= *MSB*, 221; Baylor, *Revelation and Revolution*, 80). A number of historians have commented on the connection between pedobaptism and the decline of the church in Müntzer's thought at this point. See Matheson, *Collected Works*, 184-86; Baylor, "Case of the Elect," 89; Koch, "Sakramentsverständnis," 140-41; Lohmann, 46-48; Brendler, *Geist und Faust*, 123.

74 Matheson, *Collected Works*, 191-93 (= *MSB*, 228-29; Baylor, *Revelation and Revolution*, 66-67). On the metaphor of Spirit and water in Müntzer's baptismal theology, see especially Koch, "Sakramentsverständnis," 140-41 and Lohmann, 46-48.

75 Friesen, *Muentzer*, 171-80, especially 175.

76 Matheson, *Collected Works*, 189-91, 195, 207-9 (= *MSB*, 226-28, 230-31, 239-40; Baylor, *Revelation and Revolution*, 65-66, 68, 75-76).

77 Matheson, *Collected Works*, 206-7, 218, 222 (= *MSB*, 239, 221, 223; Baylor, *Revelation and Revolution*, 75, 79, 82).

78 Bailey, "Heritage," 39, argues that Müntzer's identification of himself as a new Daniel should be read in a Joachimite context. Schwarz, *Apokalyptische Theologie*, 73-75, suggests instead a more general chiliastic context. In *Reformer without a Church*, Gritsch argued that Müntzer's apocalyptic vision was derived from his reading of Daniel and Joel. Goertz, "Geistverständnis," 94-95 argues convincingly that even in this work Müntzer's apocalyptic thought remains in service to his pneumatological-mystical understanding and that the emphasis should remain on the continuity in the church's history rather than the discontinuity. Recently Emmet McLaughlin has argued even more strenuously against treating Müntzer's thought in this work as apocalyptic. See "Apocalypticism and Thomas Müntzer," *ARG* 95 (2004): 98-131.

79 Dismer, 20-21. On the traditionalism of Müntzer's exegesis of this text, see also Ullmann, "Geschichtsverständnis," 55; Brendler, *Geist und Faust*, 134 and James Stayer, *Anabaptists and the Sword*, 2nd ed. (Lawrence, KS: Coronado Press, 1976), 83. Friesen, *Muentzer*, 202-10 regards the *Sermon to the Princes* as providing a total vision of ecclesiastical history, and while it indicates a new urgency and need for a more radical approach to the reform of the church, all of this is a necessary precondition to the reestablishment of the apostolic church.

80 Matheson, *Collected Works*, 230-32 (= *MSB*, 242-44; Baylor, *Revelation and Revolution*, 98-99). On this occasion he sees the fall of the apostolic church as a fulfillment of the prophecies in 2 Peter 2 and Acts 20.

81 Matheson, *Collected Works*, 231 (= *MSB*, 243; Baylor, *Revelation and Revolution*, 99).

82 Matheson, *Collected Works*, 230 (= *MSB*, 242; Baylor, *Revelation and Revolution*, 98).

83 Matheson, *Collected Works*, 230, 235-36, 244-45 (= *MSB*, 242, 246-48, 255-56; Baylor, *Revelation and Revolution*, 98, 100-3, 108-9). The exegesis of Daniel 2 is primarily an explanation of the importance of revelation in these dangerous times.

84 Matheson, *Collected Works*, 233-35, 237-39, 245-46, 248-52 (= *MSB*, 245-47, 248-51, 256-57, 260-63; Baylor, *Revelation and Revolution*, 100-2, 103-5, 109-10, 112-14).

85 Matheson, *Collected Works*, 231 (= *MSB*, 243; Baylor, *Revelation and Revolution*, 99).

86 Matheson, *Collected Works*, 235, 250 (= *MSB*, 247, 261; Baylor, *Revelation and Revolution*, 102, 113). Goertz, "Geistverständnis," 94-95, emphasizes the importance of Müntzer's vision of the parallel outpourings of the Spirit in these three ages.

87 Ullmann, "Geschichtsverständnis," 51.

88 Matheson, *Collected Works*, 246, 250-51 (= *MSB*, 257, 261-62; Baylor, *Revelation and Revolution*, 110, 112-13).

89 Friesen, *Muentzer*, 209-10, treats Müntzer's use of Old Testament models here as functional elements in the establishment of the new apostolic church. Insofar as this assessment is applied specifically to the advice to the princes, I think it is valid. However, as the preceding should indicate, I believe that the "church" of the Old Testament plays more than just a functional role in Müntzer's thought. For an enlightening discussion of how Müntzer's identification with different biblical figures varied according to the needs of the moment and the identity of his adversaries, see Goertz, *Apocalyptic Mystic*, 149-50.

90 Matheson, *Collected Works*, 266, 294, 341,346 (= *MSB*, 271, 294-95, 335, 340; Baylor, *Revelation and Revolution*, 116-17, 127-28, 148, 152).

91 Ibid., 270-74, 330, 338-39, 341, 346-47 (= *MSB*, 273-78, 324-25, 332-33, 335, 340-41; Baylor, *Revelation and Revolution*, 118-20, 141,146-47, 148, 152-53).

92 Ibid., 300, 327 (= *MSB*, 300, 322; Baylor, *Revelation and Revolution*, 130, 139). As a variation on this theme, Matheson, *Collected Works*, 346 (= *MSB*, 340; Baylor, *Revelation and Revolution*, 152), Müntzer identifies Luther as a false prophet, citing Ezekial and Micah.

93 Ibid., 276, 296, 308, 318-20, 329-32, 333-34, 338-41, 347 (= *MSB*, 279-80, 296, 306-7, 314-17, 323-27, 327-28, 332-33, 341; Baylor, *Revelation and Revolution*, 120-21, 128, 132-33, 136-37, 140-42, 143, 146, 152).

94 Ibid., 395-96.

95 Ibid., 152 (= *MSB*, 464-65).

96 Ibid., 312 (= *MSB*, 310; Baylor, *Revelation and Revolution*, 134).

97 Friesen, *Muentzer*, 164.

98 For example, see Matheson, *Collected Works*, 276 (= *MSB*, 279-80; Baylor, *Revelation and Revolution*, 120-21).

99 See Sider, *Karlstadt's Battle*, 40, 42 (=*WA* 15:335-36).

100 Assumptions about Karlstadt's categorical rejection of the use of force in the service of the Reformation have been challenged especially by the research of Roy L. Vice. See "Ehrenfried Kumpf, Karlstadt's Patron and Peasants' War Rebel," *ARG* 86 (1995): 153-75 and "Valentin Ickelsamer's Odyssey from Rebellion to Quietism," *MQR* 69 (1995): 75-92. On the changing interpretation of Müntzer as a revolutionary, see below.

101 The most recent and direct treatment of this topic is Josipovic and McNiel, "Müntzer as 'Disturber of the Godless,'" 431-47.

102 Stayer, *Anabaptists and the Sword*, 76.

103 Eike Wolgast, "Die Obrigkeits- und Widerstandslehre Thomas Müntzers," in Bräuer and Junghans, 195-98.

104 Baylor, "Case of the Elect," 85-86.

105 Bubenheimer, *Müntzer: Herkunft und Bildung*, 191.

106 Wolgast, "Widerstandsrecht," 199.

107 Matheson, *Collected Works*, 409 (= *MSB*, 539). Cf. Bräuer, "Kirchenverständnis," 113; Ullmann, "Geschichtsverständnis," 49-50; Baylor, "Case of the Elect," 89-90; idem, *Revelation and Revolution*, 19.

108 Matheson, *Collected Works*, 364, 369.

109 Michael Baylor's claim, *Revelation and Revolution*, 19, that this may have been a tactical move is questionable given the development of Müntzer's critique of secular authority.

110 Matheson, *Collected Works*, 183.

111 See especially, Lohmann, 39-40; Michael Baylor, "Thomas Müntzer's First Publication," *SCJ* 17 (1986), 454-55.

112 Matheson, *Collected Works*, 66-67 (= *MSB* 393-94; Baylor, *Revelation and Revolution*, 161-62).

113 Baylor, "Müntzer's First Publication," 454-55, n. 13.

114 Matheson, *Collected Works*, 69 (= *MSB*, 396-97; Baylor, *Revelation and Revolution*, 163).

115 In his letter to Count Ernst, Müntzer cites Romans 13:4 in support of his demand that the authorities rule so that people will learn to fear God alone. See Matheson, *Collected Works*, 66-67 (= *MSB*, 393-94, Baylor, *Revelation and Revolution*, 161-62).

116 Wolgast, "Widerstandsrecht," 199-200.

117 Matheson, *Collected Works*, 62 (= *MSB*, 23; Baylor, *Revelation and Revolution*, 61). See also Wolgast, "Widerstandsrecht," 199-200.

118 Wolgast, "Widerstandsrecht," 201.

119 Matheson, *Collected Works*, 246 (= *MSB*, 258; Baylor, *Revelation and Revolution*, 110). Wolgast, "Widerstandsrecht," 202-3 regards this expansion of the authority of secular government as an important development in Müntzer's thinking about authority and resistance.

120 Matheson, *Collected Works*, 250-52 (= *MSB*, 260-63; Baylor, *Revelation and Revolution*, 113-14).

121 Ibid., 246-50 (= *MSB*, 258-60; Baylor, *Revelation and Revolution*, 110-13).

122 Friesen, *Muentzer*, 207-9.

123 Ibid., 233; Baylor, "Case of the Elect," 89-90; Hinrichs, 47, 57. In this work Müntzer further emphasizes the responsibility of secular authorities in the fall of the church. See Lohmann, 53.

124 Matheson, *Collected Works*, 79-81 (= *MSB*, 404-6; Baylor, *Revelation and Revolution*, 168-69).

125 Ibid., 83-103.

126 Maron, 364.

127 See Scott, *Müntzer*, 81-88, 115-16, 147-48; idem, "The 'Volksreformation' of Thomas Müntzer in Allstedt and Mühlhausen," *JEH* 34 (1983): 194-213; Friesen, *Muentzer*, 194-96; Vogler, 174.

128 Wolgast, "Widerstandsrecht," 203.

129 Matheson, *Collected Works*, 95-103 (= *MSB*, 419-23; Baylor, *Revelation and Revolution*, 178-82).

130 Ibid., 110-13 (= *MSB*, 430-32; Baylor, *Revelation and Revolution*, 184-86).

131 Ibid., 280 (= *MSB*, 283; Baylor, *Revelation and Revolution*, 122). On the importance of the figure of Herod as the archetypical tyrant in Müntzer's thought, see Dismer, 176 and 218.

132 Matheson, *Collected Works*, 282 (= *MSB*, 285; Baylor, *Revelation and Revolution*, 123). On Müntzer's new assessment of secular authority, see Baylor, "Case of the Elect," 89-90; Wolgast, "Widerstandsrecht," 205-6.

133 Matheson, *Collected Works*, 286-88, 296-300 (= *MSB*, 288-89, 296-300; Baylor, *Revelation and Revolution*, 124-25, 128-29). See Hinrichs, 110-12; see also Scott, 100-3 and Matheson, *Collected Works*, 256-57; Goertz, *Apocalyptic Mystic*, 147-49.

134 Matheson, *Collected Works*, 327.

135 Ibid., 334-4, 342. See Hinrichs, 165; Lohmann, 64-66; Vogler, *Müntzer*, 216-18; Matheson, *Collected Works*, 324-26; Josipovic, 443-44.

136 Matheson, *Collected Works*, 137, 142, 155-56 (= *MSB*, 451, 455, 468-69; Baylor, *Revelation and Revolution*, 191-92, 195).

137 Ibid., 150, 156-59 (= *MSB*, 463, 469-72; Baylor, *Revelation and Revolution*, 193, 195-97).

138 Ibid., 144, 149-51, 156-57 (= *MSB*, 458, 462-64, 469-70; Baylor, *Revelation and Revolution*, 193-94, 195-96).

CHAPTER 3

ANABAPTIST RESTITUTION

Because God wanted one united people, separated from all other peoples, he brought forth the Morning Star, the light of his truth, to shine with all its radiance in the present age of this world. He wanted in particular to visit the German lands with his Word and to reveal the foundation of divine truth, so that his holy work would be recognized by everyone. It began in Switzerland, where God brought about an awakening.

***The Hutterite Chronicle*[1]**

Anabaptist Restitutionism

Any discussion of the Anabaptist vision of history must confront at the outset the question of whether or not the Anabaptists held to a distinctive ecclesiological vision. Over three decades ago Hans Hillerbrand and Franklin H. Littell engaged in a heated exchange about the possible existence, nature and significance of a distinctive Anabaptist view of history, and with it a unique ecclesiology.[2] A central issue in the debate was whether or not the Anabaptists, and to varying degrees other Reformation radicals, aimed at a "restitution" of the primitive church, distinct from the "reforming" agendas of the magisterial Reformers. Restitutionism, Littell had argued, is in fact a crucial defining characteristic of the Anabaptist movement. Although the most fully and clearly formulated statement of the restitutionist thesis, Littell's claims were in no way unique or unusual. In fact, assumptions similar to those held by Littell have undergirded much of the historical writing about Anabaptism carried out over the century.

The strength and pervasiveness of the restitution thesis is attested to by the fact that its fullest and clearest elucidation predated Hillerbrand's attack on it by two decades. In 1950 Littell laid out the skeleton of his thesis in an article in the *Mennonite Quarterly Review* entitled "The Anabaptist Doctrine of the Restitution of the True Church."[3] This skeleton was fleshed out two years later in his monograph, *The Anabaptist View of the Church*, subsequently revised and republished under the title *The Origins of Sectarian Protestantism*, and later translated into German.[4] Littell characterized Anabaptism as a form of "Christian primitivism" which included its own "philosophy of history: an Eden in the past, a partial Restitution in the present (wiping out the scandal of the fallen period), a divine restoration in the future." The focus on the restitution of the New Testament church in the present led the Anabaptists to reject the medieval *corpus Christianum*—a fact highlighted by their frequent identification of a Constantinian fall of the church. This radically new view of the church, argued Littell, was the most important contribution of the Anabaptists to "Christian life and history." However, Christian primitivism was not completely unique to the Anabaptists. According to Littell, a "primitivist mood" pervaded the age of the Reformation and played an especially important role in the various movements which made up the Left Wing of the Reformation, but only among the Anabaptists did this primitivism reach its fullest explication in the doctrine of restitution: "The Anabaptists were among the first to ground the church in a total and systematic application of primitivist historiography." The desire to gather and discipline a true church on the apostolic pattern was the chief characteristic distinguishing the "Anabaptists proper" from others in the Radical Reformation. Furthermore, the thorough-going primitivism of the Anabaptists was sufficiently distinct from the understanding of the magisterial Reformers that Littell claimed that the Anabaptist ecclesiology was *sui generis* and that there existed a "church of the Restitution" distinct from the "church of the Reformers."[5] The development of the church of the restitution was of profound importance for the subsequent history of Christianity. In their criticism of the Constantinian church the Anabaptists rejected the validity of the use of coercion in religious matters and paved the way for the freedom of conscience. In Littell's own words:

> The Anabaptists were in fact the first consistently to champion religious liberty in the modern sense. They believed that no individual might be compelled by the magistrate in the matter of faith, and they distinguished between political sovereignty and those controls of the church which belong to its internal discipline and integrity.[6]

Hillerbrand's response amounted to nothing less than a root and branch assault on Littell's thesis. Arguing that the sixteenth-century Anabaptist movement was notoriously heterogeneous and enigmatic, he questioned the very possibility of delineating an "Anabaptist vision."[7] Furthermore, Hillerbrand asserted, insofar as such a common vision can be pieced together from the writings of the leading "Evangelical Anabaptists"—"Anabaptists proper" in Littell's parlance—that vision has precious few of the attributes assigned to it by Littell. In response to Littell's claim that among the Anabaptists the primitivist historiography was most consistently applied to the church, Hillerbrand argued that, in fact, the early Anabaptists were not greatly concerned about or conversant with the past. "The Anabaptists were," to use Hillerbrand's own words, "not historically minded."[8] Consequently, Hillerbrand rejected the suggestion that the Anabaptists held a distinctive, "qualitatively different" notion of reform from that held by their contemporaries. All religious groups in the sixteenth century claimed to adhere to biblical ideals and norms, making problematic the suggestion that the Anabaptist vision was in some way distinctive in its appeal to the New Testament. Furthermore, the term "restitution" fails to appear in any of the writings of the mainstream Anabaptists. It is, then, a theoretical construct rather than an historical fact, and a theoretical construct of dubious linguistic and theological

pedigree.[9] The keyword to describe the Anabaptist vision of history, according to Hillerbrand, was not restitution, but continuity with the faithful of all ages. The basic assumption in the Anabaptist reading of Christian history was that the church has existed through the ages as a persecuted remnant. The apparent reappearance of scattered communities of the faithful in the sixteenth century marked no dramatic change in this basic pattern: continued faithfulness, not restitution, was the goal and program of the Anabaptist movements.[10]

At first glance Hillerbrand's most telling criticism of Littell's thesis is his observation that the sixteenth-century Anabaptists did not employ the term restitution. As a result, the restitutionist thesis must stand or fall as a theoretical concept. But it is a theoretical concept with a long and venerable history of its own. H. W. Meihuizen, who has produced the most thorough investigation to date of the roots of the concept, traces the origins of its modern usage to a footnote in Karl Wilhelm Bouterwek's *Zur Literatur und Geschichte der Wiedertäufer, besonders in den Rheinlanden*, published in 1864. In that footnote Bouterwek noted the use of the term *restitutio* in the titles of the works of five Reformation radicals: Bernhard Rothmann, Michael Servetus, Johannes Campanus, Jan Wilhelms of Roermond and Dirk Philips, and concluded only that: "The word *restitution* was favoured among the sectarians as a title."[11] One might add as well that, of these authors, only Philips can be characterized as an "Evangelical Anabaptist," and he used the term "restitution" in a far different way than Littell suggests. But, despite these humble beginnings, restitutionism quickly began to accrete further attributes. In his 1885 biography of Melchior Hoffman, Friedrich Otto zur Linden identified restitution as a central principle of Mennonitism, and at least implicitly distinguished it from the program of the magisterial Reformers by arguing that it involved carrying the ideas of the Reformation through to their logical conclusion. In 1899 Karl Rembert further clarified this distinction, connecting restitution to the Anabaptists' biblicism by tying it to New Testament roots.[12]

But by far the most complete formulation of the restitutionist thesis prior to Littell's came at the hands of Roland Bainton. Bainton recast the conversation about restitutionism by providing it with a rich theoretical superstructure: an amalgam of Arthur O. Lovejoy's theories about primitivism and the then immensely popular sociological typologies of religious groups developed by Max Weber and Ernst Troeltsch. Bainton identified the desire for a restitution of the primitive church as " a sort of Christian primitivism" and a crucial element in Protestant sect formation. Furthermore, he situated Anabaptist restitutionism in the broader context of late medieval and Reformation ecclesiastical history. He suggested that this ideal was evident among groups like the Franciscan Spirituals, and that it is identifiable as a polemical device exploited by humanist critics of the church and by the magisterial Reformers. However, the latter two groups quickly recoiled from the full implications of a complete restoration of the primitive church when faced with the Anabaptist threat.[13]

Littell's work, then, itself represented the culmination of an interpretive tradition. Not surprisingly, it received accolades almost immediately. Although he had certain misgivings about Littell's use of "primitivism" or "restitution" as the controlling idea of early Anabaptism, Harold Bender nonetheless praised *The Anabaptist View of the Church* as "a very good book, an epoch making book."[14] Specialized studies further applying the restitutionist thesis to Anabaptist sources not covered by Littell's research, and general studies incorporating the restitution thesis, abounded.[15] A crucial step in the establishment of the restitution thesis as orthodoxy undoubtedly came in 1962 when George H. Williams designated "restitutionism" as a distinguishing characteristic of the Radical Reformation. This restitutionism he described as the "sixteenth-century version of primitivism," and although it could be applied generally to the Reformation radicals, the concept was particularly apt for the Anabaptists, as Littell had indicated.[16] Aside from a very few dissenting voices, restitutionism had carried the day.[17]

Hillerbrand's challenge to Littell's thesis amounted, then, to little more than a voice crying in the wilderness. It should come as no surprise, therefore, that Hillerbrand's concerns have received little in the way of sympathetic response. The only explicit reaction came from John H. Yoder. Under the guise of downplaying the differences between the interpretations of Littell and Hillerbrand as semantic quibbles, Yoder dismissed the question of the actual use of the term "restitution" by sixteenth-century Anabaptists. His stated intention was to clearly define the label "restitution," thereby making it "objectively usable"—confusion about the use of the term "restitution" should not preclude the viability of the concept.[18] Beyond this distinction, Yoder revived the basic elements of the restitutionist arguments, in some cases even sharpening them. He reiterated the claim that the restitutionist position was central in distinguishing the vision of the Anabaptists from those of the magisterial Reformers. Furthermore, it even drew the lines between the ecclesial Anabaptists and others in the Radical Reformation, the revolutionaries and spiritualists whose perception of a dawning third age of the world made them technically not restitutionist at all.[19] In other words, the majority of those who coined the term were, by its very definition, precluded from identification with the concept. Finally, in response to Hillerbrand's claim that the Anabaptists were not historically minded, Yoder asserted that the Anabaptists took history more seriously than their contemporaries: "only the mental structure of restitutionism can be at once Christian and serious about history."[20]

Aside from Yoder's direct parry to Hillerbrand's thrust, the response from much of the academic community has been to ignore Hillerbrand—in that sense it appears that Yoder's claim that the dispute between Hillerbrand and Littell was little more than semantic quibbling has borne fruit. Instead the restitution thesis has quietly lived on in many quarters, either explicitly—as in Walter Klaassen's characterization of Anabaptism in his study of apocalypticism in the age of the Reformation—or implicitly—as in Abraham Friesen's recent treatment of Anabaptist responses to the Great Commission.[21] The continued widespread acceptance of the thesis is most evident, however, in the latest, revised edition of George Williams' *Radical Reformation*, which repeats with only limited modification the statements from the 1962 edition about restitutionism and its place in the radical Reformation and Anabaptism.[22]

Later Anabaptist Historical Visions

Restitutionism has, then, generally been considered an integral element of the Anabaptist vision. Integrated into it is an assumed distinct and unified Anabaptist vision of ecclesiastical history. The general outlines of that Anabaptist view of ecclesiastical history have been sketched by Littell. He claims that the Anabaptists looked to a golden age of the church in its early years. This pristine age came to an end with the fall of the church, usually identified by the Anabaptists with the establishment of the Constantinian church and its integration of church and state and the intrusion of the civil arm in matters of faith. Then came the "middle years" of the fallen church, during which the faithful lived in dispersion, often persecuted as heretics by the institutional church. Finally there has come the restitution of the true church, an event usually identified as growing out of the Reformation, but progressing beyond the programmes of the magisterial Reformers.[23]

Elements of the historical vision described above do appear in Anabaptist writings from the sixteenth and seventeenth centuries. The clearest and most complete example of this is contained in *The Hutterite Chronicle*, which not only describes the experiences of the Hutterites, but also attempts to locate them in the greater stream of Christian history. Within this context Constantine's conversion is described in the following terms:

> With the good intention of doing God a service, the emperor obtained peace throughout his kingdom for the pope, and for all those who called themselves Christians. Here the pestilence of deceit that stalks the darkness and the plague that destroys at midday swept in with force, abolished the cross, and forged it onto the sword. All this happened through the old serpent's deceit.[24]

Constantine's conversion, then, marked the fall of the true church and birth of the false persecuting church which subsequently came to be identified with the papacy:

> In this way the light of truth began to lose its brightness. Although a glimpse of it could be seen from time to time, the enemy, using the pope as his tool, was soon there to stamp it out. And although many groups split away on questions of faith, the popes gained the upper hand by their violence, and this abomination grew so great that it ruled wantonly over the emperor and all the kings of the Roman Empire.[25]

By way of contrast, the true church suffered persecution throughout the ages. The authors of *The Hutterite Chronicle* describe the plight of the first Christians in terms which parallel the experiences of the Hutterites and other Anabaptist groups:

> They were called enemies of the human race because they separated themselves from other people; enemies of God because they would not serve idols; useless people because they had no fellowship with robbers and corrupt men; scoundrels because they let themselves be killed for their faith. All these misfortunes happened for one reason only. And true followers of Christ are still being treated like that by the world.[26]

The authors then chronicle the persecution of true Christians throughout the ages, describing the experiences of the Donatists, the Waldensians and Fraticelli, the Lollards and Hussites, before arriving at the details of the Reformation. Consistently the account implies that medieval heretics identified in it upheld at least some aspects of Christian truth and foreshadowed the restoration of the true church in the Hutterite communities.[27]

Restoration began with the activities of the magisterial Reformers, but they lacked the fortitude to carry it through to its proper conclusion:

> These two, Luther and Zwingli, exposed all the deception and villainy of the pope and brought it to the light of day as if they

> would strike everything to the ground with thunderbolts. But they put nothing better in its place. As soon as they began to cling to worldly power and put their trust in human help, they were just as bad—like someone mending an old kettle and only making a bigger hole. They left behind a shameless people, whom they had taught to sin. To speak in a parable, they struck the jug from the pope's hand but kept the broken pieces in their own.[28]

Instead the task of restoring the true church passed into the hands of the Anabaptists whose beginnings were traced to Zurich in 1525.[29]

Individual elements of the same historical vision appear in the writings of other Anabaptist traditions which survived the sixteenth century: the Swiss Brethren and the Mennonites. A remarkably similar assessment of Constantine's conversion to that contained in *The Hutterite Chronicle* appears in a pamphlet written by a south German member of the Swiss Brethren, Hans Schnell:

> He [Constantine] was baptized by pope Sylvester, the Antichrist, the son of perdition, whose coming took place through the work of the same loathsome devil.
>
> Therefore he received the name Christian falsely. For the Christian church was at that time transformed into the antiChristian church. . . . When Constantine, the twenty-fourth emperor, assumed and accepted the name Christian, which is indeed itself a cause for lamenting, then the apostasy came, from which apostasy may God protect us eternally. Amen.[30]

Schnell failed to complement this description with an identification of the true church as the persecuted heretics of the Middle Ages, although he did characterize the true church as always suffering persecution.[31]

By way of contrast, the Mennonites paid little attention to Constantine's conversion. The most important Mennonite martyrology, Thieleman van Braght's *Martyrs Mirror*, instead identifies the beginnings of the false church with the ascendancy of the papacy:

> Besides, that in the first three centuries after the death of the apostles, nothing was known in the Roman church, as regards

> the rulers of the same, but common bishops or overseers, until the time of Constantine the Great, and from that time on until the year 600, only archbishops and patriarchs, but no popes, till after the year 606, when by the power of the Emperor Phocas, the Roman Bishop Boniface III was declared and established general head and supreme ruler of the whole church; ...[32]

This event van Braght later described as exalting the seat of the Antichrist "to its highest altitude," "whereby many superstitions and human inventions were presented to the people as the Word of God."[33] But, like *The Hutterite Chronicle*, the *Martyrs Mirror* prefaces the account of the persecution of the early Anabaptists with a developed narrative of the attempted suppression of the true church from the first through the fifteenth centuries. In this the purpose is again to show the apostolic succession of an "alternative church."[34]

In these sources, and especially in *The Hutterite Chronicle*, we have the essential outlines of Littell's description of the Anabaptist vision of ecclesiastical history, but *The Hutterite Chronicle* was begun in the 1560s, Schnell's pamphlet written sometime around 1575, and the *Martyrs Mirror* completed in 1660. The clearest evidence of an Anabaptist view of ecclesiastical history akin to that described by Littell is almost half a century removed from the beginnings of the movement. Littell allowed that the Anabaptist vision of the church evolved over time, but suggested, nonetheless, that it was fully developed in Swiss Brethren circles already in 1523.[35] Implicit in Littell's analysis is the assumption that this primitivist vision dominated subsequent reforming activities of the Anabaptists. By way of contrast, Hillerbrand has argued that insofar as Anabaptists held to a vision of the past, it was a vision determined by contemporary events and circumstances.[36] In what follows, I will argue that the Anabaptist encounter with the past can best be characterized as a relationship fitting somewhere between these two poles. That is, the Anabaptist vision of the past and reform of the church in the present interacted in a symbiotic relationship. Often Anabaptists approached the historical record with specific questions dictated by contemporary concerns, but the image of

the primitive church they constructed as a result of these forays into the past eventually began to take on normative status. In this sense the concept of "primitivism" can still be regarded as a valuable characteristic of the Anabaptist movement, but only after it has been pruned of some excessive undergrowth.

Notes

1 The Hutterian Brethren, *The Chronicle of the Hutterian Brethren*, 1 (Rifton, NY: Plough Publishing House, 1987), 43.

2 Cf. Hans Hillerbrand, "Anabaptism and History," *MQR* 45 (1971), 107-22 and Franklin H. Littell, "In Response to Hans Hillerbrand," *MQR* 45 (1971), 377-80.

3 Franklin H. Littell, "The Anabaptist Doctrine of the Restitution of the True Church," *MQR* 24 (1950), 33-52.

4 Franklin H. Littell, *The Anabaptist View of the Church: A Study in the Origins of Sectarian Protestantism* (Boston: Starr King Press, 1958), subsequently republished as *The Origins of Sectarian Protestantism: A Study of the Anabaptist View of the Church* (New York: MacMillan, 1964). The German translation appeared in 1966.

5 *Origins of Sectarian Protestantism*, . xvii, 46-57, 61-64, 77, 79; "Anabaptist Doctrine of Restitution," 33-34.

6 *Origins of Protestant Sectarianism*, 65-66.

7 Hillerbrand, "Anabaptism and History", 108.

8 Ibid., 110-11.

9 Ibid., 112-14.

10 Ibid., 117-19.

11 H. W. Meihuizen, "The Concept of Restitution in the Anabaptism of Northwestern Europe," *MQR* 44 (1970), 141-43.

12 Ibid., 143-44.

13 Roland H. Bainton, "Changing Ideas and Ideals in the 16th Century," *Journal of Modern History* 8 (1936), 428-29. Bainton further developed this thesis in "The Left Wing of the Reformation," *Journal of Religion* 21 (1941), 125-32 and *The Reformation of the Sixteenth Century* (Boston: Beacon Press, 1952), 95. Cf Meihuizen, "Concept of Restitution," 146.

14 *MQR* 27 (1953), 249-53.

15 See, for example, Frank J. Wray, "History in the Eyes of the Sixteenth-Century Anabaptists," (PhD diss., Yale, 1954); idem, "The Anabaptist Doctrine of the Restitution of the Church," *MQR* 28 (1954), 186-96; Heinold Fast, ed., *Der linke Flügel der Reformation* (Bremen: Carl Schünemann, 1962); Leonard Verduin, *The Reformers and Their Stepchildren* (Grand Rapids: Eerdmans, 1964), 11-17, 40; Cornelius Krahn, *Dutch Anabaptism: Origin, Spread and Thought* (Scottdale, PA and Kitchener, ON: Herald Press, 1981),193 and 258-60; Glanmore Williams, *Reformation Views of Church History* (Richmond, VA: John Knox Press, 1970), 15-20.

16 George H Williams, *The Radical Reformation* (Philadelphia: Westminster Press, 1962), xxvi, 236, 375, 857, 862 n. 8. Cf. Meihuizen, "Concept of Restitution," 147; James M. Stayer, "The Anabaptists," in Steven Ozment, ed. *Reformation Europe: A Guide to Research* (St. Louis, MO: Center for Reformation Research, 1982), 136-37.

17 Meihuizen, "Concept of Restitution," 144-56 qualifies strictly the extent to which the concept of restitution, as defined by Littell, can be applied to the Anabaptism of north-central Europe.

18 John H. Yoder, "Anabaptism and History: Restitution and the Possibility of Renewal," in Hans-Jürgen Goertz, ed. *Umstrittenes Täufertum 1525-1975: Neue Forschungen* (Göttingen: Vandenhoeck and Ruprecht, 1975), 244-46. Yoder admits in n. 10 on page 246 that Dirk Phillips is the only mainstream Anabaptist to use the term "restitution" and that he uses it in response to its employment by his opponents rather than as a term descriptive of his own reforming vision.

19 Ibid., 246-49.

20 Ibid., 249-53, esp. 253.

21 Walter Klaassen, *Living at the End of the Ages: Apocalyptic Expectation in the Radical Reformation* (Lanham, NY: University Press of America, 1992), 75-94. See also his "The Anabaptist Critique of Constantinian Christianity," *MQR* 55 (1981), 218-30. Abraham Friesen, *Erasmus, the Anabaptists and the Great Commission* (Grand Rapids, MI: Wm. B. Eerdmans, 1998), 98-110 .

22 George H. Williams, *The Radical Reformation* (3rd Edition; Kirksville, MO: Sixteenth Century Journal Publishers, 1992), xxxi, 189-90, 357, 575-76, 1303-04.

23 Littell, *Origins of Sectarian Protestantism*, 53, 57-63, 76, 80-82.

24 *Chronicle of the Hutterian Brethren*, 31.

25 Ibid., 32.

26 Ibid., 31.

27 Ibid., 31-39. Peter Burschel questions the extent to which *The Hutterite Chronicle* identifies a succession of heroic witnesses to the truth through the ages and how much it portrays the appearance of the Hutterite communities as a restitution of the apostolic church. See "Zur Geschichtstheologie der Täufer," *ARG* 95 (2004): 132-55. Although these themes are not stressed as fully in the *Chronicle* as they are in the *Martyrs Mirror*, as Burschel notes, and although at one point the *Chronicle* appears to leave open the question of the extent to which medieval heretics testified to the truth, the parallels drawn between the experiences of the first Christians and those of the Hutterites, and the teachings attributed to the persecuted heretics of the Middle Ages, suggest that themes of restitution and succession are there, even if muted.

28 *Chronicle of the Hutterian Brethren*, 41.

29 Ibid., 43 ff.

30 Leonard Gross, "Hans Schnell: Second Generation Anabaptist," *MQR* 68 (1994), 375-76.

31 Ibid., 373-76.

32 Thieleman J. van Braght, *Martyrs Mirror*, trans. Joseph F. Sohm (Scottdale, PA, 1950), 52. Van Braght here is refuting claims of the papal church to be the true church throughout the ages, see pp. 46-60.

33 Ibid., 213.

34 Ibid., 21-27. See also Alan F. Kreider, "'The Servant is Not Greater than his Master:' The Anabaptists and the Suffering Church," *MQR* 58 (1984), 9 and Cornelius Dyck, "The Suffering Church in Anabaptism," *MQR* 59 (1985), 6 and 24.

35 Littell, *Origins of Protestant Sectarianism*, 3, 13.

36 Hillerbrand, "Anabaptism and History," 122.

CHAPTER 4

HISTORICAL VISIONS OF THE EVANGELICAL ANABAPTISTS

Just as our forefathers had fallen away from the true God and knowledge of Jesus Christ and true faith in him, from the one true common divine Word and from the godly practices of Christian love and way, and lived without God's law and gospel in human, useless, unchristian practices and ceremonies and supposed they would find salvation in them but fell far short of it, as the evangelical preachers have shown and are still in part showing, so even today everyone wants to be saved by hypocritical faith, without fruits of faith, without baptism of trial and testing, without hope and love, without true Christian practices, and wants to remain in all the old ways of personal vices and common antichristian ceremonial rites of baptism and the Lord's Supper, dishonouring the divine Word, but honouring the papal word and the antipapal preachers, which is not like or in accord with the divine Word.

Conrad Grebel to Thomas Müntzer[1]

In the later sixteenth century and into the seventeenth, surviving Anabaptist traditions developed elaborate visions of ecclesiastical history. These visions included many, although not all, of the characteristics of the Anabaptist view of church history as outlined by Franklin Littell. Furthermore, variations of detail existed between the historical visions of the different Anabaptist traditions; different Anabaptist groups emphasized different aspects of their supposed common view of the church's history. The search for the reasons behind those variations raises a related and equally interesting issue in understanding Reformation views of history: what was the place of historical reflection in the reforming visions of the sixteenth century? Proponents of the restitution thesis usually assume that a primitivist orientation and restitutionist agenda appeared early in the development of the Anabaptist movement and were a driving force behind the reform agendas and activities of the early Anabaptists. As we will see, not all of these assumptions are warranted.

The birth of Evangelical Anabaptism is usually associated with developments in the Swiss Confederacy, especially in Zurich. As the earliest Anabaptists "proper," and early on clearly the most sectarian of the Anabaptist groups, the Swiss have a surprisingly underdeveloped historical vision even in the second half of the sixteenth century. Statements from early Swiss radicals, not only from Zurich but also the surrounding communities, provide interesting insights into restitutionist ideals of the early Anabaptists, and possibly help to explain this apparent anomaly in the Anabaptist view of the church. Among the non-Zurich Anabaptists, particularly interesting is the radical Reformer of Waldshut, Balthasar Hubmaier. Largely because of his teachings on the sword, Hubmaier has traditionally been kept at arms length from the other Swiss Anabaptists and as a result, from the study of Evangelical Anabaptism in general. However, historical writing in recent years has increasingly acknowledged Hubmaier's importance for the development of Anabaptism.

Hubmaier's thought comes out of a Swiss context, but much of his impact was felt in the South German/Austrian Anabaptist movement. This movement had different roots and different experiences than the Swiss, and as a result, manifested some different characteristics and with them variations on the Anabaptist vision of ecclesiastical history. Some of this variation can be traced to the man regarded by many as the father of South German/Austrian Anabaptism, Hans Hut. Hut had close connections to, and was strongly influenced by, Thomas Müntzer. He shared Müntzer's spiritualism and apocalypticism, but apparently not his interest in history. It is a great irony, then, that among those influenced by Hut's spiritual legacy we see some of the most impressive and ambitious historical theorizing of early Anabaptism. This fact can be explained, at least in part by another characteristic of the South German/Austrian Anabaptist movement: this movement witnessed the regular interaction of different Anabaptist and other radical reforming traditions. Especially in Strasbourg and Moravia there developed important "melting pots" of Anabaptist traditions. Out of these melting pots grew two important traditions: the Marpeckites and the Hutterites. Both groups developed elaborate visions of ecclesiastical history far more sophisticated than anything in the Swiss lands with the possible exception of Hubmaier's thought. South German/Austrian Anabaptist historical reflection culminated in *The Hutterite Chronicle*.

Among later Anabaptist writings the *Martyrs Mirror* is second only to *The Hutterite Chronicle* in the detail and breadth of its historical vision. This work marks the culmination of a long and sophisticated martyrological tradition among the Dutch and North German Anabaptists. Like Hutterite thinking about ecclesiastical history, the Mennonite vision of the past developed gradually. Also like the Hutterites, this development occurred by fits and starts which involved shifts in emphasis and ultimately some important revisions of interpretation.

Swiss Brethren

Littell's assumptions about the early appearance of the Anabaptist vision of ecclesiastical history have carried the day in much of the literature on this issue. For example, in what likely remains the most influential statement on the subject, George H. Williams has credited the letters from the Grebel group to Thomas Müntzer of September 1524 as marking the beginning of a clearly formulated restitutionist program.[2]

According to the revisionist understanding of the beginnings of Swiss Anabaptism, the Zurich radicals had not yet adopted a separatist ecclesiology in 1524. But were the early Swiss Anabaptists, or to use the language of revisionist scholarship, proto-Anabaptists, restitutionists though not yet sectarians already in 1524? The secondary literature on the subject would suggest so. Such stalwart revisionists as James Stayer and Hans-Jürgen Goertz describe the goals of the early Swiss radicals respectively, as "… the radical, literal restoration of the true church …" or the endeavour to "revive the apostolic church …."[3] The primary sources bear out this judgement, although not in an unqualified manner.

At the centre of definitions of "Evangelical Anabaptism" are the Swiss Brethren. Often the first adult baptisms undertaken by radical critics of Zwingli's Reformation in January 1525 have been identified as the birth of the movement. However, the actual baptisms are thought to lie on a continuum between the letter from the Grebel circle to Thomas Müntzer, which lays out in embryo the essentials of a new free church, and the full articulation of that vision in the Schleitheim Articles of 1527. According to traditional treatments of the rise of Swiss Anabaptism, these events are laid out on a logical, coherent and consistent evolutionary line.

Since the 1970s, however, revisionist historians have carefully scrutinized both assumptions about, and evidence for, this account. Two aspects have been subject to particular revision in interpretation. On the one hand, attention has been shifted beyond Zurich's walls to focus on the development of Anabaptist movements in other cities and rural areas of eastern Switzerland. Scholars have noted that the first refusals of infant baptism occurred not in Zurich, but in the villages of Witikon and Zollikon in early 1524. Here and elsewhere in Switzerland the early Anabaptist movement did not conform to the model of "Evangelical Anabaptism:" the earliest Anabaptist congregations were not necessarily pacifist and hardly sectarian. In fact, in several locations they were closely tied to the peasant protest movement which amounted to the Swiss contribution to the German Peasants' War. This has led James Stayer to characterize the early Swiss movement as "non-separating congregationalism."[4] In fact, initially the initiative in early Swiss Anabaptism lay with the groups outside of Zurich and only with the adult baptisms of January 1525 did it shift to the Zurich radicals.[5] The revisionists have also reexamined our understanding of the early activities of the Zurich radicals. Although admitting that the 1524 letters to Müntzer exhibit a "proto-sectarian mentality," they challenge the view that the first adult baptisms were a self-consciously sectarian or separatist act. Instead, they regard the activities of the Zurich radicals through 1525 as indicative of a radical communal Reformation agenda. Only gradually did the radicals, in the midst of their alienation from Zurich's magisterial Reformation and increasing persecution at the hands of its leaders, come to identify the separated, persecuted church of a minority as the true church. The separatist ecclesiology of the Swiss Brethren was, then, conditioned as much by the socio-political context in which the early Swiss Anabaptists found themselves as by a distinct biblical ideology. This separatist ecclesiology was first fully developed and consolidated in the Schleitheim Articles.[6] However, despite important differences between the early Anabaptist movements within and without Zurich, they shared certain common elements. Aside from their shared opposition to the direction in which Zwingli was leading the Reformation and their emphasis on the competence of the local community to reform the church, particularly important for the present study was the shared desire of the early Swiss Anabaptists to reestablish the primitive church of the apostles.[7]

The sources from the early years of the Swiss Brethren, and especially those relating to Conrad Grebel, provide possibly the clearest support for Hillerbrand's claim that the Anabaptists were not particularly interested in history. Grebel's correspondence from his student days and the early period of his allegiance to Zwingli's reform program is silent on matters pertaining to history and the history of the church. In fact, our only clue to his perception of the fall of the church is more an allusion than a statement. In 1522 Grebel appended a short poem to Zwingli's *Archeteles*. In it he fulminated against the church of the bishops in terms implying that historically the Gospel had been suppressed, but now it was being revived. While Grebel's statements might be construed as the basis of a restitutionist position, the poem contains no clearly formulated vision of the fall of the church. His commitment to Zwingli's activity at this time, and the nature of the criticism levelled at the medieval church suggest his criticism was part of a general humanist dissatisfaction with the abuses of the late medieval church.[8]

Grebel's next references to the fall of the church stem from the period after he broke with Zwingli, in July 1523.[9] Zwingli himself described this rupture in terms which stressed the sectarianism and extreme biblicism of his former allies:

> They approached us therefore in the following way: "It has not escaped our attention that there will always be those who will resist the gospel, even among those who boast the name of Christ. It is therefore never to be hoped that all souls will be so established in unity, as Christians should be permitted to live. According to the Acts of the Apostles those who had believed separated themselves from others, and then as others came to believe, they joined those who were already a new church. That is just what we must do."[10]

Zwingli wrote these words in 1527 and there is some question about the accuracy of his description and the extent to which he may have read later positions of his opponents back into their earlier statements. At the heart of interpretations of the ecclesiological visions of the early Zurich radicals are two of the most important sources for early Swiss Anabaptism: Conrad Grebel's September 1524 letters to Thomas Müntzer. These have long been recognized as crucial sources for insights into the origins of Swiss Anabaptism. Traditionally they have been treated as a "programmatic statement" of the Swiss Anabaptist reforming vision which included a clearly separatist ecclesiology and which witnessed the birth of a "distinctively restitutional type of reform."[11] The former assertion has been challenged by revisionists, especially Hans-Jürgen Goertz. Goertz argues that the letters should be treated as conversational rather than programmatic: instead of setting out hard and fast positions, they search for common ground as the basis of dialogue. Goertz does accept the traditional assumptions about the biblicism and restitutionist goals of the letters, however, seeing in the appeal to the model of the primitive church as the basis of reform a common thread in the Reformations envisioned by both Müntzer and the Grebel circle. Goertz, then, is willing to accept the Zurich radicals as restitutionists, but not separatists in 1524. Rather, he sees them as committed to the radical restructuring of the Zurich church on the basis of biblical norms.[12]

Both revisionist and traditional interpretations of the letters to Thomas Müntzer agree on the importance of the model of the apostolic church for Grebel's vision of reform. Grebel himself asserts that the church has departed from the true way, and "lived without God's law and gospel in human, useless, unchristian practices and ceremonies."[13] His call for the restoration of the "true way" suggests that the early Swiss Brethren were restitutionists, as recent scholarship has defined the term. The divine practices, sometimes called the rites of God by Grebel, can be identified from definite and clear Scripture; these are the practices instituted or commanded by Christ or practised by the apostles. Grebel identifies three specific divine practices: baptism, the Lord's Supper and the rule of Christ (discipline), but his criticisms of Müntzer's liturgical reforms at Allstedt suggest that this list is not exhaustive.[14]

Despite his restitutionist foundation, Grebel has little to say about church history more broadly. Although he was aware that Müntzer had dated the fall of the primitive church to shortly after the death of the apostles' pupils in his liturgical reforms, Grebel does not comment on this fact or provide his own speculation of when the church departed the true path.[15] In fact, the only evidence we have of Grebel's thinking on the matter stems from his statements on the practice of infant baptism and its role in the church's apostasy. At one point he reprimands the church fathers Augustine, Tertullian, Theophylact and Cyprian for their endorsement of this practice, but shortly thereafter, he cites Augustine and Cyprian to argue that adult baptism was practised for 600 years after the time of the apostles.[16] It appears that Grebel was relatively unconcerned with elaborating on the history of the early church at this point. In this sense, his appeal to the primitive church was determined more by his biblicism than any explicit historical reflection. The structure and practices of the apostolic church derived their authority from the fact that they were dictated by Christ and implemented by the apostles rather than from the fact that Grebel reflected on the place of that church in the wider panorama of salvation history. Of note, however, is the fact that when Grebel did venture into the realm of church history, he was willing to contradict the fathers and that baptism was the issue which prompted him to do so.

Other contemporary Swiss Brethren sources confirm the perceptions we glean from the letters to Müntzer. Felix Mantz's December 1524 *Petition of Defence* reveals a similar biblically-derived vision of the apostolic church as a model for contemporary reforms, with even less reflection on the history of the early church. Mantz identifies baptism and the Lord's Supper as the only two ceremonies left behind on earth by Christ. His primary concern is the former which, he claims, has been perverted since Christ's departure. Christ did not teach, nor did the apostles practise, infant baptism, which in fact is an invention of the papacy.[17] Mantz's concentration specifically on baptism to the exclusion of other characteristics of the primitive church stems, according to Martin Haas, not so much from a changed focus among the Zurich radicals as it does from the situation in which they found themselves and the need to respond to Zwingli's attacks on believers' baptism.[18] Subsequent statements of contemporaries, both among the Swiss Brethren and their enemies, suggest that they held true to these positions. If we can trust Heinrich Bullinger's account of the first public disputation on baptism held in Zurich (17 January, 1525), the Zurich radicals continued to regard the apostolic church as normative for their vision of reform. According to Bullinger, the opponents of infant baptism had cited accounts of baptism in the Gospels and Acts to argue that the apostles had not baptized infants, but only adult discerning people, and that therefore we should follow suit.[19] A little more than a year later during the tenth disputation on baptism in Zurich (March 1526), three women interrogated by the authorities, Agli Ockenfuss, Elizabeth Hottinger and Anna Widerkerin, insisted they would stand firm by their baptism which was instituted and practised by Christ and the apostles, and thereby had divine sanction.[20] Not surprisingly, Conrad Grebel's biblical concordance relies heavily on the description of the Great Commission and of apostolic examples of baptism for its discussion of true baptism.[21]

Littell's concept of "Christian Primitivism" and the importance for it of the Constantinian fall of the church are closely linked to the Anabaptist stress on separation from ungodly society. Consequently, a natural place to look for this phenomenon is in *The Schleitheim Articles*, which constitute, according to John Howard Yoder, the "crystalization point" of early Anabaptism.[22] These articles have much to say about separation from civil society and their general tone implies a position akin to Littell's interpretation of the Constantinian fall, but nowhere in them is there a specific reference to a Constantinian fall of the church or, for that matter, any historical fall of the church. One might argue that such a position is implied in the articles' description of infant baptism as "... the greatest and first abomination of the pope, ..."[23] Not surprisingly, it is on this point that Littell makes his only appeal to *The Schleitheim Articles*.[24] It appears, then, that among the early Swiss Brethren there was little explicit concern with history and historical periodization. However, there is an implied dating of the fall with specific reference to the institution of pedobaptism. But this in and of itself does not preclude the existence of a restitutionist vision among the early Swiss Brethren. In fact, sources from the beginnings of the movement suggest that the model of the primitive church was central in the reforming vision of early Swiss Anabaptism. In fact, such a vision dominates the reforming agenda of the Grebel letters to Müntzer to the extent that claims that these were the original manifesto for the restitutionist vision are not too far off the mark. The model of the primitive church, as reconstructed from New Testament sources, lies at the root of Grebel's criticism of Müntzer's liturgical reforms, it lays out the proper methods for church discipline and establishes the criteria for the correct celebration of the Lord's Supper and baptism.[25] The same vision dominates Felix Mantz's petition to the Zurich city council shortly thereafter.[26] And, not surprisingly, it is front and centre in *The Schleitheim*

Articles. There Michael Sattler bolsters his denunciation of infant baptism with an appeal to the "... reasons, testimony, practice and writings of the apostles." He also calls for the employment of brotherly admonition "... according to the command of Christ ..." as contained in Matthew 18 and clarifies the role of the shepherd in the congregation according to the "rule of Paul."[27]

In recent years revisionist studies of Swiss Brethren origins have focused increasing attention on Anabaptist movements outside Zurich, their initiative in the Anabaptist movement prior to January 1525 and the characteristics which distinguish them from the movement within Zurich's city walls. James Stayer has adopted the term "non-separating congregationalism" to characterize the important elements of Anabaptism outside of Zurich and to distinguish those movements from the separatist, or proto-separatist, ecclesiology of the early Zurich radicals. However, despite the important differences between these distinct groups in early Swiss Anabaptism, Stayer argues, a common opposition to Zwingli united them.[28] This common cause was further reinforced by a shared commitment to the restoration of the primitive church.

The limited sources available on the early Anabaptist movements in St. Gall and rural eastern Switzerland also contain frequent appeals to the primitive, apostolic church as the model for reform. This is clear in numerous descriptions contained in Johann Kessler's chronicle, *Sabbata*. For example, according to Kessler, the Anabaptists of St. Gall developed the same arguments against infant baptism as had the Zurich Anabaptists: "... it was not instituted by Christ, never practised by the apostles, but invented by the popes without foundation."[29] This criticism was fleshed out by Wolfgang Ulimann who argued in a hearing before the St. Gall City Council that Christ's order to baptize believing adults had been the norm in the primitive church for two hundred years, until the time of Cyprian.[30]

In addition to the common appeal to the practice of baptism of the apostolic church, the radicals within and without Zurich appear to have also found common ground in the description of the community of goods practised in the primitive church. James Stayer has argued that in the early years of the movement, the Swiss Brethren had a major preoccupation with the economic practices of the early church as described in Acts 2 and 4. This concern, like the focus on the correct performance of baptism and the Lord's Supper, derived from their ambition to reconstruct the practices of the New Testament church.[31] This state of affairs certainly seems to have been the case in the village of Zollikon in the first half of 1525. Again, Kessler provides us with the details:

> Now because Zollikon in general had itself baptized, and they assumed they were the true Christian church, they also undertook, like the early Christians, to practise community of temporal goods (as can be read in the Acts of the Apostles), broke the locks off their doors, chests, and cellars, and ate food and drink in good fellowship without discrimination.[32]

Central to Stayer's argument for the early Swiss Brethren preoccupation with community of goods are statements in an early congregational order now known as *The Swiss Order*. Originally thought to be a companion piece to *The Schleitheim Articles*, it has since been identified by Werner Packull as belonging to the early communal phase of Anabaptism, perhaps in Zollikon during the first half of 1525, although he allows that it could stem from any number of early communal Anabaptist movements.[33] As such, this document provides us with an interesting variation of the restitutionism of early Swiss Anabaptism. *The Swiss Order* contains a clearly restitutionist vision of the church. The introductory justification for the articles which lay out the details of the church order hearkens back to the model of the primitive church:

> Therefore, according to the command of the Lord and the teachings of His apostles, in Christian order, we should observe the new commandment in love one toward another, so that love and unity may be maintained, which all brothers and sisters of the entire congregation [*Gemein*] should agree to hold as follows ...[34]

The point is made even more forcefully in the article on community of goods which demands:

> Of all the brothers and sisters of the congregation none shall have anything of his own, but rather, as the Christians in the time of the apostles held all in common, and especially stored up a common fund, from which aid can be given to the poor, according as each will have need, and as in the apostles' time permit no brother to be in need.[35]

In early Swiss Anabaptism, then, the vision of a restored apostolic church could, and in fact did, thrive independently of a commitment to a separatist or sectarian ecclesiology, but in neither case was this restitutionist vision accompanied by the elucidation of an elaborate scheme of ecclesiastical history.

As we have seen, by far the most important source of information on the apostolic church for the early Swiss Brethren was its description in the New Testament, especially in the Acts of the Apostles. The primacy of the New Testament in Swiss Brethren hermeneutics has long been recognized. However, this emphasis did not preclude appeals to the Old Testament as well, including reliance on Old Testament texts when justifying restoration of the primitive church. Probably the best example of this appears in Felix Mantz's *Petition.* Mantz argues at one point that divinely instituted ceremonies, such as baptism, must be observed as commanded by pointing to the fate of the sons of Aaron described in Leviticus 10:1-2 after their failure to correctly observe the ceremonies in the tabernacle.[36] While such an appeal to the Old Testament in no way constitutes the identification of a "church" in the old covenant comparable to that in Müntzer's thought, it helps to explain further the "constructive misunderstanding" that developed between Swiss and Saxon radicals.

Balthasar Hubmaier

For some time in interpretations of the early Reformation Balthasar Hubmaier has sat uneasily on the fringes of the Anabaptist movement.

Particularly his views on the sword have precluded his inclusion in mainstream or Evangelical Anabaptism for many scholars. John Howard Yoder especially has been critical of Hubmaier's qualifications as a full-fledged Anabaptist, arguing that a fundamental gulf exists between his thought and that of the Swiss Brethren on many significant theological concerns.[37] However, recently Hubmaier's status within early Anabaptism has been reassessed. Reevaluations of his thought by Walter Klaassen and J. Denny Weaver have fed into a comprehensive revision of our understanding of Hubmaier's place in Anabaptism by Arnold Snyder. Noting that Swiss Brethren sources cite his writings on baptism into the seventeenth century, Snyder argues that Hubmaier was of unparalleled importance in defining the early theological core of Anabaptism.[38] Yoder had traced much of Hubmaier's divergence from the early Zurich radicals to his formal theological education, but the revision of his reputation has stressed his proximity to the Swiss Brethren on core theological issues, for example his hermeneutics are regarded as more laicist and harmonized with those of Conrad Grebel and others than Yoder would have allowed.[39]

This ambiguity in Hubmaier's place in early Swiss Anabaptism has carried over into treatments of his understanding of ecclesiastical history. Littell makes only passing reference to Hubmaier and never specifically to his understanding of the church's past.[40] On the other side of the divide, recent studies of Hubmaier's thought have characterized him as a restitutionist focused on the model of the pre-Constantinian church as the source of his reforming vision.[41] As we will see, Hubmaier had a sophisticated understanding of church history which anticipated some, although certainly not all of the elements of the Anabaptist view of church history as described by Littell. The sophistication of this vision grows out of the formal theological training once thought to separate him from the Swiss Brethren. But, perhaps more intriguing is the ecclesiological context in which he developed this vision. In sharp contrast to Littell's assumptions about the connection between the Anabaptist perception of ecclesiastical history and a separatist ecclesiology, Hubmaier has been characterized as a "sect leader who reformed towns and lordships," and his later activity in Moravia has been described as a key component of a "*Junkerreformation*" with strong clerical overtones.[42]

Hubmaier's break with the church came in the context of criticisms of it by humanist-inspired Reformers, particularly those emanating from Zwingli and the Zurich Reformation.[43] Not surprisingly, Hubmaier's earliest statements about the church's history reflect the environment out of which they arose. Initially he focused his criticisms primarily on the most recent history of the church and supplemented this with limited appeals to the model of the primitive church. A report from the 2nd Zurich Disputation (October 1523) indicates that there Hubmaier denounced the errors and abuses which had infiltrated into church practices in "the last several hundred years," especially those associated with the veneration of images of the saints and the theology of the mass.[44] His *Eighteen Theses Concerning Christian Life* from March 1524, which most commentators describe as heavily dependent on Zwingli's *67 Theses* of January 1523, focus more on the rise of scholasticism as the source of errors in the church. Hubmaier declares there that all teachings not planted by God—specifically those of Thomas, Scotus, Bonaventure and Occam—have been uprooted.[45] Increasingly in these and subsequent writings he appeals to the model of the primitive church. His own reliance on the scriptural narrative of that church is accompanied by denunciations of the fallibility of papal law, the decisions of the councils, the writings of the fathers and the pronouncements of the schools. The use of disputation to ascertain the proper direction and details of reform is defended as being in accordance with the practices of the apostles. Only with the restoration of pure baptism and the Lord's Supper will the true church be reestablished and legitimate reform of the mass should take as its model "the perfection instituted by Christ."[46]

As Hubmaier developed a more radical criticism of the established church and then of the Reformers as he moved from Waldshut to Zurich at the end of 1525 and then finally to Nicolsburg, Moravia in the spring of 1526, he deepened his understanding of the church's history and became increasingly critical of its traditions. In all of this he nowhere explicitly identifies an historical fall of the church. And yet, his discussion of the perversions of specific aspects of the religious life of western Christendom imply a deterioration of the visible church, if not an outright fall. At the centre of this perversion for Hubmaier was the practice of infant baptism, although at times he supplements his discussions of baptism with reference to other ceremonies and teachings of the church. Baptism was the issue over which he broke with the Zurich Reformation and it remained at the centre of his reforming efforts thereafter.[47] In Waldshut he attempted to reestablish the New Testament form of baptism, and likely also the Lord's Supper.[48] Certainly this is apparent in his justification for believers' baptism, *On the Christian Baptism of Believers*. Here he insists that the model for correct, adult baptism must be the "ordinances and commands" of Christ. These claims are backed up with a wealth of citations from the gospels and the book of Acts indicating that Christ commanded, and the apostles administered or practised, believers' baptism.[49] However, he supplemented his biblicist arguments for the legitimacy of his reform proposals with appeals to the history of the church. The role of historical reflection in Hubmaier's developing vision is especially evident in his response to the argument that the longevity of the practice of infant baptism guaranteed its legitimacy. To chronicle the introduction of this abomination, he turns to extra-scriptural sources from the primitive church, the books of the popes and the writings of Cyprian, Augustine and others. In fact, he concludes, papal decrees and the writings of Augustine indicate that the matter of infant baptism was a hotly contested issue 1000 to 1100 years previously.[50]

Thereafter, Hubmaier's historical research and discussion of extra-scriptural sources on the history of the early church expand considerably.[51] In *On the Christian Baptism of Believers* Hubmaier had drawn a sharp distinction between the baptism of Christ and that of John the Baptist in response to Zwingli's argument for the essential continuity between the

Old Testament and the New and the underlying unity between the old covenant and new.[52] There he had established his point with a variety of scriptural citations. In his next salvo in the war with the Swiss Reformers over true baptism, *Dialogue with Zwingli's Baptism Book*, he expands the list of authorities cited to include a number of patristic authors, including Origen, Cyril, Theophylact, Jerome and Chrysostom.[53] With his expanded scope of interest in the primitive church also came a new, more critical attitude toward the fathers. The new attitude is especially evident in Hubmaier's treatment of Augustine. In response to Zwingli's appeal to Augustine's authority to justify infant baptism, Hubmaier asserts that the father's reliance on conciliar decisions in this matter indicates that he had no scriptural authority for his claims, and then he sets the authority of Jerome over against that of Augustine.[54]

Throughout this discussion of the history of the early church Hubmaier nowhere develops an explicit account of the church's fall, but he does continue to flesh out the details of the history of baptism, and in the process he continues his appeals to extra-scriptural sources. To shore up his argument for the pedigree of believers' baptism he goes to patristic sources, citing Eusebius and the second-century bishop of Antioch, Theophilus, on the necessity of keeping baptism and faith conjoined.[55] On the other hand, he goes to great pains to establish an accurate history of infant baptism, an error in baptismal practice which, he claims, has existed for 1400 years. His historical research is especially evident in his answer to Zwingli's accusation that the Anabaptists identify the beginnings of infant baptism with the pontificate of Nicholas II (1059-1061). Hubmaier responds that "no one who has read the Decretals says that."[56] Hubmaier's lack of an explicit identification of the fall of the church is paralleled by his treatment of the true church during the "middle fallen period." He does make a distinction between the true church and "the majority," but nowhere is this distinction established historically. Instead, insofar as he takes note of historical heresies, he does so to distinguish himself and his movement from the opinions of heretical groups in the early church.[57]

This concern to establish the orthodoxy of his movement is even more evident in Hubmaier's next two writings, *Old and New Teachers on Believers' Baptism* and *On Infant Baptism Against Oecolampad*.[58] In the former work he mustered a wealth of passages from recent and especially from patristic authors to prove that he was neither a heretic nor a schismatic and that the original practice of the early church had been believer's baptism.[59] His starting point in both texts, as earlier, is baptism as commanded by Christ and practised by the apostles, and the array of scriptural texts from the Gospels and Acts mustered in *The Christian Baptism of Believers* reappears.[60] In *Old and New Teachers on Believers' Baptism* they are supplemented with an even more expanded list of patristic authors who, Hubmaier claims, testify to its legitimacy and practice in the primitive church: Origen, Basil the Great, Athanasius, Tertullian, Jerome, Cyril, Theophylact, and Eusebius.[61] But as Hubmaier's reading of patristic sources continued, so too did his willingness to challenge the church fathers he perceived to be in disagreement with him. In *Old and New Teachers on Believers' Baptism* he had rejected Augustine's appeal to the role of godparents' faith in legitimating infant baptism. At the same time he cited the decisions of Cyprian and other early church leaders at the Council of Carthage on the validity of rebaptizing those who had already undergone heretical baptism.[62] But in his response to Oecolampadius he was willing to dismiss the opinions of not only Augustine, but also Cyprian, Origen and the decrees of the Councils of Carthage (240) and Milevis (416).[63] As he had earlier answered Zwingli, he insisted that Oecolampadius's appeals to "the fathers, councils, histories and old customs" in defence of infant baptism were merely a cover for a lack of scriptural support.[64]

After his move to Moravia, Hubmaier's thoughts on the history of the church where developed in the context of two inter-related themes: his continued conflicts with his opponents in Switzerland and South Germany, and his ecclesiastical reforms in Nicolsburg under the protection of the Liechtenstein lords. Indications are that in Nicolsburg, as he had earlier in Waldshut, he sought insofar as possible to revive the religious practices and structure of the apostolic church. At the centre of this activity lay the restoration of baptism and the Lord's Supper, the only two ceremonies "instituted by Christ and left behind on earth."[65] However, he also regarded the exercise of discipline within the Christian community, in the form of admonition and ultimately the ban, as an integral element of the primitive church. Insights into Hubmaier's reforms and church life in Nicolsburg are provided by his *Catechism* and his so-called liturgical trilogy: *On Fraternal Admonition*, *A Form for Water Baptism* and *A Form of Christ's Supper*. Closely related to this group was a final work on church discipline, *On the Christian Ban*.[66] From the present perspective, of particular interest is Hubmaier's justification for his suggested reforms. He consistently appeals to apostolic practice, usually backed up with the standard citations from scriptural accounts of the early church familiar from his earlier writings. However, in exceptional cases he also backs up his claims with other sorts of historical evidence, as when he justifies the prayer schedule at Nicolsburg not only with reference to the activities of Cornelius described in Acts 10:3, but also by citing a letter of Pliny the Younger to the Emperor Trajan describing the practices of the early Christians.[67]

In the writings from Nicolsburg, Hubmaier still does not identify a specific historical "fall" of the church, but he does describe it as wandering from the true path almost since its beginning. He notes that there has been disunity in the understanding of the Lord's Supper from ancient times to the contemporary age, and the true baptismal vow has been lost for a thousand years, during which time Satan has replaced it with monastic and priestly vows. In *On the Christian Ban* he exclaims: "Oh God, how many years have we shoved the Christian ban under the bench! How long has it been completely lost!"[68] The search for the origins of this state of affairs leads to a litany which includes all the usual suspects: papal law and the scholastics; the sophists and scholastics; Thomas, Scotus, Gabriel, Occam, the decrees, decretals, legends of the saints and other scholastics; the kitchen rules, decrees, decretals, sext and Clementine commands.[69] Noteworthy in these writings is Hubmaier's increasingly critical treatment of the fathers. This trend is especially evident in the revisions to his polemical writings begun in Waldshut but only completed and first published in Nicolsburg. For example, in the preface to his *Dialogue with Zwingli's Baptism Book* he notes that "... we have wholly and completely fallen so far from the Word that nothing any longer remains with us which looks like a Christian church or a devout way of life."[70] Whereas in the text of this work, likely penned in Waldshut, he rejects Augustine's appeal to conciliar decisions in his defence of infant baptism, in the preface he holds the church father "not a little responsible" for the departure of the church from the truth over the last thousand years. Where earlier he had appealed to the authority of Jerome in response to Zwingli's appeal to Augustine, he now accuses Augustine, Jerome, Gregory, papal law and the scholastics of changing the divine writings into "a rope and net of confusion."[71] But perhaps the fruits of Hubmaier's continuing historical research are most apparent in his discussion of the original Christian missionary activity in the German-speaking lands:

> But gracious Lord, in order that no one may be too surprised by our blindness and foolishness, be it known that the pure, clear, and unadulterated Word of God has from the beginning until now never come into our German nation, already entire, seven times purged and unmixed; but as our shepherds and bishops have always and ever been from the beginning, thus they pastured their sheep. They were, however, papists from the outset: namely, monks and priests, sent out into the fields of Christ by the popes from Rome, Scotland and England, as I can prove by all the chronicles, to sow their tares, trifles, laws and doctrines. People were asleep and did not test and try their teachings by the plumb line of the Bible.[72]

Parallel to his chronicle of the perversion of the truth in the "majority" church, Hubmaier continues to shore up his own teaching with historical arguments. The focal point in this process remains the practice of believers' baptism. This is most evident in the second, revised edition of *Old and New Teachers on Believers' Baptism*. Here he expands considerably the array of sources from the early church apparently endorsing believers' baptism. These include a considerably expanded list of patristic authors and of popes from the first to the ninth century. These were supplemented with citations from decrees of church councils held between the fourth and ninth centuries.[73] Despite Hubmaier's notorious misdating of a number of these sources, it is clear that in Nicolsburg appeals to ecclesiastical history, and with them the necessity of historical research, remained a crucial component of his enterprise. His goal in this search for the historical pedigree of believers' baptism was, as Torsten Bergsten has noted, to assemble a "vast cloud of witnesses" to indicate that his teachings were in accord with the best traditions of the church.[74] Underlying this enterprise was a conviction that the true church lasted throughout the ages or, as stated in *A Christian Catechism*, an individual congregation can err, but not the universal church.[75] But while Hubmaier is clearer in his final writings that the church has departed the true path than he had been earlier, and while he continues to hold that the true church has survived through the ages, he still refuses to identify with an ongoing heretical opposition to the persecuting church.[76]

In the thought of Hubmaier, then, we see crucial elements of Littell's description of the Anabaptist perception of ecclesiastical history. While he identifies no specific historical fall of the church, Hubmaier certainly chronicles its deterioration. That deterioration was tied not to Constantine's conversion and the introduction of compulsion into matters of faith but, as with the Swiss Brethren, it is identified with the perversion of true baptism. Also in accord with the vision of the Swiss Brethren, Hubmaier appeals to the model of the primitive church for the details of his reforming vision, and looks to the restitution of the primitive church as the result of his activity. In Littell's terms he was a primitivist. However, Hubmaier's primitivism did not dictate a comprehensive historical vision which drove his reforming activity from the outset. Rather, his vision of the primitive church and of ecclesiastical history evolved in tandem with his reforming program, and the evolution of that vision chronicles his move from humanist-inspired reform of the church into Anabaptism. As he became more critical of the church and more radical in his understanding of how it should be reformed, he wrestled more and more with the early history of the church and became more willing to challenge early Christian authorities, including the fathers. His criticism of the high medieval church, and in particular of scholasticism, along with a general sense of the need to restore the primitive church gave way to an increasingly sophisticated vision of that church. The focal point in this evolution, again in accord with developments we have seen among the Swiss Brethren, was the history of baptismal practice. Also of note in this evolution is the importance of polemical exchanges in moulding Hubmaier's vision of ecclesiastical history. Particularly in his responses to Zwingli and Oecolampadius, Hubmaier reaches for the historical record.[77] Finally, although he clearly distinguishes between the true church and the church of the majority, nowhere does Hubmaier identify the former with a persecuted heretical underground church in the history of Christendom.

South German/Austrian Anabaptism

Hans Hut has long been recognized as a central figure in the development of south and central German and Austrian Anabaptism. Werner Packull has characterized Hut as "the most influential missionary of Anabaptism in central and south Germany" and in terms of his impact, as significant as Conrad Grebel for the early Anabaptist movement. Also clearly established are Hut's connections to Thomas Müntzer and the importance of Müntzer's influence on Hut's thought.[78] This influence produced in south and central German Anabaptism different nuances and emphases in some of the crucial Anabaptist themes than we see among the Swiss Brethren. Among these is a much stronger eschatological emphasis than is apparent among the Swiss. This eschatological tone had clear resonance in Hut's historical vision. George Williams characterized Hut's thought as containing an eschatological vision derived from the Danielic-

Hieronymic conception of four world empires, and yet committed as well to the idea of a return to a combined golden age, paradise and primitive church.[79] To describe Hut as a restitutionist, then, means employing the term differently than when applying it to the early Swiss Anabaptists.

At times in his writings Hut could, in fact, sound surprisingly restitutionist. In his final encyclical he clearly calls for the rebirth of the true church:

> Since almighty God, our true Father, again is building up the devastated and broken church, His own spouse which for so long has been without fruit, but now bears children in all places with knowledge of true love and faith through the power of the Holy Spirit, it is of the greatest importance that in the first place one lay before them [the children of God] the solitary example and life of Christ, ...[80]

Implicit in this statement are references to both an historical fall of the church and the call for its restitution according to an apostolic model. Elsewhere, he is more explicit about the nature of that restitution, especially as it applies to the practice of baptism and the community of goods. The former point is made clear in *On the Mystery of Baptism*:

> And so at the beginning, and first of all we treat the Judgement of Baptism, a beginning of the Christian life, and diligently we see and mark how Christ instituted it, ordained it and how it has been kept by the apostles with proof from the divine witness of Holy Scripture and not according to the good pleasure of human wisdom as it has hitherto been put out by those who boast of their gospel.[81]

Similarly, he indicates that in the restored church of Christ all things will be held in common, and nothing will be individual, according to the model of the apostolic church as described in Acts 2, 3 and 4.[82]

However, Hut's apparent restitutionism masks a fundamentally different approach to the apostolic church than that of the Swiss Brethren. As Werner Packull has noted, Hut and his followers were not committed to "pure primitivist visions from the pages of Holy Writ."[83] With reference to our immediate concerns, this is particularly relevant as it plays out in Hut's ecclesiology which, as Hans-Jürgen Goertz notes, was much more focused on the spiritual life of the individual and much less concerned with the visible order of the congregation than was the ecclesiology of the Swiss Brethren.[84] The connection between ecclesiology and history in Hut's thought can be clarified if we return to his statements about baptism and the community of goods. While Hut called for a return to the baptismal practices of the primitive church, he regarded this "external, water baptism" as a sign of an "internal, essential baptism" of tribulation. Water baptism was instituted in New Testament times, but inner baptism has existed from all time. The apostolic model of baptism, then, is normative only in a qualified sense, only insofar as it is a visible sign of true baptism.[85] Similarly, his advocacy of the community of goods was distinct from an exclusive appeal to the New Testament model and a strict biblicism. Hut argued that community of goods has been practised by the true church, the small group of the elect, since the beginning of the world. But in the coming last days, and with them the outpouring of God's Spirit, this practice will become much more general.[86] Hut's concern with community of goods was dominated less by the biblical model than by the mystical concept of *Gelassenheit* and his apocalypticism.[87]

In Hut's thought, then, the primitive church represented one stage in the progressive life of the true church. In sharp contrast to the Swiss Brethren, he drew no clear distinction between the age of the Old Testament and that of the New, between the old covenant and the new.[88] Werner Packull has described the context for Hut's apocalypticism as a trinitarian scheme of historical development with possible Joachimite influences. A central element in this trinitarian scheme was a progressive revelation of the divine will. In the last days Hut anticipated a more complete disclosure of the divine message and a more complete mission of the church.[89] Hut's thought was restitutionist, then, in the sense that he called for a return to the model of the primitive church, but that return was tied closely to his anticipation of future events and the continuous working of the Spirit. As a result, the apostolic church did not hold the same normative status in his thought as it did among the Swiss Brethren. His statements about the primitive church, however, when divorced from his expectations of the imminent apocalypse and his over-arching historical scheme, provided a possible basis for a "constructive misunderstanding" with the Swiss Brethren. Hut's final encyclical suggests that within his own lifetime he saw the value of such a misunderstanding, and the writings of some of his followers indicate not only the ease with which the transition to a more Swiss Brethren ecclesiology and restitutionism could occur, but also that some of the central elements of the Anabaptist view of church history could come out of this quasi-restitutionist position.

This becomes evident in the writings of three of Hut's most important disciples: Leonhard Schiemer, Christoph Freisleben and Oswald Glaidt. Schiemer's thought provides an interesting amalgam of Hut's Anabaptism with that of the Swiss Brethren. Schiemer retains Hut's eschatological concerns, but shifts his focus from the suffering individual to the persecuted community. Werner Packull has described this transition as the evolution from a purely internalized cross mysticism to an Anabaptist theology of martyrdom.[90] From the perspective of the present study, of note is Schiemer's ecclesiology, the importance for it of his vision of the apostolic church, and its proximity to the ecclesiology of the Swiss Brethren. Schiemer clearly regarded the contemporary, persecuted church as parallel to that of the age of the apostles. This becomes clear in a letter he wrote to the Anabaptist congregation in Rattenberg, Tyrol in 1527:

> Among us you will find the life of the church of the apostles. But whenever it is found it is called a new sect, and its members are killed even as they did the apostles. ... This church you will find clearly described in Acts 2, 4, and 5.[91]

Similar parallels are drawn in a communal order, *The Church Discipline*, which may have been written by Schiemer. Although it contains no elaborate vision of the history of Christianity, *The Church Discipline* appeals on occasion to the model of the apostolic church, as in its justification for voluntary community of goods "as among the Christians at the time of the apostles."[92] *The Church Discipline* may have served as the congregational order at Rattenberg. More importantly, as Werner Packull has convincingly argued, it is a reworking of *The Swiss Order*.[93] In his amalgamation of south German and Swiss Anabaptism, Schiemer clearly moved closer to the Swiss style of restitutionism but, interestingly, he did not supplement this move with the development of a detailed historical vision.

Similar conclusions can be drawn from the writings of Christoph Friesleben. In 1528 Freisleben penned a pamphlet entitled *On the Genuine Baptism of John, Christ and the Apostles*. In it he charged the church fathers Tertullian, Cyprian and Augustine with placing too much emphasis on outer baptism. This emphasis led ultimately to the official sanctioning of pedobaptism by Nicholas I in 862 C.E., a practice Freisleben identified with the work of the Antichrist and source of further unchristian and superstitious rites and fallacious doctrines.[94] Freisleben wrote this work while under the influence of Wilhelm Reublin, one of the contributors to *The Schleitheim Articles*, when the south German and Austrian Anabaptist movement was coming under the increasing influence of the Swiss Brethren.[95] As a reflection of this movement toward the radical sectarianism of the post-Schleitheim Swiss Brethren, Freisleben's work might have involved deeper reflection on the history of sectarian Christianity. But in the end, Freisleben's appeal to history remains in the service of the same program as the more limited historical allusions of the Swiss Brethren.

Also in 1528 Oswald Glaidt, a prominent member of the early Anabaptist community in Moravia, wrote a hymn entitled "Awake, You People, in These Last Days." In it Glaidt claimed that the conversion of Constantine the Great had transformed the church into a temporal power from which the Spirit of God had departed. Originally a convert of Hubmaier, Glaidt had in Nicolsburg in 1527 fallen under the sway of Hut. At the time he wrote his hymn his thought, and particularly his ecclesiology, was still dominated by Hut's eschatology.[96] Glaidt likely collaborated with Hubmaier on the latter's *Old and New Teachers on Believers' Baptism*.[97] It is tempting to see in this collaboration the source of Glaidt's historical interest. Later Glaidt was to bring together a separatist ecclesiology and identification of a Constantinian fall of the church.[98] Interestingly, he first voices his criticism of the Constantinian church independently of that ecclesiology only after the lords of Liechtenstein had supported Hubmaier in a conflict with Hut at Nicolsburg and then expelled Hut and Glaidt from their territories.

Marpeckites

Prominent among the spiritual heirs of Hans Hut are Pilgram Marpeck and his circle of followers. Stephen Boyd has argued that Marpeck's decision to resign his post as mining magistrate in Rattenberg—a crucial step in his journey to Anabaptism—was likely occasioned by Schiemer's martyrdom. Furthermore, Boyd sees in Marpeck's early writings the influence of Schiemer and another of Hut's followers, Hans Schlaffer.[99] Marpeck and his circle were largely lost to history until the latter part of the nineteenth century when they and their writings were rediscovered by historians. Study of this group of Anabaptists has since flourished, due in no small part to the Marpeckites' attempts to unify Anabaptist groups in the 1540s and 1550s and because their reforming vision appears almost an Aristotelian *via media* between the legalism of the Hutterites and the Swiss Brethren on one hand and the anti-institutionalist impulses of the Spiritualists on the other. However, despite this resurgence of interest in Marpeck and his companions, there has been little awareness of, or concern with, their historical vision. Littell makes only passing reference to them. William Klassen has remarked on this lacuna in Littell's study on several occasions; he argues that Marpeck's thought poses serious challenges to both Littell's characterization of Anabaptism as primitivist and/or restitutionist and his portrayal of the Anabaptist vision of history.[100] Like many of the other early Anabaptists, Marpeck nowhere employs the term "restitution" and at times his references to the continuity of the church among the faithful appear to support Hillerbrand's description of Anabaptist thought more than Littell's. But, as we will see, the Marpeck circle was one of the first groups among the "Evangelical Anabaptists" to develop something approaching a comprehensive historical vision which included a number of details described by Littell.

While Marpeck and his followers developed a more detailed and sophisticated historical vision than did the early Swiss Brethren, this vision did not appear fully formed at the beginning of the movement. Rather it coalesced gradually. Many of the essential outlines appear in Marpeck's earliest writings, his 1531 answers to the criticisms of the Spiritualizers Hans Bünderlin and Christian Entfelder: *A Clear Refutation* and *A Clear and Useful Instruction.*[101] Details of this vision were fleshed out the following year in Marpeck's *Confession* submitted to the Strasbourg city council and his anonymously published denunciation of the use of force in matters of faith, *The Exposure of the Babylonian Whore.*[102] And they were further elaborated on in *The Confession to Jan von Pernstain* of the later 1530s and the writings from Marpeck's conflict with Caspar von Schwenckfeld in the 1540s: *The Admonition* and *Reply to Caspar von Schwenckfeld.*[103]

The evolutionary nature of Marpeck's developing vision of ecclesiastical history becomes evident when placed in the context of his debts to Hut's Anabaptism and the Strasbourg Anabaptist community in which it began to evolve. Indications are that the earliest Anabaptists in Strasbourg held to a restitutionist position like that of the early Swiss Brethren.[104] Marpeck likely shared this view when he arrived in Strasbourg in 1528. Stephen Boyd has speculated that Marpeck carried with him to the imperial city a copy of *The Church Discipline*, the contents of which he may have tried to implement as part of his efforts for communal poor relief.[105] As we have seen, *The Church Discipline* contains no elaborate vision of the history of Christianity, and yet the nature of the community envisioned in it, and the scriptural texts cited to justify such a community, point to the apostolic community as normative for the contemporary reform of the church.[106] The starting point for Marpeck's historical reflection, then, was much the same as it was for the early Swiss Brethren, but as he became embroiled in conflicts with the Spiritualizers, the Strasbourg clergy and finally Caspar Schwenckfeld on the one hand, and the Swiss Brethren on the other, his historical vision quickly filled in.

In spite of the evolution of his historical vision, Marpeck retains throughout his writings a constant appeal to the model of the apostolic church as normative for his vision of the restored church. Neal Blough has indicated that in Marpeck's thought all manifestations of Christian faith qualify as "ceremonies" and, therefore, as extensions of the Incarnation.[107] Marpeck's appeal to the model of the apostolic church should be understood in this context. In the early writings against the Spiritualizers, he is particularly concerned with justifying the apostolic pattern for the observation of the ceremonies of baptism and the Lord's Supper:

> But whoever retains, practises and accepts such ceremonies according to the command, attitude, form, essence and example of Christ and the apostles, indeed according to the urging and instruction of the free Spirit, participates without blemish, misunderstanding, or abomination in the truly reenacted, spiritual apostolic order.[108]

The *Confession* to the Strasbourg City Council of 1532 describes adult baptism as "the baptism of the apostolic church" and *The Admonition* asserts that the true church exists only where the Word is proclaimed and the true baptism and the Lord's Supper are observed. Repeatedly in the latter work the reformation of baptism and the Lord's Supper according to the commands of Christ and the practices of the apostles is demanded.[109] In the *Confession to Jan von Pernstain* Marpeck calls for the reestablishment of the apostolic church according to the commands of Christ and repeatedly in his *Reply* he chides Schwenckfeld for neglecting the outward things instituted by Christ, including teaching, preaching, baptism, the Lord's Supper, and Scripture.[110]

Marpeck's ongoing interaction with ecclesiastical history led him to a more sophisticated understanding of the nature and history of the apostolic church. A crucial stage in this development is marked by the *Admonition* of 1542. As Frank Wray has alerted us, the *Admonition* is a carefully reworked rendition of Bernhard Rothmann's *Confession of Two Sacraments*, but despite its provenance, it provides us with interesting insights into the perceptions of the Marpeck circle.[111] *The Confession of Two Sacraments* called repeatedly for the restoration of the ceremonies of the primitive church. In an attempt to establish a legitimate pedigree for his description of baptism and the Lord's Supper, Rothmann argued that these practices survived as he described them into the early history of the church. To make his case he called on the witness of a number of church fathers, often relying on the histories of the early church by Heinrich Bullinger and Sebastian Franck, both of whom he also recommends to his readers.[112]

Indications are that his reworking of Rothmann's argument led Marpeck to a more detailed and sophisticated understanding of ecclesiastical history. His interpolations into Rothmann's text certainly suggest that he was grappling with the sources directly. In several places he supplements Rothmann's historical details and, although retaining the recommendation of the works of Bullinger and Franck, he warns his readers to approach these works with caution.[113] The increasing sophistication of Marpeck's vision is evident in his treatment of two aspects of the history of the primitive church: its practice of community of goods and the dissension which at times threatened the early church. If we accept Boyd's speculation that Marpeck attempted to institute at least parts of *The Church Discipline* in Strasbourg in 1528, it is evident that at that time he saw voluntary community of goods as an important characteristic of the apostolic church.[114] However, in the *Admonition*, although he did not reject the voluntary community of goods described in Acts 4, he did qualify its meaning and normative nature. He emphasized more than previously that the first Christians in Jerusalem could have kept their own possessions and pointed out that community of goods was not the practice among the churches of the Diaspora.[115] A similar trend is discernible in Marpeck's vision of the troubles that beset the apostolic church almost from the outset. In *A Clear and Useful Instruction* he pointed to dissension in the Jerusalem community described in Acts 6 when responding to arguments that the Anabaptist communities were not the true church because their infighting contrasted with the unity of the apostolic church. In his letter to Helena Streicher, one of Schwenckfeld's followers, written around the same time as the *Admonition*, Marpeck responds to the same argument with a much more detailed discussion of dissension among the early Christians not only in Jerusalem, but in the churches throughout the Roman empire.[116] And in his response to Schwenckfeld he not only takes up the theme of dissension in the apostolic church, but also expands the scope of investigation to include disagreements between the "ancient teachers," in most cases the church fathers, on a number of theological topics.[117]

According to Littell's portrayal of the Anabaptist view of church history, most Anabaptists thought the primitive church fell after Constantine's conversion. The issue of the church's fall comes to the fore in Marpeck's response to the arguments of the Spiritualizers in *A Clear Refutation* and *A Clear and Useful Instruction* that the abuse of apostolic ceremonies invalidated them. He grants that the Antichrist has perverted those ceremonies and, one could argue, implicitly acknowledges a fall of the visible church, but he rejects the claim that they have been superseded as a result.[118] This exchange seems to have served as a catalyst for further reflection on the question of when historically the church fell and what occasioned that fall. Jan Kiwiet has argued that in his *Confession* Marpeck identified this fall with the introduction of pedobaptism.[119] While Marpeck makes no explicit attempt to date the fall of the church in this work, he does describe the teaching that unbaptized children are condemned as "the mother and root" of all other apostasies and refers to the baptism of children as the "root of the Roman harlot."[120]

However, at about the same time he wrote his *Confession* Marpeck identified clearly a Constantinian fall of the church in *Exposure of the Babylonian Whore*. True to Littell's characterization of the Anabaptist position, Marpeck ties his denunciation of Constantinian Christianity to the integration of the church and secular power, and the introduction of force and compulsion in matters of faith:

> It was also the case among the ancient Christians, from the time of the apostles until the time of the emperor Constantine, that neither physical power nor the sword were used among Christians, nor according to the commands of the Master were these established, but alone the sword of the word. And whoever did not listen to this they regarded a heathen and an unbeliever. Then, however, the pope, as a servant of the church, married himself to the Leviathan, that is the temporal authority, under the appearance of Christ. Then the Antichrist was made and born, as has now been revealed, ...[121]

Thereafter, Marpeck's statements suggest a general sense of the historical fall of the church associated with several distinct events. While the events identified remain consistent, the exact relationship between them is not clarified. On several occasions in the *Admonition* he endorses Rothmann's vision of the demise of the apostolic church. He takes over lengthy extracts of Rothmann's argument that the true church fell when the teaching of the Word was neglected, pedobaptism replaced true baptism and the Lord's Supper became the Catholic mass.[122] Marpeck frequently elaborates on Rothmann's arguments, in some cases adding historical detail to bolster their effectiveness. Both men were particularly concerned with the pernicious effects of infant baptism which Marpeck credited with desolating and despoiling the Christian church and planting the kingdom of the Antichrist:

> ... *infant baptism is an introduction* to the realm of the Antichrist, a true and real entrance, beginning, door, and reason for its being, and an instigation to all evil and idolatry which is maintained through his deceptive disguise of Christ, a secure anchor to deceive people. As soon as infant baptism were to be abolished, the disruption of the realm of the Antichrist would immediately follow. The devil has undermined the true Christian baptism and done away with it. Consequently, the Christian church has become desolated and soiled and, because of infant baptism, has, instead, planted the kingdom of the Antichrist. The abolition of the infant baptism and the reinstatement of true baptism, based on faith in Christ, would

> destroy the kingdom of the Antichrist, *and would restore the true holy church, purified and cleansed of all unclean animals.*[123] [italicized words are Rothmann's]

But this focus on the perversion of apostolic ceremonies did not imply a retraction of his criticism of the Constantinian church. Regularly in the *Admonition* Marpeck supplemented his own and Rothmann's discussions of apostolic ceremonies with warnings against the baneful effects of compelling the conscience, and this theme reappeared regularly in his subsequent writings. While the connection to the establishment of the Constantinian church is nowhere as explicit as in the *Exposure of the Babylonian Whore*, Marpeck's allusions are still clear.[124]

From his earliest conflicts with the Spiritualizers Marpeck was clear that he regarded the activities of the Anabaptists as the restoration of the primitive church. The point is probably made most clearly in the *Confession to Jan von Pernstain* where he asserts that although the true church has been "darkened and led astray by the great ravager," it is now being brought back to the light of day. Marpeck echoes nationalist sentiments from other Reformation quarters when he points to the significance of the reappearance of the true Gospel in the German-speaking lands which had been Christianized only after its perversion.[125] The significance of this restoration is underscored by the fact that the reawakening of the Gospel faces similar opposition to that accompanying its original proclamation.[126]

Marpeck's identification of parallels between the first appearance of the Gospel and its reappearance points to a broader pattern in his understanding of salvation history. Already in his conflict with the Spiritualizers he was, by his own assessment, drawn into a discussion of Old Testament history by his opponents,[127] and he began to discern parallels between the historical experiences of ancient Israel and contemporary events. In the repeated Old Testament pattern of apostasy and redemption he saw a model for understanding contemporary events. This point was used to particularly good effect to argue against the Spiritualizers' claim that a new divine commission was needed to restore the practices and ceremonies of the apostolic church. Marpeck responded that no new commission was required, just as none was necessary throughout the Old Testament when the Israelites returned to the true worship of Yahweh. However, in all of this Marpeck in no way compromises the distinctiveness of the Incarnation. He resolutely rejects the possibility that the abrogation of the Old Testament ceremonies at the inauguration of the new covenant can be applied to the ceremonies of the new covenant.[128]

In Marpeck's thought, then, we can see the essential outlines of the Anabaptist view of church history as described by Littell. However, conspicuous by its absence is his treatment of the true church during the "middle fallen period." He suggests that the true church has existed since the Incarnation despite the perversion of the institutional church, but these suggestions are not developed into a history of the persecuted remnant. Even more importantly, in Marpeck's thought the lines of ecclesiastical history are not as clearly drawn as Littell's thesis suggests they should be. The different events Marpeck identifies with the church's fall can be reconciled, but nowhere does Marpeck draw them together into a coherent and comprehensive vision.[129] This fact reflects the *ad hoc* manner in which Marpeck's historical vision was put together in response to the challenges of a variety of opponents.

Hutterites

As we have seen, in the second half of the sixteenth century the Hutterite communities in Moravia produced the most comprehensive historical vision, and that closest of any Anabaptist groups to Littell's description of the Anabaptist view of church history. Robert Friedmann has described the Hutterites as the most historically minded of the sixteenth-century Anabaptist groups. In addition to *The Great Chronicle*, as *The Hutterite Chronicle* is more accurately titled, the existence of their archives and historical library at Neumühle as well as numerous individual chronicles, often excerpted from *The Great Chronicle*, attest to this fact.[130] We are faced, as a result, with the question of why the Hutterites stand out in this way.

Despite the influence of some historically minded individuals like Hubmaier and Marpeck on early Moravian Anabaptism, there appears among the early Hutterites nothing approaching a comprehensive historical vision. A survey of Hutterite statements on the subject suggests that the Hutterite vision of church history evolved as the Hutterite movement itself developed.

Voices from the early years of Moravian Anabaptism suggest that Anabaptists there were initially no more historically oriented than they were elsewhere. Among the communitarian groups which paved the way for, and in some cases fed into, the Hutterites—the group under the leadership of Jacob Wiedemann at Nicolsburg and then Austerlitz, the Gabrielites at Rossitz and the Philipites at Auspitz—we again see a biblically derived restitutionism with little reference to the history of the church. The earliest communitarian experiment, that of the Wiedemann group after their break with Hubmaier in Nicolsburg, was justified in terms of the description of the primitive church in Acts 2 and 4. This appeal was reinforced after they moved to Austerlitz and were joined by refugees from the Tyrol who brought with them from Rattenberg *The Church Discipline*.[131] Similarly, Philipite teaching and congregational polity appear to have shared the restitutionism of the early Swiss Brethren.[132] However, in none of these cases were appeals to the primitive church placed in a broader historical context.

This restitutionist position was carried over by the first generation Hutterites, as is especially evident in their central teaching on the community of goods. Jacob Hutter's reorganization of the practice of community of goods is regarded as of paramount importance in its subsequent institutionalization in Hutterite communities, but as in earlier experiments with community of goods, Hutter continued to appeal to the description of the primitive church in Acts 2 through 5.[133] He did point to a greater historical tradition for his movement, suggesting it shared in the experiences of "... all prophets, Christ the Lord, His apostles, and in short all saints from the beginning of the world," but he failed to develop this suggestion into any significant vision of ecclesiastical history.[134] The limited, tentative nature of early Hutterite appeals to church history is further evident in Ulrich Stadler's *Cherished Instructions on Sin, Excommunication, and the Community of Goods*. Initially a member of Wiedemann's Austerlitz community, Stadler joined the Hutterites in 1537 or 1538; his *Cherished Instructions* were written about that time. Stadler's restitutionist orientation is clear in his insistence that in the Hutterite communities the deacons exercise the ban as commanded by Christ and the apostles.[135] More interesting from the current perspective, however, is Stadler's treatment of community of goods. The cornerstone of his argument is not the usual appeal to the practices of the primitive church described in Acts 2 to 5, but instead the claim that all things were created free and in common, and according to divine law should remain that way.[136] In fact, the primitive church appears in Stadler's argument as a challenge to the practice of community of goods. On behalf of his opponents Stadler introduces the argument that community of goods was practised among the first Christians only at Jerusalem and then only for a brief period of time. Therefore, it is not binding on the true church. Apparently outflanked on the historical front, Stadler instead explains the differences in practice of community of goods between the primitive church and contemporary Hutterites by appealing to the different circumstances in which they found themselves:

> Answer: I say there is a great difference in the times. There, they [the primitive Christians] were left in their own homes and not at once driven into misery, but now the children of God have no place in the whole Roman Empire. For the Babylonian whore who sits on the dragon with the seven heads, I mean the Roman Church, a synagogue of the living devil, spews out all the children of God and only drives them into the wilderness, unto their place, as declared above.[137]

The Hutterite practice of community of goods, then, is a response to the desperate situation in which the brethren found themselves. The contrast is stark between the later Hutterite engagement with ecclesiastical history and Stadler's refusal to rise to this challenge.

However, already among the first generation Hutterites we see the beginnings of a more detailed and sophisticated understanding of ecclesiastical history. This development is clear a few years later in Peter Riedemann's *Account of Our Religion, Doctrine and Faith*. Written in 1540, the *Account* anticipates Riedemann's tenure as elder of the Moravian Hutterite communities from 1542 to 1556. Under his leadership, the Hutterites moved to their more settled second generation.[138]

In comparison to Stadler's *Cherished Instructions*, Riedemann's *Account* comes across as remarkably historically-minded. In general, it is pervaded more fully with an historical awareness and orientation. This is evident already in Riedemann's description of the Hutterites as a separated people, which includes a lengthy excursus on the history of the Israelites as the chosen people. Unfortunately, when Riedemann gets to the Incarnation the historical narrative breaks off and he shifts his focus to "how the house of the Lord should be built up in Christ."[139] Nonetheless, scattered throughout the *Account* are a number of the elements of the assumed Anabaptist vision of church history. While he provides no explicit statement about the fall of the institutional church, Riedemann alludes to such an event on several occasions. He refers to the "deception and seduction by papistry" which has led people from worshipping the creator to adoring creatures, and elsewhere he bemoans the manifold abuses and practices which afflict the church, including perversions of baptism, the Lord's Supper and fasting.[140] Perhaps most enlightening is Riedemann's discussion of "wood and stone temples." Here he suggests that the roots of current idolatry were laid when the German-speaking lands were first Christianized:

> With regard to the buildings of stone and wood—these originated, as the history of several showeth, when this country was forced by the sword to make a verbal confession of the Christian faith. Further, men dedicated temples to their gods, and then made them "Churches," as they are wrongly named, of the Christians. Thus, they originated through the instigation of the devil and are built up through sacrifices to devils, ...[141]

These activities contravened the Old Testament commands to root out the shrines and altars of the Canaanites and fed the idolatrous practices as the pagan gods became so-called Christian saints.[142] In this way, Riedemann not only reinforced the historical continuity between the chosen people of the old covenant and the Hutterites, and thereby anchored the movement in an historical continuum, but he also provided an historically-based criticism of the introduction of compulsion in matters of faith.

The increasing historical orientation of the Hutterites and the greater sophistication of their vision of ecclesiastical history is probably clearest in Riedemann's reconstruction of the primitive church as a model for contemporary reform. Riedemann provides no single, concise description of the primitive church; its structure must still be extrapolated from his proposals for the reform of specific ceremonies and practices. For example, when outlining the proper procedure for choosing ministers for a congregation he appeals to apostolic practice, including the reliance on drawing lots to ascertain the will of the Spirit, as described in Acts 1:21-26.[143] But Riedemann's historical orientation is especially clear in his discussion of baptismal practice. Riedemann's justification for believers' baptism continues the earlier demand that baptism be performed as commanded by Christ and practised by the apostles. Beyond that, however, he is much more concerned with discussing the introduction of infant baptism than had been his predecessors. He begins with the usual claim that there is no evidence in Scripture that the apostles ever baptized infants, but he goes beyond this point by arguing that papal decrees declaring that children who can recite the Lord's Prayer and the Apostles' Creed can be baptized indicate that the baptism of children had not been an accepted practice previously. Therefore, he argues, the baptism of children was a teaching planted by men and, consequently, it should be rooted out.[144] The details of Riedemann's arguments are still vague; nowhere does he indicate to which papal decrees he is referring, but they are more sophisticated than were Stadler's and point to a more detailed historical critique of contemporary baptismal practice.

Perhaps the clearest indication of the greater sophistication of Riedemann's historical arguments is evident in his defence of Hutterite community of goods. This becomes immediately apparent in his response to the challenge earlier faced by Stadler: that the community of goods practised by the first Christians in Jerusalem was the exception rather than the rule for the property relations of the primitive church. As we have seen, Stadler's response to this argument was to appeal to the prelapsarian order established by God and to contemporary circumstances to override the normative nature of the primitive church on this issue. Riedemann, while sharing Stadler's appeal to the order established at creation and other theological foundations of his position, takes a different tack. He contends that even if the case of the Jerusalem community were unique among the early Christians, this does not invalidate it as a model for contemporary organization of the church. Rather, in the primitive church there were limited opportunities and time for the proper organization of communal structures; at the present time these opportunities exist. Furthermore, the Epistles indicate that the apostles prescribed *Gelassenheit*, or true surrender, which Riedemann equates with community of goods, for all Christians, and Paul's references to the zeal of the Macedonian churches in 2 Corinthians 8:1-5 suggest that the first Christians responded enthusiastically to these prescriptions.[145] By implication, then, the experience at Jerusalem was not as unique as his opponents would have us believe. At this point, though, Riedemann is still making his historical argument rather tentatively, almost as a second line of defence behind the requirement of *Gelassenheit*.

Riedmann's historical reflections set the stage, however, for the more sophisticated musings of second generation Hutterites, especially under the leadership of Peter Walpot. At the centre of the mature Hutterite historical enterprise is *The Great Chronicle* which George H. Williams has described as the first comprehensive church history from the pen of an Anabaptist.[146] Certainly comprehensive, it attempts to cover the history of the earth from creation to the year 1665. Caspar Braitmichael likely carried the narrative through to 1542, at which point it was taken up by others after his death. Particularly interesting from the perspective of the present study is *The Chronicle's* treatment of history from creation to the beginning of the Reformation. Here played out briefly is the history of God's people from ancient Israel, through the primitive church and the persecuted church of the Middle Ages to the eve of the restitution of the true church in the Hutterite communities of Moravia. To write this panorama of history, Braitmichael relied on the Bible, the works of Josephus and Eusebius and especially on the *Chronica* of Sebastian Franck.[147] However, as we will see, Braitmichael sifted and sorted this material to suit the needs of the mid sixteenth-century Hutterites.

In many ways the historical vision contained in *The Great Chronicle* is the extension and culmination of the historical reflection witnessed among Hutterite authors to this point. Throughout the history of God's people, their alternating episodes of fidelity and apostasy, their frequent persecution, Braitmichael focuses consistently on the activities of the faithful remnant as the backdrop to the activities of the Hutterites. In this Riedemann's implicit appeal to the ancient Israelites as the spiritual ancestors of the Hutterites is made explicit. Braitmichael opens his account:

> Here is a simple but thorough summary of history from the beginning of the world until the present time telling as accurately as possible how God began his work and carried it out among his people.[148]

When he gets to the age of the apostolic church, Braitmichael's identification with the contemporary Hutterites gets much more explicit. Frequently his discussion of the various persecutions faced by the first Christians concludes with the refrain that these events still happen today.[149] His focal point throughout the discussion of the primitive church is the persecution and rejection of the first Christians, and Braitmichael devotes surprisingly little attention to the practices of the primitive church. For example, he disposes of the communism of the church of Jerusalem in two brief sentences:

> All who believed stayed together and held their goods in common, but unbelievers were not allowed to join them. There were about five thousand men who believed, gathered together, united in heart and soul.[150]

Persecution by the world is also a central theme in his identification of the faithful with persecuted heretical groups in the Middle Ages. Braitmichael consistently contrasts the false, persecuting church, established by Constantine's conversion and renewed through the alliance between the papacy and the Carolingians, with the persecuted witnesses to the true gospel. In the process he takes every available opportunity to identify other abuses introduced to Christendom by this unholy alliance of papal and imperial authority: the substitution of human for divine teachings in canon law; the introduction of new, godless ceremonies, including infant baptism; encouragement of the sectarianism of religious orders; the exercise of papal authority over secular rulers and the spreading of the new, heathen gospel with the sword.[151] By way of contrast, the "righteous heretics," from Donatus in the third century to Hus and prominent Hussites in the fifteenth, are identified with practices and teachings dear to the Hutterites: practice of community of goods and opposition to the papal hierarchy, canon law, the exercise of temporal authority of the papacy and Catholic ceremonies and teachings including infant baptism and the mass. But in the end the primary defining feature of the "righteous heretics" is the fact that they opposed the church and were, therefore, persecuted by it.[152]

Interestingly, another important source from the last years of Walpot's tenure as elder or shortly thereafter, *The Great Article Book*, contains a somewhat different, although by no means incompatible, view of ecclesiastical history. The oldest extant copy of this work dates from 1583. Assumptions that Walpot himself was its author have recently been called into doubt. However, it still provides valuable insights into historical thinking among the Hutterites at the end of his time as elder, and for reasons of convenience and clarity I will continue to refer to Walpot as the author of this work. Composed of five articles dealing with central practices of the Hutterites: baptism, the Lord's Supper, community of goods, the sword and the questions of marriage and divorce between a believing and an unbelieving spouse, its format is drastically different from that of *The Hutterite Chronicle*. And yet the grasp of history in the work and its reliance on historical argumentation suggest that it belongs in the same tradition as *The Hutterite Chronicle*.[153]

Throughout the five articles of *The Great Article Book* runs the underlying assumption of *The Hutterite Chronicle* that salvation history is a unified whole from ancient Israel, through the primitive church to the contemporary Hutterite settlements. This continuity provides the basis for an appeal to the normative nature of biblical examples and biblical statements. Unlike *The Hutterite Chronicle*, no comprehensive vision of the church's history is laid out here, but crucial elements of that vision can be pieced together from scattered statements in each of the articles. At the centre of this vision is the basic restitutionist assumption that the primitive or apostolic church is normative for reform of the contemporary church: Christ's commands as enshrined by apostolic practice become the model for the practices and teachings of the Hutterite communities. Throughout the five articles, Walpot relies on a standard pattern to make his case: he establishes the commands or examples of Christ on the basis of Gospel descriptions or statements in Paul's epistles, and then he reinforces these claims with reference to the activities of the apostolic church, usually drawn from Acts, although occasionally extrapolated from the statements of Paul and/or Peter.[154] These biblically-based arguments are also shored up with evidence from extra-biblical sources on the history of early Christianity. For example, to make his case for the legitimacy of believers' baptism, Walpot quotes a variety of sources from the history of the early church, including Jerome, Augustine, Bede, papal decrees and conciliar statements, to indicate that instruction in the essentials of Christian teaching and a confession of faith preceded baptism throughout much of the church's early history. Similarly, he appeals to positions taken by Tertullian, Augustine and quotations from canon law to argue against the teaching on the real presence in the Lord's Supper and to argue that the doctrine of transubstantiation was still not apparent in the Carolingian age. Finally, he draws on Augustine, Chrysostom, canon law and conciliar decisions from as late as the fifth century to argue against the use of the sword by Christians. Like Braitmichael, Walpot relies heavily on Sebastian Franck's *Chronica* for the identification of these extra-biblical sources, although he may have drawn as well on historical references in some of Hubmaier's writings.[155] Throughout, *The Great Article Book* reveals a much greater historical sophistication than earlier polemical works like Riedemann's *Account*.

This new historical sophistication is most evident in the treatment of community of goods in article 3 of *The Great Article Book*. The attention to historical detail here is not surprising given the centrality of this teaching to the Hutterites and their distinctiveness. Walpot's primary concern is to prove that their practice marks the Hutterites as the sole heirs of the early Christian church. Their life is that prophesied in the Old Testament and practised by the early Christians throughout the New.[156] This becomes especially evident in the answer to the apparently perennial challenge to Hutterite teaching on community of goods: that the biblical example derived from Acts 2 and 4 applied only to the Jerusalem community and only for a limited time. On behalf of his opponents, Walpot presents a vast array of New Testament texts suggesting that the early Christians outside of Jerusalem had private property. Even more vast, however, is the array of biblical "evidence" suggesting that community of goods has been part of the history of God's people throughout the ages. He begins with the example of the Levitical priesthood which had no inheritance in the promised land and then moves quickly to the teachings of Christ and the example of the common purse among the disciples.[157] His primary concern, however, is to establish that this was general practice among the early Christian churches, a task he undertakes by scouring descriptions of the church in the Acts of the Apostles and the epistles of Paul. Included among these is Riedemann's unusual reading of 2 Corinthinans 8:3-4.[158] These claims he then backs up with evidence from extra-biblical sources. He appeals to Eusebius' *Ecclesiastical History* and the fifth epistle of the Pseudo-Clementine corpus to reinforce his assertion that the original Christians outside of Jerusalem also practised community of goods, and he cites patristic sources, specifically Jerome and Augustine, to indicate that the church recognized the importance of community of goods at least until the end of the fourth century. In both cases he draws extensively on Sebastian Franck's *Chronica* for these sources of information.[159]

The result of these forays into the history of the early church is a vision of Christian beginnings that departs from Braitmichael's in subtle but important ways. This is probably most obvious in Walpot's failure to clearly identify a Constantinian fall of the church. He does identify with the underlying theme of Braitmichael's criticism of Constantinian Christianity, the use of compulsion in matters of faith.[160] Citing a variety of sources from the ancient church, again borrowed primarily from Franck's *Chronica*, he argues that as late as the fifth or even the sixth century important voices in the church stood against compelling consciences.[161] Here he does not so much contradict Braitmichael's history as supplement it.

This becomes clear in other articles where he identifies other dates and events with the fall of the church. In the first article he describes infant baptism as the beginning of the desolation and fall of the church, and he asserts that the true church cannot be restored until believer's baptism is reinstituted.[162] Later he traces the historical perversion of believers' baptism into infant baptism. A crucial event in this devolution was the declaration by pope Nicholas I in 862 that children able to recite the Lord's Prayer should be baptized.[163] Similarly, the perversion of the Lord's Supper into the mass has ushered in the growth of a false Christianity prophesied by Christ in the Gospels and by John in Revelation. In this case it appears that the desolation advanced more slowly. At one point he claims that there is no evidence of the doctrine of transubstantiation as late as the Carolingian age, and elsewhere he asserts that this doctrine did not appear until the middle of the eleventh century.[164]

The Great Article Book suggests, then, that even as *The Great Chronicle* was being written, its vision of the primitive church did not hold exclusive sway within Hutterite circles. Its reconstruction of Christian history does not directly challenge Braitmichael's, but it does emphasize different events and themes in fleshing out the details of that history. Like the earliest Anabaptists, Walpot's view and use of history do not follow one consistent narrative, but are determined by the task at hand. Interestingly, again like the earliest Anabaptists, insofar as he identifies one crucial event or element in the church's fall, it is the beginning of infant baptism, not Constantine's conversion. However, his vision parts company with those of the earliest Anabaptists in the extent of its detail and sophistication of its knowledge. This greater sophistication is due in large part to Walpot's reliance on Franck's *Chronica* as a mine of citations and evidence, and it indicates, furthermore, that the Hutterite vision of ecclesiastical history was still a living and evolving organism during the Walpot years.

Mennonites

At the centre of the rich tradition of Mennonite historical writing was the vision of Menno Simons. Menno regularly appealed to historical arguments to support his claims. In particular, he was fond of citing the ecclesiastical history of Eusebius and the writings of the church fathers.[165] However, like many other early Anabaptists, Menno did not lay out a comprehensive vision of ecclesiastical history in a specific work dedicated to the subject. Rather, his historical vision also must be gleaned from his discussions of particular issues. Nonetheless, a coherent vision of the history of the church arises from those references. The legacy of Menno's historical knowledge and interest is clear in the *Martyrs Mirror*. As we have seen, the great seventeenth-century Mennonite martyrology combined the common Anabaptist restitutionism with a sophisticated understanding of the church's history. However, in contrast to *The Hutterite Chronicle* it focused more on the history of the persecuted, minority church than it did on the persecuting majority. Many of the important outlines of this distinctive variation on the Anabaptist view of history were laid down by Menno, but they subsequently were revised and then reinforced by the experiences of later Mennonites.

Menno's writings make it clear he regarded the primitive, apostolic church as the true church; that he believed the institutional church subsequently fell; and that he regarded the teachings and practices of the apostolic church as normative for the restoration of the true church in his own age. References to the historical fall of the true church—on one occasion Menno identifies it as "the most holy city and temple"—and its subsequent desolation by the Antichrist for many centuries until its restoration in the last days of unbelief and abomination pervade Menno's writings.[166] These references indicate that the church's fall is manifested in many ways, although usually they involve a departure from the life, practices and teachings of the apostolic church especially relating to baptism, the Lord's Supper and the ban.[167] Of these marks of the true church, Menno focuses especially on baptism and, of course identifies the true baptism commanded by Christ and practised by the apostles with believers' baptism.[168] Less frequently he connects the deterioration of the primitive church to perversion of teaching and practice relating to the Lord's Supper and the ban.[169]

Menno establishes no hard and fast date for the church's fall. Instead, he develops a vision of its decline, focused especially on its perversion of the apostolic practice of believers' baptism. This was a gradual process apparently spanning several centuries. Scripture clearly indicates, Menno asserts, that the apostles baptized only adult believers. However, even during the lifetimes of some of the apostles, or shortly after their deaths, perversions of baptismal practice were introduced. Menno claims to have scriptural evidence of this fact, citing Paul's reference to the baptism on behalf of the deceased in I Corinthians 15:29, and he reinforces this claim with an appeal to the statements of Tertullian and Rufinus that early in its history the primitive church witnessed the invention of new ceremonies. Such an early dating of the perversion of true baptism likely had polemical value in response to claims of his opponents that statements by Origen and Augustine indicated infant baptism had existed since the time of the apostles.[170] Thereafter, a slow but steady decline set in. While he does not chronicle all the details of that decline, Menno does highlight several important stages along the way. In the middle of the second century the tenth pope, Hyginus, instituted the office of godfathers, and at the beginning of the fifth century Pope Innocent I confirmed by decree the practice of infant baptism.[171]

The early appearance of infant baptism in the church's history, however, in no way invalidates or supersedes the apostolic practice of believers' baptism which continued concurrently with the new practice. Again citing Tertullian and Rufinus, Menno claims that among the earliest ancients infant baptism was not common and most continued the practice of adult baptism. The sophistication of Menno's historical understanding and research is evident at this point in his appeal to Beatus Rhenanus' annotations on Tertullian to make his point. Furthermore, as late as the third century, Cyprian was still leaving the baptism of infants optional and, according to Eusebius, into the fourth century Alexander of Alexandria refused to baptize infants in his church.[172] In response to arguments from patristic sources in favour of infant baptism, Menno lays the blame for this perversion of apostolic practice, at least in part, at the feet of the church fathers. The endorsement of infant baptism by Tertullian, Origen, Cyprian and Augustine calls forth the retort that there is no scriptural justification for such a position. On another occasion, the actual perversion of baptismal practice is attributed to Origen, Augustine, Jerome and Lactantius.[173] In response to the argument of his counterpart in the Reformed Church, Gellius Faber, that infant baptism was practised already at the time of Augustine, therefore before the reign of Antichrist had been fully established, Menno responded that Antichrist was already in full honour in Augustine's day.[174]

The general outlines of Menno's vision suggest then that almost at the beginning of the church's history a process began which led to the perversion of baptism and with it to the fall of the church. Subsequent centuries witnessed slow but steady deterioration until baptism and the visible church saw complete deterioration at the end of the fourth and beginning of the fifth centuries in the teachings of Augustine and Jerome and the decrees of Pope Innocent. Menno's other references to the history of baptism fit this general scheme. For example, on the question of the legitimacy of rebaptizing, or more accurately to his mind, baptizing those who had already undergone an heretical form of baptism, he appealed to the teachings of Cyprian and the decrees of the Councils of Carthage and Nicaea, that is to statements of an age when true baptism had not yet been completely subverted.[175] Menno's references to the historical fate of other practices of the primitive church provide slight variations on this theme. When discussing the true practice and teaching of the Lord's Supper he appeals to Tertullian's description of it as a "brotherly meal" or a "love feast" among the earliest Christians. However, elsewhere he claims that his understanding of the Lord's Supper and his position on the oath are in accord with the teachings of the church fathers. This suggests the possibility that he believed patristic teachings on these issues had not deteriorated as quickly as they had on baptism.[176]

Despite this fairly detailed sense of the church's fall, Menno nowhere makes reference to a Constantinian fall of the church, the assumed cornerstone of the Anabaptist view of church history. Behind *The Hutterite Chronicle's* criticism of Constantinian Christianity lies an attack on the use of compulsion in matters of faith. Menno also opposes the coercion of religious belief, even though he fails to mention Constantine's conversion. Throughout Menno's writings we see repeated appeals to the witness of the persecuted church. But even in *The Cross of Saints*, which has been characterized as epitomizing Menno's theology of martyrdom, no reference is made to Constantine or the Constantinian church.[177] He does, however, trace the histories of the persecuted, true church and the persecuting, false church from both Testaments of Scripture. New Testament examples are then reinforced with citations from patristic sources indicating that the early Christians did not persecute religious dissenters.[178] Gradually religious compulsion infected the church; like the perversion of true baptism this was a gradual process. At first the Arians were expelled from the church "in misery." And ultimately the "bloody tyranny of Antichrist gained the upper hand." Menno provides few details about this process, but it is clear that he identifies it with the growth of papal power, culminating in the ascendancy of the "papal Antichrist" above all potentates on earth. The only specific example Menno identifies in this process makes no reference to Constantine and Pope Sylvester, but to Emperor Frederick Barbarossa and Pope Alexander III.[179]

Despite his perception that the true church has suffered persecution throughout the ages, Menno nowhere identifies with a medieval sectarian tradition. On one occasion he cites approvingly Hus' statements on the swearing of oaths,[180] but he treats Hus more as an important harbinger of the Reformation than as the culmination of an ongoing dissenting tradition in the medieval church. Elsewhere Menno goes to great pains to distance himself from those tainted with the charge of heresy, and reveals a sophisticated understanding of the heresies which rent the primitive church and of their doctrinal deviations. He is particularly at pains to refute charges of his opponents that his movement has revived the Circumcellian, Donatist and Arian heresies. In fact, he goes so far as to identify the Catholics, Zwinglians and Lutherans, along with Arians, Circumcellians and Münsterites, as sectarians who rely on doctrines of men and validate their teachings with the sword. He challenges the Diet of Speyer's revival of the death penalty for rebaptism, arguing that the original mandate of Theodosius was directed against the evil deeds of heretical groups rather than the act of rebaptism.[181] In reading Menno's statements, one is struck not by his identification of an ongoing sectarian tradition, but by his attempts to establish the orthodoxy of his movement in the mainstream of church history.

James Stayer has argued that by the time of his death in 1561, Menno had moved the Melchiorite movement along the road to nonconformist respectability.[182] The process of attaining this status involved once again appeals to the history of the church. In the first place, Menno looks to the church fathers in an appeal for toleration for his movement. In 1537, in the *Foundation of Christian Doctrine*, he cited Cyprian in support of his claim that the persecution of religious dissenters is contrary to the true

Christian spirit.[183] This practice of justifying toleration from the writings of the fathers increases in Menno's writings from the early 1550s, in which he campaigned for open toleration for the Mennonites and crossed swords with the Lutheran and Calvinist theologians of the establishment.[184] At the same time, in these polemical works Menno began to develop a clearly formulated ecclesiology which identified the suffering of persecution as a mark of the true church and the exercise of tyranny as that of the Antichrist's church.[185] An important element in the development of this doctrine was Menno's reading of Eusebius' account of the persecutions of the primitive church. These examples are repeated frequently in Menno's polemical works from the early 1550s and culminate in the claim that the church "always suffers enmity, tumult, violence and the tyranny of the wicked."[186] This identification of persecution as a basic mark of the true church throughout the ages is an important step toward an identification with a tradition of ongoing heretical opposition to the institutional church, and with it the full-blown historical vision of the *Martyrs Mirror*. While Menno was unwilling to take this final step, others in the movement were less reticent.

Menno's scattered historical references were taken up by Dirk Philips and incorporated into an explicit and systematic history of the church, tracing its cosmic conflict with the world from prehistory to the end of history.[187] Dirk clearly identifies the church with the faithful of all ages. The angels in heaven formed the first church and established the subsequent pattern of apostasy and redemption for ecclesiastical history. The fall of Adam and Eve established a similar pattern among humans. To this the actions of Cain and Abel added the related pattern of the persecution of the true church by the world. The first restitution of the church occurred with the promise of the coming Saviour and in this sense the church existed in Christ from the beginning. Dirk traces these patterns in detail through the history of the Old Testament.[188]

With the Incarnation, Dirk argues, the conflict between good and evil was heightened and reached a new climax in history. As well, the nature of the church changed significantly. Although the true congregation has existed through all ages, Dirk regards Old Testament practices and institutions as merely "shadowy types" of apostolic practices and institutions.[189] Although he argued that the rebuilding of the temple in Jerusalem after the Babylonian Captivity foreshadowed the restoration of the true Christian congregation, the apostolic church remained uniquely normative as a model for the church of the restitution in Dirk's thought.[190] Throughout his writings Dirk consistently holds up the commands of Christ and the practices of the apostles as an absolute norm for the reform of the church.[191]

Despite the changes, historical patterns established before the Incarnation continued to affect the congregation of God, and persecution remained the fate of true believers throughout the ages.[192] Also carried forward was the pattern of apostasy and restitution which marked the earlier history of the church. Dirk agreed with Menno that already during the New Testament age the apostolic church had begun to accommodate itself to the world, a fact evidenced already by the end of persecution and increasing prosperity of the church during the Roman Empire.[193] However, Dirk's understanding of subsequent Christian history diverged slightly from Menno's. Where Menno tended to regard all who disagreed with his understanding of the church as sectarians, and therefore their communities as sects, Dirk regarded Catholics and major Protestant denominations as false or Antichristian churches. As communities they had apostatized as had Israel and Judah before the Babylonian Captivity. But, as with the Old Testament communities, they included individuals who had remained faithful despite the general apostasy. This opened the door to the possibility that true believers could be found throughout the church's history. Dirk never identified with medieval heretical opposition to the hierarchical church, and he always vehemently rejected the accusation of heresy whenever it was levelled against the brethren from any quarter.[194] However, his assertion that the faithful have existed throughout the ages opened the door, ever so slightly, to such an identification.

The creation of a clear and comprehensive history of persecuted martyrs was slow in coming to the Mennonites. Two years after Dirk completed *The Church of God* the first great Mennonite martyrology, *The Sacrifice unto the Lord* appeared. This work provides little evidence of Mennonite reflection on the history of the church. After a brief treatment of the biblical faithful who died for their faith in its preface, the martyrology itself begins with the martyrdom of Stephen described in Acts 7 and then jumps to that of Michael Sattler. Brad Gregory has highlighted this aspect of the martyrology, suggesting that its author was more interested in how the patterns of contemporary martyrdoms fit the scriptural template than in tracing the history of the persecuted faithful throughout the ages. At this point the Mennonite martyrologists were not yet inspired to write church history.[195] However, as we have seen, when pushed on doctrinal points Menno especially betrayed a clear sense of ecclesiastical history. Over the next half century the details of a more comprehensive historical vision were filled in. In 1615 a group of editors under the leadership of the Waterlander elder Hans de Ries published a *History of the Martyrs or Genuine Witnesses of Jesus Christ*. This work not only included predecessors from the Old and New Testaments of contemporary Anabaptist martyrs, but even some medieval witnesses who opposed infant baptism.[196] Two years later this work was republished by the Old Frisian Mennonites under the leadership of Peter Jans Twisk with a modified preface and new title, *History of the True Witnesses of Jesus Christ*.[197] Finally, in 1631-32 the Waterlanders published the first martyrology entitled the *Martyrs Mirror* with an historical scope equal to that of the 1660 edition of the same work. The prologue to the 1631-32 edition emphasized the continuity both of persecution and the true church of the martyrs throughout the ages, and it filled in the narrative between the martyrs of the primitive church and those of the sixteenth century by drawing on descriptions in Eusebius and the *Ecclesiastical Annals* of Caesar Baronius.[198]

CHAPTER 4

Anabaptist Restitution

Were the early Anabaptists restitutionists? The early Swiss Brethren, the supposed founders of "Evangelical Anabaptism," appealed to the model of the primitive church in their reforming endeavours in a fashion that distinguishes them from the humanists and magisterial Reformers, and even many of the other Reformation radicals. From the Grebel Letters to *The Schleitheim Articles*, Swiss Brethren sources hold up the apostolic church as a model to be emulated. Furthermore, *The Congregational Order* indicates that the primitivism of the early Swiss Brethren could operate independently of, and even precede, a commitment to a free church ecclesiology. In none of the early Swiss Brethren sources, however, is this restitutionism supplemented by an elaborate historical vision along the lines described by Littell. Their primitivism, if one can use this term for their vision, was determined more by their approach to the Bible than their thoughts about history.

Swiss Brethren sources were not unique in this regard. My survey of early Anabaptist sources from a variety of traditions has turned up relatively few detailed historical references. Rather, the earliest Anabaptists seemed unconcerned with elaborating detailed historical visions or with situating themselves within them. The exceptions to this rule, for example the detailed historical references in the arguments of Balthasar Hubmaier, Pilgram Marpeck or Menno Simons, stand out because they are exceptional. In his final salvo against Littell, Hillerbrand charged that the immediate experiences of the sixteenth-century Anabaptists, not their visions of the past, determined their activities. In Hillerbrand's own words: "Their own experience came first; theoretical reflection followed."[199] In terms of the fully articulated Anabaptist view of the church as identified by Littell, Hillerbrand's observations appear to be accurate. *The Hutterite Chronicle* and the *Martyrs Mirror* stem from more settled and relatively more tolerant circumstances which, in the latter case at least, James Stayer has identified as the end of the Radical Reformation.[200] Only after the initial brutal attempts to suppress the movement had abated could the Anabaptists afford the luxury of elaborate historical reflection.

But does this fact invalidate the restitutionist thesis *in toto*? Or, to put it another way, do the early Anabaptists still qualify as restitutionists despite these disclaimers? If we are willing to restrict significantly the meaning of the term, I believe that they do. Particularly among the southern Anabaptist traditions—the Swiss Brethren, Marpeckites, Hutterites—the primitive church was a beacon for reforming visions in a way unparalleled among other reformers of the sixteenth century. Despite their appeals to the model of the early Christian community, humanists and magisterial Reformers never hung as tenaciously to this vision or strove with equal vigour to see it revived. Other Reformation radicals, although no less interested in the history of the early church, similarly tended not to share in the fervent desire for its complete revival. But in labelling the early Anabaptists restitutionists we must not forget the extent to which we have qualified the definition of that title. The desire to revive the primitive church did not necessarily imply a commitment to a separatist ecclesiology, although the two were often united. It did not immediately commit one to a specific and detailed vision of ecclesiastical history which included a Constantinian fall of the church and a necessary rejection of the medieval *corpus Christianum*, although many Anabaptists eventually came to hold these opinions. And finally, it did not make one the only serious or honest student of history among the sixteenth-century reformers. Many non-Anabaptists of the age were interested in the history of the church, especially the early church.

Notes

1 Harder, 285 (=*QGTS* 1:13).

2 George H. Williams, *Radical Reformation*, 3rd edn.(Kirksville, MO: Sixteenth Century Journal Publishers, 1992), 189-90.

3 James M. Stayer, *The German Peasants' War and Anabaptist Community of Goods* (Montreal and Kingston: McGill-Queen's University Press, 1991), 95-99, 104-5; idem, "The Radical Reformation," in Thomas A. Brady, Jr., Heiko A. Oberman and James D. Tracy, eds., *Handbook of European History, 1400-1600: Late Middle Ages, Renaissance and Reformation*, vol. 1: *Visions, Programs and Outcomes* (Grand Rapids, MI: Eerdmans, 1996), 255; Hans-Jürgen Goertz, "'A common future conversation': A revisionist

interpretation of the September 1524 Grebel letters to Thomas Müntzer," in Werner O. Packull and Geoffrey L. Dipple, eds., *Radical Reformation Studies: Essays Presented to James M. Stayer* (Aldershot: Ashgate Publishing, 1999), 84.

4 James M. Stayer, "Die Anfänge des schweizerischen Täufertums im reformierten Kongregationalismus," in Hans-Jürgen Goertz, ed. *Umstrittenes Täufertum 1525-1975: Neue Forschungen* (Göttingen: Vandenhoeck & Ruprecht, 1975), 19-49; Martin Haas, "Der Weg der Täufer in die Absonderung," in Ibid., 50-78; Heinold Fast, "Conrad Grebel: The Covenant on the Cross," in Hans-Jürgen Goertz, ed. *Profiles of Radical Reformers: Biographical Sketches from Thomas Müntzer to Paracelsus* (Kitchener, ON: Herald Press, 1982), 118-31.

5 Stayer, "Anfänge des schweizerischen Täufertums," 38.

6 Ibid., 20, 25-26, 37-39; Fast, "Covenant on the Cross," 130. For critiques of the revisionist reading of the beginnings of Swiss Anabaptism, see Charles Nienkirchen, "Reviewing the Case for a Non-Separatist Ecclesiology in Early Swiss Anabaptism," *MQR* 55 (1982), 227-41, and especially Andrea Strübind, *Eifriger als Zwingli: Die frühe Täuferbewegung in der Schweiz* (Berlin: Duncker & Humblot, 2003).

7 For the common opposition to Zwingli and shared emphasis on the competence of the local community to enact reform, see Stayer, "Anfänge des schweizerischen Täufertums," 34 and Fast, "Covenant on the Cross," 127. The shared desire to revive the primitive church has been highlighted for various aspects of the movement, see Stayer, *Anabaptists and the Sword*, 2nd ed. (Lawrence, KS: Coronado Press, 1976), 95, 102, 330 and *The German Peasants' War and Anabaptist Community of Goods* (Montreal and Kingston: McGill-Queen's University Press, 1991), 95-106. On this point more traditional interpretations of the beginnings of Swiss Anabaptism agree with the revisionist interpretation. See for example Harold S. Bender, *Conrad Grebel c. 1498-1526: The Founder of the Swiss Brethren Sometimes Called Anabaptists* (Goshen, IN: Mennonite Historical Society, 1950), 89, 93, 213.

8 Leland Harder, ed., *The Sources of Swiss Anabaptism: The Conrad Grebel Letters and Related Documents* (Scottdale, PA and Kitchener, ON: Herald Press, 1985), 185 (= ZW, vol. 1, 327). Grebel derides the church's meddling in matters of temporal authority along with other abuses of the upper echelons of the ecclesiastical hierarchy, but from no clear doctrinal perspective. On Grebel's relationship with humanism and Zwingli in 1522, see Bender, *Conrad Grebel*, 16-88; Robert Kreider, "Anabaptism and Humanism: An Inquiry into the Relationship of Humanism to the Evangelical Anabaptists," *MQR* 26 (1952), 123-41; Dale Schrag, "Erasmian and Grebelian Pacifism: Consistency or Contradiction?" *MQR* 62 (1988), 431-54.

9 On Grebel's break with Zwingli, see Stayer, "Anfänge des schweizerischen Täufertums," 35.

10 Harder, 278.

11 On the separatist ecclesiology in the letters to Müntzer, see Bender, *Conrad Grebel*, 171, 175 and Nienkirchen, 231. Williams, *Radical Reformation*, 189-90, sees in these letters the first clear appearance of restitutionism.

12 Hans-Jürgen Goertz, *The Anabaptists*, translated by Trevor Johnson (London: Routledge, 1996), 70, 87-88 and "A Common Future Conversation," 78, 82-88. Andrea Strübind, who is critical of Goertz's interpretation on so many other issues, describes the vision of the Müntzer letter as the establishment of the visible church of Jesus Christ according to the standard of Scripture. See *Eifriger als Zwingli*, 290-91.

13 Harder, 285 (= *QGTS* 1:13).

14 Ibid., 285-94 (= *QGTS* 1:13-21). See also Grebel's biblicist criteria for the reform of the mass at the Second Zurich Disputation, ibid., 244.

15 Ibid., 286, 293 (= *QGTS* 1:14, 20).

16 Ibid., 290-91 (= *QGTS* 1:17-18). Strübind, *Eifriger als Zwingli*, 216-18, suggests that the Zurich radicals took over these rudimentary historical details from Müntzer's *Protestation*.

17 Harder., 312-15 (= *QGTS* 1:24-28). On the importance of the primitive church in Manz's reforming vision, see Ekkehard Krajewski, "The Theology of Felix Manz," *MQR* 36 (1962), 76-87. Strübind, *Eifriger als Zwingli*, 306-7, 556, highlights the importance of the identification of the papal origins of infant baptism for the Zurich Anabaptists' criticism of the institution.

18 Haas, "Weg der Täufer," 51.

19 Harder, 335.

20 Ibid., 446-47.

21 *QGTS* 2:271-73; C. Arnold Snyder, *Anabaptist History and Theology: An Introduction* (Kitchener, ON: Pandora Press, 1995), 54-55. Strübind's argument, *Eifriger als Zwingli*, 485-509, that Hans Krüsi significantly reworked Grebel's concordance suggests that the historically vague primitivism of the early Zurich Anabaptists was shared by their counterparts in eastern Switzerland.

22 John Howard Yoder, ed. and trans., *The Legacy of Michael Sattler* (Scottdale, PA: Herald Press, 1973), 7 and 29.

23 Ibid., 36 (= *QGTS* 2:28-29).

24 Franklin H. Littell, *The Origins of Sectarian Protestantism: A Study of the Anabaptist View of the Church* (New York: MacMillan, 1964), 83.

25 Harder, 286-91, 293 (= *QGTS* 1:14-18, 20).

26 Harder, 311-15 (= *QGTS* 1:23-28).

27 Yoder, *Legacy of Michael Sattler*, 36-39 (= *QGTS* 2:28-31).

28 Stayer, "Anfänge des schweizerischen Täufertums," 19-49.

29 Harder, 381 (= *QGTS* 2:608).

30 Williams, *Radical Reformation*, 223-24. On Ulimann see John Horsch, "The Swiss Brethren in St. Gall and Appenzell," *MQR* 7 (1933), 205-26.

31 Stayer, *German Peasants' War and Anabaptist Community of Goods*, 95-106.

32 Harder, 345 (= *QGTS* 2:601).

33 Werner O. Packull, *Hutterite Beginnings: Communitarian Experiments During the Reformation* (Baltimore and London: Johns Hopkins University Press, 1995), 37-46.

34 Yoder, *Legacy of Michael Sattler*, 44.

35 Ibid., 45.

36 Harder, 314 (= *QGTS* 1:27); Strübind, *Eifriger als Zwingli*, 329.

37 John Howard Yoder, "Balthasar Hubmaier and the Beginnings of Swiss Anabaptism," *MQR* 33 (1959), 15-17. For an excellent summary of scholarly reticence to include Hubmaier as a full-fledged member of Swiss Anabaptism, see Christof Windhorst, *Täuferisches Taufverständnis: Balthasar Hubmaiers Lehre zwischen traditioneller und reformatorischer Theologie* (Leiden: E.J. Brill, 1976), 2-3.

38 See Walter Klaassen, "Speaking in Simplicity: Balthasar Hubmaier," *MQR* 40 (1966), 139-40; J. Denny Weaver, "Discipleship Redefined: Four Sixteenth-Century Anabaptists," *MQR* 54 (1980), 255-56, 276; Snyder, *Anabaptist History and Theology*, 63-64.

39 Cf. Yoder, "Hubmaier and the Beginnings of Swiss Anabaptism, 7; Klaassen, "Speaking in Simplicity," 140 and Snyder, *Anabaptist History and Theology*, 163.

40 Littell, *Origins of Sectarian Protestantism*, 17, 38, 87-88.

41 Windhorst, *Täuferisches Taufverständnis*, 144-45; H. Wayne Pipkin, "The Baptismal Theology of Balthasar Hubmaier," *MQR* 65 (1991), 51.

42 See Stayer, *Anabaptists and the Sword*, 141-45 and *The German Peasants' War and Anabaptist Community of Goods*, 140; Martin Rothkegel, "Die Nikolsburger Reformation 1526-1535: Vom Humanismus zum Sabbatarianismus" (ThD diss., Charles University Prague, 2000), 101-4 and "Die Nikolsburger Reformation 1526-1535," *MGBl* 59 (2002), 185.

43 See Torsten Bergsten, *Balthasar Hubmaier: Anabaptist Theologian and Martyr*, Irwin J. Barnes and William R. Estep, trans., William R. Estep, ed., (Valley Forge, PA: Judson Press, 1978), 68-87.

44 H. Wayne Pipkin and John H. Yoder, eds. and trans., *Balthasar Hubmaier: Theologian of Anabaptism* (Scottdale, PA and Kitchener, ON.: Herald Press, 1989), 23, 27.

45 Ibid., 33 (= *QGT* 9:73).

46 Ibid., 31, 53, 70, 75 (= *QGT* 9:72, 88-89, 102).

47 Bergsten, *Anabaptist Theologian*, 157.

48 Ibid., 233 and 237.

49 Pipkin and Yoder, *Hubmaier: Theologian of Anabaptism*, 118, 124, 129-36 (= *QGT* 9:137, 142, 146-51).

50 Ibid., 137-39 (= *QGT* 9:153-55).

51 Bergsten, *Anabaptist Theologian*, 280.

52 Pipkin and Yoder, *Hubmaier: Theologian of Anabaptism*, 101-14, 118 (= *QGT* 9:123-34, 137); Williams, *Radical Reformation*, 224-26, 232.

53 Pipkin and Yoder, *Hubmaier: Theologian of Anabaptism*, 188-91, 208-11 (= *QGT* 9:181-84, 196-98).

54 Ibid., 221-22, 224-25 (= *QGT* 9:205, 207-8). On Hubmaier's treatment of Augustine and Jerome, see Bergsten, *Anabaptist Theologian*, 281-83.

55 Pipkin and Yoder, *Hubmaier: Theologian of Anabaptism*, 194 and 197 (= *QGT* 9:185, 188).

56 Ibid., 186, 212, 224-25 (= *QGT* 9:180, 198, 207-8).

57 Ibid., 212, 224-25. Jarold Zeman has noted Hubmaier's "puzzling failure to appeal to Hus and the legacy of the Czech Reformation even in his Moravian writings." See *The Anabaptists and the Czech Brethren: A Study in Origins and Contacts* (The Hague and Paris: Mouton, 1969), 141-42, 72-73. Zeman speculates that in Moravia Hubmaier may have been too preoccupied with practical church matters to take the opportunity to look into the Czech Reformation. Equally likely is the explanation that Hubmaier's concern to establish the orthodoxy of his movement discouraged him from identifying with the heretical Bohemians.

58 Although not completed and published until Hubmaier's stay in Moravia, these works were likely begun earlier. Much of the text of *Ancient and New Teachers* was likely written in Waldshut and the response to Oecolampadius was written sometime in 1525. See Pipkin and Yoder, *Hubmaier: Theologian of Anabaptism*, 246 and 275.

59 Ibid, 245-46.

60 Ibid, 261-62, 277, 279, 288 (= *QGT* 9:238-39, 259, 260-61, 265).

61 Ibid., 250-55 (= *QGT* 9:230-32). As Christof Windhorst has noted, Hubmaier cites approvingly patristic statements on the necessary relationship between faith and baptism, but remains silent when the fathers disagree with him on the subject of infant baptism. The result, according to Windhorst, is a vision maintaining that the true church lasted from the time of the apostles until the fifth century when it was scattered until its restoration in Hubmaier's day. See Windhorst, *Täuferisches Taufverständnis*, 108-12.

62 Pipkin and Yoder, *Hubmaier: Theologian of Anabaptism*, 254-55, 266 (= *QGT* 9:232, 244-45).
63 Ibid., 279-81 (= *QGT* 9:260-61).
64 Ibid., 290-91 (= *QGT* 9:267).
65 Ibid., 355 (= *QGT* 9:318). On restitutionist and biblicist themes in the Nicolsburg Reformation, see Rothkegel, "Nikolsburger Reformation: Humismus zum Sabbatarianismus," 101-35, especially 114-32.
66 On the relationship between Hubmaier's writings and the reforms undertaken in Nicolsburg, see Pipkin and Yoder, *Hubmaier: Theologian of Anabaptism*, 372, 386, 393 and 409.
67 Ibid., 349, 374-75, 393, 544-45 (= *QGT* 9:314, 339, 355, 476-77).
68 Ibid., 319-20, 325, 349, 422 (= *QGT* 9:290-91, 294-95, 314, 375-76).
69 Ibid., 176, 326, 343, 422 (= *QGT* 9:172, 295, 309, 375-76).
70 Ibid., 176 (= *QGT* 9:172).
71 Ibid., 175-76 (= *QGT* 9:172).
72 Ibid., 343 (= *QGT* 9:309).
73 Ibid., 264-74 (= *QGT* 9:243-49).
74 Bergsten, *Anabaptist Theologian*, 281.
75 Pipkin and Yoder, *Hubmaier: Theologian of Anabaptism*, 352 (= *QGT* 9:315).
76 This is probably clearest in his sharp distinction between believers' baptism and the heretical rebaptism of the Novatians and Hemerobaptists in the early church, see Ibid., 391 (= *QGT* 9:352).
77 Windhorst, *Täuferisches Taufverständnis*, 21, has noted the importance of Hubmaier's dialogue with Scripture, with the fathers, and with contemporary theologians for the development of his understanding of baptism. The same point can be made with reference to the evolution of his understanding of ecclesiastical history.
78 For a good overview of interpretations of Hut's place in Anabaptism and of his relationship to Müntzer, see Werner O. Packull, *Mysticism and the Early South German-Austrian Anabaptist Movement 1525-1531* (Scottdale, PA and Kitchener, ON: Herald Press, 1977), 62-66 and *Hutterite Beginnings*, 56-57.
79 Williams, *Radical Reformation*, 1304.
80 "Ein Sendbrief Hans Huts," in Adolf Laube, at al., eds., *Flugschriften vom Bauernkrieg zum Täuferreich (1526-1535)*, vol. 2 (Berlin: Academie Verlag, 1992), 858.
81 Hans Hut, "On the Mystery of Baptism," in Gordon Rupp, *Patterns of Reformation* (Philadelphia: Fortress Press, 1969), 382. See also Hut's further comments on 383.
82 Hans Hut, "Eine christliche Unterrichtung," in Laube, et al., *Flugschriften vom Bauernkrieg zum Täuferreich*, 694.
83 Packull, *Mysticism and the South German-Austrian Anabaptist Movement*, 87.
84 Goertz, *The Anabaptists*, 92-93.
85 Hut, "On the Mystery of Baptism," 390-91, 394-97. For a thorough analysis of Hut's baptismal theology, see Gottfried Seebass, "Das Zeichen der Erwälten: Zum Verständnis der Taufe bei Hans Hut," in Goertz, ed., *Umstrittenes Täufertum*, 138-64, especially 144.
86 Hut, "Eine christliche Unterrichtung," 694.
87 Packull, *Mysticism and the South German-Austrian Anabaptist Movement*, 81; Stayer, *German Peasants' War and Anabaptist Community of Goods*, 114 and 117.
88 Packull, *Mysticism and the South German-Austrian Anabaptist Movement*, 81.
89 Ibid., 67; Hut, "Eine christliche Unterrichtung," 688-95.
90 Packull, *Mysticism and the South German-Austrian Anabaptist Movement*, 110-12.

91 Leonhard Schiemer, "A Letter to the Church at Rattenberg, 1527-1528," in Walter Klassen, ed., *Anabaptism in Outline: Selected Primary Sources* (Kitchener, ON and Scottdale, PA: Herald Press, 1981), 105.

92 Robert Friedmann, "The Oldest Church Discipline of the Anabaptists," *MQR* 29 (1955), 162-66.

93 On the background to this order, see Packull, *Hutterite Beginnings*, 34-37 and 136; Stayer, *German Peasants' War and Anabaptist Community of Goods*, 152-53.

94 Packull, *Mysticism and South German/Austrian Anabaptist Movement*, 145-46.

95 Ibid., 145.

96 Daniel Liechty, *Andreas Fischer and the Sabbatarian Anabaptists: An Early Reformation Episode in East Central Europe* (Scottdale, PA: Herald Press, 1988), 46-49; W. Wiswedel, "Oswald Glaidt von Jamnitz," *ZKG* 56 (1937), 555, 561-62.

97 Packull, *Hutterite Beginnings*, 104.

98 Ibid., 104-6.

99 Stephen Boyd, *Pilgram Marpeck: His Life and Social Theology* (Durham, NC: Duke University Press, 1992), 22-25.

100 See Littell, *Origins of Sectarian Protestantism*, 24-25 and William Klassen, "The Relation of the Old and New Covenants in Pilgram Marpeck's Theology," *MQR* 40 (1966), 98, 109; idem, *Covenant and Community: The Life, Writings and Hermeneutics of Pilgram Marpeck* (Grand Rapids: Eerdmans, 1968), 24-25; idem, "The Limits of Political Authority as Seen by Pilgram Marpeck," *MQR* 56 (1982), 361.

101 The identification of Marpeck's opponents in 1531 has not been without its disputes. See Klassen, *Covenant and Community*, 30-31, 36-45, 150, 156; idem., "Pilgram Marpeck: Liberty Without Coercion," in Goertz, ed. *Profiles of Radical Reformers*, 171; William Klassen and Walter Klaassen, eds. and trans., *The Writings of Pilgram Marpeck* (Kitchener and Scottdale: Herald Press, 1978), 3-44, 69 (hereafter *WPM*); Neal Blough, *Christologie Anabaptiste: Pilgram Marpeck et l'humanité du Christ* (Geneva: Fides et Labor, 1984), 44, 45; idem, "Pilgram Marpeck and Caspar Schwenckfeld: The Strasbourg Years," in Jean-Georges Rott and Simon L. Verheus, eds., *Bibliotheca Dissidentium: Scripta et Studia* 3 (Baden-Baden and Bouxwiller: Éditions Valentin Koerner, 1987): 371-80; Boyd, *Pilgram Marpeck*, 62 and 84-90; Packull, *Hutterite Beginnings*, 133-34 and 157; Williams, *Radical Reformation*, 406; Snyder, *Anabaptist History and Theology*, 134 and 309-14.

102 On Marpeck's authorship and the dating of the *Exposure* see Hans Hillerbrand, "An Early Anabaptist Treatise on the Christian and the State," *MQR* 32 (1958), 30; Walter Klaassen, "Investigation into the Authorship and Historical Background of the Anabaptist Tract *Aufdeckung der Babylonischen Hurn*," *MQR* 61 (1987), 255-56; Neal Blough, "*The Uncovering of the Babylonian Whore*: Confessionalization and Politics Seen from the Underside," *MQR* 75 (2001), 39, 42-43; Werner Packull, "Preliminary Report on Pilgram Marpeck's Sponsorship of Anabaptist *Flugschriften*," *MQR* 75 (2001), 81, 84n.39.

103 On Marpeck's authorship of *The Confession to Jan von Pernstain* and the date of its composition see Boyd, *Pilgram Marpeck*, 98-99. There is no clear consensus on when the two parts of the *Reply* were composed. See Klassen, *Covenant and Community*, 47-50; Boyd, *Pilgram Marpeck*, 140 and John Rempel's introduction to the English translation of the pamphlet in Walter Klaassen, Werner Packull and John Rempel, trans., *Later Writings by Pilgram Marpeck and His Circle*, vol. 1: *The Exposé, A Dialogue, and Marpeck's Response to Caspar Schwenckfeld* (Kitchener, ON: Pandora Press, 1999), 68.

[104] See my "Pilgram Marpeck, the Spiritualizers and the Anabaptist View of Church History," in C. Arnold Snyder, ed., *Commoners and Community: Essays in Honour of Werner O. Packull* (Kitchener, ON: Pandora Press, 2002), 219-20.

[105] Boyd, *Pilgram Marpeck*, 52, 54-55, 61-62. On the background to this document and its possible reliance on an earlier *Swiss Order*, see Packull, *Hutterite Beginnings*, 43-37, 136.

[106] See above, p. 140-41 and Friedmann, "Oldest Church Discipline," 162-66.

[107] Neal Blough, "Pilgram Marpeck and Martin Luther on the Humanity of Christ," *MQR* 61 (1987), 204-8.

[108] *WPM*, 64. For further discussion of the restoration of baptism and the Lord's Supper, see 48-54, 64-66, 104-5.

[109] Ibid., 127, 172, 179-81, 186, 199, 203, 213, 267, 272, 277-78 (= *QGT* 7:449-50).

[110] Hans Hillerbrand, "Ein Täuferbekenntnis aus dem 16. Jahrhundert," *ARG* 50 (1959), 48; J. Loserth, ed., *Quellen und Forschungen zur Geschichte der oberdeutschen Taufgesinnten im 16. Jahrhundert: Pilgram Marpecks Antwort auf Kaspar Schwenckfelds Beurteilung des Buches der Bundesbezeugung von 1542* (Vienna and Leipzig: Carl Fromme, 1929), 529-30, 570-71. Elsewhere in the *Reply* Marpeck makes similar claims with reference to specific ceremonies. See ibid., 62, 70-71, 119, 138-39, 159-60, 433, 435, 454-59, 481. For English translations of many of these passages, see *Later Writings by Marpeck*, 1:77, 86-87, 99-100, 105-8, 111.

[111] Frank J. Wray, "The 'Vermanung' of 1542 and Rothmann's 'Bekenntnis,'" *ARG* 47 (1956): 243-51. On the value of the *Admonition* as a window into the ideas and attitudes of the Marpeckites, see Klassen, *Covenant and Community*, 46 and *WPM*, 159-60.

[112] *WPM*, 253-54, 279-82, 285, 288.

[113] Ibid., 277-78.

[114] See above, p. 143. In the *Exposure* Marpeck advocated a limited form of community of goods and identified property as the source of all government, but did not appeal to the model of the primitive church in so doing. See *Aufdeckung*, Aiij(b)-(c), Cij(b)-Ciij, in Hillerbrand, "Early Anabaptist Treatise," 37 and 44; Stayer, *Anabaptists and the Sword*, 71-72; Packull, *Hutterite Beginnings*, 136-37.

[115] *WPM*, 278-79; Snyder, *Anabaptist History and Theology*, 244-45.

[116] Compare Marpeck's comments in *WPM* 103-4 and 386.

[117] *Antwort*, 72-73, 88, 190, 547-48. For English translations of some of these passages, see *Later Writings by Marpeck*, 1:11, 87, 128-29.

[118] *WPM*, 44-46.

[119] Jan Kiwiet, *Pilgram Marbeck: Ein Führer der Täuferbewegung in süddeutschen Raum* (Kassel: J.G. Oncken Verlag, 1957), 133.

[120] *WPM*, 110-12, 127, 129-31, 140-41, 142-47, 152-55. See especially 130 and 145 (= *QGT* 7:420-23, 449-50, 456-59, 481-85, 486-501, 512-15; especially 458 and 498).

[121] *Aufdeckung*, Cii(b) - Ciii in Hillerbrand, "Early Anabaptist Treatise," 44.

[122] *WPM*, 297-98. For his treatment of each of these "perversions" of the truth, see also ibid., 204, 214-16, 253-54, 281-82.

[123] Ibid., 259-60.

[124] Ibid., 209, 539-40; *Antwort*, 303 (= *Later Writings of Marpeck*, 1:97).

[125] Hillerbrand, "Täuferbekenntnis," 46-47.

[126] *WPM*, 163.

[127] *WPM*, 46.

[128] Ibid., 47-51, 58, 63-66; Hillerbrand, "Täuferbekenntnis," 46-47. As Marpeck confronted arguments drawn from the Old Testament in his exchanges with the magisterial

Reformers of Strasbourg and Schwenckfeld, and in his response to the events at Münster, he further emphasized the distinctions between the old covenant and the new. See Kiwiet, *Pilgram Marbeck*, 93-94, 102-9; Klassen, *Covenant and Community*, 101-47, 156-64; *WPM*, 222-41, 556-59.

129 *Antwort*, 564-65, 569; see also *Later Writings by Marpeck*, 136.

130 Robert Friedmann, *Hutterite Studies* (Goshen, IN: Mennonite Historical Society, 1961), 151, 153-54.

131 Williams, *Radical Reformation*, 353; Packull, *Hutterite Beginnings*, 35-36.

132 Packull, *Hutterite Beginnings*, 98.

133 Friedmann, *Hutterite Studies*, 82.

134 Hutter's "Last Epistle" in ibid., 204.

135 Ulrich Stadler, "Cherished Instructions on Sin, Excommunication and the Community of Goods," in *SAW*, 276, 278.

136 Ibid., 278-79. George Williams saw in Stadler's statements echoes of statements made in the fifth letter of Clement of Rome or the writings of Cyprian. He further implies the possibility that Stadler learned of Clement's writing through Sebastian Franck's *Chronica*. This is highly unlikely given the limitations of Stadler's historical vision. See Williams' comments in the introduction to *Cherished Instructions* in *SAW*, 272-73.

137 Stadler, "Cherished Instructions," *SAW*, 282-83. See also, Stayer, *German Peasants' War and Anabaptist Community of Goods*, 155.

138 For the importance of Riedemann's eldership in the evolution of the Hutterite movement, see Robert Friedmann, "Second Generation Anabaptism as Illustrated by the Walpot Era of the Hutterites," *MQR* 44 (1970), 391. Friedmann's conclusions were seconded by George H. Williams, *Radical Reformation*, 637-38, 648 and recently confirmed by Andrea Chudaska, *Peter Riedemann: Konfessionsbildendes Täufertum im 16. Jahrhundert* (Gütersloh: Gütersloher Verlagshaus, 2003), esp. 273-330, 340-42, 364-66. James Stayer has highlighted the importance of Riedemann's leadership for the institutionalization of Hutterite teachings on the sword and on community of goods in *Anabaptists and the Sword*, 175 and his *German Peasants' War and Anabaptist Community of Goods*, 144.

139 Peter Ridemann, *Account of Our Religion, Doctrine and Faith Given by Peter Rideman of the Brothers Whom Men Call the Hutterians* (Rifton, NY: Plough Publishing House, 1970), 139-65.

140 Ibid., 68-69, 24-25, 149, 188-94.

141 Ibid., 94.

142 Ibid., 93-95.

143 Ibid., 80-81.

144 Ibid., 68-69.

145 Ibid., 90-91. On the shared features of Stadler's and Riedemann's defences of Hutterite community of goods, see Chudaska, 283-89.

146 Williams, *Radical Reformation*, 1076.

147 On *The Chronicle's* reliance on Franck, see my "'Yet from time to time there were men who protested against these evils': Anabaptism and Medieval Heresy," in Bruce Gordon, ed., *Protestant History and Identity in Sixteenth-Century Europe*, vol. 1: *The Medieval Inheritance* (Aldershot: Scolar Press, 1996), 134-35.

148 *Chronicle of the Hutterian Brethren*, 1.

149 Ibid., 29-31.

150 Ibid, 27.

151 Ibid., 31-35.

152 Ibid., 32-38. Peter Burschel has accurately noted Braimichael's reluctance to identify openly medieval heretics as the true church. However, his claim that the Hutterites saw the appearance of their community more in an eschatological than a restitutionist light overstates the extent to which Braitmichael saw the Hutterites breaking with the past. See "Zur Geschichtstheologie der Täufer," *ARG* 95 (2004): 132-55.

153 Friedmann, *Hutterite Studies*, 195-97, has suggested that this work betrays an "amazing" knowledge of church history and the history of Christian thought. On the authorship of this work, see Astrid von Schlachta, *Hutterische Konfesssion und Tradition (1578-1619). Etabliertes Leben zwischen Ordnung und Ambivalenz* (Mainz: Verlag Philipp von Zabern, 2003), 202.

154 For example, see *QGT* 12: 60-85 (baptism), 125-74 (Lord's Supper), 248-86 (sword), 303-17 (divorce).

155 Ibid., 116-22, 170-7, 288-89.

156 Stayer, *German Peasants' War and Anabaptist Community of Goods*, 155.

157 *QGT* 12: 177, 198-200 (= Kathleen Hasenberg, trans., "A Notable Hutterite Document: Concerning True Surrender and Christian Community of Goods," *MQR* 31 (1957), 26, 39-40)

158 *QGT* 12:184, 187-88, 200-03, 224-27 (= Hasenberg, 30, 32-33, 40-42, 54-56).

159 Ibid, 231-32, 234-38 (= Hassenberg, 59, 61-62). On this work's reliance on Franck, see Friedmann's comments in the introduction to Kathleen Hassenberg's translation of Article 3, Hassenberg, 24; Williams, *Radical Reformation*, 651-54 and Stayer, *German Peasants' War and Anabaptist Community of Goods*, 156.

160 This theme runs throughout article 4 of *The Great Article Book* on the sword, although it is stated most clearly and forcefully in points 43, 80 and 81 of that article. See *QGT* 12: 256, 281-83.

161 Ibid., 288-90.

162 Ibid., 68; see also 73-74.

163 Ibid., 103-4, 121-22.

164 Ibid., 134-36, 165-68, 170-71.

165 *CWMS*, 4.

166 Ibid., 189, 192, 361-62, 502, 581, 964. Cornelius Krahn has described the restitution of the apostolic church as one of Menno's primary concerns, see "Menno's Concept of the Church," in Cornelius J. Dyck, ed., *A Legacy of Faith: A Sixtieth Anniversary Tribute to Cornelius Krahn* (Newton, KS: Faith and Life Press, 1962), 19, 27, 29.

167 *CWMS*, 92, 502.

168 Ibid., 237-84, 287, 304, 570-71, 630, 775.

169 Ibid., 81, 304, 515, 517, 724, 962.

170 Ibid., 137, 248, 276, 279-80.

171 Ibid., 128, 276.

172 Ibid., 137, 248, 258-59, 279-80, 695.

173 Ibid., 278-79, 695.

174 Ibid., 775.

175 Ibid., 141, 271, 570-71, 630.

176 Ibid., 304, 515, 520-21, 571.

177 Ibid., 582-98. See also Hans Hillerbrand, "Anabaptism and History," *MQR* 45 (1971), 115.

178 *CWMS*, 65, 202, 232, 539, 544-45, 587-602, 732-44.

179 Ibid., 65, 151-52.

180 Ibid., 520.

181 Ibid., 175, 199, 219, 231-32, 525-26, 730, 758, 760-61.
182 Stayer, "Radical Reformation," 39.
183 *CWMS*, 202.
184 Ibid., 779-80.
185 Ibid., 743-44.
186 Ibid., 544-5, 595, 751, 755.
187 William Keeney, *The Development of Dutch Anabaptist Thought and Practice from 1539-1564* (Nieuwkoop: B. De Graaf, 1968), 175.
188 Dietrich Philips, "The Church of God," in *SAW*, 228-34 (= *WDP*, 351-58; Kolb, 369-76). Cf. Keeney, 176-77.
189 Philips, "Church of God," *SAW*, 242-48 (= *WDP*, 365-70; Kolb, 386-92); Keeney, 36, 177. A detailed discussion of the relationship between the symbolic history of the "church" in the Old Testament and its literal history in the New Testament is included in *On Spiritual Restitution*, Kolb, 321-63 (= *WDP*, 316-48).
190 Keeney, 147-48, *WDP*, 342-48 (= Kolb, 365-62).
191 *WDP*, 71, 83, 107, 175, 195, 218, 596-97, 608-9.
192 Ibid., 213-14, 336-37, 347, 373-74, 384-87, 390, 404-5, 423-24, 596, 609.
193 Keeney, 178. See *On Spiritual Restitution*, *WDP* 341-44 (= Kolb, 354-57).
194 *WDP*, 59, 135, 609.
195 Brad Gregory, *Salvation at Stake: Christian Martyrdom in Early Modern Europe* (Cambridge, MA: Harvard University Press, 1999), 228; idem., "Prescribing and Martyrdom: Menno's *Troestlijke Vermaning* and *Het Offer des Heeren*," *MQR* 71 (1997), 606-7.
196 Gregory, *Salvation at Stake*, 237, 240, 243.
197 Ibid., 241.
198 Ibid., 243.
199 Hillerbrand, "Anabaptism and History," 122.
200 Stayer, "Radical Reformation," pp. 273-74. For the circumstances surrounding the writing of *The Hutterite Chronicle*, see Dipple, "Anabaptism and Medieval Heresy," 135-37.

CHAPTER 5

THE SPIRITUALIST ALTERNATIVE

In an addendum affixed to his translation of *A Chronicle or Description of Turkey* (1530), Sebastian Franck referred to three newly arisen beliefs—the Lutheran, Zwinglian and Anabaptist—and then noted:

> [a] fourth is on the way, which will clear out of the way all outward preaching, ceremonies, sacraments, the ban and callings as unnecessary, and simply assemble an invisible, spiritual church in the unity of the Spirit and belief among all people, and will establish through the eternal, invisible word alone, [a church] ruled directly by God without any external means, from which the apostolic church departed shortly after [the time] of the apostles.[1]

Students of Franck's writings have described this statement as the birth announcement of a new Spiritualist church.[2] While the spiritualist character of the anticipated movement is clear, its identification as a church, and especially one modelled on the apostolic church, may strike us as odd. As an archetypical Spiritualist, Franck's vision of Christianity should have been fundamentally individualistic and nonhistorical, and yet, his translation of *A Chronicle or Description of Turkey* was intended to anticipate the appearance of his *Chronica*, a massive compendium of world history from creation to his own day.[3] Franck, then, challenges us to re-examine accepted notions about both the existence and nature of a distinct

Spiritualist movement in the Reformation, and the possible role of historical reflection in the thought of such a movement.

Walter Klaassen's identification of spiritualism as an underlying principle running through the Reformation has posed a serious challenge to the identification of a distinct Spiritualist movement in it. Yet, James Stayer's attempt to rehistoricize the categories we use in discussing the groups of the Radical Reformation continues to employ some of the important characteristics of Troeltsch's ideal types. If spiritualism and biblicism are not polar opposites, but instead different ends of a continuum as Klaassen argues, there remains the question of what to do with those thinkers at the spiritualist end of the continuum who played down the importance and value of all religious externals, including baptism. On this issue the present study takes as its point of departure Emmet McLaughlin's position that Spiritualism constitutes a distinct movement in the Reformation, and is not just a morphological category.[4]

McLaughlin's use of the term movement in this context assumes a different definition for that term than is often employed when it is applied to the more cohesive Anabaptist groups or the confessional churches. The individuals he identifies as members of the Spiritualist movement—Caspar Schwenckfeld, Sebastian Franck, Jakob Kautz, Johannes Bünderlin and Christian Entfelder—represent a wide variety of opinions on aspects of reform, although they are clustered around similar stances on the issues of the relationship between the Spirit and the letter, the intrinsic value of external religious observances and the nature of the visible church. In this sense the emphasis on the individualism of the Spiritualists is valid. However, as we saw above, this diversity of opinions did not preclude Franck from anticipating the appearance of a movement with sufficient cohesion to be labelled a church. Furthermore, the diversity of opinions among the Spiritualists has led some historians to further subdivide the type. For example, George H. Williams distinguished between revolutionary Spiritualists, represented by Müntzer, Karlstadt and the Zwickau Prophets; rationalist Spiritualists, identified with Franck; and Evangelical Spiritualists, associated with Schwenckfeld.[5] Heinold Fast retained the categories and characteristics of evangelical and rationalist Spiritualists, but rejected the category of revolutionary Spiritualism—for Müntzer, *et al.* he prefers the term *Schwärmer*. He also added the new category mystic Spiritualists which included individuals such as Paracelsus, Valentin Weigel and Jakob Böhme.[6] Among Walter Klaassen's criticisms of attempts to categorize Reformation radicals has been the reliance on sociological categories to distinguish between essentially theological positions.[7] This concern appears to have been addressed in Emmet McLaughlin's more recent attempts to distinguish between spiritualist traditions based on biblical and neo-Platonic assumptions. McLaughlin identifies Müntzer with a more strictly biblical tradition, Schwenckfeld with a sacramentalist Spiritualism with strong medieval roots but deriving ultimately from neo-Platonic assumptions, and Franck with a more radical neo-Platonic noetic Spiritualism.[8]

The present chapter focuses on statements about the history of the church made by two prominent Spiritualists: Caspar Schwenckfeld and Sebastian Franck. In particular, it addresses the question of whether we can identify a Spiritualist vision of history in the way that people often speak about an Anabaptist historical vision. Traditional assumptions about the nature of Reformation Spiritualism suggest that in comparison to the Anabaptists, the Spiritualists were relatively unconcerned with the details of the historical record. However, as we will see, both Schwenckfeld and Franck developed comprehensive historical visions to justify their theological and especially ecclesiological positions. Those visions contain both important similarities and significant differences. Characterizations of Schwenckfeld as an evangelical or a sacramentalist Spiritualist, and of Franck as a rationalist or a noetic Spiritualist, would suggest that the former would be the more historically minded of the two, and yet Franck holds the place of honour as the great chronicler of the early Radical Reformation. The apparent anomalies presented by the historical reflections of the Spiritualists challenge us to reflect further not only on our characterizations of Reformation radicals, but also on the role of historical reflection in Reformation thought.

CHAPTER 5

Caspar Schwenckfeld

Although Schwenckfeld's thought has been characterized in a variety of ways by different interpreters, there has been general agreement among them that he is the most institutionally oriented of the major Reformation Spiritualists. This is evident in George H. Williams' and Heinold Fast's characterization of him as an "Evangelical Spirtualist." According to this interpretation, Schwenckfeld belongs in a tradition deriving from patristic and medieval Christianity which emphasizes an experiential relationship with the Holy Spirit, and yet allows for the formation of fellowships for common study and prayer.[9] No less obvious is Schwenckfeld's traditionalism according to the characterization of his thought in the more theologically-oriented categories employed by Emmet McLaughlin. McLaughlin suggests that Schwenckfeld's Eucharistic theology, his emphasis on the clarity of Scripture for those enlightened by the Spirit, and the designation of his fellowships as schools of Christ place his thought between the poles of noetic and sacramental Spiritualism and make him the most Catholic of Reformation Spiritualists.[10] In the context of usual assumptions about Reformation Spiritualism and its perceptions of history, it would be natural to assume that of the Spiritualists Schwenckfeld would be most likely to take seriously the lessons of history, certainly more likely to do so than the more radically spiritualist Franck.

The full development of Schwenckfeld's Spiritualism was a gradual process identified by Schwenckfeld himself with three divine visitations in 1519, 1525 and 1529. The initial visitation apparently coincided with his identification with the reforming movement emanating from Wittenberg. Schwenckfeld was drawn especially to works of Luther which reflected the thought of late medieval mysticism. He identified himself with the Wittenberg reform until 1524 when his disenchantment with its inability to produce visible improvement in the lives of its adherents or in society generally led to a second visitation or conversion experience in 1525. Schwenckfeld's disillusionment and increasingly more radical spiritualism is evident in his call at that time for a suspension of the celebration of the Eucharist because it had become a source of division among Christians and failed to effect any improvement in the morals of those who partook of it. Schwenckfeld later dated his mature religious life from this second visitation. The worsening political situation in Silesia led to Schwenckfeld's voluntary exile from his homeland in April 1529, and with it his third visitation which led him to a thorough denigration of all externals in matters spiritual. In the wake of this experience and in the context of conflicts with a variety of religious reformers in his new home, Strasbourg, Schwenckfeld called for a suspension of the sacrament of baptism as well.[11]

According to Emmet McLaughlin's account of the evolution of Schwenckfeld's theology, his historical vision was recast in 1527.[12] Like so many Reformation Radicals, Schwenckfeld does not lay out a comprehensive vision of ecclesiastical history in one place. Rather, historical references are scattered throughout his writings in the context of different reforming suggestions and polemical utterances. Nonetheless, these scattered references yield a fairly consistent vision of ecclesiastical history and of the significance of the fall of the church in that vision.

It appears that Schwenckfeld saw in the flow of sacred history two distinct but complementary patterns. At times he refers to a cyclical process in which periods of ignorance are punctuated by moments of divine visitation and knowledge,[13] but these cycles occur within the context of a general progression toward greater spiritual awareness. Established shortly after creation, the church has been subject to the effects of both processes. A crucial stage in the increased spiritual awareness of humanity came with the Incarnation. In the Old Testament external faith, religion and worship were regulated by the law of Moses and when necessary enforced with the sword or physical punishment. However, since the coming of Christ the demands of the law have been fulfilled by the office of the Spirit, and the gospel of grace and true spiritual worship have replaced the external religion of the old covenant. However, the cycles of ignorance and revelation have intervened and the progress toward greater spiritual awareness has not been direct. After the apostolic age the papacy reimposed the legalistic measures of the Old Testament, and as a result the spiritual understanding of Scripture and the sacraments was lost.[14]

The role and place of the apostolic church in Schwenckfeld's reforming vision needs to be understood in the context of the historical patterns described above. His spiritualist definition of the true church would seem to undermine the validity of the apostolic church as a model for contemporary reforms. In response to the question of where the true church, with which Christ had promised to remain throughout the ages, has been for the preceding centuries if the visible church had fallen, Schwenckfeld responds by defining the true church as the elect throughout the ages, sometimes visible and sometimes not. In the latter case, however, the church is no less present—God is a spirit and so is His body. The true church is in no essential way tied to the external elements like the performance of the sacraments or preaching of the word. Christ can sustain the church in the Spirit alone as He has throughout the centuries when the visible church was dominated by the papacy.[15] Nonetheless, Schwenckfeld does allow that the "first" church, the visible church at the time of the apostles, was filled with the Spirit and its gifts to the degree that it can be identified with the true church. As a result, the apostolic church serves as a standard in Schwenckfeld's thought to criticize contemporary abuses in the church and as a model for reforms in the contemporary church. For example, on several occasions Schwenckfeld calls for a reform of the sacraments of baptism and the Lord's Supper so that they conform to those practised by the apostles and church fathers according to the ordinance of Christ.[16]

Schwenckfeld's appeal to the model of the pristine church implies that historically that church fell. Emmet McLaughlin suggests, I believe correctly, that Schwenckfeld never identified a specific date or event as the occasion of the church's fall. Rather, he defined that fall as a gradual loss of the church's spiritual understanding of Scripture and of the sacraments instituted in the apostolic church.[17] The perversion of the sacraments and loss of the true gospel message loom large in Schwenckfeld's assessment of ecclesiastical history and the fall of the apostolic church. Schwenckfeld regarded the increasing "creatureliness" of the sacraments, particularly the Eucharist, as a clear sign that under the papacy the church had fallen.[18] On several occasions he ties the perversion of the Lord's Supper into the contemporary mass, with its focus on the doctrine of transubstantiation, teaching about the real presence and adoration of the host, directly to a general fall of the church.[19] Parallel to the perversion of the Lord's Supper, Schwenckfeld regarded the introduction of pedobaptism as no less significant in obscuring the truth of the Gospel:

> I regard the baptism of infants to be the beginning of papistry and the foundation of all error and ignorance in the church of Christ, and, moreover, the destruction of all piety and ... the apostolic ministry. I am not able to think otherwise, with good conscience, until I shall have been better informed from the Scriptures.[20]

Behind the perversion of the sacraments, Schwenckfeld saw a more fundamental loss of spiritual truths and their replacement with human laws, resulting in the introduction of compulsion in matters of faith. As we have seen, although Schwenckfeld regarded an element of compulsion in religious matters as appropriate under the old law, it does not apply under the gospel. The reintroduction of compulsion in spiritual matters by the papacy led to a falling away from Christ and darkening of the light of the gospel.[21]

Despite the scattered nature of Schwenckfeld's historical references, he produces a fairly consistent vision of the church's history. On one occasion he appeals to Berengar of Tours' challenge to the teaching on transubstantiation in the eleventh century to argue for the novelty of the Roman teaching,[22] but much more common are references to the fall of the church much earlier in its history.

> And since almighty God, out of his boundless mercy, has in our days allowed a wonderful light to arise, by which we are able to see and recognize in what serious errors we were in past times, and how far we fell from His Word, from true worship and from the truth. And since that fall lasted so many hundreds of years, indeed we can say since shortly after the time of the apostles, and since it grew with so many errors, it is not possible that all things can be put right in such a short period of time and in the face of such resistance restored to the first apostolic order and to the fullness of the pure teaching.[23]

Schwenckfeld notes that already at the time of Paul the forces of disintegration were at work in the apostolic church, and gradually thereafter it was supplanted by the papal church. After the deaths of the apostles and servants of the Spirit, their offices were occupied by the ambitious and unworthy. The perversion of these offices led to the introduction of Jewish and heathen practices. This was a gradual process, and the faith and lives of the martyrs of the "first church" are a witness to the continued presence of the Spirit in it.[24] The final fall of the church appears not to have occurred until the end of the patristic age, likely around the end of the fourth and beginning of the fifth century. In one place he traces the beginnings of compulsion in the matters of faith to the time of Arius, possibly suggesting a critique of the Constantinian church.[25] However, if this is a critique of the Constantinian settlement, Schwenckfeld is not consistent in his identification of this event as the introduction of compulsion into matters of faith. A variation on the theme appears elsewhere when he identifies compelled consciences already in the third century, at the time of Tertullian, or even in the late second century as a result of the activities of the emperor Commodus and the "Roman Bishop" Victor.[26]

But Schwenckfeld's other criteria for identifying the fall of the church point again to the gradual nature of the process. He suggests that infant baptism did not become a common practice until later in the patristic age, arguing that church fathers like Jerome, Ambrose, Gregory Nazianzus and Augustine were baptized as adults despite the fact that they had

Christian parents. Furthermore, several of the church fathers manifested the presence of the Spirit by standing up for their beliefs even in the face of persecution and exile.[27] Furthermore, Schwenckfeld's citations of patristic authors suggest that until the end of the fourth or beginning of the fifth century the "first church" remained, in part at least, true to the teachings of the Spirit. Frequently he appeals to the authority of Ambrose, Augustine, Chrysostom, Cyprian, Cyril and Jerome in various combinations.[28] However, he also saw evidence of the church's decline in the writings of the fathers. He claimed that some of them did not fulfill their offices with the same zeal as was manifested by their predecessors. His observation that Augustine changed his position on the possibility of true sacraments existing outside of the church as a result of his confrontations with the Donatists indicates that the purity of the "first church's" teachings was in decline as well.[29]

Under the dominance of the papacy the true church was only a spiritual entity, and Schwenckfeld refused to identify an ongoing sectarian opposition to the persecuting church directly with the true church. He did suggest at one point that the late medieval mystics had separated themselves from the fallen church, but nowhere treated them as anything other than members of the invisible church.[30] However, contemporary events indicated to him that the renewed gospel was making its presence felt.[31] Through the activity of the Spirit the apostolic church would be restored. That church would be marked by unity, purity and the charismatic gifts of the Spirit. Preeminent among the gifts of the Spirit evident in the restored church would be the liberty suppressed by the papal church. In his confrontations with the Anabaptists in Strasbourg, Schwenckfeld increasingly emphasized the importance of the manifestation of the fruits of the Spirit in the restored apostolic church.[32] Nonetheless, the restored church would be a visible assembly modelled on the early church or the church of the fathers brought together by the activities of "... the Holy Spirit, who, it is clear, plans to erect a Christian church with the correct use of the sacraments, brotherly admonitions, ban, and consequent betterment of Christian living."[33]

CHAPTER 5

Sebastian Franck

Even more than Schwenckfeld, Sebastian Franck qualifies as the archetypical Reformation Spiritualist. In fact, it was in his 1892 biography of Franck that Alfred Hegler first coined the term "Spiritualist," and Hegler's subsequent research began the process of establishing connections between such prominent Reformation Spiritualists as Franck, Schwenckfeld, Michael Servetus, Hans Denck and Johannes Bünderlin.[34] The perceived existence of a distinct Spiritualist tradition within the Reformation derives in no small part from an awareness of the connections between Franck and Schwenckfeld. Likely the two men met for the first time in Strasbourg in 1531. Over much of the next decade they cooperated with each other in a variety of ways. However, possibly as early as 1534 and certainly by 1536, both men were aware that their paths were diverging. This parting of ways was indicative of fundamental theological differences, or as Emmet McLaughlin has so aptly noted "the two men simply did not breathe the same spirit."[35]

A number of explanations have been advanced for the different emphases in the spiritualism of Franck and Schwenckfeld, although one I believe deserving of more attention is the paths the two men followed on their Reformation journeys and the individuals they encountered along the way. Franck's early years as a Reformer parallel those of Schwenckfeld in important ways, but also diverge from them in other important areas. Like Schwenckfeld, Franck was initially drawn to the reforming movement emanating from Wittenberg. After studying in Ingolstadt and Heidelberg he had first served as a priest in the diocese of Augsburg. In 1525 or 1526 while serving as chaplain in the village of Büchenbach, he committed himself to the Wittenberg reform movement. In 1527 he moved to the village of Gustenfelden, where in 1528 he married Ottilia Behaim, possibly the sister of two of "the three Godless painters of Nuremberg." There has been no small amount of speculation about whether Franck was introduced to radical reforming ideas and circles through his wife and her connections. Also in 1528 Franck translated from

Latin into German Andreas Althamer's *Dialloge*, a detailed response by the Lutheran pastor to Hans Denck's *He Who Truly Loves the Truth*. In the autumn of that year Franck gave up his pastorate in Gustenfelden and moved to Nuremberg where he may have worked in the printing industry and certainly continued his literary activity. His translation of *A Chronicle or Description of Turkey* was published in Nuremberg and Franck began work on his *Chronica* there. The latter work was first published in Strasbourg in 1531 where Franck moved in 1530.[36]

An obvious difference between the reforming journeys of Schwenckfeld and Franck is the latter's connection to the traditions of the Saxon Radicals. Even his contemporaries drew parallels between Franck's thought and some of the radicals, especially Denck and his associate Ludwig Hätzer,[37] and it appears that such charges were not without a basis in fact. For example, Franck's descriptions of the teachings of Denck, Hätzer and even Thomas Müntzer in the *Chronica* indicate that he had much more than a passing acquaintance with their thought.[38] Not surprisingly, interpreters of Franck's writings have stressed the influence especially of Denck on his thought, in some cases going so far as to speculate that Franck may have met Denck during his days as a student at Ingolstadt.[39] The most obvious and definite source for Franck's introduction to Denck's thought was Althamer's *Dialloge*. Althamer may have commissioned Franck to translate this work, and Franck appears to have approached the task as a conscious member of the evangelical movement. The resulting translation has been characterized as an almost literal rendering of the Latin original, but Franck also appended his own foreword to the text and this has been the source of significant scholarly interest about the extent to which Franck's comments there remain within the bounds of Lutheran orthodoxy and the extent to which they anticipate his later, mature Spiritualist teachings. Most scholars agree that the translation and Denck's thought were an important catalyst for the development of Franck's Spiritualism.[40] Recently, the growing awareness of the connections between Müntzer and Denck has added substance to earlier observations of parallels between Franck's thought and Müntzer's.[41] If, as these observations suggest, Franck belongs in at least a loose tradition going back to Müntzer, this raises interesting questions about the development of that tradition and the place of historical visions in that development.

Usual assumptions about historical visions in the Reformation would lead one to assume that Franck's radical spiritualism would have led him to ignore history and historical references, but nothing could be further from the truth. Schwenckfeld's sketchy outline of ecclesiastical history contrasts sharply with the breadth and depth of Franck's vision. The clearest and fullest statement of that vision appears in the *Chronica*, and in that form it had its greatest impact on Franck's contemporaries and on posterity. The *Chronica* went through five printings in the year of its publication, 1531, and a total of 16 or 17 printings in German and seven printings in Dutch during the sixteenth century.[42] This work is actually composed of three distinct chronicles. The first covers the history of humanity from creation to the Incarnation. The second focuses on secular affairs from the Incarnation to the present day, organized as a history of emperors from Augustus to Charles V. The third deals with ecclesiastical history for the same period in eight distinct books: a history of the papacy from Peter to Clement VII; a history of ecclesiastical councils; an alphabetically arranged compendium of heretics from throughout the history of the Christian church; a chronicle of Roman orders or sects; a chronicle of temples, icons, the veneration of the saints, and the mass; a discussion of the origins of idolatry; a chronicle of papal infidelity and deceit against emperors and councils; and a chronicle of the Antichrist and last days.

The full title of the *Chronica, Zeitbuch oder Geschichtsbibel* already indicates the importance of historical reflection in the thought of Franck, and students of his writings have been almost unanimous in seeing a close connection between his historical reflection and his religious vision.[43] Franck's use of the term *Geschichtsbibel* betrays his view that the study of history is a valuable complement to the study of Scripture. In its introduction Franck elaborates on that value. The lessons of history, he argues, are a crucial corrective to the weakness of human faith.

> Because we rely so much on experience and do not believe, we hold history above all other books of teaching. For history lives, but teaching is a dead letter. Had Adam seen an example of his fall, and not just the teaching and command, he might still be in paradise. ... Therefore, no teaching may be so cleverly contrived, not even the commands of God Himself, as to change an evil heart. Yet experience, if we will learn from others, can help us to understand, for experience is a key to Scripture for both the child of the world and the blessed person.[44]

This is only one of many statements in which Franck emphasizes both the intellectual and spiritual value of the study of history.[45]

Several important assumptions underlie Franck's perception of the pedagogic value of history. His vision of sacred history is impressed by the belief that both divine and human natures are constant. As a result, the relationship between God and humanity remains fundamentally the same throughout history. In each age human interaction with the divine follows a pattern similar to all other ages. From this observation Franck draws the further conclusion that there is a direct correspondence between the history of the individual and universal history—the individual is a microcosm of both nature and history.[46]

Franck's application of these assumptions to the lessons of history appear reminiscent of Müntzer's use of the *ordo rerum*. The term *ordo rerum* appears nowhere in Franck's writings, but this does not preclude the possibility that he shared Müntzer's assumptions about the pedagogic value of history. James Stayer has noted that Ulrich Bubenheimer's description of the role of the *ordo rerum* in Müntzer's thought sounds remarkably like Werner Packull's description of Hans Hut's gospel of all creatures,[47] and parallels to Hut's gospel of all creatures are evident in Franck's writings. In the preface to the *Chronica*, he justifies his undertaking in the following terms:

> And so God will lead you, as He did Abraham, from one thing to the next, and [He] will preach with His work, through and in all creatures, so that the whole world and all creatures will become for you nothing other than an open book and living Bible, from which, without any instruction, you can study God's ways and learn His will.[48]

I believe that Franck is here formulating in less technical terms a hermeneutical principle similar to Müntzer's. Furthermore, I am convinced that this principle lies at the root of Franck's historical investigations. This fact is evident in two of his earliest and best known works: the *Chronica* and his survey of world geography published in Tübingen in 1534, the *World Book*. Taken together, these two works look suspiciously like an attempt to read history and nature through the lens of the *ordo rerum*, and it seems that Franck intended them to be a unified work. In the conclusion to *A Chronicle or Description of Turkey*, he points his readers to his forthcoming compendium of world history, the scope of which appears to encompass both the *Chronica* and the *World Book*.[49] Several interpreters of Franck's writings have noted these comments and suggested that the *Weltbuch* comprises a missing, fourth chronicle of the *Chronica*.[50]

Particularly valuable for understanding Franck's vision of the fall of the church is the third part of the third chronicle in the *Chronica*, *The Chronicle of Roman Heretics*.[51] It amounts to a slight reworking of an earlier *Catalogue of Heretics* by the Dominican Bernard of Luxembourg, but Franck's new spin on this material yields drastically different conclusions than those contained in the original catalogue. In the preface to this work, Franck warns his readers that the title is meant ironically. Those included in the register are not necessarily heretics according to Franck's criteria, but have been judged so by the Roman Church. In fact, many of them might be more justly honoured as saints.[52] Nonetheless, as Christoph De Jung has noted, the portrayal of individuals and groups in *The Chronicle of Roman Heretics* amounts to more than a simple reversal of appraisals.[53] In other words, those included as heretics are not automatically to be counted as members of the true, invisible church. Rather, Franck's purpose is to highlight the fallacy of all existing organized churches through a critique of their mutual exclusivity and denunciations. To understand Franck's intentions in this work, we need to look at his definition of heresy.

At the conclusion of his register of heretics, Franck launches into a definition of heresy and then musters an array of opinions against the persecution of the heretics. Developing an etymological analysis of the Greek root of the term "heresy," Franck defines it primarily as separatism or sectarianism. It applies first and foremost to those who rend Christian unity under the guise of, and with the help of, an idiosyncratic reading of the Gospel.[54] Franck's frequent denunciations of sectarianism throughout the text of *The Chronicle of Roman Heretics*, and in many of his other works, indicate the sincerity of this definition.[55] Equally important for our purposes is Franck's identification of the root of all sectarianism in biblical literalism and the consequent obsession with ceremonies and the externals of religion. Already in the preface to the third chronicle of the *Chronica*, in which *The Chronicle of Roman Heretics* is contained, Franck makes this point clearly,[56] and in his definition of heresy he reiterates it even more forcefully, directly contrasting sectarian, outward divisions with the true, spiritual church which is unified:

> [Heretic] means not an external enemy, but a Judas among the Apostles, a secret foe in the house of God, a wolf among the sheep and flock of Christ, who wishes to be called brother, and yet tears asunder the spiritual unity of the church, and establishes his own direction. In summary, under the name and title of Christ and the Gospel he believes and teaches against Christ and the Gospel, and develops his own following which then becomes a special church, a sect, an alternate way, a separate teaching. And these are especially those who, with their own ceremonies, bind the invisible, spiritual gifts of God to external elemental things of this world, whether of time, person, ceremonies, orders, and do not allow the spiritual assembly to remain free in the Spirit, and bound alone to God's invisible Word.[57]

This definition of heresy, when combined with Franck's heralding of the birth of the Spiritualist church with which this chapter opened, indicates clearly his place among the Spiritualist reformers of the Reformation. It also highlights the importance of historical arguments in establishing the legitimacy and necessity of the new Spiritualist church. By highlighting the exclusion and persecution of so-called heretics throughout Christian history, Franck is able to undermine the legitimacy of all existing dogmatic "churches." This agenda lies behind Franck's discussion of the fall of the church.

A crucial component in that discussion is the relationship between the invisible, spiritual church and the visible apostolic church. As we have seen, Schwenckfeld regarded the apostolic church as a brief, visible manifestation of the true church. Franck allows that the apostolic church is to be identified with the true church, but in contrast to Schwenckfeld he insists that the true church became visible during the apostolic age as a concession to human weakness. Outward signs, like the sacraments, he regards as concessions to the church in its infancy, like the gift of a doll to a child.[58] These assumptions had important implications for Franck's assessment of both the fall and the possibility of restitution of the visible church.

In a number of his writings Franck states clearly that the visible church fell immediately after the age of the apostles; in the letter to John Campanus he explicitly juxtaposes his opinion with that of some of his contemporaries, presumably the Anabaptists, who held to a Constantinian fall of the church. After the age of the apostles the Antichrist adapted for his own purposes the outward ceremonies instituted by Christ: baptism became infant baptism and the Lord's Supper was turned into the mass.[59] However, like Schwenckfeld, Franck believed that the fall of the visible church included as well a process of decline. For the first three hundred years of its history, the visible church remained relatively pure, at least when compared with its subsequent history.[60] In both his letter to Campanus and the variety of individual chronicles making up the third chronicle of his *Chronica* Franck identifies a number of events contributing to that decline. These suggest that the process began with the perversion of true teachings. Franck indicates in the *Chronica* that all councils after the first apostolic council described in Acts 15 have served only to circumscribe the freedom of the Spirit and substitute for it renewed Mosaic legalism. He warns Campanus that even the teachings of the church fathers, among whom he includes Clement, Irenaeus, Tertullian, Cyprian, Chrysostom, Hilary, Cyril and Origen, have perverted the truth of the Spirit.[61]

A crucial component in the church's decline was the rise of the papal Antichrist, its alliance with secular authority and imposition of compulsion in matters of faith. Franck appears at times to be undecided about the significance of the establishment of the Constantinian church in this process. As noted above, in the Campanus letter he challenged the opinion of others who identified the fall of the church with Constantine's conversion. In the *Chronica* he responds to the claim that Pope Sylvester was the first Antichrist by suggesting that this pope's predecessors were no better than he was. But elsewhere in the same work he suggests that the alliance between the pope and emperor marked an important stage in the Devil's control of both the papacy and the church.[62] In the end, the establishment of the Constantinian church remained only one element in the larger process of decline. For example, when concentrating specifically on the perversion of the mass, Franck focused on the reigns of the emperors Arcadius (395-408) and Honorius (395-423) as the time when apostolic practices were perverted and the church desolated,[63] and the freedom of the Spirit was further restricted by the growth of papal power especially during the pontificates of Gregory the Great and Leo III.[64]

The Chronicle of the Roman Heretics provided Franck with the perfect opportunity to identify an alternate ecclesiology focused on an ongoing tradition of sectarian opposition to the false, papal church, but his radical spiritualism precluded Franck from taking that step. As has been noted, Franck's adoption of the Roman definition and identification of heresy and heretics was meant ironically, but that in no way means that he accepted those heretics as the true church. Heresy played an important dialectical role in Franck's vision of history; its regular challenge to prevailing opinion served to undermine the enshrining of orthodoxy in Christian teachings.[65] But identifying the heretics through the ages with the true church ran the risk of enshrining their teachings and practices as an alternative orthodoxy. In the end Franck stood against all "sects," and the radical spiritualism behind this position led him to a very different opinion about the restitution of the apostolic church than that held by Schwenckfeld. In the letter to Campanus, he insisted that without a special divine mandate the visible church could not be restored:

> To be brief, my dear brother Campanus, that I may say it in summary fashion and openly and be understood by thee, I maintain against all ecclesiastical authorities that all outward things and ceremonies, which were customary in the church of the apostles, have been done away with and are not to be reinstituted, although many without authorization or calling undertake to restore on their own the degenerated sacraments.[66]

Franck's writings, then, bring together a comprehensive vision of ecclesiastical history and a clear-cut spiritualist definition of the church. Clearly, these two aspects of his thought are closely related. However, the connections between them may be even more extensive than first appears. In fact, Franck's vision of the Spiritualist church likely developed in tandem with his engagement with history. Horst Weigelt has argued convincingly that Franck's disaffection from the Lutheran Reformation developed in three stages: at first he criticized Luther's soteriology, then he attacked the ecclesiology of the magisterial Reformers, and finally he repudiated the basis of their entire enterprise by undermining their *sola scriptura* emphasis with his full blown Spiritualist teaching on the inner word. Although there are not clear cut chronological divisions between Franck's points of criticism, Weigelt argues that different perspectives dominate at different times.[67] Within this scheme, Franck's criticism of the Reformers' ecclesiology becomes prominent in 1530 or 1531 and it first comes to the fore in the letter to Campanus and the *Chronica*.[68] In other words, the important transition from Franck's criticism of the

Reformation's soteriology to his criticism of its ecclesiology, a cornerstone of his spiritualism, occurred at precisely the time he was most fully immersed in the study of history.

In early 1529 Franck wrote a short poem or song entitled "On the Four Divided Churches."[69] In this work, he states clearly his unwillingness to join any of the existing "sects" within western Christendom: the Catholic, Lutheran, Reformed or Anabaptist.[70] He then goes on to reject the claims of all of the above "sects" and warns anyone who wants to follow Christ to flee all of them. In the *Chronicle or Description of Turkey*, published the following year, his position is more clearly defined and the themes of the letter to Campanus and the *Chronica* are laid out in embryonic form. His translation and additions to the existing text highlight the theme of the divisions within Christianity so central to the Campanus letter and especially *The Chronicle of Roman Heretics*.[71] He concludes his addendum to this work with his announcement of the birth of the Spiritualist church.[72] We see here in an embryonic form the central themes of the Campanus letter and *Chronica*. Philip Kintner has described *The Chronicle or Description of Turkey* as the announcement of a new Spiritualist church, for which the *Chronica* and Franck's subsequent *World Book* were the major apologetic treatises. Franck's subsequent works were, then, an attempt to define an "undogmatic theology" for the new Spiritualist church.[73]

Conclusion

The close integration of historical reflection and developing spiritualism in the thought of Sebastian Franck challenges a simple characterization of the Spiritualists as nonhistorical. Although historical reflection does not play nearly as prominent a role in the thought of Schwenckfeld, he too relies on historical evidence and argumentation at crucial junctures in his thought. In fact, the historical visions of these two Spiritualists share important elements. Both men date the fall of the church to shortly after the deaths of the apostles, but see the effects of that fall worked out in a process of gradual decline. They both also emphasize the importance of doctrinal orthodoxy, with a consequent loss of the freedom of the Spirit, and the increasing "creatureliness" evidenced by the growth of ceremonialism within the church as crucial elements in its decline. Furthermore, their spiritualist assumptions kept both men from identifying heretical opposition to the medieval church as an alternate tradition of apostolic succession, despite Franck's concern with the history of those heretical traditions. On the basis of these similarities, we can identify a distinctive Spiritualist historical vision. And yet, there are important differences between the historical visions of Franck and Schwenckfeld. Franck's more radical spiritualism led him to qualify the identification of the apostolic church with the true spiritual church and, therefore, to reject the possibility or desirability of its restitution. He also identified a more abrupt decline of the visible church and with it a more thorough rejection of ecclesiastical tradition, as evidenced especially in his treatment of the church fathers in the Campanus letter. Just as the Spiritualists held to no entirely consistent theology, so their perceptions of the history of the church were not uniform, but, as we have noted with other Reformers of the sixteenth century, historical reflection was an important element in their reforming thought.

According to the assumptions of Ernst Troeltsch and subsequent interpreters of Reformation Spiritualism, the Evangelical or Sacramental Spiritualist Schwenckfeld should have shown the greater interest in history and tradition. Indeed, more of the church's traditions and teachings retained validity for him than they did for Franck. However, as we have seen, while rejecting many of those traditions, Franck devoted more time and effort to investigating the historical record than did Schwenckfeld and the lessons of history played a much more prominent role in his thought than they did in Schwenckfeld's. Franck, not Schwenckfeld or even the Anabaptists, became the chronicler of the early Radical Reformation. These observations indicate, I believe, that we need to rethink how we apply the term "nonhistorical" to the Spiritualists, and with that term the place of historical reflection in their thought. The Spiritualists were nonhistorical to varying degrees insofar as they rejected the continued validity of teachings, traditions and practices of the church's past. In this sense Franck was "more nonhistorical" than Schwenckfeld, and certainly more so than the Anabaptists. His deep interest in history and the lessons it teaches, then, came from another source than the desire to restore the apostolic church. Ultimately, the pervasiveness and force of historical arguments in the sixteenth century meant that those who rejected ecclesiastical traditions, possibly even more than those who endorsed them, were forced to confront the record of the past. In many ways, the burden of proof was on their shoulders. In the case of Franck, that onus was reinforced by an intellectual tradition, likely going back to Thomas Müntzer, which saw in the lessons of history an important locus of divine revelation. To untangle that tradition we need to turn to the so-called Spiritualizing Anabaptists.

Notes

1 Franck, *Werke* I: 304.

2 Phillip Kintner, "Studies in the Historical Writings of Sebastian Franck (1499-1542)," (PhD diss., Yale, 1957), 44.

3 According to Phillip Kintner, if the *Chronicle or Description of Turkey* announced the birth of the new Spiritualist church, the *Chronica* and another treatise, the *World Book*, were intended as its major apologetic treatises. See Kintner, "Historical Studies of Franck," 44 and my "Sebastian Franck in Strasbourg," *MQR* 73 (1999): 796-97.

4 R. Emmet McLaughlin, "Schwenckfeld and the Strasbourg Radicals," *MQR* 59 (1985), 278.

5 *SAW*, 31-35. More recently Williams reworked his categories: evangelical or conventical spiritualists (Schwenckfelders), conformist spiritualists (Nicodemites, Epicureans) and prophetic or revolutionary spiritualists. See *Radical Reformation*, 3rd ed. (Kirksville, MO: Sixteenth Century Journal Publishers, 1992), 1298.

6 Heinold Fast, ed. *Der linke Flügel der Reformation: Glaubenszeugnisse der Täufer, Spiritualisten, Schwärmer und Antitrinitarier* (Bremen: Carl Schünemann Verlag, 1962), xxii-xxxi.

7 Walter Klaassen, "Spiritualization in the Reformation," *MQR* 37 (1963), 69.

8 R. Emmet Mclaughlin, "Spiritualismus," in *TRE* 31:702-4; idem., "Reformation Spiritualism: Typology, Sources and Significance," (Typescript), 13-17.

9 *SAW*, 34-35; Fast, *Linke Flügel der Reformation*, xxvi.

10 McLaughlin, "Spiritualismus," 703-4; idem., "Reformation Spiritualism," 15.

11 R. Emmet McLaughlin, *Caspar Schwenckfeld, Reluctant Radical: His Life to 1540* (New Haven and London: Yale University Press, 1986), 14, 39-56, 106, 136-37; idem., "Reformation Spiritualism," 14-15; Williams, *Radical Reformation*, 201-11.

12 McLaughlin, *Reluctant Radical*, 107-8.

13 *CS* III, 659; McLaughlin, *Reluctant Radical*, 139-40.

14 *CS* II, 500-1, 640; *CS* III, 870-71; Williams, *Radical Reformation*, 1268; McLaughlin, *Reluctant Radical*, 107-9, 143. Cf. Karl Ecke, *Schwenckfeld, Luther und der Gedanke einer apostolischen Reformation* (Berlin: Martin Warneck, 1911), 157-59.

15 *CS* III, 657-59, 901-10. On the relationship between the visible, apostolic church and the invisible, spiritual church in Schwenckfeld's thought, see Ecke, 108-13, 154 and Gottfried Maron, *Individualismus und Gemeinschaft bei Caspar von Schwenckfeldt: Seine Theologie, dargestellt mit besonderer Ausrichtung auf seinen Kirchenbegriff* (Stuttgart: Evangelisches Verlagswerk, 1961), 116-38.

16 *CS* III, 814, 821.

17 McLaughlin, *Reluctant Radical*, 107-8.

18 Maron, *Individualismus und Gemeinschaft bei Caspar von Schwenckfeld*, 98-99.

19 *CS* II, 325-33, 501, 640; *CS* III, 649-52; cf. McLaughlin, *Reluctant Radical*, 74-76, 107-8.

20 Quoted in Paul L. Maier, *Caspar Schwenckfeld on the Person and Work of Christ: A Study of Scwenckfeldian Theology at its Core* (Assen: Van Gorcum, 1959), 23; *CS* III, 820-23, 858.

21 *CS* III, 870, 872-73; cf. III, 650.

22 Ibid., 652, 654.

23 Ibid., 863.

24 Ecke, 157-58.

25 *CS* IV, 756. McLaughlin, *Reluctant Radical*, 143, treats this as a reference to the establishment of the Constantinian church. Ecke, 158-59, also emphasizes the importance of this event in the fall of the apostolic church for Schwenckfeld.

26 *CS* IV, 190.

27 Ecke, 133, 158.

28 *CS* III, 863-63, 919-23; *CS* IV, 182, 193-95.

29 *CS* IV, 192; Ecke, 158.

30 *CS* IV, 199; Maron, *Individualismus und Gemeinschaft bei Caspar von Schwenckfeld*, 110, 122-24; Ecke, 159.

31 *CS* III, 864.

32 *CS* III, 825; *CS* IV, 204-5; Williams, *Radical Reformation*, 209; Maier, 29. On the importance of liberty among the gifts of the Spirit, see Maron, *Individualismus und Gemeinschaft bei Caspar von Schwenckfeld*, 133-35.

33 Quoted in McLaughlin, *Reluctant Radical*, 109; *CS* III, 103. Cf. McLaughlin, *Reluctant Radical*, 138-39.

34 Alfred Hegler, *Geist und Schrift bei Sebastian Franck: eine Studie zur Geschichte des Spiritualismus in der Reformationszeit* (Freiburg: J.C.B. Mohr, 1892), v and 21. On Hegler's place in the definition of the Spiritualist type among Reformation radicals, see Kintner, "Historical Studies of Franck," 234-44; A.G. Dickens and John Tonkin, *The Reformation in Historical Thought* (Oxford: Basil Blackwell, 1985), 216 and Williams, *Radical Reformation*, 394.

35 R. Emmet McLaughlin, "Sebastian Franck and Caspar Schwenckfeld: Two Spiritualist Viae," in Jan-Dirk Müller, ed., *Sebastian Franck (1499-1542)* (Wiesbaden: Harrasowitz Verlag, 1993), 71-86, especially 71-72.

36 The most thorough English summary of Franck's life during these years is Patrick Hayden-Roy, *The Inner Word and Outer World: A Biography of Sebastian Franck* (New York: Peter Lang, 1994), 3-42.

37 This observation was made most forcefully in 1535 by the Ulm pastor Martin Frecht during one of his campaigns to have Franck expelled from the city. See Will-Erich Peuckert, *Sebastian Franck: Ein Deutscher Sucher* (Munich: R. Piper & Co., 1943), 284-85; Siegfried Wollgast, *Der deutsche Pantheismus im 16. Jahrhundert. Sebastian Franck und seine Wirkungen auf die Entwicklung der pantheistischen Philosophie in Deutschland* (Berlin: VEB, 1972), 95-96.

38 *Chronica*, clviii(b)-clx(b), clxiiii-clxv, clxvii(b)-clxxxix(b); Wollgast, *Deutsche Pantheismus*, 113-20; idem, "Zu Sebastian Francks philosophischen Auffassungen," *Daphnis: Zeitschrift für Mittlere Deutsche Literatur* 25 (2-3) (1996), 221-28, 230-31.

39 Already Ernst Troeltsch, *The Social Teachings of the Christian Churches* (London: George Allen and Unwin, 1931), II:768-69, identified Denck as an important influence on Franck's thought and that conclusion continues through to the most recent interpretations, for example Hayden-Roy, *Inner Word and Outer World*, 30-36.

40 For example, see Hegler, *Geist und Schrift*, 28-48; Eberhard Teufel *"Landräumig." Sebastian Franck, ein Wanderer an Donau, Rhein und Neckar* (Neustadt an der Aisch: Verlag Degener & Co., 1954), 24-27; Christoph DeJung, *Wahrheit und Häresie: Eine Untersuchung zur Geschichtsphilosophie bei Sebastian Franck* (Zurich: Samisdat, 1980), 105-8; Hayden-Roy, *Inner Word and Outer World*, 11-17.

41 Wollgast, "Francks philosophischen Auffassungen," 225-31.

42 Philip Kintner, "Sebastian Franck and the Problem of History," (typescript of paper presented at the Sixteenth Century Studies Conference, Toronto, ON, October, 1994), 4 lists 17 German printings while Williams, *Radical Reformation*, 396, lists 16.

43 The groundwork for this interpretation was laid at the outset of modern Franck studies, see Hegler, *Geist und Schrift*, 243-44 and Troeltsch, *Social Teachings of the Christian Churches*, II, 761.

44 *Chronica*, av-av(b).

45 For a summary of Franck's position on the spiritual relevance of historical study, see Peuckert, 105-6; Kintner, "Historical Writings of Franck," 45-64; Steven Ozment, *Mysticism and Dissent: Religious Ideology and Social Protest in the Sixteenth Century* (New Haven and London: Yale University Press, 1973), 148-49.

46 Kintner, "Historical Writings of Franck," 45-64, 175-83.

47 James M. Stayer, "Theologians of Revolution in the Peasants' War? The Cases of Balthasar Hubmaier and Thomas Müntzer," (typescript), 9. On Hut's gospel of all creatures, see Werner O. Packull, *Mysticism and the Early South German-Austrian Anabaptist Movement 1525-1531* (Scottdale, PA and Kitchener, ON: Herald Press, 1977), 67-74.

48 *Chronica*, aiiii(b)

49 Franck, *Werke*, I, 326-27.

50 Kintner, "Historical Writings of Franck," 34-35; Peuckert, *Franck*, 153-55; Hayden-Roy, *Inner Word and Outer World*, 108-9.

51 Williams, *Radical Reformation*, 396-97, calls this the most original and valuable portion of the *Chronica*.

52 *Chronica*, lxxxi(v) - lxxxii. See also Kintner, "Franck and the Problem of History," 6.

53 De Jung, *Wahrheit und Häresie*, 32. Hayden-Roy, *Inner Word and Outer World*, 85-86 seconds DeJung's judgement on this point.

54 *Chronica*, cci(v) - ccii. Hayden-Roy, *Inner Word and Outer World*, p. 70, has noted the significance of this definition, describing the theme of the divisions in Christianity as the most urgent in the *Chronica*.

55 For example, Franck states in his article on the Antichrist that all sects belong to the Antichrist, in *Chronica*, xcii. Elsewhere he claims that God is against all sects, ibid., cxciii(v).

56 Ibid., iii - iiii. See DeJung, *Wahrheit und Häresie*, 19, on the significance of the prefaces in Franck's works for recovering his own voice.

57 *Chronica*, cci(v).

58 *SAW*, 149-50 (= *QGT* 7 (1): 304-5). Kintner, "Historical Writings of Franck," 183-210, provides a detailed discussion of the relationship between the spiritual church and the apostolic church in Franck's thought.

59 Franck makes these claims most clearly and forcefully in the letter to Campanus, see *SAW*, 148-52 (= *QGT* 7(1): 302-9). However, he also alludes to problems in the apostolic and post-apostolic church in the *Chronica*, for example xvi(b), lxiiii, ccliiii-ccliiii(b).

60 *Chronica*, ccliiii-ccliiii(b); Kintner, "Historical Writings of Franck," 208-9, 213.

61 *Chronica*, lxii(b)-lxiii; *SAW*, 148-52 (= *QGT* 7(1): 302-9).

62 *Chronica*, xxiii(b)-xxiiii; ccliiii(b).

63 Ibid., ccxliiii(b)-ccxlv(b).

64 Ibid., ccxlvi(b)-ccxlvii(b). cclv(b), [ccv-ccv(b)— Kaiserchronik]

65 Kintner, "Historical Writings of Franck," 225-26; Hayden-Roy, *Inner Word and Outer World*, 85-86.

66 *SAW*, p. 150 (= *TAE* I: 306).

67 Horst Weigelt, *Sebastian Franck und die lutherische Reformation* (Gütersloh: Gerd Mohn, 1972), 20, 34, and "Sebastian Franck und die lutherische Reformation. Die Reformation im Spiegel des Werkes Sebastian Francks," in Müller, ed., *Sebastian Franck*, 41.

68 Weigelt, *Reformation*, 20 and 34 suggests that this process begins as early as 1529 in *The Chronicle or Description of Turkey*. However, in "Spiegel," 42 he emphasizes instead 1531 and the *Chronica*.

69 Peuckert, *Franck*, 99.

70 Ibid., 100.

71 *Franck Werke*, I: 288-90, 298-300.

72 Ibid., 304.

73 Kintner, "Historical Writings of Franck," 44.

CHAPTER 6

VARIATIONS ON AN ANABAPTIST THEME

Just as in the time of the physical captivity the physical and yet spiritual Israelites, [who lived] without priests, offerings, a temple or ceremonies, remained blameless in the sight of God, so I have no doubt that the good Father keeps even to this day in many places and corners of the earth many of his children, [just like] the seven thousand men who would not kneel to Baal...

Christian Entfelder, *Von den mannigfaltigen Zerspaltungen*[1]

While we can speak of both Anabaptist and Spiritualist historical visions developing during the Reformation, among neither group were these visions uniform. Different elements of these two movements emphasized different aspects of their common heritage. Especially among the Anabaptists, the development of a consistent, shared interpretation of the Christian past emerged only gradually. In the cases of both the Anabaptists and Spiritualists, historical visions were less the engines of reforming agendas, in the sense that they dictated clear-cut outlines of reform to be undertaken, than they were outgrowths of those agendas. Only as reform-minded individuals sought to define for themselves the nature of the true church, and to convince others of the accuracy of their vision, did they flesh out the details of its historical past.

As we have also seen, the process involved in formulating historical visions in the Radical Reformation calls into question some of the basic assumptions about how Anabaptists and Spiritualists related to the past and to religious tradition. Matters are further complicated if we look at individuals and groups who do not fit neatly into the traditional categories of the Radical Reformation. Here we will focus on two such traditions: the Spiritualist Anabaptists, sometimes also referred to as Spiritualizing Anabaptists or Spiritualizers, and elements of the Melchiorite Anabaptist movement. The Spiritualizers manifest characteristics often associated with both Spiritualists and Anabaptists. In his attempt to rehistoricize the Radical Reformation, James Stayer has characterized them as Saxon-style Spiritualists who became immersed in the Anabaptist movement as the result of a "constructive misunderstanding" and gradually disentangled themselves from it as they realized the extent and nature of that misunderstanding.[2] The central piece of this process occurred in Strasbourg in the early 1530s. Conflicts among religious reformers in Strasbourg were a strong impetus to the elaboration of historical visions not only by the Spiritualizers, but also by Spiritualists and Anabaptists. In addition, these events provide the context for the formulation of Melchior Hoffman's mature theology. Hoffman's thought, and that of his spiritual heirs, has been characterized as an unsteady amalgam of Anabaptism and Spiritualism.[3] Included in that mix was a comprehensive historical vision which was closely integrated with Hoffman's apocalypticism. The tensions between these aspects of Hoffman's thought were such that they could play out as both the Old Testament literalism of Anabaptist Münster and the radical Spiritualism of Obbe Philips and David Joris.

The Spiritualizers

Historians have come to no clear agreement on who qualifies as a Spiritualist Anabaptist and what criteria should be used to determine inclusion in that category. A more restrictive definition identifies this term with a group of reform-minded individuals who are assumed to have close intellectual, if not personal, ties to each other. All of these individuals were at some point involved with the Anabaptist movement, but all ended their lives as committed Spiritualists. Included in this group are Hans Denck, Ludwig Hätzer, Jacob Kautz, Johannes Bünderlin and Christian Entfelder. A broader definition of the term allows one to expand this list considerably and to include on it such prominent Melchiorite Anabaptists as Obbe Philips and David Joris. Without intending to weigh in on the issue of who should be included among the Spiritualist Anabaptists, the present study will treat Obbe Philips and Joris as part of the Melchiorite tradition. Denck, Hätzer, Kautz, Bünderlin and Entfelder will be treated as a group and referred to as Spiritualizers. The term Spiritualist Anabaptists will be used more broadly to designate those who straddled the line between Spiritualism and Anabaptism. Recent scholarship on the thought of the Spiritualizers tends to see in their thought and reforming activity the gradual evolution of a more radical and clearly-defined Spiritualism.[4] Interestingly, this process seems to have involved as well the elaboration of a much more comprehensive and detailed vision of salvation history. The thought of the Spiritualizers, then, further challenges us to rethink our assumptions about the connections between historical thinking and various groups in the Radical Reformation.

Although they never formed a tightly knit, cohesive organization like that of the Swiss Brethren, the lives of these men intersected at several crucial points during their reforming careers. At the centre of the group looms the figure of Hans Denck. In Nuremberg, and possibly subsequently in Mühlhausen, he imbibed the ideas of Müntzer and Karlstadt, and then encountered early Anabaptism in a visit to Switzerland in 1525.[5] Denck, then, seems to embody the "constructive misunderstanding" which James

Stayer has identified as the basis of the Spiritualist Anabaptist phenomenon. While in Augsburg between September 1525 and October 1526, he baptized Hans Hut, and likely also Bünderlin. Assumptions that Denck also met Hätzer in Augsburg, possibly taking over from him leadership of an Anabaptist conventicle there, now seem untenable. Denck's writings from this time and his choice of Pentecost as the date for Hut's baptism suggest that his activities had more to do with the thought of Müntzer and Karlstadt than with that of the Swiss Anabaptists.[6]

From Augsburg Denck went to Strasbourg where he certainly crossed paths with Hätzer. The very different experiences the two men had in the city—Hätzer enjoyed the hospitality of the Strasbourg Reformer Wolfgang Capito while Denck was regarded as a "sly hypocrite" by the Strasbourg pastors — reinforces suspicions that they had not met in Augsburg and that they first became acquainted in Strasbourg.[7] By early 1527 Denck and Hätzer were working closely together in Worms where they won over two of the local preachers, Jacob Kautz and Hilarius, to their reforming vision. While Denck and Hätzer devoted themselves to a new translation from Hebrew of the Old Testament books of the prophets, Kautz looked to practical aspects of reform. On the Friday before Pentecost, Kautz posted *7 Articles* on the door of the Dominican church in Worms. These were intended as the basis for a disputation with the city's Lutheran pastors. The pastors refused the challenge and on 1 July Kautz and Hilarius were expelled from the city.[8] Denck and Hätzer left Worms around the same time. They may have travelled together to Augsburg where Denck participated in the Martyrs' Synod. Although they were fortunate enough to elude capture in the wake of that meeting, both men perished shortly thereafter, Denck from the plague in Basel in 1527 and Hätzer by the executioner's axe in Constance in 1529.

Kautz, meanwhile, had moved on to Strasbourg where he was soon jailed together with the more sectarian Anabaptist Wilhelm Reublin and eventually banished from the city,[9] but his role as a spiritualizing force in the imperial city was quickly adopted by Bünderlin and Entfelder, both of whom arrived in 1529. Although historians usually group Bünderlin and Entfelder together, like Hätzer and Denck before them, they had remarkably different experiences in Strasbourg. Bünderlin was expelled almost immediately, but not before leaving behind three lengthy tracts with the Strasbourg printers. Entfelder was able to stay on in the city, likely until 1533.[10]

Hans Denck has long been regarded as both a pivotal and an enigmatic figure in the annals of Reformation radicalism. Most treatments of his career bracket his reforming activity with two common bookends: his baptism of Hans Hut in Augsburg in 1526 and his so-called "recantation," more aptly titled *Protestation and Confession*, written shortly before his death. Not surprisingly, Denck has been seen as leaving an ambiguous legacy. He can be justifiably claimed as both the father of south German/Austrian Anabaptism, and also as a crucial member of the early Spiritualist movement.[11] In a 1527 letter to Oecolampadius requesting refuge in Basel Denck asserted: "I disagree greatly with those, whoever they might be, who excessively bind the Kingdom of God with ceremonies and elements of this world, although I cannot deny that I had adhered to things of this kind for some time."[12] Debate continues over the extent of Denck's retreat from Anabaptism at the end of his life and its significance for the legacy he left for both Anabaptism and Spiritualism. Was he repudiating all of his earlier Anabaptist activities, or merely excesses associated with some of them? Those who see in Denck the father of South German Anabaptism opt for the latter explanation while those who see his subsequent legacy more among the Spiritualists opt for the former.[13]

The difficulty in categorizing Denck as either a Spiritualist or an Anabaptist is especially evident when one looks at his collaboration with Hätzer and Kautz in Worms. Martin Bucer asserted that the posting of Kautz's *7 Articles* was an attempt to initiate an Anabaptist Reformation in Worms similar to that attempted by Baltasar Hubmaier in Waldshut. Both contemporaries and later historians have seen in these articles the clear influence of Denck. Reports indicate that both Denck and Hätzer signed at least some copies of the articles, and in a response to the articles, entitled *A Faithful Warning*, the Strasbourg clergy referred repeatedly to the baneful influence of Denck on Kautz, a man with whom they had earlier had a congenial relationship.[14] Historians have since accepted suggestions that the articles reflect important aspects of Denck's thought,[15] and there is no reason to challenge these conclusions. The traditional touchstone of Denckian Spiritualism, a sharp dualism between the internal and the external, the spiritual and the carnal, pervades the articles. Article 1 distinguishes clearly the inner, spiritual from the external, literal word of God. Article 2 contrasts more generally the efficacy of spiritual content with the emptiness of the physical sign alone in all manner of ceremonies and activities; articles 3 and 4 apply this same reasoning to the contentious issues of the Lord's Supper and baptism. The final three articles focus on matters relating to Christology and the nature of Christ's atonement and are of less direct relevance for the topic at hand.[16]

However, the tone of these articles stands in sharp contrast to certain charges made by the Strasbourg clergy in *A Faithful Warning*. This report makes it appear that Kautz, Denck and Hätzer were assembling a gathered church much on the model of Swiss Brethren groups. Specifically, the Strasbourg clergy attributed to the Worms radicals Swiss Brethren sounding positions on secular authority, the oath, community of goods and separation from godless society.[17] Hans Werner Müsing has argued that in the response to Kautz's articles, Bucer, the likely author of the report, was in fact responding to events in both Strasbourg and Worms. Responses dealing with matters of the Spirit were directed at Kautz, Denck and the others in Worms while those on traditional Swiss Brethren concerns were aimed at Sattler and other radical biblicists in Strasbourg.[18]

Debates about the applicability of Bucer's accusations to the situation in Worms call to mind ongoing disputes about the authenticity of parts of Denck's *Concerning True Love*.[19] Final segments of that work deal with ostensibly Swiss Brethren topics such as baptism, the ban, the oath and secular authority. These portions are included in the original 1527 publication in Worms, but are omitted from a subsequent 1531 edition. They seem out of place when compared with Denck's discussions in earlier parts of *Concerning True Love* and other writings from this time. However, parallels between the accusations of the Strasbourg clergy and the disputed parts of *Concerning True Love* raise the possibility that Denck may have been involved in activities in Worms that he later retracted in his letter to Oecolampadius.

Unfortunately, Denck's references to the history of the church provide little help in establishing how we should characterize his activity in Worms or his reforming vision more generally. In an apparent confirmation of Troeltsch's characterization of the Spiritualists, Denck and Hätzer have little to say about history, and the evidence from the reforming activities in Worms provides no historical context. This seems all the more surprising if we accept the influence of Müntzer on Denck. Yet, Denck's scattered references to the history of the church suggest that he took over the essentials of Müntzer's vision. Like Müntzer he saw all of creation manifesting an order which was a crucial form of divine revelation, and his scattered references to the progress of salvation history suggest that for Denck, too, history manifested that order.[20] Like Müntzer he saw history as a gradual progression towards greater spiritualization and therefore a process of diminishing importance of the external and ceremonial, arguing at one point that ceremonies and an external order were essential for the people of Israel because spiritual speech was foreign to them.[21] Even more clearly indicative of Denck's adherence to Müntzer's historical scheme is his statement that the church fell after the deaths of the apostles when undue emphasis on the authority of Scripture led to numerous sects and divisions.[22] While Denck makes no clear statement of a desire to restore the apostolic church, such is implied in his lament that, as in the present, in past times there were many sects and heresies, and his claim that unity can be restored only through the leadership of the Spirit. This statement suggests further that Denck also shared Müntzer's view of the primitive church as primarily a pnuematological community.[23]

Denck's references to the history of Christianity are few and far between, and they tend to be concentrated in his earlier writings from 1525 and 1526. Consequently, we have no direct evidence of how he may have construed the relationship between his reforming activity in Worms and the model of the primitive church. Unfortunately, Hätzer is no more forthcoming. What indications we have of his historical vision are also scattered references from his earlier literary activity, but these suggest a vision similar to Denck's at least in its general outlines. Like Denck, Hätzer sees Israel's pattern of disobedience and reconciliation as instructive for understanding the life of the believer. He also hints at a process of increasing spiritualization throughout salvation history, although on this issue he may have been slightly more apocalyptic than was Denck. Finally he hints that the apostolic church should serve in some way as the model for the reform of the contemporary church.[24]

Historical references in the writings of Denck and Hätzer are not particularly helpful in understanding their activity in Worms. However, they may provide some insights into the "constructive misunderstanding" that drew Spiritualists like Denck and Hätzer into Anabaptism, and they make more comprehensible Kautz's subsequent activity in Strasbourg. In October 1528 Kautz was arrested there together with Pilgrim Marpeck, Fridolin Meyger and Wilhelm Reublin. In subsequent affairs Kautz's name has become closely linked especially to Reublin's. After attempts to convert the two men failed, they were banished from Strasbourg, but not before leaving us with some interesting and informative statements in their exchanges with the Strasbourg clergy and authorities.[25] Reublin indicated in a joint profession of faith with Kautz that the two men were not in harmony on all matters.[26] Nonetheless, historians have emphasized the fact that the two men could work so closely together as an indication of the extent to which the lines between Anabaptism and Spiritualism had yet to be clearly drawn.[27] Beyond that fact, however, these documents provide valuable insights into Kautz's thought and the evolution of Reformation Spiritualism.[28]

From what we can ascertain from these sources, Kautz appears to have stuck closely to the principles that had guided his reforming activity in Worms. He continued to make a clear and sharp distinction between the visible church and the invisible. He also insisted that those commissioned to assemble the visible church from all lands needed a divine calling distinct from any earthly calling. Finally, he insisted that the invisible church had no connection to "external elements."[29]

Yet, other elements of Kautz's vision suggest he attempted to establish a gathered church. All indications are that Kautz and Reublin felt they had received a divine commission to assemble the true visible church, a fact they appear to have contrasted with the calling of the Strasbourg clergy.[30] While asserting that external elements and ceremonies were not essential to the invisible church, they allotted them a crucial role in the assembling of the visible. Water baptism was important in marking entrance to a community whose unity was maintained through the breaking of bread and a judicious use of the ban.[31] But behind this Swiss Brethren sounding attempt to revive the apostolic church, Kautz remains loyal to the fundamentals of Denck's thought. In the end, water baptism remains nothing more than a mere external sign.[32]

In all of this Kautz appeals to the structure and practice of the apostolic church as a model for contemporary reforms in a way that sounds reminiscent of the biblicist restitutionism of the early Swiss Brethren. Frequently in his discussion of the visible church he appeals to the commands of Christ and practices of the apostles. Strasbourg's Reformation is denounced with the contention that clergy are capable only of tearing down the old church, not of building up a new one. They have singularly failed to establish a community (*Gemeinde*) according to Christ's commands and their conduct is contrasted with that of the apostles, which becomes normative for those called to assemble the visible church.[33] On the crucial issue of baptism, Kautz asserts that there is no scriptural precedent for pedobaptism and he appeals to the Great Commission and the activities of the early church described in Acts to justify believers' baptism.[34] All of this is strongly reminiscent of the activities of the Swiss Anabaptists, and it suggests a likely point of agreement between the visions of Kautz and Reublin. And yet none of it necessarily contradicts the fundamentals of Kautz's earlier activity or thought. The apostolic church could still be defined first and foremost as a Spirit-filled community which also exhibited certain external marks.

According to accepted typologies of the evolution of Reformation Spiritualism, the spiritualist impulse of Denck and Kautz gave way to the more complete spiritualism of people like Entfelder and Bünderlin. On the basis of similarities in their thought and writings, it is assumed that Entfelder and Bünderlin were intellectual if not personal companions.[35] And yet, their drastically different experiences in Strasbourg should alert us to the possibility of important differences in their thought and reforming visions. These differences are not without implications for our understanding of the development of Spiritualism and its early relationship to Anabaptism.

The Spiritualist credentials of Bünderlin and Entfelder become clear if we look at their stances on the crucial hermeneutic question of the relationship between the Spirit and the letter. Denck and those associated with him had frequently distinguished between the living Spirit and the dead letter, and they repeatedly warned against undue reliance on the latter without the former. Here lay the basis for their criticisms of "literalists" (*Schriftgelehrten*). Entfelder and Bünderlin take up this distinction and, if anything, they sharpen the contrast between the Spirit and the letter. Like Denck, they argue that Scripture can serve as a witness to the living Word, but is not itself that Word.[36] Thereafter they both sharpen and extend the focus of their attack. Undue reliance on the external word, they claim, only leads to the elevation of the authority and importance of external ceremonies and ultimately to divisiveness and sectarianism.[37] This new concern with and criticism of ceremonialism, as we will see, reflects events in Strasbourg at the time and provides us with a good example of the interaction between historical vision and lived experience.[38] But while Entfelder and Bünderlin shared the criticism of ceremonialism, they parted ways on how one should deal with this problem, and their respective justifications for these different paths were firmly rooted in their visions of salvation history.[39]

The first thing to note about Entfelder and Bünderlin is that both men are remarkably historically minded for Spiritualists. In contrast to Denck, Hätzer and Kautz, they explicate elaborate historical schemes and weave them tightly into their visions of the nature of Christianity and its reform. The basic outlines of these historical schemes remain true to the sketchy references of Denck, but the details are much more fully fleshed out. Entfelder explicitly accepts Müntzer's position of the revelatory value of the order of things, although he identifies it with the same language as Hans Hut, that is, as the gospel of all creatures.[40] Bünderlin, by way of contrast, makes no explicit reference to the *ordo rerum* or the gospel of all creatures and, as we will see, some of the subtleties of its historical value are lost on him. Nonetheless, it is clear that he recognized the value of historical reflection and argumentation. As well he, like Entfelder, saw in human history a clear pattern of progressive spiritualization, but within this pattern there were important differences of detail.

For Bünderlin underlying all salvation is a basic dialectic pattern of divine revelation and human response. History consists of a series of spiritual disclosures and their subsequent perversion through human focus on the carnal means of the revelation rather than on its spiritual message.[41] But despite the dialectical interaction, the overall pattern is one of progressive spiritualization. The earliest manifestations of the divine in nature were revealed and understood in primarily carnal terms. This set the context for the establishment of the covenant with Israel. But here, too, the carnal means of revelation overwhelmed its spiritual message: Scripture became a substitute for the experience of the divine and religious practice was reduced to formal ceremonialism.[42] Within the context of such a fleshly understanding of the divine law, it is no wonder that God had to come to humanity incarnate. But the Incarnation still served as a dividing line between the past age and a present, increasingly spiritual epoch. Gradually those physical aspects of religion which still clung to the primitive church are giving way to a truly spiritual community. From this vision Bünderlin draws the expected conclusions: the age of the external church has passed and the true church exists only in the hearts of true believers.[43] Among the outmoded physical aspects of Christianity to which people still cling, Bünderlin is especially critical of baptism which he claimed stood in the place of Israel's idolatry under the old dispensation. Of particular interest is Bünderlin's identification of the clergy as those responsible for the most recent externalization of religion.[44] It is likely that we have here an echo of Müntzer's anticlericalism.

Entfelder's view of history followed many of the same outlines as Bünderlin's, although he saw progressive revelation occurring according to an explicitly trinitarian pattern: the age of the Father ran from creation to the revelation of the law, that of the Son from the law to Christ's ascension, and that of the Spirit began with Pentecost.[45] Like Bünderlin, he believed that the earliest human responses to the traces of God in nature gave birth to pagan notions of the divine and forms of worship focused on external ceremonies — as creaturely beings the pagans assumed that God wanted to be honoured in creaturely ways.[46] Within this context God established his covenant with the Jews in a way they could understand: the divine nature and activity was attached to earthly signs.[47] But the chosen people became tied up in the signs instead of looking to the spiritual reality that lay beneath them. As a result when Christ came to earth he did so in an earthly body and made use of external ceremonies for the sake of "fleshly Israel." Insofar as the apostolic church serves as a model for Entfelder, it does so as a pneumatic community. The true church is a community in which the gifts of the Spirit, the offices of Christ and the power of the Father are evident, but none of these are tied necessarily to the practices and ceremonies of the early church. In fact, these ceremonies were only of limited, instrumental value, and remained valid only for the duration of the lives of those commissioned to institute them.

Shortly after the age of the apostles, the early church failed to heed these strictures and went into decline.[48]

At this point, however, Entfelder parts ways with Bünderlin and develops an historical vision that is not characterized by simple linear progression. Like Müntzer before him, Entfelder appears to have believed that cross-references between different ages in the history of the church were instructive. Lessons from one age of the church could be enlightening in another. This tactic is most obvious in his discussion of the three "translations" of the church in both the Old and New Testaments. In this Entfelder describes three parallel ages. The first is an age of peace and harmony, in which the church was not fraught with divisions and the people lived in true fear of God. In the New Testament it is identified with the early church in Jerusalem, composed of only Jewish followers of Jesus, and in the Old with the kingdom of Israel during the early peaceful and prosperous years of Solomon's reign. The second age witnessed in the New Testament the expansion of the church's mission to the gentiles and with it disputes over the applicability of the law and conflict about both baptism and the Lord's Supper. In the Old Testament this age is represented by Solomon's later reign, his taking of foreign wives and idolatry, and the divisions and dangers all of this entailed. During this age Paul had abstained from baptizing and placed greater emphasis on the preaching office. The final age witnessed the complete perversion of all legacies from the first church. The Antichrist has swept in and everything has been turned upside down. All that was spiritual has become fleshly and all that was fleshly is honoured as if it were spiritual. This age had its Old Testament parallel in the break-up of the Hebrew monarchy and the subsequent fate of Judah, including the Babylonian Captivity.[49]

This description of the progression of the church provides valuable insights into Entfelder's perception of the nature of the visible church as a community in his own age. Clearly, he identifies contemporary events as an extension of the Babylonian Captivity. Consequently, that age in which the people of God had no temple or sacrifices, no priesthood or ceremonies, stands as a model for the organization of the contemporary church. Entfelder calls on all true spiritual Israelites to boycott the perverted ceremonies of the institutional churches. He further admonishes them to follow the examples of Tobias in Ninevah and Daniel in Babylon and to perform ceremonies truly pleasing to God: prayer, acts of charity and "safe-guarding the house of knowledge."[50] Entfelder's rejection of the ceremonies of the existing churches, then, did not implicitly involve a withdrawal from community or heightened individualism. He exhorts his readers to continue to learn together and to admonish one another and, one could extrapolate, maintain the cohesiveness of the community despite the hostile environment, as the people of Israel did in Babylon.[51] Finally, his closing exhortation to await a new Cyrus suggests that he regarded the contemporary state of affairs as temporary.[52] His repudiation of ceremonies, then, should be regarded as a *Stillstand* more than a categorical rejection. That is, he never dismissed the possibility of a new calling from God to reinstitute purified ceremonies in the church.[53]

In the greater scheme of things this divergence of paths followed by Bünderlin and Entfelder may appear a minor matter. However, I think it is important for understanding the nature of the Spiritualist movement in Strasbourg at the beginning of the 1530s. On the one hand, the different experiences of Bünderlin and Entfelder begin to make more sense. While the radical rejection of all ceremonialism by Bünderlin would hardly have endeared him to the Strasbourg Reformers, Entfelder's position would have found more welcoming ears in the city. In 1527, while a guest of Capito, Martin Cellarius developed a similar argument about the parallels between the contemporary church and the people of Israel during the Babylonian Captivity and Capito gave Cellarius' work a hearty endorsement.[54] On the other hand, we see interesting similarities between the historical visions of Entfelder and Schwenckfeld and between those of Franck and Bünderlin. Combined with Franck's effusive praise of Bünderlin in his letter to John Campanus, this suggests that groups were forming within the Spiritualist camp writ large in Strasbourg already at the beginning of the 1530s.

The Spiritualizers present interesting challenges to the traditional typologies of the Radical Reformation and the characteristics associated with them. Denck, Hätzer and Kautz appear to fit the mould of Spiritualists who for a time became enmeshed in the early Anabaptist movement. As such, their infrequent historical references provide us with few surprises. Insofar as they do reflect on the church's past, their comments appear to echo the biblically-inspired restitutionism of the early Swiss Brethren. This vision of the apostolic church was likely at the centre of the "constructive misunderstanding" that developed between individuals like Kautz and Reublin. However, beneath these similarities were fundamental differences in how the Spiritualizers and the Swiss Brethren viewed the primitive church. Like Schwenckfeld or Franck, Denck, Hätzer and Kautz saw the church of the apostles primarily as a spirit-filled community — other details of its organization and practices were of secondary importance. The provisional nature of such "external elements" as models for reform becomes clear in light of remarks by Denck and Hätzer about long-term developments in salvation history. The progressive spiritualization of humankind undermines the potential for any external structures of the church to have lasting value.

In the thought of Denck, Hätzer and Kautz references to the apostolic church and to the broader flow of salvation history tend to be vague and infrequent. In the writings of Bünderlin and Entfelder they are much more specific and detailed. As a result, the fundamental differences between how they and the Anabaptists viewed the apostolic church and history were clearer. In this regard, their positions can be described as more radically spiritualist than those of Denck, Hätzer and Kautz. Given the traditional assumptions about the interaction of Spiritualists with history and tradition, it seems ironic that when the Spiritualizers did develop more detailed visions of the past, they did so in the context of a more developed spiritualist vision of the church, in which the value of the apostolic church as a model for reform had diminished. This suggests that sophisticated historical schemes and arguments were developed among the Spiritualizers not to defend a primitivist ecclesiology, but to undermine it. In this sense, our qualifications of Troeltsch's characterization of the Spiritualists apply as well to the Spiritualizers. They were nonhistorical in the sense that they diminished the importance of the objective and historical elements of Christianity, but they were not nonhistorical in the sense that they ignored the past or avoided arguments from it. Rather, like their counterparts who remained committed to the Anabaptist vision, they found themselves relying increasingly on such arguments to defend their own understanding of the essence of Christianity.

Melchiorites

From its outset Melchiorite Anabaptism contained a highly developed historical vision. Melchior Hoffman himself formulated an elaborate scheme of historical periodization stretching from creation to the end of time, and historical reflection was intimately tied to crucial elements of his thought, including his hermeneutics and his eschatology. This historical sense Hoffman bequeathed to subsequent Melchiorites among whom it became a powerful social force. Hoffman's historical vision was not static, and its evolution allows us to follow the development and radicalization of his reforming thought. While the general outlines remain relatively consistent, details were modified as Hoffman moved from being a radical Martinian on the Baltic coast and in Scandinavia to an Anabaptist heresiarch in Strasbourg. Charting the development of his historical vision, then, provides another interesting study in the interaction of historical reflection and development of reforming vision.

Historical reflection was integral to both Hoffman's hermeneutics and his eschatology. Apocalyptic themes dominated his theology and his thought, but for Hoffman divine revelation about the end times was most evident not in signs and wonders in the natural world, but in the signs of history. Similarly, he was convinced that integral to biblical interpretation was the assumption that present and future events were "prefigured" in the events and the visions of the Old and New Testaments.[55]

Hoffman's fully developed schematization of salvation history was trinitarian: he divided the course of human affairs into three ages, each of which was identified with a person of the Trinity. As humanity moved through these three ages it progressed, albeit at times unevenly, to a greater spiritual awareness. The first age, identified with the Father and temporally with the events of the Old Testament, was characterized by the literal law and an incomplete human righteousness before God. With the Incarnation began the second age, the age of the Son which stretched until Hoffman's own day. This epoch witnessed the restoration of human free will, originally lost during the fall, and with it greater moral and spiritual responsibility. Hoffman thought that he and his contemporaries were living at the dawn of the third age or age of the Spirit when God's law would be written directly in the hearts of humankind. While this vision of history saw human development as progressive, this was not a linear process. During each age greater spiritual awareness was inhibited by humanity's attachment to creaturely concerns, as exhibited especially in a tendency toward legalism and sacramentalism.[56] Developing parallel to the three ages of salvation history was a distinct stream of secular history. Hoffman's periodization here was based on the idea of eight world empires: Egypt, Babylon, Greece, Macedonia, Judea, Rome, the Papacy, and the Holy Roman Empire. Hoffman saw his own age witnessing an apocalyptic conjunction of events: the parallel end of an independent stream of secular history witnessed by the demise of the last world empire and the dawning age of the Spirit.[57]

Hoffman's vision of progressive spiritualization suggests that at least technically he was not a restitutionist. His primary focus was forward to the new church of the Spirit instead of backward to the apostolic church of the New Testament. However, his understanding of the events of the second age of salvation history allowed for a normative role for the apostolic church in his reforming vision, in at least a provisional sense.

As has been noted, Hoffman saw the manifestations of the Spirit in history constantly thwarted by the human proclivity for legalism and sacramentalism. In this context he did allow for an historical fall from the norm of the primitive church. The details of this fall, and the reasons for it, varied somewhat as Hoffman's reforming vision developed, but its general pattern remained consistent. Furthermore, despite the progressive nature of humanity's spiritual awakening, Hoffman did allow for possible symmetry between the successive outpourings of the Spirit. In this sense the apostolic church was normative for the impending church of the Spirit. Throughout his writings, Hoffman makes repeated references not only to the impending age of the Spirit, but also to its relationship to the outpouring of the Spirit in the apostolic church.[58] Hoffman's description of the parallels between those events suggests that in his vision of Christian beginnings the church of Pentecost looms large, but, as we will see, other aspects of the primitive church also held a strong grip on his imagination.

Hoffman's earliest descriptions of the primitive church and its subsequent fall are found in his 1526 commentary on the twelfth chapter of the book of Daniel. When he wrote the commentary, Hoffman still regarded his own activity as part of the reforming movement stemming from Wittenberg. However, he had already crossed swords with the Lutheran clergy in Livonia, and he may be regarded at this time as a radical Martinian. On the important theme of ecclesiology he advocated local parish autonomy based on a radicalized version of Luther's doctrine of the priesthood of all believers, possibly reflecting the teachings of Karlstadt.[59] Hoffman's thought in this work is restitutionist in the sense that his calls for congregational autonomy are rooted in his vision of the primitive church, especially as embodied in Paul's description in I Corinthians 14. From this description Hoffman derives the right of the congregation to elect its own pastor and the right of all Christians to prophesy publicly and to interpret the Bible. Again, Hoffman's vision focuses primarily on the church as the spirit-filled community of Pentecost, but he also advocates the return to more institutional aspects of the primitive church, demanding that the Lord's Supper and the ban be practised as they were in the early church.[60]

Between the primitive church and its contemporary restitution was its fall. Hoffman's identification of the reasons for that fall reaffirm the perception that at the time of the writing of the *Commentary on Daniel 12* he is best characterized as a radicalized member of the Wittenberg reform movement. The root cause of the demise of the primitive church was the activity of the papal Antichrist who suppressed the Gospel with lies and false laws. Klaus Deppermann has suggested that Hoffman's identification of the papacy as the Antichrist and his perception that the unmasking of the Antichrist heralded the imminence of the Last Judgement were likely derived from Luther's *Church Postil*. According to Hoffman, the papacy has used a variety of means to suppress the gospel and the true church, but he consistently returns to two themes: an underlying anticlericalism which identifies the fall of the church with congregational loss of autonomy and authority, and a consistent denunciation of the papal assumption of secular authority. Opposite the divine trinity stands a devilish trinity of Pope, emperor and false doctors. Hoffman's treatment of the universities is interesting in this context. He fulminates against the "learned servants of the belly" and charges that "our most respected schools are not fountains of divine teaching."[61]

Hoffman's historical vision as outlined in his commentary on Daniel 12 was fleshed out, and in some cases modified, in his subsequent writings. The modifications introduced to that vision reflected the further development of his reforming thought, especially after he broke with the Wittenberg Reformers and then after he was exposed to the intellectual hothouse of Strasbourg.[62] The more detailed vision is especially evident in a series of works published in 1530: *Commentary on the Revelation of St. John*, *Prediction*, *Prophecy or Prediction*, and *The Ordinance of God*. Further elaborations also appear in Hoffman's 1533 *Commentary on Paul's Letter to the Romans*.

The general outline and organizing structure for Hoffman's historical vision is laid out in his *Commentary on the Revelation of St. John*. There he traces the history of the Christian church during the world's second age according to the pattern of the seven churches described in Revelation.

The first two churches, those of Ephesus and Smyrna, he identifies with the primitive church. Ephesus he equates with the church of the apostles or the original Jewish Christian congregation. This church was scattered with the destruction of Jerusalem. Smyrna is characterized as both the church of the martyrs and the original gentile congregation. It was persecuted both by those who claim to be Jews but in truth belong to the Synagogue of Satan and by pagan Rome. Both churches represent, then, the primitive church before its corruption.[63]

Pergamon, the third church of the Apocalypse, Hoffman identified with the fallen church in which the divine truth had been diluted and perverted. By his calculations the church fell immediately after the age of the martyrs, that is around the reign of Constantine. Hoffman regarded the Donation of Constantine as evidence of the continuity between persecuting pagan Rome and the persecuting papal church.[64] His description of this event sounds familiar to those versed in later Anabaptist criticisms of the Constantinian church:

> for by this means the *Endchrist* received from his father and Satan the throne to the Roman Empire over all the godless, and … the pope and Antichrist were very pleased to accept the same and the power, authority and strength of the worldly rule, and this dragon was the emperor from whom the pope received the authority of the Roman throne … and all the splendour and power which power and strength and authority was very great to receive.[65]

From its beginnings, then, the church of Rome was a fallen church, and Hoffman lays primary responsibility for its degeneration at the feet of the clergy. In the *Commentary on the Revelation of St. John* he identifies some of the basic steps in this process: prohibitions on marriage and enforced abstention from meat.[66] Hoffman fleshed out this list in some of his other writings from this time as he dealt with specific reform issues. In *Prophecy or Prediction* he adds to the list the substitution of the idolatrous mass for Christ's true sacrifice. *The Ordinance of God* is more comprehensive, suggesting that the introduction of infant baptism—elsewhere he lays the blame for this at the feet of Innocent I (401-17) and Martin I (649-55) — and departure from the true practice of the ban undermined the voluntary nature of the church, and with it destroyed the church. The introduction of the cult of saints as mediators between man and God is added as an important perversion of the true church in *Prediction*.[67] By Hoffman's reckoning, the medieval church reached its low point around 1200 when papal claims to secular authority completely perverted the pastoral office. Werner Packull suggests that Hoffman is likely alluding to the pontificate of Innocent III with this reference. In his exegesis of Revelation, Hoffman identified the fourth and fifth churches of John's vision with further details of the apostasy of the Roman church. Thyatira, the fourth church, he identifies with the Bohemians and others who resisted papal perversions, but nonetheless retained some human customs and doctrines. The fifth, the church of Sardis, he identified with "present teachers" who made moves to reform but were unable to follow Scripture to its inner meaning.[68]

In spite of this blanket condemnation of the medieval church, Hoffman fails to identify an ongoing tradition of opposition to it. His only references to a medieval precedent for contemporary challenges to Rome's authority focus exclusively on the activities of Jan Hus. The frequency with which Hoffman refers to the Czech Reformer is a clear indication of the significance he has in Hoffman's reforming vision.[69] But throughout these references Hus consistently appears as a herald of the Reformation rather than as the culmination of a tradition of medieval heretical opposition to the Roman church. Already in the commentary on Daniel 12 Hoffman describes Hus' activity as the reawakening of the Gospel and his martyrdom as a witness to the devilish alliance of the pope and emperor.[70] This role was clarified and apocalyptic dimensions added to it in the *Commentary on the Revelation of St. John*. Here Hoffman identified three outpourings of the Spirit during the second age of the world: at the time of the apostles, during Hus' days and at the end of the age.[71]

At one level, at least, Hoffman's thought contains many of the crucial elements of the Anabaptist view of church history as defined by Littell.

Throughout his writings he is critical of the persecuting church, and in the *Commentary on the Revelation of St. John* he supplements this criticism with an explicit identification of a Constantinian fall of the church. *The Ordinance of God* adds to the list of steps in the church's degeneration the rejection of apostolic practices of the ban and baptism, and with them the loss of the original voluntary nature of the apostolic church. Yet there remain matters which modify the characterization of Hoffman as a restitutionist and primitivist in Littell's mould. In response to the martyrdom of some of his followers in December 1531, Hoffman suspended the practice of baptism. He explained this drastic step by equating the contemporary form of adult baptism with the imperfect service to God of the apostolic church before Pentecost. With the coming of the Spirit a more perfect form of baptism would be instituted.[72] Subsequently, Hoffman took a more radical step: in a partial recantation of his teachings in 1539 he agreed on the authority of Pseudo-Dionysius, Irenaeus, Origen and possibly Tertullian, but especially on the authority of Paul's statements in I Corinthians 15 about the allowance of baptism for the dead, that infant baptism was practised in the primitive church and it was, therefore, permissible.[73] Clearly, at the centre of Hoffman's "primitivism" was a vision of the primitive church as the church of Pentecost. The outpouring of the Spirit on the community of the faithful was primary; the specific practices and institutions of that community were relegated to a secondary role.

Melchior Hoffman left a powerful legacy in the form of north German and Dutch Anabaptism. Shorn of its apocalyptic and spiritualist elements, his historical vision was passed on and laid the groundwork for the historical musings of Menno Simons, Dirk Philips and the later Mennonite tradition, but it also lived on in forms closely integrated with apocalypticism and Spiritualism. Especially in the Anabaptist rule of Münster in 1534-35 we see further developments of Hoffman's integration of apocalypticism and historical reflection, and in the writings of David Joris, among his followers and in the person Obbe Philips we see the continued development of historical reflection on a spiritualist basis.

The events of the rise and fall of the Münster Anabaptist government are generally well known and need be rehearsed here only in the most general outline. The Reformation movement in the city can best be summed up as a theologically Reformed movement in a politically Lutheran context. Tensions increased as the reforming movement became even more radical with the arrival in the city of the Wassenberg preachers, who not only reinforced a Sacramentarian understanding of the Lord's Supper, but also began questioning the practice of infant baptism. Theological squabbles in Münster were played out against a tense political backdrop pitting three powerful groups against each other: Catholics, Evangelicals allied with the city council and Evangelicals allied with the guilds. The arrival in the city in January 1534 of apostles of the self-proclaimed Dutch Melchiorite prophet, Jan Matthijs, strengthened the hand of the more radical Evangelical party. This strength became apparent in city elections held on 23 February, when Anabaptist supporters took control of the city council. Shortly thereafter Matthijs himself arrived in the city, and on 27 February the Bishop of Münster began his siege. Anticipating the impending end of the world, Matthijs led a suicidal sortie against the besiegers and was killed on Easter 1534. He was succeeded by Jan of Leyden who, not satisfied with the informal power wielded by Matthijs as prophet, instituted new constitutional forms ostensibly derived from biblical history: first a Council of Twelve and then a revival of the monarchy of King David. As the siege dragged on the instruments of terror favoured by desperate regimes began to appear, and the manifestations of power and their justifications became more and more bizarre. The days of the Anabaptist kingdom were clearly numbered after the Bishop's forces were able to impose a total blockade on the city, although it still required an act of treachery to capture the city on 25 June 1535.[74]

In assessing the Münsterite historical vision and the role that historical reflection played in the radicalization of Anabaptist Münster we are concerned especially with the thought and writings of the city Reformer and later mouthpiece of the Anabaptist leadership, Bernhard Rothmann.

Of particular concern are several pamphlets written before and after the establishment of Anabaptist rule. *The Confession of Two Sacraments* was written in collaboration with the Wassenberg preachers and provides important insights into the reforming vision in Münster on the eve of the Anabaptist takeover. After the arrival of Jan Matthijs, Rothmann wrote a series of pamphlets justifying the regime and attempting to rally support for it: *Restitution of True Christian Teaching* (October 1534), *On Vengeance* (December 1534), *On the Hiddenness of Scripture* (February 1535) and *On Earthly and Temporal Power* (unfinished at the fall of Münster in June 1535). Initially the driving force behind the city's Reformation, Rothmann seems to have been relegated to a back seat role after the arrival of Jan Matthijs. His writings, then, appear more as *ex post facto* justifications for policies and activities in Münster than statements of, or proposals for, those policies.[75] Nonetheless, these writings provide interesting and valuable insights into the self-understanding of the Münsterite mission.[76] From the perspective of the present study they provide invaluable information about Rothmann's perception of the flow of human history and the significance of that perception in explaining and justifying events in Münster.

As we have seen, perceptions of history were closely integrated with theorizing about the endtimes in the thought of Melchior Hoffman, and as a result they were closely intertwined in the thought of Bernhard Rothmann as well. Already prior to his rebaptism Rothmann was working out a view of ecclesiastical history, likely under the influence of Hoffman's theology, and in general Hoffman exercised a decisive influence on Rothmann's view of history.[77] Rothmann developed a comprehensive outline of the history of the world, which reaches its fullest development in his propaganda efforts to justify the Anabaptist regime: *Restitution of True Christian Teaching, On the Hiddenness of Scripture*, and *On Earthly and Temporal Power*. Like Hoffman he divides the history of the world according to a tripartite scheme. The first age runs from creation to the biblical flood. During this time a basic pattern of human falls and restitutions was established which would characterize human relations with the divine and dominate subsequent historical ages. This age also witnessed the origins of subsequent human institutions, most importantly human government. As a result of the fall of Adam and Eve, human government and justice were necessitated, although the actual beginnings of political history belong to the second age.[78] The second age, which ran from the time of Noah to the restitution Rothmann assumed was imminent, continued the pattern laid out in the first age. The coercive authority necessitated by Adam's fall was itself subject to a fall. This event Rothmann associated with the mythical founder of world empires, Nimrod, usually associated in the medieval mind with the origins of tyranny. Thereafter, political history progressed according to the pattern of the four world empires laid out in the vision of Daniel 2. The second age also witnessed the divergence of the paths followed by secular and sacred history. At the time that Nini, the grandson of Nimrod, was establishing the Assyrian empire God called Abraham out of Mesopotamia and set the history of the chosen people on a separate path. But at the time of the restitution heathen secular authority would come to an end and the streams of secular and sacred history would be reunited.[79] In the restitution peace and justice would be the hallmarks of a physical and temporal reign of the returned Christ and the saints.[80] While many of the individual details of Rothmann's vision are distinctive, he was likely indebted to Hoffman for its general outlines, particularly its apocalyptic orientation, tripartite scheme and series of falls and restitutions.[81]

Within this comprehensive view of world history the Incarnation occupies a special place, despite the fact that it does not act as a dividing line between historical ages. Rothmann describes it as the greatest restitution which, however, was followed by the most abysmal fall.[82] However, Rothmann's treatment of the Incarnation, and with it the history of the early church, appears to change through the course of his writings. In his early works the primitive church appears as a model for reform in a manner already familiar. Especially in the *Confession of Two Sacraments*, which some commentators have described as a "classic peaceful Anabaptist statement," Rothmann's treatment of the apostolic church sounds like the biblically-oriented restitutionism of other early Anabaptists.[83] In this work Rothmann identifies the true church as a voluntary assembly in which the true preaching of the Gospel and the true practice of baptism and the Lord's Supper are present. The proper observation of these two sacraments is determined by the commands of Christ and the practices of the apostles. Rothmann further adds that community of goods was a characteristic of the apostolic church. His restitutionist credentials are reinforced by the methods employed to back up his claims. Evidence of apostolic practice from scriptural sources is supplemented with citations from a number of patristic and other ancient sources as well as from some contemporary authors developing similar historical arguments, most notably Sebastian Franck.[84] According to Frank Wray, who has investigated Rothmann's views of the early church most intensively, Rothmann here treats the apostolic church as a model for a practical reform program of the contemporary church. Furthermore, in his rejection of his opponents' argument for infant baptism on the basis of the circumcision model of the Old Testament he draws a sharp distinction between the pre-Christian and Christian faithful. As a result, Wray argues, in this work Rothmann regards the age of Christ and the apostles as a watershed in salvation history.[85] However, thereafter in Rothmann's writings the significance of the apostolic church appears to diminish. In *Confession of Two Sacraments* Rothmann had not yet laid out his broader scheme of world history. When he first indicated the outlines of this vision in *Restitution of True Christian Teaching*, the restitution effected by the Incarnation remained distinct from earlier restitutions and the apostolic church was still held up as normative for the reform of the contemporary church.[86] Thereafter in Rothmann's writings references to the apostolic church dwindle, and apparently with them its role as a model for reform.

The changing role of the primitive church as a model for reform appears to be reflected in Rothmann's developing assessment of the dates and reasons for its fall. Even before his rebaptism Rothmann focused attention on the perversion of apostolic baptism as a crucial factor in the church's fall. In *Answer to the Council of the Theologians of Marburg* of August 1533 Rothmann and his fellows concentrated on denying the lineage of infant baptism. They said that this practice was not instituted by Christ, the apostles, or the early church, and that its establishment marked the beginning of the devastation (*Verwüstung*) of the church.[87] Shortly thereafter, in *Confession of the Two Sacraments*, Rothmann expanded his attack on infant baptism, and tied it to a criticism of the contemporary understandings of the Lord's Supper.[88] Here he suggested that the abuse of baptism had begun already in Paul's time, although this perversion had not gained the upper hand until much later. Rothmann again claimed that with the establishment of infant baptism the church was laid waste and infested with all manner of evils.[89] However, ultimately it was the perversion of the Word, baptism and the Lord's Supper that heralded the arrival of the Antichrist's troops.[90]

In his subsequent writings Rothmann identifies the fall of the church as having occurred within the first century after Christ's death and ascension. In these works his identification of the primary reasons for the fall change somewhat. The fall is no longer so much a question of the practices of the early church as it is a general criticism of the development of human wisdom and teachings and the process by which they supplanted divine teachings. Rothmann reserves special venom for the learned and the universities in this process. Such an approach has significant polemical value in the symmetry it provides between the events of the restitution of the apostolic age and that of the contemporary age. At the time of the apostles God's message was revealed to the simple, but it was subsequently perverted by the learned. In the restitution currently underway, however, the reawakened Gospel was first proclaimed by the learned, here identified with the magisterial Reformers, but after their failure to recognize its full truth and implications, it was taken up by the simple such as Melchior Hoffman and Jan Matthijs.[91]

Frank Wray has described Rothmann's changing analysis of the church's fall as an outgrowth of a growing anti-intellectualism in his thought and writings.[92] As will become evident below, I am inclined to agree with this assessment insofar as we treat this anti-intellectualism as a propaganda tool. In addition, however, Rothmann's statements are also indicative of his need to confront the historical record and to deal with tradition in the context of the radicalization of his thought. Although he identified the beginnings of the church's devastation already within a century of the time of the apostles, Rothmann saved his sharpest criticisms for the church of the high middle ages, and especially for the development of scholasticism. In a now familiar refrain he claimed that the gospel had been supplanted by the teachings of the universities — especially the teachings of Aristotle and Thomas — and by canon law and the decisions of the councils.[93] The suspicion that his criticism here reflected attacks on scholasticism by both humanist and magisterial Reformers is reinforced by a rather cryptic reference of Rothmann to himself as merely a simple "Grammarian," unlearned in the subtleties of dialectics.[94] Interesting in this context is a growing critique in his later writings of the church fathers, who had earlier been cited as evidence of baptismal practice in the early church.[95] As we have seen with other Reformation radicals, the move to a more comprehensive criticism of contemporary church and society occasioned for Rothmann as well a more thorough-going critique of Christian traditions. In addition, in his later works Rothmann began laying the groundwork for the identification of an ongoing tradition of heretical opposition to the Babylonian church, although this line of thought was never fully developed. He argues that those who opposed the perversion of the gospel by the learned have traditionally been branded and persecuted as heretics by the church. Unfortunately, Rothmann provides us with no details or further identification of these heretics, but interestingly, the primary teaching on the basis of which they have been singled out is their understanding of scriptural references to the endtimes.[96]

In Rothmann's later writings the place of the apostolic church as a model for contemporary reform activities appears to be supplanted by the kingdom of Christ. With this shift comes an important reorientation of Rothmann's thought. Christ's return is increasingly identified with the reign of Solomon: as the peaceful reign of Solomon developed on the foundations laid by the conquests of David, the way for Christ's return must be prepared by the revived Davidic monarchy.[97] Rothmann's changed orientation, then, is closely connected to a new willingness by the Münsterites to employ force in the defence of the Gospel. Historians have long noted this connection and commented on the evolution of Rothmann's thought from a New Testament suffering ethic to an Old Testament crusading ethic.[98] However, the role of appeals to the Old Testament in Rothmann's vision, their relationship to his apocalypticism, and the significance of both of these elements of his thought for Münsterite self-understanding remain matters of controversy. Noting that Rothmann's propaganda efforts to justify the Anabaptists' use of force develop parallel legal and eschatological arguments, Willem de Bakker has questioned the value of relying on his eschatological statements as the primary key to understanding what the Münsterites were doing. Instead, he argues, in appealing to eschatological themes, Rothmann was playing the one viable card he held to rally support for the regime from its only potential supporters, north German and Dutch Melchiorites. Rather than an unambiguous mirror of Münsterite self-perception, Rothmann's eschatological utterances in his propaganda for the Anabaptist kingdom appear more as a clever public relations move.[99] More recently, Ralf Klötzer has argued for the essential compatibility of rational Reformation strategies and eschatological hopes in the Münsterite vision.[100] From the present perspective, of interest is Rothmann's use of history in both of his parallel propaganda strategies. In many ways, historical arguments bridge the gap between legalistic and eschatological arguments in his writings. More importantly, they provide important insights into the roles of history and historical arguments in Münster. The shift of focus in Rothmann's writings from New Testament to Old Testament models of reform was not a paradigm shift driving the agendas and self-perceptions of the Münster Anabaptists. Rather, appeals to Old Testament parallels to the coming kingdom of Christ were more *ad hoc* justifications for the apocalyptically determined actions and reforms undertaken by the Anabaptist leadership. During the reign of Jan of Leyden, historical vision did not so much dictate actions as actions dictated historical visions.

Traditionally the willingness of the Münsterites to employ force in their own defence has been seen as inherent in the movement, at least from the time of the arrival of Jan Matthijs in Münster.[101] One of the more significant revisions in our understanding of Münster Anabaptism is the realization that the decision to employ the sword was a gradual process in response to external conditions and internal power struggles. Initially the Münster Anabaptists were ambivalent or undecided about the use of the sword and only gradually did they come to espouse its employment.[102]

This evolution in thinking on the sword among the Münster Anabaptists is reflected in the writings of Rothmann, especially in his statements justifying its use and, with them, his evaluations of the origins and nature of secular authority. Rothmann's rationalization for the employment of the sword, and with it his thinking about political authority, was an ongoing process from the beginning of Anabaptist rule in Münster until its demise. At the beginning of this process, Rothmann's political ethic can probably best be characterized by what James Stayer has labelled the Christian Realpolitik of Ulrich Zwingli.[103] His writings from the period prior to his rebaptism by the emissaries of Jan Matthijs in January 1534 suggest that his political ethic, like many of his theological positions, owed a strong debt to the Reformed tradition of southwest Germany and Switzerland. Notable is the latitude Rothmann gives to the secular authorities in matters broadly defined as ecclesiastical. While he adopts the common Reformation position that secular authorities should be obeyed in all things that do not contravene divine commandments, he also stresses the complementary roles of spiritual and secular authority. He argues for the possibility of, and desirability of, the establishment of godly rulers, and he calls on the authorities to suppress false teaching.[104]

This faith in secular authorities appears to have been eroded somewhat after Rothmann's break with the Münster city council in the summer of 1533. Thereafter Rothmann was much less willing to allow interference from the secular arm in matters of religion, although he continued to hope for the establishment of godly authorities.[105] Of note, though, is his continued respect for, and calls for obedience to, established temporal authority. This respect for secular authority continued to influence his thinking and statements on the relationship of the Münster Anabaptists to the sword. On 23 February 1534 a new city council dominated by the Anabaptists was elected in Münster; in other words, the Anabaptists came to power there by legal means.[106] This event likely reinforced Rothmann's respect for secular authority. It certainly aided him in justifying the activities in Münster. In the spring of 1534, after the bishop's armies were already besieging the city, Rothmann completed his *Confession of the Belief and Life of the Community of Christ at Münster*. In this work, he characterizes the Anabaptists' decision to resort to arms as the justifiable activity of a legally constituted government in response to the tyrannical activities of the bishop of Münster.[107] As numerous interpreters of Rothmann's writings have noted, this legitimation of a legal defensive war continues in Rothmann's writings throughout the seige.[108]

Behind these arguments lie continued references to the legitimacy of temporal authority, at least insofar as it has been established by divine ordinance. In Rothmann's later works the origins of temporal power continue to be described in "quasi-Lutheran" terms as the divine remedy for human wickedness. In his *Restitution of True Christian Teaching*, printed in October 1534, Rothmann makes this point clearly. He argues that temporal authority has resulted from the human fall from obedience to

God and righteousness to disobedience and unrighteousness. The resulting conflicts between humans led God to establish the sword, in the form of temporal authority (*Obrigkeit*), to protect the righteous and exact vengeance on the unrighteous.[109] Even in *On Earthly and Temporal Power*, Rothmann's extended exposé on the origins, nature and history of temporal authority, left behind as an unfinished fragment after the fall of Münster, secular authority is described as divinely instituted and derived from human wisdom and the law of nature.[110] Yet, as Stayer notes, these claims are increasingly overshadowed by Rothmann's denunciations of existent temporal authority in his later writings.[111] Parallel to his continued claims that the office of the temporal sword has been instituted by divine decree, Rothmann argues that the exercise of that authority throughout history has departed from its divine origins and become heathen and tyrannical. In *Restitution* Rothmann argues that early in its history secular authority had been perverted by human pride and self-interest. He claims that for a long time secular authorities have not only forgotten and abused the divine commands for their offices, but also have turned their authority against God Himself and His Word. This, Rothmann asserts, is clear today, especially among rulers who call themselves "Christian."[112] Shortly thereafter, in *A Report on Vengeance*, printed in December 1534, he contrasted the need for obedience to divinely established authority in the form of the revived Davidic kingship of Jan of Leyden with the need to resist the tyranny of the "Babylonian rulers."[113] This process comes to full fruition in *On Earthly and Temporal Power*, in which Rothmann develops a detailed historical argument to justify his claims that existing secular authority derives from heathen, godless roots. He traces the origins of temporal authority to Nimrod, the son of Ham, and the cursed line among Noah's descendants. Although instituted by divine decree, this authority was perverted by Nimrod's pride and transformed into tyranny, which is the chief characteristic among Nimrod's successors to the present day.[114]

It is interesting to note that Rothmann's critique of existing temporal authority begins in *Restitution of True Christian Teaching*, and this raises the question of why he first turned to this tactic in the autumn of 1534. The answer to this question likely lies in the constitutional history of Anabaptist Münster. As has been noted, with the elections to the city council of 23 February 1534 the Anabaptists were able to assume authority by legitimate means. Although this seizure of power resulted in a significant change in the practical locus of authority, largely through the extra-institutional role of the prophet exercised by Jan Matthijs, the institutional structure of the city government remained largely untouched. Indeed, the transfer of power from the old to the new city council occurred according to the usual forms.[115] All of this changed, however, at Easter 1534 with Matthij's suicidal sortie against the besieging army. Jan of Leyden's attempt to "institutionalize charisma" was accompanied by a thoroughgoing constitutional change. The established city council was replaced by an Elders' Constitution, supposedly derived from biblical models.[116] After a failed attempt to storm the city on 31 August, the Elders' Constitution was supplanted by the kingship of Jan of Leyden, again a political form purportedly with biblical precedent. Both of these new constitutions were seen as marking a sharp break with all existing political forms and traditions. They were of divine, not human, origin. Unlike existing power structures, they synthesized both temporal and spiritual authority in one institution, and their appearance was understood to be integral to the establishment of a new age of world history.[117] The novelty of Münsterite political forms, then, provided the opportunity, even the necessity, for Rothmann's criticism of all existing political structures, and with it a reassessment of political history.

In addition to providing a justification for Münster's constitutional experiments, Rothmann's reflections on the origins and nature of political authority also helped to explain Münsterite relations with the world beyond the city walls. Parallel to his developing denunciations of governments outside Münster there emerged detailed arguments for the Anabaptists to take up the sword and assume an active role in the great apocalyptic crusade of the dawning new age. This theme appears first in

Restitution and is expanded in subsequent writings. It is especially well developed in *On Vengeance* when Rothmann calls on the righteous to lay aside the spiritual weapons of the apostles and take up the physical weapons of the restored Davidic kingdom. Later in *On the Hiddenness of Scripture* he calls on the saints to put an end to "Babylonian authority" and to do away with all unrighteous rulers.[118]

Rothmann's developing views on the sword were intimately tied to his understanding of history and his speculations about the Apocalypse.[119] The latter connection is obvious. The rationalization for the righteous to take up arms is rooted in the idea of an apocalyptic crusade emanating from Münster and then filling the entire world. In the works written after the establishment of the Davidic kingdom of Jan of Leyden, Rothmann calls on the faithful to cleanse the world of the wicked in preparation for the return of Christ. This theme is implicit in *Restitution* and then appears with increasing frequency and takes on added significance in *On Vengeance* and *On the Hiddenness of Scripture.*[120] But for Rothmann, a proper understanding of the apocalyptic timetable, and of the scriptural references to it, required a careful reading of history and understanding of one's own place in it, and he frequently advises his readers to pay careful attention to these matters.[121] One's place in history determined, among other things, how one read the Scriptures and the proper ethic for the righteous.[122] This lies at the basis of Rothmann's statements in *On Vengeance* that the time has come for the righteous to lay aside the weapons of the apostles and take up those of the Davidic kingdom. The age of suffering was giving way to the age of vengeance.

Rothmann's call for the establishment of the kingdom of Christ led him to rely increasingly on Old Testament models to justify the activities in Münster. The Davidic kingdom of Jan of Leyden was the necessary precursor to the return of Christ who would reign as a peaceful Solomon. In this he made effective use of Hoffman's identification of parallels between different ages of the church. The progress of events in Münster indicates that rather than a comprehensive vision dictating activities of the Anabaptist kingdom, Rothmann's exegesis amounted to an *ex post facto* justification of the constitutional changes and apocalyptic agenda of the Anabaptist leadership. In this sense, Rothmann's apparent growing anti-intellectualism appears as a sophisticated propaganda tool. Under the influence of circumstances in Münster Hoffman's exegetical method, which was influenced by his spiritualism, evolved into a form of Old Testament literalism.

Events in Münster and Rothmann's explanation of their significance had important consequences for others in the Melchiorite movement. Involved in these was the development of his historical vision which helped to highlight the potential dangers in Melchior Hoffman's amalgamation of Spiritualism and Anabaptism. Rothmann's earliest writings suggest that the starting point for that vision was a biblically-based restitutionism similar to that of many early Anabaptists, although the availability of Franck's *Chronica* and other resources provided him with more detailed knowledge of the history of the early church. However, that image was subsequently subsumed under a broader Spiritualist vision of the progressive spiritualization of humanity's interaction with the divine and a general pattern of falls and restorations in salvation history. This was a gradual process, and at first the primitive church retained some of its status as a model for contemporary reform. In his first writings after the establishment of Anabaptist rule in Münster, Rothmann continues to accord the restitution effected by the Incarnation a distinct status in the general pattern. However, in his later writings that status fades and with it the value of the apostolic church as a model for reform. The shift in Rothmann's focus is evident in the changing reasons identified as the cause of the primitive church's fall: he begins to focus less on the perversion of apostolic practices and more on the substitution of human teachings for divine. This allows him to contrast favourably the divine wisdom of Hoffman and the Anabaptist leadership with the human wisdom of the learned divines. Gradually the coming kingdom of Christ rather than the apostolic church becomes the dominant image. Hoffman's teaching on the parallels between different ages in the church's history allowed Rothmann to still justify his claims historically, but the overall tenor of the later writings is much more eschatological than restitutionist.

As we saw in chapter four, Menno and his followers responded to these developments by refocusing attention on the primitive church. In their eyes, the church of the apostles was the true church, and its teachings and practices were normative for the restoration of the true church on earth. In Menno's writings, the focus on the apostolic church tends to avoid further reflection on the broader contours of salvation history. Dirk Philips, by the way of contrast, was willing to place the apostolic church in a more general pattern of falls and restorations. However, unlike Rothmann, he insisted on the unique significance of the Incarnation within that pattern, and with it the importance of the apostolic church as a model of the true church on earth.

Others in the Melchiorite movement were unwilling to return to this restitutionist position. In their attempts to understand and explain the failure of the Münster Anabaptist kingdom, the Davidjorites and Obbe Philips were led to disentangle the Anabaptist and spiritualist elements in Melchior Hoffman's thought and to develop a spiritualist understanding of the church more radical than that of many of the south German Spiritualizers. With this radical spiritualism they also moved away from appeals to, and arguments from, history and historical precedent in a way unparalleled by most of the Reformation Radicals studied so far.

David Joris' career as a Reformer presents a classic case of evolution from an Anabaptist to a Spiritualist position. With that evolution he developed a familiar spiritualist understanding of salvation history. He described the development of the human spirit as a process of maturation. The spiritual childhood of humanity he identified with the "shadowy Gospel" of Old Testament Law. This gave way over time to the "Gospel according to the flesh" with the Incarnation. Ultimately, humanity would encounter the "Gospel according to the Spirit" when spirit-filled men would progress beyond the need for outmoded religious forms and ceremonies. After his discussion with the Melchiorite elders in Strasbourg, Joris formulated this progression in a strictly trinitarian pattern of three epochs each associated with a person of the trinity.[123]

Joris provides little detail about the history of the church within this pattern, but his scattered references suggest a general outline of how he saw its development. In *Of the Wonderful Working of God*, in which he attempted to account for the failure of the Münster Anabaptist kingdom, Joris dealt explicitly with the concept of restitution. Like other Melchiorites, he saw human history as marked by a series of falls and restitutions. Preeminent among the restitutions was that occurring at the time of Christ and the apostles, but that restitution found humanity spiritually unprepared and its effects were quickly undermined by the activities of the Antichrist. The next and final restitution, which Joris thought was imminent, would reestablish the apostolic church, but on the new foundation of the spirit-filled who had attained a state of innocence. In preparation for the impending restitution, Joris' primary concern was with the process of individual conversion, not the communal structure of the spirit-filled people. At times he appears to be advocating a restoration of the apostolic church, but in the end his belief in the greater spiritual maturity of the final age meant that in his vision the church of the coming restitution would supersede that of the apostles.[124] Joris' opinion about the relationship between the church of the coming restitution and the church of the apostles is evident in his treatment of baptism. Consistently he identifies true baptism with the baptism of the Spirit, of which water baptism is the external sign. Gradually in his writings the significance of water baptism diminishes. By the early 1540s he was describing the debate over the validity of infant baptism as of little concern. He declared that the practice was "free and unnecessary" and argued that participation in it did no good, but also no real harm if one placed no trust in it. In the end, water baptism is merely an "image, figure, shadow and letter" of spirit baptism, and spirit baptism has superseded water baptism as Christ has superseded John.[125]

More details of the Davidjorite vision of ecclesiastical history are provided by Joris' lieutenant and son-in-law, Nicholas Meyndertzs van Blesdijk, during his polemical campaign against the Mennonites in the late 1540s. Blesdijk characterized the Davidjorites as New Testament Christians who regarded the New Testament as authoritative in religious matters. He also stated that their goal was the restitution of the church, which he also referred to as the Tabernacle of David. The true church had originally fallen through the sin of Adam and his descendants, was restored by Christ and the apostles, and then fell again as a result of the activities of the Antichrist. It would be restored again through the work of a promised new David who would set the stage for the return of Christ and his reign as a peaceful Solomon.[126] Despite his apparent appeals to historical models and precedents for the coming restitution, Blesdijk's vision of that restitution moves it beyond historical examples of the church. Again, this is most apparent in his treatment of infant baptism. He regarded this practice as an abuse, but not necessarily as idolatry or blasphemy as the Mennonites claimed. On the basis of Christian freedom, one could choose to participate in this ceremony without detriment. Interestingly, to make his case he appealed to the example of the Corinthian baptisms on behalf of the dead mentioned by Paul. In fact, Blesdijk claimed, it is not even clear whether or not the apostles baptized infants. As James Stayer has indicated, Blesdijk moved the discussion of baptism to a supra-historical horizon which rendered irrelevant Mennonite arguments about the history of baptism. He identified external, water baptism as a concession to the spiritual immaturity of humanity in the apostolic age. In the coming restitution spiritual baptism, the true baptism of Christ, would replace the water baptism of John.[127] Further, he charges that appeals to scriptural evidence, and one can assume that includes descriptions of the apostolic church, consistently run the danger of deteriorating into crass proof-texting which can, in the end, justify any position. What is needed instead is the proper discernment of the Spirit.[128] Obbe Philips came to similar conclusions, but with a less developed historical vision. He agreed with his detractors that the apostolic church had been destroyed in early times by the Antichrist, but he denied that there was any justification for its restoration. Rather, people should serve God in simplicity without teachers, preachers or external assemblies. Those who attempted to restore the apostolic church were involved in an enterprise parallel to the ancient Hebrews' demand for a monarchy.[129]

Conclusion

While we can speak of Spiritualist and Anabaptist historical visions, it is difficult to identify anything approaching a common vision of the past among those frequently identified as Spiritualist Anabaptists or others on the fringes of the Anabaptist movement. The variations in approaching the record of the past among the Spiritualist Anabaptists are clearest when we compare the visions of Bünderlin and Entfelder with those of Obbe Philips and Blesdijk. The elaborate schemes of salvation history developed by the former stand in sharp contrast to the relatively abrupt manner in which the latter dismiss historical arguments. These observations reinforce suggestions that the Spiritualist Anabaptists were a group of individuals caught in the grey area somewhere between the Anabaptism of Conrad Grebel or Menno Simons and the Spiritualism of Caspar Schwenckfeld or Sebastian Franck. Yet, the extent to which these individuals appeal to the authority of the past is not indicative of where they belong on the continuum between Anabaptism and Spiritualism. Bünderlin's spiritualist rejection of religious externals is no less radical than Obbe Philips'. Like Franck, and to a significant degree like Entfelder, Bünderlin developed an elaborate historical vision not to bolster arguments for a restitutionist position, but to undermine them.

The willingness to appeal to the authority of the past appears, then, to be determined less by what lessons the individual involved took from history than by the circumstances in which the appeal to history was made. Historians have pointed to events in Strasbourg as the catalyst for unravelling the "constructive misunderstanding" that produced the Spiritualist Anabaptists. There the simmering tension between Denck and Sattler escalated to the open conflict which pitted Bünderlin and Entfelder against Marpeck. As the inherent tensions within the Spiritualizers' positions were clarified, so were the contradictions in their historical visions. In the thought of Denck, Hätzer and Kautz, an appeal to the apostolic church , defined primarily as a Spirit-filled community but one with a distinct structure and practices, sat uneasily alongside a vision of salvation history which assumed the progressive spiritualization of humanity's relations with the divine. In the thought of Bünderlin and Entfelder, those two visions of the past could no longer be reconciled. For them the structure and practices of the apostolic church had become stumbling blocks on the path to greater spiritual understanding.

Melchior Hoffman's historical vision, which matured in the context of the Strasbourg debates, integrated the restitutionist appeal to the apostolic church with the Spiritualist understanding of the flow of salvation history. To this Hoffman added a strong sense of apocalyptic urgency. All of this he bequeathed to the Melchiorite movement in the north, where Spiritualist and Anabaptist historical visions were disentangled in a process that ran parallel to the events in Strasbourg. The Münsterites inherited Hoffman's vision. Under the pressure of events, and the apocalyptic lens through which they viewed those events, they turned increasingly to the Spiritualist scheme of salvation history which they grafted on to an Old Testament literalism. This union of two apparently irreconcilable positions was facilitated by Hoffman's teaching on the symmetry between different ages of the church. In spite of the disaster of Münster, both Anabaptist and Spiritualist visions of history remained current among the Melchiorite Anabaptists. Initially, Menno and his followers adopted a clearly restitutionist position while Obbe Philips and the Davidjorites opted for a more clearly Spiritualist position. However, as we will see, these visions of the past continued to interact with each other.

NOTES

1 Christian Entfelder, *Von dem mannigfaltigen Zerspaltungen inm Glauben, die in diesen Jahren entstanden sind*, Laube II: 963.

2 James M. Stayer, "The Radical Reformation," in Thomas A. Brady, Jr., Heiko A Oberman and James D. Tracy, eds., *Handbook of European History, 1400-1600: Late Middle Ages, Renaissance and Reformation*, vol. 2: *Visions, Programs and Outcomes* (Grand Rapids: Eerdmans, 1996), 258-59, 263-65.

3 Ibid., 267.

4 James Stayer has described the appearance of a distinct spiritualist tradition as the result of a process whereby anti-Lutheran spiritualists gradually disentangled themselves from the Anabaptist movement into which they had earlier immersed themselves, see "Radical Reformation," 254-59. This process was earlier noted by, among others, Heinold Fast, *Der linke Flugel der Reformation: Glaubenszeugnisse der Täufer, Spiritualisten und Antitrinitarier* (Bremen: Carl Schunemann Verlag, 1962), xvii, xxv-xxvi and Werner Packull, *Mysticism and the South German-Austrian Anabaptist Movement 1525-1531* (Scottdale, PA and Kitchener, ON: Herald Press, 1977), 156, 174-75, 182-83.

5 As Packull, *Mysticism and the South German-Austrian Anabaptist Movement*, 33-36, notes, the question of Denck's connections to Müntzer is particularly contentious in the confessionally-charged debates about Anabaptist beginnings. Jan Kiwiet, "The Life of Hans Denck," *MQR* 31 (1957): 235-43 and "The Theology of Hans Denck," *MQR* 32 (1958), 3-8; David Steinmetz, "Hans Denck (1500?-1527): The Universal Word," in *Reformers in the Wings* (Philadelphia: Fortress Press, 1971), 211; Claus-Peter Clasen, "Nuernberg in the History of Anabaptism," *MQR* 37 (1965): 25-27; Heinold Fast, "Hans Denck and Thomas Müntzer," *MQR* 45 (1971): 82-83 and Clarence Bauman, *The Spiritual Legacy of Hans Denck: Interpretation and Translation of Key Texts* (Leiden: E.J. Brill, 1991), 29-32 all reject any significant influence of Müntzer on Denck and dismiss the report of Oecolampadius that after his expulsion from Nuremberg Denck moved on to Mühlhausen. On the other side of the fence, Gustave Roehrich, *Essay on the Life, Writings and Doctrine of the Anabaptist Hans Denck*, trans. by Claude R. Forster, William F. Bogart, Mildred Van Sice (Lanham, MD: University Press of America, 1983), 4-6, 21; Alfred Coutts, *Hans Denck 1495-1527: Humanist and Heretic* (Edinburgh: Macniven and Wallace, 1927), 20 and 34; Rufus Jones, *Spiritual Reformers in the 16th and 17th Centuries* (Macmillan, 1914; reprint ed., Boston: Beacon Press, 1959), 19; Frederick L. Weis, *The Life, Teaching and Works of Johannes Denck* (Pawtucket, RI, 1925), 15-18, 26; Walter Fellmann, *QGT* VI (2), 10-11; Packull, *Mysticism and the South German-Austrian Anabaptist Movement*, 35-41 and "Hans Denck: Fugitive from Dogmatism," in Hans-Jürgen Goertz, ed. *Profiles of Radical Reformers: Biographical Sketches from Thomas Müntzer to Paracelsus* (Kitchener, ON and Scottdale, PA: Herald Press, 1982), 63; George H. Williams, *The Radical Reformation*, 3rd ed. (Kirksville,, MO: Sixteenth Century Journal Publishers, 1992), 247-54; James M. Stayer, *The German Peasants' War and Anabaptist Community of Goods* (Kingston and Montreal: McGill-Queens University Press, 1991), 4, n. 14 argue for significant influence of the Saxon Radicals on Denck and some for at least the possibility that Denck went to Mühlhausen. The most recent publication on Denck, Matthias Gockel's "A Reformer's Dissent from Lutheranism: Reconsidering the Theology of Hans Denck (ca. 1500-1527)," *ARG* 91 (2000): 130, accepts Denck's sojourn there as fact.

6 On Denck's baptism of Bünderlin, see Packull, *Mysticism and the South German-Austrian Anabaptist Movement*, 156-57; Williams, *Radical Reformation*, 257 and Alexander Nicoladoni, *Johannes Bünderlin von Linz und die oberösterreichischen Täufergemeinden in den Jahren 1525-1531* (Berlin: R. Gaertners Verlagsbuchhandlung, 1893), 107. On the possible existence of a baptist fellowship in Augsburg at this time and the possible roles of Denck and Hätzer in it, see Weis, 80-89; Coutts, 42-44; Kiwiet, "Life of Denck," 243-47; Fellmann, *QGT*, VI (2), 12; Packull, *Mysticism and the South German-Austrian Anabaptist Movement*, 92-93; Williams, *Radical Reformation*, 255; Gockel, 131.

7 For suggestions that Hätzer was Denck's right-hand man in Strasbourg, see Kiwiet, "Life of Denck," 247-52; Steinmetz, "Universal Word," 211-12; Williams, *Radical Reformation*, 260-63 and Weis, 120-39. Hans-Werner Müsing, "The Anabaptist Movement in Strasbourg from Early 1526 to July 1527," *MQR* 51 (1977): 98-105 and Klaus Deppermann, *Melchior Hoffman: Social Unrest and Apocalyptic Visions in the Age of Reformation*, trans. Malcolm Wren and ed. Benjamin Drewery (Edinburgh: T.&T. Clark, 1987), 180-87 suggest that only gradually did the activities of Denck and Hätzer coalesce in Strasbourg.

8 On the activities in Worms, see Coutts, 69-77; Kiwiet, "Life of Denck," 252-54; Bauman, 15-17; Williams, *Radical Reformation*, 261-68 and Weis, 140-53.

9 On Kautz's activity in Strasbourg and his relationship with Wilhelm Reublin, see Frank Muller, "Jacob Kautz," in *Bibliotheca Dissidentium* 17 (1995): 8-9; Deppermann, *Melchior Hoffman*, 190-91.

10 Nicoladoni, 118-21, 129-30; Gäbler, 9, 13: Packull, *Mysticism and the South German-Austrian Anabaptist Movement*, 163-64; Williams, *Radical Reformation*, 398-400; Laube, II, 973.

11 For an overview of the disputed historiography on Denck, see Packull, *Mysticism and the South German-Austrian Anabaptist Movement*, pp. 35-36, 155-56.

12 Bauman, 244 (= *QGT* VI (3), 134-35).

13 For a recent defence of Denck as an Evangelical Anabaptist, see Baumann, 245. Clear arguments for Denck's repudiation of his Anabaptist practices at the end of his life have been made by Steinmetz, 213 and Packull, "Fugitive from Dogmatism," 65-67 and *Mysticism and the South German-Austrian Anabaptist Movement*, 60.

14 On Denck and Hätzer as signatories to the articles, see Williams, *Radical Reformation*, 168 and James Beck, "The Anabaptists and the Jews: The Case of Hätzer, Denck and the Worms Prophets," *MQR* 75 (2001): 414. For the comments of the Strasbourg clergy, see *QGT* VII: 92, 95, 106-7, 109, 113-15.

15 Packull, *Mysticism and the South German-Austrian Anabaptist Movement*, 57-58, and idem., "Fugitive from Dogmatism," 64-65, calls Denck the "spiritual father" of the articles. Beck, 412, suggests the articles were "strongly influenced" by Denck. Bauman, 16, is somewhat less enthusiastic, referring to the articles as encapsulating Denck's ideas in a more crude and controversial fashion. For a detailed analysis of Denck's influence on the articles, see Laube, I: 702-7.

16 Laube I: 702-4.

17 *QGT* VII: 109.

18 Müsing, 118-19.

19 See Bauman, 178 and Packull, *Mysticism and the South German-Austrian Anabaptist Movement*, 59 for the details of the disputes about the authenticity of this material. For the text of the disputed material, see Bauman, 192-201.

20 Denck makes references to the order and its revelatory value throughout his writings. See Bauman, 56-57 (*Nuremberg Confession* = Furcha, 15; *QGT* VI [2], 21), 86-87, 94-95, 98-99 (*Whether God is the Cause of Good and Evil* = *QGT* VI [2], 32, 36, 38), 146-47 , 156-57

(*The Law of God* = Furcha, 62, 70; *QGT* VI [2], 60, 65), 212-23 (*The Order of God* = Furcha, 77-78; *QGT* VI [2], 89). Several scholars have noted his use of the concept of the order of God or order of things without tying it to his historical vision. Williams, *Radical Reformation*, 1268, includes Denck as a proponent of the Gospel of all Creatures and Jan Kiwiet, "Theology of Denck," 12-13, argued that Denck took the concept of the order of God from the *Theologia Deutsch*. A clear example of Denck's treatment of history as a revelation of the divine will is his description of the history of Israel as recurring cycles of disobedience to, and then reconciliation with, God and therefore as paradigmatic of the life of the believer. See Bauman, 112-15 (*Whether God is the Cause of Good and Evil* = *QGT* VI [2], 45-46).

21 Bauman, 132-35, 152-55 (*Concerning the Law of God* = Furcha, 50-52, 66-60; *QGT* VI [2], 53-54, 63-64).

22 Bauman, 56-59 (*Nuremberg Confession* = Furcha, 16; *QGT* VI [2], 22).

23 Bauman, 164-65 (*He Who Truly Loves the Truth* = Furcha, 134-35, *QGT* VI [2], 68). Coutts, 175-79, 239 has come to similar conclusions.

24 See Hätzer's preface to Oecolampadius' *Von Sacrament der Dancksagung* (1526), in Paul Visser, *The Anabaptist, Mennonite and Spiritualist Reformation* (Leiden: IDC, 1977ff), #53, aij-avj(f). J.F. Gerhard Goeters, *Ludwig Hätzer (ca. 1500 bis 1529), Spiritualist und Antitrinitarier: Eine Randfigur der frühen Täuferbewegung* (Gütersloh: C. Bertelsmann Verlag,1957), 76, 82-85, claims that under the influence of Karlstadt, Hätzer was moving in an increasingly spiritualist direction at this time. Such claims, when combined with Hätzer's own vociferous denial of any connections to Anabaptism, suggest a vision of the apostolic church more akin to Denck's. For Hätzer's possible earlier dependence on the thought of Karlstadt, see Charles Garside, Jr. "Ludwig Haetzer's Pamphlet Against Images: A Critical Study," *MQR* 34 (1960): 20-36. See also Goeters' (p.61) discussion of Hätzer's vision of the normative nature of the apostolic church in his earlier pamphlet *Von den evangelischen Zechen*.

25 Muller, 8-9; C. Arnold Snyder, *Anabaptist History and Theology: An Introduction* (Kitchener, ON: Pandora Press, 1995), 133.

26 *QGT* VII: 195.

27 Snyder, *Anabaptist History and Theology*, 133; Stephen Boyd, *Pilgram Marpeck: His Life and Social Theology* (Durham, NC: Duke University Press, 1992), 59.

28 See *QGT* VII: 195. Reublin's claim about the differences between his position and Kautz's comes immediately after the Strasbourg preachers' discussion of the threat posed to scriptural authority by Kautz's thought. It seems logical, therefore, that the area of clearest divergence between them was on the authority of the written word. Snyder, *Anabaptist History and Theology*, 139, n. 32, suggests that the written response of the Strasbourg clergy aimed more at the statements of Kautz than those of Reublin.

29 *QGT* VII: 201-4.

30 Ibid., 199.

31 Ibid., 198, 204-5. See also 213 and 217.

32 Ibid., 198.

33 Ibid., 199, 204-5.

34 Ibid., 198-99 and 210-11.

35 See Jones, 31-34, 41; Williams, *Radical Reformation*, 381, 398; Packull, *Mysticism and the South German-Austrian Anabaptist Movement*, 161, 163-64, Laube, II: 973. For an overview of the debate over whether or not this represents the "legitimate" line of Denck's legacy, see Packull, *Mysticism and the South German-Austrian Anabaptist Movement*, 155-56.

36 Christian Entfelder, *Von Gottes vnnd Christi Jesu unnsers Herren erkandtnuß/ ...*, in Köhler, *Early Modern Pamphlets*, fiche 1343, Nr. 3527, Cv(c); idem., *Zerspaltungen*, 939-40, 942-43; see also the summary in Packull, *Mysticism and the South German-Austrian Anabaptist Movement*, 171. On Bünderlin, see Claude R. Foster, "Hans Denck and Johannes Bünderlin: A Comparative Study," *MQR* 49 (1965), 115-24, especially 122-23; Packull, *Mysticism and South German-Austrian Anabaptist Movement*, 161-62 and Johannes Bünderlin, *Erklerung durch Vergleichung der Biblischen geschrifft, das der Wassertauf sampt anderen eüsserlichen gebreuchen, in der Apostolischen kirchen geübt*, in Köhler, *Early Modern Pamphlets*, fiche 1167-68, Nr. 246, Aiiii(b)-Av.

37 Entfelder, *Erkandtnuß*, Cv(b), *Zerspaltung*, 936-38, 948-51; Nicoladoni, 145-46. On the extent to which this amounts to a radicalization of Denck's criticism of the Anabaptists, see *Zerspaltung*, 976-77, n. 14.

38 Packull, *Mysticism and the South German-Austrian Anabaptist Movement*, 164-65, has commented on this convergence.

39 Compare, Entfelder, *Zerspaltung*, 936-38, 941 and Bünderlin, *Erklerung*, Eiii-Eiiii(b), Gii(b)-Gv. See also Packull, *Mysticism and the South German-Austrian Anabaptist Movement*, 164.

40 *Erkandtnuß*, Av(c), Biij. See also Williams, *Radical Reformation*, 1268 and Packull, *Mysticism and the South German-Austrian Anabaptist Movement*, 173.

41 See Packull, *Mysticism and the South German-Austrian Anabaptist Movement*, 159; Johannes Bünderlin, "The Reasons Why God Descended and Became Man in Christ, Through Whom, and How, He Atoned For and Restored Man's Fall and Man Himself Through the Messiah Whom he Sent," trans. and ed., Claude R. Foster, Jr. and William Jerosch, *MQR* 42 (1968), 269-75.

42 *Erklerung*, Aiiii, Av(f)-Biiii(b), Bv(b)-C(b); "Reasons Why God Descended," 262-63; Nicoladoni, 135-38; Jones, 37-38; Ulrich Gäbler, "Johannes Bünderlin," in *Bibliotheca Dissidentium* 3 (1982), 35-37.

43 *Erklerung*, Cii(b)-Ciii, Ciiii, D-Ev(d), Ev(f)-Ev(g), Fv(b)-Fv(c); "Reasons Why God Descended," 262-63, 269, 275-77; Nicoladoni, 136-38, 147-53; Jones, 37-39; Gäbler, "Bünderlin," 27-30, 34-37, 40-42.

44 Gäbler, "Bünderlin," 41.

45 Packull, *Mysticism and the South German-Austrian Anabaptist Movement*, 174. See *Erkandtnuß*, Aiij(b)-Aiiij, Av(g)-Av(h)

46 *Erkandtnuß*, Bij(b)-Biij.

47 Ibid, Biij(b)-Biiij.

48 *Zerspaltung*, 939, 941, 952, 955-57, 959-64, 971.

49 Ibid., 964-66.

50 Ibid., 963, 966-68.

51 Ibid., 967-68.

52 Ibid., 967.

53 Ibid., 936, 938, 939, 970.

54 Deppermann, *Melchior Hoffman*, 192-93.

55 Ibid., 241-62; especially 241-42 and 245. Werner Packull, "A Reinterpretation of Melchior Hoffman's *Exposition* Against the Background of Spiritualist Franciscan Eschatology with Special Reference to Peter John Olivi," in I.B. Horst, ed. *The Dutch Dissenters: A Critical Companion to Their History and Ideas* (Leiden: E.J. Brill, 1986), 32-33, emphasizes the importance of Revelation for Hoffman's understanding of the rest of Scripture.

56 Deppermann, *Melchior Hoffman*, 245-46, 256. A number of Hoffman scholars have pointed to the proximity of his historical periodization to that of Joachite and Pseudo-Joachite texts, see Packull, "Reinterpretation of Hoffman's *Exposition*," 34.

57 James Stayer, *Anabaptist and the Sword*, 2nd ed. (Lawrence, KS: Coronado Press, 1976), 217.

58 See, for example, *Auslegung der heimlichen Offenbarung des Apostels und Evangelisten Johannes, Vorrede* in Laube, I:492-93. See also Packull, "Reinterpretation of Hoffman's *Exposition*," 53, 56-57, 63 and Walter Klaassen, "Eschatological Themes in Early Dutch Anabaptism," in Horst, ed. *Dutch Dissenters*, 21.

59 Deppermann, *Melchior Hoffman*, 63, 67-70.

60 Ibid., 69; Klaus Deppermann, "Melchior Hoffmans Weg von Luther zu den Täufern," in Hans-Jürgen Goertz, ed. *Umstrittenes Täufertum 1525- 1975: Neue Forschungen* (Göttingen: Vandenhoeck & Ruprecht, 1975), 183-84; Klaus Deppermann, "Melchior Hoffman: Contradictions Between Lutheran Loyalty to Government and Apocalyptic Dreams," in Hans-Jürgen Goertz, ed. *Profiles of Radical Reformers: Biographical Sketches from Thomas Müntzer to Paracelsus* (Kitchener, ON: Herald Press, 1982), 182, 189.

61 Deppermann, *Melchior Hoffman*, 64 and "Hoffmans Weg," 80.

62 Deppermann, "Hofmanns Weg," 188-90.

63 Packull, "Reinterpretation of Hoffman's *Exposition*," 51-52.

64 Stayer, *Anabaptists and the Sword*, 217 and Deppermann, *Melchior Hoffman*, 248 had taken Hoffman's references to the binding of Satan for 1,000 years at the time of Paul's mission to the gentiles as evidence that in the *Commentary on the Revelation of St. John* he had dated the fall of the church much later. Consequently, Hoffman's dating of the fall to the end of the first century CE in his *Commentary on Paul's Letter to the Romans* appeared as a significant alteration in his vision of ecclesiastical history. More recently, however, Werner Packull, "Reinterpretation of Hoffman's *Exposition*," 53-54, 56, has argued convincingly that Hoffman's millennial references are subordinate to his main theme of a Constantinian fall of the church.

65 *Offenbarung*, Pvii(a) as quoted and translated in Packull, "Reinterpretation of Hoffman's *Exposition*," 54.

66 Packull, "Reinterpretation of Hoffman's *Exposition*," 55.

67 Deppermann, *Melchior Hoffman*, 248-49.

68 Packull, "Reinterpretation of Hoffman's *Exposition*," 54-55.

69 See ibid., 43.

70 Deppermann, *Melchior Hoffman*, 72-73, 80.

71 Ibid., 248-49; Stayer, *Anabaptists and the Sword*, 218.

72 Stayer, *Anabaptists and the Sword*, 212.

73 See Williams, *Radical Reformation*, 450; Werner Packull, "Melchior Hoffman — A Recanted Anabaptist in Schwäbisch Hall?" *MQR* 57 (1983), 100, 102. The sources of this information, the relevant parts of Hoffman's recantation and a report of it by Nicolaas Meyndertsz. van Blesdijk, are reproduced in translation in Packull, "Melchior Hoffman — Recanted Anabaptist?" 108-9.

74 There are a number of excellent summaries of the history of the Münster kingdom available in English. See Williams, *Radical Reformation*, 553-82; Willem De Bakker, "Bernhard Rothmann: The Dialectics of Radicalization in Münster," in Goertz, ed., *Profiles of Radical Reformers*, 191-202 and idem., "Bernhard Rothmann: Civic Reformer in Anabaptist Münster," in I.B. Horst, *The Dutch Dissenters*, 105-16; James M. Stayer, *Anabaptists and the Sword*, 227-39; idem., "Christianity in One City: Anabaptist Münster, 1534-35," in Hans Hillerbrand, ed. *Radical Tendencies in the Reformation:*

Divergent Perspectives (Kirksville, MO: Sixteenth Century Journal Publishers, 1988), 117-34; idem., *German Peasants' War and Anabaptist Community of Goods*, 125-30.

75 See James M. Stayer, "The Münsterite Rationalization of Bernhard Rothmann," *Journal of the History of Ideas* 28 (1967), 180, 192; De Bakker, "Dialectics of Radicalization," 191-99; Williams, *Radical Reformation*, 574; Snyder, *Anabaptist History and Theology*, 148.

76 The value of Rothmann's writings as sources for Münsterite self-understanding has been especially stressed by Ralf Klötzer, *Die Täuferherrschaft von Münster: Stadtreformation und Welterneurung* (Münster: Aschendorf, 1992) and Willem de Bakker, "Civic Reformer in Münster," 105-16.

77 Stayer, *Anabaptists and the Sword*, 240-48; Deppermann, *Melchior Hoffman*, 342-43, 345-46; Martin Brecht, "Die Theologie Bernhard Rothmanns," *Jahrbuch für Westfälische Kirchengeschichte* 78 (1985), 64-66.

78 *SBR*, 213-15 (*Restitution*), 332-33 (*Hiddenness of Scripture*), 380-82 (*Earthly and Temporal Power*). Good overviews of Rothmann's outline of human history are available in Stayer, *Anabaptists and the Sword*, 240-48 and Deppermann, *Melchior Hoffman*, 345-47.

79 *SBR*, 333-34, 336 (*On the Hiddenness of Scripture*), 382-89, 392-93, 401-4 (*On Earthly and Temporal Power*).

80 Ibid., 296-97 (*On Vengeance*), 333, 350, 352, 360-68 (*On the Hiddenness of Scripture*). See also Stayer, *Anabaptists and the Sword*, 240.

81 See Stayer, *Anabaptists and the Sword*, 216-17, 242 and Deppermann, *Melchior Hoffman*, 342-48.

82 *SBR*, 213-15 (*Restitution*). See also Stayer, *Anabaptists and the Sword*, 245.

83 This characterization of *Confession of Two Sacraments* has been adopted especially by Stayer, "Anabaptism in One City," 121 and *German Peasants' War and Anabaptist Community of Goods*, 126-27, and by de Bakker, "Civic Reformer," 109-10.

84 *SBR*, 142, 145-49, 155-58, 178, 180-87, 191, 194-95.

85 Frank J. Wray, "Bernhard Rothmann's Views on the Early Church," in Franklin H. Littell, ed., *Reformation Studies* (Richmond, VA, 1962), 230-32.

86 *SBR*, 235-43, 255-58; Wray, "Rothmann's Views on the Early Church," 232.

87 *SBR*, 134-35.

88 Brecht, "Theologie Rothmanns," 69-70.

89 *SBR*, 158-59, 161-65, 170-71.

90 Ibid., 194-95.

91 Ibid., 216-18, 242-43 (*Restitution*), 304, 337, 354 (*On the Hiddenness of Scripture*). See also Wray, "Rothmann's Views on the Early Church," 233, 237.

92 Wray, "Rothmann's Views on the Early Church," 237.

93 *SBR*, 217-18, 242-43.

94 Ibid., 375 (*On Earthly and Temporal Power*).

95 Ibid., 218 (*Restitution*), 337 (*On the Hiddenness of Scripture*).

96 Ibid., 337, 354 (*On the Hiddenness of Scripture*).

97 Ibid., 218-19, 270-76, 278 (*Restitution*), 286-87, 294-95 (*On Vengeance*), 352, 356-57, 364, 366-67 (*On the Hiddenness of Scripture*).

98 Williams, *Radical Reformation*, 553-54; Cornelius Krahn, *Dutch Anabaptism: Origin, Spread, Life and Thought* (Scottdale, PA and Kitchener, Ont.: Herald Press, 1981), 140-41. The most detailed analysis of this transition has been undertaken by Frank Wray, "Rothmann's Views on the Early Church," 229-38.

99 De Bakker, "Civic Reformer," 105-16.

100 Ralf Klötzer, "Hoffnungen auf eine andere Wirklichkeit. Die Erwartungshorizonte in der Täuferstadt Münster 1534/35," in Norbert Fischer and Marion Kobelt-Groch, eds.,

Aussenseiter zwischem Mittelalter und Neuzeit: Festschrift für Hans-Jürgen Goertz zum 60. Geburtstag (Leiden: E.J. Brill, 1997), 153-69.

101 This interpretation has been espoused most recently by Brecht, "Theologie Rothmanns," 72-73.

102 Of crucial importance in this revision has been the work of Karl-Heinz Kirchhoff, "Was There a Peaceful Anabaptist Congregation in Münster in 1534," *MQR*, 44 (1970), 357-70. See also Williams, *Radical Reformation*, 553-54, 562-64; Stayer, *Anabaptists and the Sword*, 228, 230-33 and "Radical Reformation," 269; Richard van Dülmen, *Reformation als Revolution: Soziale Bewegung und religiöser Radikalismus in der deutschen Reformation* (Munich, 1977), 288-98; de Bakker, "Civic Reformer," 107-11.

103 On Zwingli's political thought, see Stayer, *Anabaptists and the Sword*, 49-69.

104 Brecht, "Theologie Rothmanns," 52-58, 64-65; de Bakker, "Dialectics of Radicalization," 194-95; Klötzer, *Täuferherrschaft von Münster*, 139-40.

105 Cf. Brecht, "Theologie Rothmanns," 66-67 and Taira Kuratsuka, "Gesamtgilde und Täufer: Der Radikalizierungsprozeß in der Reformation Münsters: Von der reformatorischen Bewegung zum Täuferreich 1533/34," *ARG* 76 (1985), 249.

106 Stayer, *Anabaptists and the Sword*, 234.

107 *SBR*, 206-8. See also Brecht, "Theologie Rothmanns," 73 and on the question of dating this work, *SBR*, 195, de Bakker, "Civic Reformer," 111, n.13 and Klötzer, *Täuferherrschaft von Münster*, 204.

108 Stayer, *Anabaptists and the Sword*, 235, 238-39; de Bakker, "Civic Reformer," 112.

109 *SBR*, 276-77. On the characterization of Rothmann's thought about the origins of temporal authority as 'quasi-Lutheran,' see Stayer, *Anabaptists and the Sword*, 241, 243.

110 *SBR*, 376-77, 380-82, 387. See also Stayer, *Anabaptists and the Sword*, 243.

111 Stayer, *Anabaptists and the Sword*, 235-36.

112 *SBR*, p. 277.

113 Ibid., 287, 296.

114 Ibid., 376-77, 382-87, 392, 399.

115 Eike Wolgast, "Herrschaftsorganization und Herrschaftskrisen im Täuferreich von Münster 1534/35," *ARG*, 67 (1976), 180-81.

116 Ibid., 182-83, n. 14. Wolgast surmises that the model for Münster's government of twelve elders was an amalgam of the description of the Israelite tribal leadership contained in Numbers 1 and the title elder from the New Testament.

117 Ibid., 181-89. Further on the novelty of these political forms and their union of temporal and spiritual authority, see Gerhard Brendler, *Das Täuferreich zu Münster 1534/35* (Berlin, 1966), 128-29 and Klötzer, *Täuferherrschaft von Münster*, 89-93, 103-5. The fact that Rothmann's rationalization for Münster's constitutional experimentation first appeared after the Davidic monarchy had replaced the Elders' Constitution is explained by the time lag involved in the writing and printing of Rothmann's justifications. As James Stayer has noted, Rothmann's justifications for activities of the Anabaptists in Münster were often out of step with events. See "Christianity in One City," 133-34.

118 *SBR*, 281-82, 287, 290, 292-95, 297, 307, 350-56, 365-66.

119 Stayer, *Anabaptists and the Sword*, 240.

120 *SBR*, 278, 287, 290, 292, 295, 297, 346, 350-52, 355, 357, 364-67. See also Stayer, *Anabaptists and the Sword*, 249 and Deppermann, *Melchior Hoffman*, 347.

121 *SBR*, 281, 288, 332, 335. On the importance of history for Rothmann's hermeneutics, see Stayer, "Rothmann's Rationalization," 181 and Deppermann, *Melchior Hoffman*, 344.

[122] *SBR*, 212-19, 239-43, 255-56, 332-35, 349, 382-99.
[123] Deppermann, *Melchior Hoffman*, 365-66.
[124] Gary K. Waite, ed. and trans., *The Anabaptist Writings of David Joris 1535-1543* (Kitchener, ON and Scottdale, PA: Herald Press, 1994), 110-25; Gary K. Waite, *David Joris and Dutch Anabaptism 1524-1543* (Waterloo, ON: Wilfred Laurier University Press, 1990), 97-100.
[125] Waite, *Anabaptist Writings of David Joris*, 278-79.
[126] James M. Stayer, "Davidite vs. Mennonite," in I.B. Horst, ed., *The Dutch Dissenters*, 156.
[127] Ibid., 149-53.
[128] Ibid., 153.
[129] Obbe Philips, "Confession," in *SAW*, 207.

CHAPTER 7

DIALOGUE, HISTORY AND ANABAPTIST CONFESSIONALISM

Dear Brother Thomas:
For the sake of God please do not let it surprise you that we address you without title and ask you as a brother henceforth to exchange ideas with us by correspondence, and that we, unsolicited and unknown to you, have dared to initiate such future dialogue. God's Son, Jesus Christ, who offers himself as the only Master and Head to all who are to be saved and commands us to be brethren to all brethren and believers through the one common Word, has moved and impelled us to establish friendship and brotherhood and to bring the following theses to your attention. Also the fact that you have written two books on phony faith has led us to write to you. Therefore, if you will accept it graciously for the sake of Christ our Saviour, it may, if God wills, serve and work for the good. Amen.

Conrad Grebel and Friends to Thomas Müntzer, September 1524[1]

Hans-Jürgen Goertz's suggestion that the Grebel letters to Thomas Müntzer should be treated as an invitation to dialogue rather than as a programmatic statement provides an interesting and valuable approach to understanding some of the dynamics of the Radical Reformation. Applied to the formation of historical visions, this model suggests that visions evolved and were clarified over time, much as ideas develop in the course of human conversation. Various individuals and groups in the Radical Reformation did not encounter each other with fully developed and clearly formulated visions of ecclesiastical history. Rather, like their reform plans, their understandings of history tended to be vague and nebulous at the outset, but gradually coalesced in the course of dialogue. The conversation itself was, then, crucial to the process of formulating historical visions.[2]

The apparent starting point for this process came in Strasbourg at the beginning of the 1530s as Spiritualists and Anabaptists clarified their reforming visions in direct confrontation with one another. Here Sebastian Franck's *Chronica* was published. At roughly the same time, Bünderlin and Entfelder were publishing works with elaborate visions of salvation history and Pilgram Marpeck was developing an historical vision that, with the exception of Balthasar Hubmaier's, was probably the most detailed of any by the early Anabaptists. As we will see, the developments in Strasbourg were anticipated in important ways elsewhere. Nonetheless, they retain their status as the beginning of serious and extended dialogue about history among the Reformation radicals. This dialogue continued among Moravian and Melchiorite Anabaptists, and it contributed to the formulation of the historical visions contained in *The Hutterite Chronicle* and the *Martyrs Mirror*. The relative absence of such dialogue among the Swiss Brethren goes a long way toward explaining their comparatively less enthusiastic engagement with history.

This process, which saw close interaction between inter-group dialogue and the formulation of historical visions, suggests further that appeals to history played an important role in the formation of confessional identity, especially among the Anabaptist groups. We have seen that the fully formulated Anabaptist view of church history appeared rather late in the history of those groups. Among the Hutterites, it was a product of the last three decades of the sixteenth century and among the Mennonites it appears at the beginning of the seventeenth. That is to say, the Anabaptist view of church history was formulated most clearly when the radicalism of the Radical Reformation is assumed to have already passed, when the non-conformity of groups like the Anabaptists had already become legitimate. James Stayer's comment that the *Martyrs Mirror* celebrated a Radical Reformation that was already a concluded chapter of history may point us toward further processes at work in the creation of Radical Reformation histories.[3] The more developed historical visions of the Radical Reformation were not the products of the early years of the movements involved, but instead appeared in the context of a later, more settled existence. Scholars of Anabaptism have recently begun focusing more attention on developments in the later sixteenth and seventeenth centuries, and they have highlighted different dynamics at work in this later time. Their conclusions suggest that by the seventeenth century, Anabaptist groups were less voluntary communities than nonconformist variations on the denominational churches into which people were born.

Recognition of these changed circumstances points us toward recent research into the extent to which Anabaptists shared the experiences of their contemporaries in the territorial churches during Europe's confessional age. Confessionalism, the process whereby the religious denominations of early modern Europe created their own communities with distinct ideologies, institutions and systems of rituals, is usually discussed with reference to Catholics, Lutherans, Calvinists and Anglicans.[4] While some scholars of confessionalism have allowed that the Anabaptists shared in the processes of this phenomenon, until recently the idea of Anabaptist confessionalism has been treated essentially as an oxymoron.[5] One of the enduring legacies of Harold Bender's "Anabaptist Vision" has been an emphasis on the ethical dimensions of the movement rather than its theological, and by extension confessional, dimensions. Recently, however, the topic of Anabaptist confessionalism has drawn increasing attention.[6] Michael Driedger has argued in his study of Mennonite identities in the confessional age that confessional identities become most fixed, clearest and most significant during public controversies.[7] In other words confessional identities are closely tied to some of the same dynamics we have observed at work in the elaboration of historical visions.

The connection between historical writing and confession building, long recognized in the literature of the magisterial Reformation, has recently been confirmed by the research of Irena Backus, who emphasizes the importance of history as a court of appeal in the struggles for religious identity in the sixteenth century.[8] The full flowering of confessional historical writing is evident in Lutheran quarters with the publication between 1559 and 1574 of *The Magdeburg Centuries* and in the Catholic response to it, Caesar Baronius' *Ecclesiastical Annals*. Interesting from the perspective of the present study is that while Lutheran historical writing initially had not paid close attention to the church in the first four or five centuries of its existence, this became an important battleground in the contest between the *Magdeburg Centuries* and the *Ecclesiastical Annals*.[9] The contexts in which the more detailed Anabaptist histories were written in the later sixteenth and seventeenth centuries, and the contents of those histories, suggest that similar confessional agendas were at work in the historical writing of some of the Reformation radicals.

Strasbourg

The works of Franck, Bünderlin and Entfelder indicate most clearly the interaction between religious controversy and the formation of historical visions in the early years of the Reformation. None of these men first turned to serious reflection on the lessons of history in Strasbourg, but events there provided encouragement for processes already underway. As we have seen, Franck's historical interest was closely intertwined with his developing criticism of the magisterial Reformation and the evolution of his own Spiritualist theology. I have argued elsewhere that Franck's writings in Strasbourg should also be regarded as contributions to the conflict between Marpeck and the Spiritualizers over the restitution of the ceremonies and practices of the primitive church. As a result, key elements of Franck's thought, most notably his definition of heresy and its place in the history of Christianity, matured in the context of this conflict.[10] This is not to say that the Strasbourg environment was responsible for the formulation of that vision *in toto*; clearly Franck's statements in *A Chronicle or Description of Turkey* and the fact that he had already begun work on the *Chronica* in Nuremberg indicate that he had recognized the pedagogical value of history and laid out the essentials of his historical vision long before arriving in Strasbourg. But the environment in Strasbourg, and especially the interaction between the radicals there, was important for the full formulation of that vision.

Some of Franck's comments in his letter to John Campanus suggest that he knew Johannes Bünderlin personally and that Bünderlin's thought may have influenced his own evolving theology. The exact ways in which Franck's historical vision may have been influenced by the other religious dissidents in Strasbourg are difficult to ascertain, but it is likely that Bünderlin, and possibly also Christian Entfelder, further encouraged his historical research. Likely both men had developed their own elaborate historical visions independently of Franck before their arrivals in Strasbourg. Werner Packull speculates that they may have come to the imperial city with manuscripts of some of their writings already in hand.[11] Both men were connected to the Nicolsburg Reformation before moving to Strasbourg.[12] It is reasonable to assume, then, that they were exposed to the detailed historical arguments in Hubmaier's works. It seems, in fact, that historical reflection and argumentation may have already been common in some circles of Moravian Anabaptism. In 1529 Clemens Adler, possibly a Gabrielite missionary in Silesia, penned the treatise *The Judgement Concerning the Sword with its Distinct Power in the Three Realms*. A justification for pacifism strongly influenced by Spiritualist assumptions, this work contains an elaborate theology of history.[13] The Radical Reformation in Moravia and Silesia witnessed the interaction of Anabaptist and Spiritualist themes that was to reappear in Strasbourg,[14] and it appears that the same forces may have been at work encouraging historical reflection there as we witness in Strasbourg.

If debates in Strasbourg only reinforced an already established appeal to history in the thought of Franck, Bünderlin and Entfelder, in others, most notably for Pilgram Marpeck and Melchior Hoffman, it provided the initial impetus to serious historical reflection. If, as Stephen Boyd suggests, Marpeck arrived in Strasbourg with a copy of *The Church Discipline* in hand, we can assume that his reflections on history at that time amounted to little more than the biblically-oriented restitutionism shared by so many early Anabaptists. But in the arguments formulated against the Spiritualizers in *A Clear Refutation* and *A Clear and Useful Instruction* we see the beginnings of a more detailed understanding of ecclesiastical history. The vision developed there is further fleshed out in his writings from subsequent conflicts with other Anabaptists, Spiritualists and magisterial Reformers, but the initial impetus for that vision came from the conflict with the Spiritualizers.[15] Hoffman was not an obvious participant in the Strasbourg conflict over restitution of the ceremonies and practices of the primitive church, although like Franck he, too, might have been on its fringes.[16] In any case, the Strasbourg conflicts provide an important context for the development of Hoffman's historical musings as they do for the development of his theology more generally. His historical references before his first arrival in the city, especially in the 1526 *Daniel 12 Commentary*, suggest a commitment to a restitutionist agenda and a vague primitivism with little historical detail. However, his understanding of the historical past changed dramatically after the move to Strasbourg, as is evident in his writings from 1530.

While Hoffman passed on his historical vision directly to the Melchiorites of the north, Marpeck's influence was less direct in this regard. Nonetheless, Marpeck contributed to further historical reflection among Anabaptists not only as an author, but likely also as a sponsor and editor of Anabaptist publications. Given his connections to Anabaptist congregations in Moravia, it is reasonable to assume that he provided part of the impetus to the further development of historical thinking there. The method of that influence is clarified by Werner Packull's recent research into the publishing activity of the Marpeckites in Augsburg during the 1540s. Included among the works published, or republished, by Marpeck and his circle are a number which contain significant historical reflection. Of Marpeck's own works these include *The Exposure of the Babylonian Whore*, the *Admonition* and the *Reply to Caspar Schwenckfeld*. These works were supplemented by materials from other authors, most notably Hubmaier's *Old and New Teachers on Believer's Baptism* and *Dialogue with Zwingli's Baptism Book*. Marpeck himself indicated on one occasion that he had provided Moravian Anabaptists with copies of one of his books, likely the *Admonition*. It is also possible that the influence of the Marpeckites continued after the end of their publishing activity in the 1540s. The *Kunstbuch* contains, among others, writings by Sebastian Franck and Christian Entfelder and it is likely that Marpeckite manuscripts remained influential among the Swiss Brethren in the later sixteenth century and into the seventeenth.[17]

Hutterites

Given the contacts between the Moravian Anabaptist communities and the dissenters in Strasbourg, it is not surprising that we hear echoes of the historical arguments used in the Strasbourg debates in Moravia, but these arguments were further developed in the context of continued discord and polemic. As we have seen, the elaboration of the Hutterite historical vision was a slow evolutionary process, spanning much of the middle half of the sixteenth century. Robert Friedmann traced the origins of Hutterite historical awareness to some of the earliest interactions between factions in Moravian Anabaptism. He identified the schism of 1533 between the Hutterites, Gabrielites and Philippites and later dialogue between the Hutterites and Gabrielites in 1545 as "external impulses for a more systematic history with its necessary substratum of salvation history as its prehistory."[18] The essential outlines of Friedmann's explanation for the development of Hutterite perceptions of ecclesiastical history appear solid, although the process was more gradual than he suggested, and one most allow for internal dynamics of the movement as well.

If, as Friedmann suggested, the initial impetus for Hutterite reflections on ecclesiastical history came from the schism of 1533, there is little immediate evidence of this fact, especially evidence that Hutterites began looking into the long term history of the church. As we have seen, one of the earliest apologetic works of the Hutterites, Ulrich Stadler's *Cherished Instructions*, indicates the adherence to at best a general New Testament primitivism, akin to that espoused by other early Anabaptist movements. When challenged on the value of the primitive church as a normative model for the communal life Stadler, in fact, conceded the historical argument to his opponents. Instead, he chose to defend Hutterite practices on the basis of eternal divine decrees and contemporary circumstances.[19]

Therefore, if the initial impetus came from the 1533 schism, it took some time to develop and percolate through the movement. By the early 1540s it was showing signs of bearing fruit. As we noted earlier, Peter Riedemann's *Account of Our Religion, Doctrine and Faith* marks an important advance in the development of a distinctive Hutterite vision of ecclesiastical history. This is immediately obvious in his more general historical orientation. He exhibits a clearer and more definite sense of the normative nature of the apostolic church and appears to be searching for a clear conception of the date and historical circumstances associated with the fall of the institutional church. Riedemann's more historical orientation is most obvious in his defence of community of goods. He refuses to concede the historical precedent as Stadler had, and instead searches Scripture for evidence of the practice of community of goods by the apostolic church outside Jerusalem. Riedemann's reflections did not occur in a vacuum, however. The *Account* was written while he was imprisoned in Hessia, composed at least in part as an explanation to the Landgrave Philip of the teachings and practices of the Hutterites. As such it responds as much to the concerns of Hessian Anabaptists as it does to matters in Moravia. But in the end, Riedemann's contacts with Moravia while he was writing the *Account* give it more than local significance.[20] We can assume, then, that it reflects Riedemann's experiences from earlier conflicts and dialogues as well. From 1537 to 1539 he played a central role in dialogues with other Anabaptist groups, including some of the parties to the schism of 1533. Especially important were his discussions in 1538 and 1539 with Philippites who had returned to the Reich and with Melchiorites in Hessia. A crucial element in these discussions, as so often in discussions involving Hutterites and other Anabaptist groups, was community of goods.[21]

According to Friedmann's explanation for the rise of Hutterite historical thinking, the effects of the schism of 1533 were reinforced by the 1545 dialogue and ultimately reunion with the Gabrielites. The background to this dialogue and its details, indeed, provide us with important insights into the development of the Hutterite historical vision. At the centre of Hutterite-Gabrielite relations looms the character of Gabriel Ascherham. Ascherham has been recognized as an important goad for Hutterite thinking about history. Werner Packull suggests that an account he wrote of Anabaptist beginnings in Moravia was an important factor in Braitmichael's decision to chronicle the early history of the Hutterites.[22] But of more immediate impact than Gabriel's description of early Moravian Anabaptism was likely his *Distinction Between Divine and Human Teaching*. Written between 1540 and Gabriel's death in 1545, this tract was a response to the perceived poaching of his followers by Hutterite missionaries after the breakup of his community and its expulsion from Moravia in 1535.[23]

As part of a general denunciation of papists, Lutherans and so-called Brethren, Gabriel levels a scathing attack on Hutterite teaching and practice from a decidedly Spiritualist position. The basis for his denunciation of "the Brethren" in particular is their legalism and excessive concern with the external and creaturely. Given that it is the spiritual, not the external, that saves, he argues that these concerns, in fact, lead to a new form of idolatry.[24] In service of this argument, Gabriel challenges directly the Hutterite perception of ecclesiastical history. He accepts the claim that the apostolic church is normative for contemporary reform of the church, and in that sense he can be identified as a primitivist. However, his vision of the apostolic church is dominated by the image of Pentecost. The distinguishing characteristic of the community of the first Christians is their reception of the gift of the Spirit; where the Spirit is, there the true church is. This true church has existed through the ages, although it is not always to be identified with the visible church. In Gabriel's metaphor for the true church, the stones have fallen, but not the foundation, the Word of God. Gabriel is not completely clear on when exactly the "stones" fell, although his suggestions point to sometime around 1,400 to 1,500 years before he was writing. But in the dawning new age of grace, the church will be restored. The crucial matter in this restoration is the reception of the Spirit, and it has nothing to do with external matters.[25]

Gabriel's identification of the true, spiritual church lays the groundwork for a withering attack on the legalism and externalism of the Hutterites. He charges them with thinking that since they have faith, baptism, community and a separated life preached to them according to the witness of Scripture, they need nothing more. In fact, though, they have never heard the Gospel of the faith of the Spirit. Their concern with establishing the correct form of baptism has led to a new idolatry which places more trust in the water than in the Spirit. In light of the discord generated by disagreements over the external practice of baptism, Gabriel suggests that it is better to let go of the external rite than to fight over it.[26]

Given the centrality of discussions of community of goods in relations between Anabaptist groups in Moravia, it is not surprising that this topic plays a central role in Gabriel's polemics. He takes a slightly different tack than other critics of the Hutterites by keeping his attention focused firmly on the example of the first church in Jerusalem. He acknowledges that community of goods was practised there, but he argues that unlike the practice of contemporary "Brethren" it was a voluntary community of goods. The first Christians' spontaneous alienation of their goods to the community was the natural outgrowth of their reception of the Spirit. Where this voluntary renunciation and the presence of the Spirit are lacking, one is not following the model of the apostolic church. In their legislated community of goods the Hutterites are, in fact, trying to buy their way into the kingdom of God, and therefore they are establishing a new form of works righteousness.[27]

The impact of Gabriel's criticism on Hutterite thinking about church history is immediately evident in Peter Walpot's *Five Articles of the Great Controversy Between Us and the World*. Inserted in *The Hutterite Chronicle* under the year 1547, this work occupies a pivotal position in the evolution of Hutterite historical thinking; it grew out of the dialogue with the Gabrielites in 1545 and amounts to the earliest incarnation of the text which became eventually *The Great Article Book*.[28] Its connections to the elucidation of the Hutterite historical vision are evident, particularly in the role it played in establishing the importance of historical precedent and the nature of the model portrayed by the apostolic church. With particular reference to the history of baptism and community of goods, *The Five Articles* develop the essential outlines of the argument employed in *The Great Article Book*, but these outlines lack the full detail of the arguments in the latter work. The most obvious omissions in *The Five Articles* are the references to extra-biblical sources of information on the practices of the apostolic and post-apostolic church.[29] The impact of the exchange with the Gabrielites, and especially the impact of Gabriel's polemics, are particularly evident in the *Five Articles'* treatment of community of goods. As Friedmann notes, Walpot relies in his argument for the necessity of community of goods on the model of the apostolic church, but he roots his argument as well in the teaching on *Gelassenheit*.[30] In this way he attempted to answer Gabriel's charge that the determining feature in the practice of the true church was the presence of the Spirit, and consequently more the disposition of Christians than their external activities. But beyond this he set out to establish the practice of community of goods as normative for the people of God. The assembling of biblical sources outlining the practice of community of goods not only in the primitive church, but also in the history of Israel anticipates the basic structure of the argument in *The Great Article Book*.[31]

The step from the vision of *The Five Articles* to that of *The Great Article Book* amounted largely to the addition of extra-biblical sources and appeal to the history of the church after the apostolic age. The likely source of most of this information was Sebastian Franck's *Chronica*. It is tempting, therefore, to posit a direct connection between the availability of the *Chronica* and the further development of the Hutterite vision of ecclesiastical history. Certainly, by the late 1540s there was sufficient interest in history and historical arguments among Hutterite polemicists to make reaching for the treasure trove of historical information in Franck's work a natural reaction. But experiences of the Hutterites in the second half of the sixteenth century appear to have made historical research even more attractive to those polemicists. The decisions to establish archives and an historical library at Neumühle, the assumed connections between the activities of Walpot and Braitmichael, and the *Chronicle's* reliance on historical sources besides the *Chronica*, particularly Josephus and Eusebius, all suggest that this was something more than fortuitous borrowing from Franck's text.

The transition to the sophisticated portrayals of the history of Christianity presented in *The Hutterite Chronicle* and *The Great Article Book* did, in fact, occur in the context of dialogue not only with other Reformation radicals, but also with representatives of the magisterial Reformation. In 1557 a group of Lutheran theologians assembled at Worms published a damning critique of the Anabaptists. The Hutterite reply, a *Handbook* against the charges levelled at them, likely written by Peter Walpot between 1558 and 1560, is regarded by many as one of the great doctrinal works of the Hutterites. As such, it highlights the continued importance of the polemical context for the further development of Hutterite thought. It is noteworthy that in this work Walpot began moving beyond the exclusive use of biblical sources to defend believers' baptism and appealed as well to the authority of Origen, Jerome and Augustine, as well as to conciliar decisions.[32] Not surprisingly, the final impetus to the vision contained in *The Great Article Book* also came in the context of dialogue and conflict. In 1567 members of Swiss Brethren groups in Moravia wrote a lengthy book detailing seven points of disagreement between them and the Hutterites. The Hutterites replied with *Seven Articles* of their own. During and after the writing of the *Seven Articles* from 1567 to 1571 they also were engaged in dialogue with the Polish Brethren. In contrast to the discussion in the *Handbook*, the justification for, and correct practice of, community of goods returns to centre stage in the *Seven Articles*. The conclusion of the first article highlights the fruit of continued historical reflection when applied specifically to this subject by insisting that community of goods was practised by the church not only in New Testament times, but that the practice continued to the time of Augustine, when it fell into abeyance until reinstituted by the Hutterites.[33]

Together with a greater historical awareness, we see in the Hutterite sources of the later sixteenth century increasing theological sophistication and a clearer definition of group identity. In fact, the milestones in the evolution of their historical vision appear in some of the most important Hutterite theological writings of the sixteenth century: Riedemann's *Account of Our Religion, Doctrine and Faith*, Walpot's *Five Articles*, *The Great Article Book*, and the *Handbook*.[34] It seems logical, then, to treat the development of a more sophisticated vision of ecclesiastical history as an integral component of confession building in the emerging Hutterite movement.

The interaction between historical vision and confessionalism becomes clearer if we examine the context in which these developments occurred. Robert Friedmann has schematized the development and institutionalization of the Hutterite movement. The first generation, which he associates with the leadership of Jacob Hutter and Peter Riedemann from approximately 1530 to 1555, he sees as representative of the "sect" type in its purest form. The second generation, the golden years of the movement under the leadership of Peter Walpot (1565-1578), gives evidence of the increasing institutionalization of the movement. During the third and fourth generations Friedmann sees further standardization and the movement of the Hutterites toward a denominational type of church. These trends are especially evident during the leadership of Andreas Ehrenpreis from 1630 to 1661.[35]

The greatest strides in the creation of a Hutterite historical vision were made in the last years of the first and throughout the second generation of the movement, at precisely the time, according to Friedmann, when it evolved from the sect type to a denominational form of the brotherhood church.[36] In the early years of the movement we see a combination of charisma and a vague primitivism. For example, Jakob Hutter's regularization of community of goods involved an appeal to the model of the primitive church, but little more by the way of historical argumentation. Under the leadership of Peter Riedmann, however, the Hutterites moved from their first to their second generation, with a significant elaboration of their historical vision. As we saw, this is evident especially in Riedemann's treatment of the history of community of goods in the *Account*. Riedemann is credited with institutionalizing Hutter's charisma on this practice. Clearly that process included appeals to history.[37]

The integration of confessionalism and historical writing becomes closest, however, during the Walpot years. Then a burst of historical activity coincided closely with the rapid institutionalization of the movement.[38] Taken together, the writings of the Walpot era reveal the twin prongs of a confessionalist strategy. Braitmichael himself described his work as a "mirror to guard against division and error."[39] To do so he attempts to explain how the frequent persecution suffered by the Hutterites fits into God's plan, and in the process exhorts them to steadfastness in the face not only of that persecution, but also in response to the temptation of a more tolerant world. It is in this context that we see the importance of his emphasis on the Constantinian fall of the church and the subsequent dichotomy between the persecuting world and the persecuted church. The historical vision contained in *The Great Article Book* focused more on answering another perceived threat to the Hutterites:

challenges from other religious groups, especially other Reformation radicals, but at times magisterial Reformers as well. In addition to the lure of the world, there was the appeal of false shepherds to be countered. In this case, emphasis on the continuity, and therefore legitimacy, of Hutterite teachings and practice was an important strategy in maintaining the allegiance of the faithful.

Mennonites

Like the Hutterites, Mennonites developed in the midst of controversy an elaborate vision of the past that played an important role in confessionalist strategies within the movement. William Keeney has suggested that conflicts involving the early Mennonite movement can be periodized in the following manner. From 1530 to 1540 the Mennonite leadership squared off against Catholics on the right and other Anabaptist groups on the left. From 1540 until roughly 1554/55 primary challenges to the movement came from the Reformed on the right and Spiritualists on the left. The third period of controversy in the early movement, which reached its highpoint between 1565 and 1568, was marked especially by internal divisions in the movement.[40]

Interestingly, despite the sophistication of the Melchiorite historical vision from the outset and the confrontational environment in which the movement found itself, the historical vision of Menno and his immediate successors remained fairly static. Menno scholars are generally agreed that the thought of the Anabaptist leader evolved significantly over the course of his career.[41] No such development is evident, however, in Menno's historical vision. Instead, that vision and most of its details remain consistent throughout his writings, in spite of his frequent confrontations not only with Münsterites, Davidjorites and various Spiritualists, but also with representatives of the Reformed establishment. This controversial context likely explains a prominent theme in Menno's historical arguments, his emphasis on the orthodoxy of the movement and refusal to identify it with a tradition of heretical dissent from the visible church.[42]

As with Menno's historical vision, we see no obvious development in Dirk Philips' historical understanding. Like Menno, Dirk remains consistent throughout his writings in his appeals to history and historical argumentation, despite the fact that his thought also developed amidst controversy. Like Menno he sought to steer a path between Münsterite literalism on the one hand and Spiritualism on the other. As late as 1559 Dirk still felt compelled to respond to the arguments of Bernhard Rothmann in his *On Spiritual Restitution*.[43] Challenges to the Mennonite movement intensified in the spiritualist crisis of 1564 to 1567 related to the publication and then translation into Dutch of two of Sebastian Franck's letters.[44] Dirk's *Answer to Sebastian Franck* indicates the underlying restitutionism of his position, but lacks further historical reflection. A focal point in his response is Franck's claim that the true church has fallen and there has been no divine commission for its restoration. Dirk grants the first assertion, but challenges the second. He identifies the contemporary Mennonite community with the visible congregation of the Lord, but does not go to great pains to establish his case historically. He draws parallels between the fall and restitution of the visible church and other biblical examples of restitutions following falls, for example the cases of Adam and Eve and the restitution of circumcision after its perversion. In his closest allusion to an historical precedent, he points to Elijah's restitution of worship in Israel as a model for the need to restore the visible church.[45] Beyond this, however, there are few historical references, and none to the medieval church and its opposition.

By way of contrast, subsequent controversy within northern Anabaptism encouraged extensive historical reflection. The history of Dutch Anabaptism in the later sixteenth and seventeenth centuries is the history of repeated schisms punctuated by attempts to reunify the various groups. Although the details of these schisms and attempted unifications are complex, the basic outlines will be laid out here. Disagreement over the rigorous application of the ban led to a division in 1557 between the Waterlanders and the more rigorous mainstream Mennonite movement. In 1566-67 this more rigorous group again split between Frisian and

Flemish factions, ostensibly over questions of congregational autonomy but other ethnic and cultural concerns were operating behind the scenes. In 1587 there occurred a further schism between the Old and Young Flemish, followed shortly by a similar division among the Frisians. The divisiveness of the early Melchiorite Anabaptists was counteracted by attempts at unification coming often, but not exclusively, from the Waterlanders.[46] The schisms within Dutch Anabaptism were driven by a variety of dogmatic, practical and personal factors, but the situation was further complicated by the continuing influence of Spiritualist ideas on the movement. Even after the danger from the Münsterites, Obbenites and Davidjorites abated, the Spiritualist challenge continued. The publication of Franck's letters in 1564 provoked a Spiritualist crisis for the young Mennonite movement, and subsequently, Spiritualist ideals were especially influential among the Waterlanders. An important source of Spiritualist ideas, and especially the influence of Franck, was the Spiritualist reformer Dirck Volckertsz Cornheert whose thought resonated with the Waterlander elder Hans de Ries.[47]

Not surprisingly, greater historical sophistication among the Mennonites was connected closely to the development of a martyrological tradition. The connection is not apparent, however, at the beginning of that tradition as is evidenced in the first edition of *The Sacrifice Unto the Lord*.[48] But in the century between the publication of this work and van Braght's edition of the *Martyrs Mirror* sectarian controversy and a changing social and political environment influenced extensively the writing of Anabaptist martyrologies.[49] Brad Gregory has examined this process against the backdrop of tensions within north German and Dutch Anabaptism. In the gradual expansion of *The Sacrifice Unto the Lord* after the initial edition of 1562/63 he sees evidence of an Old Frisian appropriation of the Anabaptist martyrology. Against that appropriation, he sets evidence of other Melchiorite groups pulling together their own martyrological traditions by assembling pamphlets on martyrs excluded from *The Sacrifice*. Competing matyrologies, then, were important weapons in conflicts between different factions within the movement, but history and martyrs could also serve a role in attempts to overcome those divisions. The vastly expanded list of martyrs, and with it the broader scope of Christian history, contained in Hans de Ries' *History of the Martyrs or Genuine Witnesses of Jesus Christ* (1615) betrays a strategy of inclusiveness as part of attempts to unify the splintered Anabaptist movement in the north. The importance of church history as a polemical weapon was highlighted immediately thereafter in Peter Jan Twisk's *History of the True Witnesses of Jesus Christ*, which was little more than an Old Frisian appropriation of de Ries' materials accomplished by asserting in a new preface that all the martyrs were unanimous in their faith and adhered to an Old Frisian Confession of Faith included in the martyrology. By way of contrast, the Waterlander response, the 1631/32 edition of the *Martyrs Mirror*, again betrays a strategy of inclusiveness. Its widened historical perspective complemented its broadened criteria for the inclusion of martyrs: teachings common to all Anabaptist groups but distinct from those of Protestants and Catholics. At the same time, de Ries points to another concern of the martyrologists by warning against the lure of the world in the form of new found tolerance and prosperity.[50]

A similar concern with the temptations of the world pervades the expanded and more famous *Martyrs Mirror* edited by van Braght. According to van Braght, in the past Satan had persecuted true Christians as a "roaring lion," but now he tempts them with prosperity and a "crossless Christianity." On one level, then, the *Martyrs Mirror* is a call to reform through an appeal to the "bloody army of spiritual champions" of the past.[51] But the lure of the world was not the only challenge faced by van Braght and his fellows. Michael Driedger has called attention recently to the neglect, especially in English language treatments of the *Martyrs Mirror*, of the immediate polemical context in which this work appeared, the so-called "War of the Lambs."[52] This conflict pitted conservative elements within the Dutch Mennonite community against a preacher of the Amsterdam Church *bij het Lam*, Galenus Abrahamsz, and his supporters. Abrahamsz was also a member of the spiritualist-inclined

Collegiant movement in the Netherlands and it was his connection to the Collegiants that sparked the original conflict in the Church *bij het Lam*.[53] The "War of the Lambs," then, came out of the ongoing spiritualist challenge to Dutch Anabaptism in the tradition of Obbe Philips, the Davidjorites, Sebastian Franck and Dirck Volckertzs Cornheert, and from that tradition Galenus took a scathing critique of the Mennonite restitutionist agenda.

In 1655 a request by Amsterdam Collegiants to use the chapel of the Church *bij het Lam* for their meetings raised the ire of conservatives in the congregation and led to concerns about Abrahamsz's connections to the group. To clarify his position, in 1657 Abrahamsz and a supporter, David Spruyt, submitted to the church leadership nineteen articles outlining their beliefs. In the articles they contrasted sharply the churches of the seventeenth century, including their own congregation, with the apostolic church. They acknowledged that the church of the apostles had possessed the gifts of the Spirit, but argued that the true church on earth had subsequently fallen. After the deaths of the apostles spiritual decay had gradually set in. While this stance could have been reconciled with Mennonite restitutionist assumptions, Abrahamsz and Spruyt went further and denied that there was any divine commission for the restitution of the true church on earth. As a result, no contemporary church offices had apostolic authority and the ceremonies and practices of the contemporary church were different from those of the apostolic church. In 1659 the nineteen articles, which by agreement were to be circulated only in manuscript form, were published with an unfavourable introduction. Galenus and Spruyt responded with *Further Explanation of the Nineteen Articles*. In this work they strengthened their criticism of the restitutionist position by linking their criticism of contemporary churches with prevailing Collegiant millennial thinking, and insisting that the restitution of the true church would only occur in the millennium. In the meantime, the only option available to the faithful was to meet in informal groups without pretense to being the true church, as the Collegiants did.

Later the same year *Refutation of the Work Entitled: Answer by Means of Remarks, Questions and Reasons, Given to Laurens Hendricksz* filled in further historical details about the fall of the apostolic church. This work claimed that the gifts of the Spirit given to the early church had been extraordinary; they had made the leaders of the first church truly apostolic teachers. These gifts persisted through the early persecutions of the church, but the conversion of Constantine led to the corruption of the church by secular forces and to its spiritual decay. Thereafter, gifts of the Spirit were still dispensed, but these were granted only on an individual basis to make possible personal salvation. They did not include the prophetic or teaching abilities granted to the early church.[54] In Galenus' thought, then, we see a clearly formulated spiritualist historical vision which reformulates some of the central elements of the Anabaptist historical vision, but derives from them radically different conclusions which challenge directly the whole restitutionist tradition.

The controversy stirred up by the exchanges between Galenus and his opponents continued to escalate, leading to a conference of conservative Mennonite leaders from around the Low Countries in Leiden in 1660, ultimately splitting the congregation of the Church *bij het Lam* and leading to aftershocks in Mennonite communities throughout the Netherlands. The chairman of the Leiden meetings was the Dordrecht Elder Thielemann Janz van Braght. Van Braght's edition of the *Martyrs Mirror* appeared in print about one month after the beginning of the meetings in Leiden and had obviously been in the works long before the calling of the meeting. Nonetheless, Driedger argues that contemporaries would have recognized in it, and especially in its doctrine of the church, an anti-Galenist writing.[55]

In the *Martyrs Mirror* van Braght takes up directly the challenge of Abrahamsz and the Collegiants. Part I of the massive martyrology consists of a history of baptism and of martyrs to the true faith from the time of Christ to the eve of the Reformation. Van Braght identified this as his original contribution to the martyrological tradition.[56] Van Braght's introduction to the book and this first section, when read in the context of the opening salvos of the "War of the Lambs," indicate clearly the polemical nature of the work.

Van Braght shared with his opponents both the assumption that the institutional church had fallen and the belief that there remained a faithful remnant. At the outset he claimed:

> This bloody army of the spiritual champions, who fought unto blood and death for the Lord, commenced with the beginning of the world, as though God's saints were born to suffer and fight; and as though God had designed that His church should be tried from the beginning and all through, even as gold in the furnace, that her purity might become more manifest.[57]

In true Augustinian fashion, van Braght then traces the interaction of the persecuting false church and persecuted true church throughout history, beginning with Cain and Abel. From the time of David, he indicates, the true church has been a visible entity, although at times it was obscured, for example during the Babylonian captivity. Furthermore, while the true church has remained essentially the same throughout the ages, at different times God has prescribed different ceremonies and different ordinances for it.[58]

To this point van Braght's depiction of the church's history could be reconciled with the views of the Collegiants. But as van Braght continues, the fundamental opposition between the two visions of the church and its history becomes apparent. Van Braght allows that even after the Incarnation at times the true visible church was obscured. Nonetheless, he insists that it remains in existence:

> It is settled, therefore, that the visible church of Jesus Christ (for this is the one in whom the preaching of the holy Gospel, faith, baptism and whatever there is more besides have place) shall exist through all time, even unto the consummation of the ages; for otherwise, the promise. "Lo, I am with you all the days," etc., can not be fulfilled in her.[59]

Integral to this true visible church are the "external ceremonies" instituted by Christ:

> Even as, besides preaching and faith, baptism shall continue in the church to the end of time, so also the holy supper. ... it follows that there will be, throughout the ages to the end of the world, a church which will observe the external ordinance of Christ not only in respect to holy baptism, but also to the holy supper, ...[60]

Van Braght then follows up with a history of the succession of the true church not only in persons, but also in correct doctrine from the apostolic church to the contemporary age. Van Braght's version of the *Martyrs Mirror* was, then, much more than a further elaboration of the Mennonite martyrological tradition. It was at the same time a refutation of the Collegiant understanding of ecclesiastical history and the perceived spiritualist threat it posed to Mennonite congregations in the Netherlands.

Recent research indicates that these conflicts which rent Dutch Anabaptism at the end of the sixteenth century and the beginning of the seventeenth and contributed to the development of a more sophisticated historical vision were themselves the consequences of Mennonite confession building. Faced both with escalating tensions and divisions within the movement and decreasing persecution and further integration of the movement into larger Dutch society, Mennonite leaders looked to unify their followers and clearly demarcate the boundaries between themselves and the larger society. Karl Koop has undertaken a detailed study of Mennonite confessions of faith and concluded that they enter a new phase between 1577 and 1632 when they become more comprehensive, systematic and doctrinal.[61] Disputes among Mennonites at this time were based largely on divisions over this strategy and reached a climax in the 1660s, especially in the conflict between Galenus Abrahamzs and conservative leaders at the Church *bij het Lam*. Van Braght's *Martyrs Mirror*, insofar as it is a product of that conflict, provides us with an historical vision that is also a tactic in a confessionalist strategy.[62]

Studies of Mennonite martyrologies of the sixteenth and seventeenth centuries have indicated their importance as tools for confession building. They are integral parts of a process of formalizing distinctive characteristics of early Anabaptism, often at the time when these are being lost to the life of the movement. The result is a crucial component of a strategy Michael Driedger has termed "conforming nonconformity."[63] The historical vision portrayed in the *Martyrs Mirror* indicates that much the same process is at work for historical visions generally.

In addition to the challenges of the frequent schisms which rent the Anabaptist community, Mennonite confessionalist strategies needed to respond as well to the lure of the world in a context of increasing prosperity and toleration for Anabaptists in the wider society of the Dutch Golden Age. These concerns are evident already in the 1631/32 edition of the *Martyrs Mirror* edited by Hans De Ries. There it appears that resisting the draw of the world is of greater concern than reuniting the splintered Anabaptist movement.[64] Clearly, this was also a primary concern for Thieleman van Braght. In the *Martyrs Mirror* he describes the temptations of prosperity and tolerance as more dangerous than those of persecution:

> These times are certainly more dangerous; for then Satan came openly, through his servants, even at noon-day, as a roaring lion, so that he could be known, and it now and then was possible to hide from him; besides his chief design was to destroy the body: but now he comes as in the night, or in the twilight, in a strange but yet pleasing form, and, in a two-fold way, lies in wait to destroy the soul; partly to trample under foot, and annihilate entirely, if this were possible, the only saving Christian faith; partly to destroy the true separated Christian life which is the outgrowth of faith.[65]

In his move to guard against the temptations of the world, van Braght appears to overcome the earlier divisiveness of the martyrological tradition and to speak of the baptist-minded in general, seemingly in the tradition of de Ries and the Waterlanders.[66] However, an underlying confessionalist agenda is still evident in this work. In the introduction to the *Martyrs Mirror* he highlights the significance of correct doctrine in the succession of the true church:

> The latter [the succession of doctrine] is a sign and evidence of the former [the succession of persons], so that the former cannot subsist without the latter. Where the latter is, the former need not be looked for so carefully. But where both are found in truth and verity, it is not to be doubted that there is also the true and genuine church of God, in which God will dwell and walk; which has the promise of an eternal and blissful life; and about which the holy Scriptures glory and teach so much.[67]

Doctrinal matters are, then, crucial in the identification of contemporary Mennonite churches as heirs of the apostolic church:

> Here the words of Tertullian are applicable. He says: "The Christian church is called apostolic but not just because of the succession of persons, but on account of the kinship of doctrine, since she holds the doctrine of the apostles." *Lib. de praescript, etc.*
>
> This doctrine everyone who boasts of the true succession must prove from the apostolic writings, as the means by which the church was originally instituted, subsequently established, and maintained through all times (we speak of the Christian and evangelical church). Therefore this doctrine must necessarily, also in these last times, be the mark of true succession.[68]

In his emphasis on the importance of doctrinal succession van Braght echoes *The Magdeburg Centuries*, on which he might have modelled the organization of the first part of the *Martyrs Mirror*.[69] The details of the faith of the martyrs through the ages indicates van Braght's adherence to the Mennonite confessionalist agenda. As evidence of the faith professed by contemporary Mennonites, and ultimately by the true church throughout the ages, van Braght includes in the introduction to the *Martyrs Mirror* texts of *The Apostles' Creed* and three seventeenth-century Mennonite confessions of faith: the *Olijftacxken* (1626), the *Jan Cents*

Confession (1630), and the *Dordrecht Confession* (1632). The apparently increasing complexity of true doctrine evident in the increasing length and complexity of the confessions of faith van Braght explains as a natural elaboration of matters of faith as a consequence of human contention. These amount, then, to differences of style, but not the essentials of the faith. The Mennonite confessions included were key components of Mennonite confessionalist strategies and were, in fact, the confessions agreed to at a synod held in Haarlem in 1649 and reconfirmed at the Leiden Synod of 1660.[70]

Swiss Brethren

The Swiss Brethren represent an exception to the general trend of increasing historical sophistication of the various Anabaptist groups in the later sixteenth and seventeenth centuries. Hans Schnell's book includes elements of what has been identified as the Anabaptist view of church history, but that vision is limited and relatively unusual among known Swiss Brethren sources. We are faced with the question, then, of why the Swiss Brethren stand out in this way. Recent research into the manuscript traditions of the Swiss Brethren in the late sixteenth and early seventeenth centuries has led Arnold Snyder to suggest that some revisions in our understanding of their later history might be in order. While Snyder has pointed the way some of those revisions may lead, he is also clear that we are only at the beginning of the process of understanding them.[71] Our conclusions about the historical visions of the later Swiss Brethren are, then, provisional at best.

The avoidance of elaborate historical arguments by the later Swiss Brethren is further a mystery because they appear to have had a number of important building blocks for the development of such a vision: they were involved in religious controversies which might have generated historical reflection and they had access to some important sources which would have aided in developing such a vision. In the second half of the sixteenth century the Swiss Brethren frequently crossed swords with other radicals and with representatives of the magisterial Reformation. Documents from these conflicts, especially the protocols from disputations with the Lutheran and Reformed clergy, would seem a natural place to look for the development of historical arguments. A series of such disputations aimed at winning the Swiss Brethren back to the respective territorial churches culminated in the 1571 Frankenthal Disputation in the Palatinate.[72] The protocols, in fact, reveal a lack of historical reflection on the part of the Swiss Brethren even on such obvious topics as the legitimacy of infant baptism or the celebration and understanding of the Lord's Supper. Even when their opponents appealed directly to historical arguments—as, for example, at Frankenthal when citing the writings of the church fathers to indicate that early on the church had baptized infants and claiming that even if believers' baptism were apostolic practice, it had fallen into abeyance shortly after the time of the apostles until it was revived by Nicholas Storch in 1522—the Swiss Brethren fail to respond with historical arguments.[73] Schnell's pamphlet suggests in addition that by the second half of the sixteenth century the Swiss Brethren had access to at least some of the materials required to develop a more sophisticated historical vision. This suspicion is confirmed by recent research into Marpeckite influences on the Swiss Brethren in the second half of the sixteenth century.[74] For example, Arnold Snyder has discovered that among sources taken into the Swiss Brethren manuscript tradition in the wake of the Frankenthal Disputation were such historically sophisticated works as Hubmaier's *Old and New Teachers on Believers' Baptism* and *Dialogue with Zwingli's Baptism Book*.[75]

It may be that as research into late sixteenth- and early seventeenth-century Swiss Brethren manuscript traditions progresses we will find more evidence of a vigorous engagement with ecclesiastical history by these least-historical of the Anabaptists. However, in the absence of such evidence, I will hazard an explanation for the Swiss Brethren failure to engage more fully with history. It appears that two issues are relevant here: the impetus to go to the historical record and the opportunity to undertake such research. In both cases, the experience of the Swiss Brethren distinguishes itself from that of other Anabaptist groups. Although they regularly confronted other religious traditions, the Swiss Brethren were from early in the movement's history free of the sorts of spiritualist challenges that regularly confronted other Anabaptists.[76] As we have seen, the clash between Anabaptists and Spiritualists seems to have been especially profitable in terms of the historical research it generated. The Swiss Brethren also likely lacked the opportunity for detailed historical reflection afforded their Hutterite and Mennonite cousins in the more stable environments of the Netherlands and Moravia.

Notes

1 Harder, 285 (=*QGTS* 1:13).

2 Hans-Jürgen Goertz, "'A Common Future Conversation:' A Revisionist Interpretation of the September 1524 Grebel Letters to Thomas Müntzer," in Werner O. Packull and Geoffrey Dipple, eds., *Radical Reformation Studies: Essays Presented to James M. Stayer* (Aldershot: Ashgate, 1999), 73-90. Andrea Strübind has argued that in these letters the Zurich radicals take over Müntzer's vision of ecclesiastical history, see *Eifriger als Zwingli: Die frühe Täufer Bewegung in der Schweiz* (Berlin; Dunker & Humblott, 2003), 216-19. Strübind's observations appear valid for some of the details of Grebel's vision, but I believe both parties had their own sense of the church's historical fall.

3 James M. Stayer, "The Radical Reformation," in James A. Brady, Jr., Heiko A. Obermann, and James D. Tracy, eds. *Handbook of European History: Late Middle Ages, Renaissance, and Reformation*, vol. 2: *Visions, Programs and Outcomes* (Grand Rapids, MI: Eerdmans, 1995), 274. For Stayer's comments on the passing of the Radical Reformation and the growing respectability of the Anabaptists in the later sixteenth century, see ibid., 251, 266-67, 273; idem., "The Passing of the Radical Moment in the Radical Reformation," *MQR* 71 (1997): 147-52.

4 Good definitions of confessionalism are developed in Ernst Walter Zeeden, *Die Enstehung der Konfessionen: Grundlagen und Formen der Konfessionsbildung im Zeitalter der Glaubenskämpfe* (Munich and Vienna: R. Oldenbourg, 1965), 9-10; R. Po-Chia Hsia, *Social Discipline in the Reformation: Central Europe 1550-1750* (London and New York: Routledge, 1989), 4-5 and Heinz Schilling, "Confessional Europe," in Brady, Oberman, and Tracy, eds. *Handbook of European History*, vol. 2, 641.

5 See Schilling, "Confessional Europe," 643.

6 See, for example, Karl Koop, *Anabaptist-Mennonite Confessions of Faith: The Development of a Tradition* (Kitchener, ON: Pandora Press, 2004); Hans-Jürgen Goertz, "Zwischen Zweitracht und Eintracht. Zur Zweideutigkeit täuferischer und mennonistischer Bekenntnisse," *Mennonitischer Geschichtsblätter* 43/44 (1986/87): 16-46; idem., "Kleruskritik, Kirchenzucht und Sozialdisciplinierung in den täuferischen

Bewegungen der Frühen Neuzeit," in Heinz Schilling, ed., *Kirchenzucht und Sozialdisciplinierung im frühneuzeitlichen Europa* (Berlin: Duncker und Humblot, 1994), 183-98; idem., "Zucht und Ordnung in nonkonformistischer Manier. Kleruskritik, Kirchenzucht und Sozialdisciplinierung in der Bewegungen der Täufer," in *Antiklerikalismus und Reformation: Sozialgeschichtliche Untersuchungen* (Göttingen: Vandenhoeck und Ruprecht, 1995), 103-14; Michael Driedger, *Obedient Heretics: Mennonite Identities in Lutheran Hamburg and Altona during the Confessional Age* (Aldershot: Ashgate, 2002); Astrid von Schlachta, *Hutterische Konfession und Tradition (1578-1619): Etabliertes Leben zwischen Ordnung und Ambivalenz* (Mainz: Verlag Philipp von Zabern, 2003).

7 Driedger, *Obedient Heretics*, 172-78, especially 173.

8 See Gerald Strauss, "The Course of German History: The Lutheran Interpretation," in *Enacting the Reformation in Germany: Essays on Institution and Reception* (Aldershot: Variorum, 1993), I: 665-86 and Irena Backus, *Historical Method and Confessional Identity in the Era of the Reformation (1378-1615)* (Leiden and Boston: E.J. Brill, 2003), especially 61, 390-91.

9 Enrico Norelli, "The Authority Attributed to the Early Church in the *Centuries of Magdeburg* and the *Ecclesiastical Annals* of Caesar Baronius," in Irena Backus, ed. *The Reception of the Church Fathers in the West: From the Carolingians to the Maurists* (Leiden: E.J. Brill, 2001) II: 745-74, especially 746-47, 753-54. For a good overview of the developing Lutheran treatment of the early church, see Backus, *Historical Method*, 326-91.

10 Geoffrey Dipple, "Sebastian Franck in Strasbourg," *MQR* 73 (1999), 783-802.

11 Werner O. Packull, *Hutterite Beginnings: Communitarian Experiments during the Reformation* (Baltimore and London: Johns Hopkins University Press, 1995), 133-39.

12 Werner Packull, *Mysticism and the Early South German/Austrian Anabaptist Movement 1525-1531* (Scottdale, PA and Kitchener, ON: Herald Press, 1977), 103; Martin Rothkegel, "Die Nikolsburger Reformation 1526-1535: Von Humanismus zum Sabbatarismus" (ThD diss., Charles University Prague, 2000), 42-43, 105.

13 See Packull, *Hutterite Beginnings*, 106-19.

14 Rothkegel, "Von Humanismus zum Sabbatarismus," 134-35, 180.

15 Geoffrey Dipple, "Pilgram Marpeck, the Spiritualizers and the Anabaptist View of Church History," in C. Arnold Snyder, ed., *Commoners and Community: Essays in Honour of Werner O. Packull* (Kitchener, ON: Pandora Press, 2002): 217-32.

16 Stephen Boyd, *Pilgram Marpeck: His Life and Social Theology* (Durham, NC: Duke University Press, 1992), 62, 84-90.

17 Werner O. Packull, "Preliminary Report on Pilgram Marpeck's Sponsorship of Anabaptist *Flugschriften*," *MQR* 75 (2001): 75-88; Heinold Fast, "Vom Amt des 'Lesers' zum Kompilator des sogenannten Kunstbuches: Auf den Spuren Jörg Malers," in Norbert Fischer and Marion Kobelt-Groch, eds. *Aussenseiter zwischen Mittelalter und Neuzeit: Festschrift für Hans-Jürgen Goertz zum 60. Geburtstag* (Leiden: E.J. Brill, 1997), 187-217. On the impact of Marpeckite writings in the Swiss Brethren in the later sixteenth century, see below, p. 276.

18 As quoted in Packull, *Hutterite Beginnings*, 381, n. 65. For the details of the 1533 schism, see ibid., 224-35.

19 See above, pp 150-51.

20 Werner O. Packull, "Weite Weg von Mähren nach Hessen. Die zweite Missionsreise Peter Riedemanns," in Fischer and Kobelt-Groch, eds., *Aussenseiter zwischen Mittelalter*

und Neuzeit, 171-85; idem., "The Origins of Peter Riedemann's *Account of Our Faith*," *SCJ* 30 (1999): 61-69; Andrea Chudaska, *Peter Riedemann: Konfessionsbildendes Täufertum im 16. Jahrhundert* (Gütersloh: Gütersloher Verlagshaus, 2003), 53-62, 216-45.

21 See Chudaska, 175-86, 195-202; Robert Friedmann, "The Philippite Brethren: A Chapter in Anabaptist History," *MQR* 32 (1958), 285-87; *The Chronicle of the Hutterian Brethren* (Rifton, New York: Plough Publishing, 1987), 163-69, 176-86.

22 Packull, *Hutterite Beginnings*, 225.

23 Ibid., 123, 292-93; Wilhelm Wiswedel, "Gabriel Ascherham und die nach ihm benannte Bewegung," *ARG* 34 (1937), 7-10. Astrid von Schlachta has commented on the significance of the challenges posed by Ascherham and Pilgram Marpeck for the development of Hutterite teachings on community of goods, in *Hutterische Konfession und Tradition*, 185-86.

24 Wiswedel, "Gabriel Ascherham," 23, 31-32, 35, 234. For a good overview of Gabriel's thought, see Packull, *Hutterite Beginnings*, 127-30, 292-302.

25 Wiswedel, "Gabriel Ascherham," 22-23, 26-28, 30-31.

26 Ibid., 237-40.

27 Ibid., 241-51; Packull, *Hutterite Beginnings*, 128-29.

28 See George H. Williams, *The Radical Reformation*, 3rd ed. (Kirksville, MO: Sixteenth Century Journal Publishers, 1992), 1073 and the comments of Robert Friedmann in Kathleen Hasenberg, trans., "A Notable Hutterite Document: Concerning True Surrender and Christian Community of Goods," *MQR* 31 (1957), 22-23.

29 *Chronicle of the Hutterian Brethren*, 251-94, especially 251-57 and 265-75.

30 Friedmann in Hasenberg, 23.

31 *Chronicle of the Hutterian Brethren*, 265-75.

32 Robert Friedmann, *Hutterite Studies* (Goshen, IN: Mennonite Historical Library, 1961), 221-22; Williams, *Radical Reformation*, 1219-20; Wilhelm Wiswedel and Robert Friedmann, "The Anabaptists Answer Melanchthon," *MQR* 29 (1955), 215-16, 226.

33 C. Arnold Snyder, *Anabaptist History and Theology: An Introduction* (Kitchener, ON: Pandora Press, 1995), 242-43; Leonard Gross, *The Golden Years of the Hutterites: The Witness and Thought of the Communal Moravian Anabaptists During the Walpot Era, 1565-1578* (Scottdale, PA and Kitchener, ON: Herald Press, 1980), 164-93; von Schlachta, *Hutterische Konfession und Tradition*, 192-99. On exchanges between the Hutterites and Swiss Brethren and Gabrielites at this time, see *The Chronicle of the Hutterian Brethren*, 388-91, 394, 411-26; Gross, *Golden Years*, 150-63; Williams, *Radical Reformation*, 1091-98. For a good summary in English of the discussions between the Hutterites and the Polish Brethren, see Stanislaw Kot, "Polish Brethren and the Problem of Communism in the XVIth Century," *Transactions of the Unitarian Historical Society* 11 (1956): 38-53.

34 On the theological significance of these works, see Williams, *Radical Reformation*, 1076. Also Friedmann, *Hutterite Studies*, 151, 195, 224; idem., "Peter Riedemann: Early Anabaptist Leader," *MQR* 44 (1970), 30-31; idem., "Second Generation Anabaptism as Illustrated by the Walpot Era of the Hutterites," *MQR* 44 (1970), 391-92; Hasenberg, 25; Packull, "Origins of Riedemann's *Account*," 61-62; idem., "Weite Weg von Mähren," in Fischer and Kobelt-Groch, eds. *Aussenseiter zwischen Mittelalter und Neuzeit*, 171.

35 Friedmann, "Second Generation Anabaptism," 391. Subsequent research has begun pointing to the details of this confessionalist strategy. Werner Packull, "Origins of Riedemann's *Account*," 68-69, has suggested the existence of a confessionalist strategy in Riedemann's *Account*; Andrea Chudaska has elaborated on Riedemann's importance as the founder of Hutterite confession building and Leonard Gross, *The*

Golden Years of the Hutterites, 202-3, identifies Walpot's strategy in *The Great Article Book* with the confessionalist practices of the magisterial Reformers.

36 Friedmann, "Second Generation Anabaptism," 391-92 and *Hutterite Studies*, 151.

37 On Riedemann's role in institutionalizing community of goods, see Chudaska, 283-89; James Stayer, *The German Peasants' War and Anabaptist Community of Goods* (Kingston and Montreal: McGill-Queen's University Press, 1991), 144; Friedmann, *Hutterite Studies*, 82. Astrid von Schlachta notes Riedemann's importance in anticipating later institutionalization of the Hutterite movement, see *Hutterische Konfession und Tradition*, 9, 15, 246-47.

38 A number of historians have commented on the connection between consolidation in the Hutterite movement and active concern with its history. See Friedmann, "Second Generation Anabaptism," 391-92; idem, *Hutterite Studies*, 151, 279; Gross, *The Golden Years of the Hutterites*, 200-1; Williams, *Radical Reformation*, 1076. The most thorough and recent treatment of this subject, particularly as it pertains to developments at the end of the sixteenth and beginning of the seventeenth centuries is Astrid von Schlachta's *Hutterische Konfession und Tradition*, especially 16-17, 132-79, 220-33, 272, 393.

39 *The Chronicle of the Hutterian Brethren*, lxxiv.

40 William Keeney, *The Development of Dutch Anabaptist Thought and Practice from 1539-1564* (Nieuwkoop: B. DeGraaf, 1968), 22-23.

41 See Snyder, *Anabaptist History and Theology*, 341-42. Snyder identifies 1546 as the watershed between Menno's early thought and his later thought.

42 Williams, *Radical Reformation*, 596.

43 Jacobus ten Doornkaat Koolman, *Dirk Philips: Friend and Colleague of Menno Simons 1504-1568*, trans., William Keeney, ed., C. Arnold Snyder (Kitchner, ON: Pandora Press, 1998), 99-100; Douglas Schantz, "The Ecclesiological Focus of Dirck Philips' Hermeneutical Thought in 1559: a Contextual Study," in H. Wayne Pipkin, ed., *Essays in Anabaptist Theology* (Elkhart, IN: Institute of Mennonite Studies, 1994), 200.

44 See Williams, *Radical Reformation*, 749-50.

45 *WDP*, 455-64.

46 S. Zijlstra, *Om de Ware Gemeente en de Oude Gronden. Geschiednis van de Dopersen in de Nederlanden 1531-1675* (Hilversum and Leeuwarden: Uitgeverij Verloren and Fryske Akademy, 2000), 270-401.

47 On Cornheert and his influence on de Ries, see Williams, *Radical Reformation*, 1187-90; Gerrit Voogt, *Constraint on Trial: Dirck Volckertsz Cornheert and Religious Freedom* (Kirksville, MO: Truman State University Press, 2000) and Zijlstra, *Om de Ware Gemeente*, 317-26. A good overview of the Spiritualist pressure on Dutch Anabaptism is provided by H.W. Meihuizen, "Spiritualistic Tendencies and Movements among the Dutch Mennonites of the 16th and 17th Centuries," *MQR* 27 (1953): 259-304.

48 See above, p. 167.

49 Brad Gregory, "Prescribing and Describing Martyrdom: Menno's *Troestlijke Vermaninge* and *Het Offer des Heeren*, *MQR* 71 (1997), 608; idem, *Salvation at Stake: Christian Martyrdom in Early Modern Europe* (Cambridge, MA: Harvard University Press, 1999), 231-35.

50 Gregory, *Salvation at Stake*, 231-45.

51 Alan F. Kreider, "The Servant is Not Greater than his Master: The Anabaptists and the Suffering Church," *MQR* 58 (1984), 6-7, 25.

52 Driedger, *Obedient Heretics*, 56-57.

53 On the Collegiants and the role of Galenus Abrahamzs in the movement, see Andrew Fix, *Prophecy and Reason: The Dutch Collegiants and the Early Enlightenment* (Princeton: Princeton University Press, 1991), especially pp. 84-112. For discussions of the ongoing spiritualist challenges to the Dutch Mennonites, see Samme Zijlstra, "Anabaptists, Spiritualists and the Reformed Church in East Frisia," *MQR* 75 (2001), 57-73; Mirjam G.K. van Veen, "Spiritualism in the Netherlands from David Joris to Dirck Volckertsz. Cornheert," *SCJ* 33 (2002), 129-50.

54 On the role of Galenus Abrahamsz, his place in the escalating conflict in the Church *bij het Lam*, and the details of his writings, see Meihuizen, "Spiritualistic Tendencies," 284-304; idem., *Galenus Abrahamsz 1622-1706: Strijder voor een onbeperkte verdraagzaamheid en verdediger van het Doperse Spiritualisme* (Haarlem: H.D. Tjeenk Willink & Zoon N.V., 1954), 54-76; Fix, *Prophecy and Reason*, 93-103; idem., "Mennonites and Collegiants in Holland 1630-1700," *MQR* 64 (1990), 165-67; Driedger, *Obedient Heretics*, 53-55; Zijlstra, *Om de Ware Gemeente*, 402-17.

55 Driedger, *Obedient Heretics*, 54-57. On the subsequent events in the War of the Lambs and the relations thereafter between the Lambists and the Zonists, see Zijlstra, *Om de War Gemeente*, 417-29.

56 *Martyrs Mirror*, 19.

57 Ibid., 12.

58 Ibid., 21-26.

59 Ibid., 24.

60 Ibid.

61 Koop, *Anabaptist-Mennonite Confessions of Faith*, 11-13. For details of the divisions within Dutch Anabaptism and their relationship to the confessions of faith of the age, see pp. 114-34. See also Goertz, "Zwischen Zweitracht und Eintracht," 33-43; "Kleruskritik, Kirchenzucht und Sozialdisciplinierung," 194; "Zucht und Ordnung in nonkonformistischer Manier," 109. Although he disagrees with Koop about the extent to which Mennonite confessionalism of the late sixteenth and early seventeenth centuries represents continuity with the earlier ideals of the movement, Goertz does recognize its importance for its seventeenth-century history.

62 Driedger, *Obedient Heretics*, 51-57.

63 Goertz, "Zwischen Zweitracht und Eintracht," 38-42; "Kleruskritik, Kirchenzucht und Sozialdisciplinierung," 194-98; "Zucht und Ordnung in nonkonformistischer Manier," 109-14. Goertz sees in this formalization process a loss of the early radicality, and by implication the original ideals, of the movement. Koop, *Anabaptist-Mennonite Confessions of Faith*, 150-51, although he disagrees with Goertz on the extent to which confessionalism amounted to a departure from the original ideals of the Anabaptists, does see in the increasing formalization of the movement significant changes in its characteritics.

64 Gregory, *Salvation at Stake*, 243-45. S. Zijlstra, *Om de Ware Gemeente*, 464-93 provides a good overview of the interaction between the Mennonites and wider Dutch society from the late sixteenth to the late seventeenth centuries.

65 *Martyrs Mirror*, 8. On the importance of the lure of the world for van Braght's enterprise and the context in which this occurred, see Gregory, *Salvation at Stake*, 245-47; Cornelius Dyck, "The Suffering Church in Anabaptism," *MQR* 59 (1985), 7; Kreider, "The Servant is not Greater Than His Master," 6-7, 24-25; Cornelius Krahn, "Anabaptism and the Culture of the Netherlands," in Guy F. Herschberger, ed., *Recovery of the Anabaptist Vision: A Sixtieth Anniversary Tribute to Harold Bender*

(Scottdale, PA: Herald Press, 1957), 219-36; Mary Sprunger, "The Golden Age: Prosperity and Martyr Tradition," *Mennonite Life* 45 (1990), 28-31.

66 Gregory, *Salvation at Stake*, 247.

67 *Martyrs Mirror*, 26.

68 Ibid., 26-27.

69 Gregory, *Salvation at Stake*, 247 notes the organizational parallels between the *Martyrs Mirror* and *The Magdeburg Centuries*.

70 *Martyrs Mirror*, 26-44. See especially pp. 19 and 27. On the relationship of the *Martyrs Mirror* to the confessionalist strategy, see Driedger, *Obedient Heretics*, 54-57.

71 C. Arnold Snyder, "The (Not-So) 'Simple Confession' of the Later Swiss Brethren. Part I: Manuscripts and Marpeckites in the Age of Print," *MQR* 73 (1999): 679; idem., "The (Not-So) 'Simple Confession" of the Later Swiss Brethren. Part II: The Evolution of Separatist Anabaptism," *MQR* 74 (2000), 120.

72 Williams, *Radical Reformation*, 1227. For the details of these disputations, see ibid., 309, 918-22, 1219, 1227-29; John Oyer, ed. and trans., "The Pfeddersheim Disputation, 1557," *MQR* 60 (1986): 304-51; John Howard Yoder, *Anabaptism and Reformation in Switzerland: An Historical and Theological Analysis of the Dialogues Between Anabaptists and Reformers*, trans. by David Karl Stassen and C. Arnold Snyder, ed. by C. Arnold Snyder (Kitchener, ON: Pandora Press, 2004); Jess Yoder, "A Critical Study of the Debate between the Reformed and the Anabaptists, Held at Frankenthal, Germany in 1571" (PhD diss., Northwestern University, 1962); idem., "The Frankenthal Debate with the Anabaptists in 1571: Procedure, Participants," *MQR* 36 (1962): 14-35.

73 Jess Yoder, "Critical Study," 187, 194, 223-24, 236; idem., "Frankenthal: Procedure, Participants," 128, 136.

74 See Snyder, "(Not-So) 'Simple Confession,' Parts I and II"; idem. "The 'Perfection of Christ' Reconsidered: the Later Swiss Brethren and the Sword," in Packull and Dipple, eds., *Radical Reformation Studies*, 53-69; John Roth, "Harmonizing the Scriptures: Swiss Brethren Understandings of the Relationship between the Old and New Testament during the Last Half of the Sixteenth Century," in ibid., 35-52.

75 Snyder, "(Not-So) 'Simple Confession,'" 687, 697-98.

76 Snyder, *Anabaptist History and Theology*, 172 makes this point specifically about Swiss Brethren hermeneutics.

CONCLUSION

Studies of historical reflection in the Radical Reformation tend to rest on two basic assumptions. On the one hand, they assume that the historical thinking of the age was dominated by a primitivism that manifested itself most clearly in an appeal to the apostolic church as the golden age of the church. On the other hand, they view this primitivism and the visions of the past it produced as driving forces in the agendas of religious reformers of the age. For example, the Anabaptists are regarded as being sectarian because they were primitivists—their commitment to a gathered church grew out of their belief that the primitive church was both a voluntary community and the true church. As we have seen, there is an element of truth to these assumptions. However, the full range of historical reflection of the age was much more complicated and nuanced than this picture would suggest.

The late medieval and early modern periods in European history can be characterized generally as primitivist in the sense that the teachings and institutions of the past were often attributed greater authority than those of the present. The pervading assumption about historical development was that it involved a process of deterioration rather than progress. This fundamentally medieval mode of thought was reinforced by the events and mindsets of the Renaissance and Reformation. The Renaissance humanists further enshrined the authority of the ancients with their *ad fontes* methodology. This approach was reinforced by the biblicism of the magisterial Reformers. In both cases an appeal to the authority of ancient texts could naturally be extended to an appeal to ancient institutions and practices as models for contemporary reforms. However, this primitivism amounted to much more than the simple juxtaposition of the contemporary church with the pristine, apostolic church. The writings of Erasmus and other Renaissance humanists suggest that there was no simple or single golden age of the church in the past. The humanist understanding of the historical development of the church was much more sophisticated than that. However, there was a common sense of the church's historical deterioration, and a shared perception that the rise of scholasticism was an important factor in that decline. This position was initially a rallying point for reform-minded individuals of all stripes. It united a variety of humanists, including those who would ultimately remain loyal to the church and those who would leave it in the end. It also formed a common ground between humanists and magisterial Reformers and facilitated the movement from the former camp into the latter. Most surprisingly, it was also the starting point for the historical reflections of a number of early Reformation radicals.

However, the visions of the past developed by these reformers were initially less driving forces in the development of their reforming agendas than they were mirrors to reflect contemporary abuses. This is evident in the evolution of the historical visions of those who opted for the Reformation. As their reforming visions evolved and more practices and teachings of the contemporary church came under censure, Reformers like Luther, Zwingli and Eberlin searched further into the church's past for the sources of contemporary abuses. Interestingly, the same process is also apparent in the development of the historical visions of a number of the early Reformation radicals. For example, Karlstadt, Müntzer, Grebel and Hubmaier all initially identified the rise of scholasticism as the root of the church's deterioration, but quickly came to the conclusion that it was only the latest manifestation of problems that went much deeper.

While a number of the early Reformation radicals started their historical reflections in the same place as the humanists and magisterial Reformers, they quickly came to very different conclusions about the events and lessons of ecclesiastical history. The radicalness of their rejection of contemporary ecclesiastical institutions is evident in their willingness to identify the fall of the visible church at almost the beginning of its history. Among those often identified as Evangelical Anabaptists, this accompanied the elevation of a biblically-based image of the primitive church as a normative model for the reform of the contemporary church. The structure, practices and teachings of the true church were those handed down by Christ and practiced by the apostles. In this appeal to the primitive church the Anabaptists were restitutionist in a way that the humanists and the magisterial Reformers were not. We can characterize their agenda as primitivist in the sense that the apostolic church existed in the past, but their appeal to that model was more biblicist than historical. Initially among these Anabaptists there was usually little further reflection on church history between the apostolic age and contemporary events. What reflection did occur tended to be associated with justifying specific reform proposals, most often the practice of believers' baptism. The driving force in these proposals was, then, much more the Anabaptists' biblicism than a primitivism derived from any sort of developed theory about a past golden age or an elaborate historical vision.

The initial, vague primitivism of the early Anabaptists evolved into an elaborate vision of ecclesiastical history in at least some of the surviving Anabaptist traditions. However, this was a slow and gradual process. Some Anabaptists, like Hubmaier, very quickly turned to history for arguments to support their reforming agendas; others like Conrad Grebel or Michael Sattler never developed detailed visions of the church's history. The surviving evidence from Swiss Brethren sources suggests that the development of a sophisticated understanding of ecclesiastical history was not a foregone conclusion. In the long run, it appears that a crucial factor in the formulation of more detailed historical visions was involvement in controversies which forced participants to actively confront history to justify positions they had adopted. Particularly fruitful in encouraging historical reflection were controversies involving Anabaptists and Spiritualists.

At one level the Spiritualist reforming vision, too, can be labelled restitutionist: it focused on restoring the church of Pentecost. This was an underlying feature in the visions of Müntzer and Karlstadt, and it is a central image in Müntzer's insistence on worshipping a speaking God. It likely also explains Denck's baptism of Hut on Pentecost and possibly the timing of the reforming activities of Kautz, Hätzer and Denck in Worms. Initially, the Spiritualists and Spiritualist Anabaptists regarded the structure and practices of the apostolic church as possible elements of the restored church of the Spirit. Both Müntzer's liturgical reforms at Allstedt and Kautz's alliance with Reublin and activities in Strasbourg are understandable in this context. On this basis, it appears that the shared restitutionist agenda of the Spiritualists and Anabaptists played a crucial role in the constructive misunderstanding that developed between them. However, the restitutionism of the Spiritualists was not the restitutionism of the Anabaptists. Although the Spiritualists wanted to emulate the primitive church insofar as it manifested the gifts of the Spirit, they saw it and the apostolic age as one stage in the progression of humanity toward spiritual maturity. As a result, the apostolic church never had the same status and authority as the visible church on earth for the Spiritualists as it did for the Anabaptists. Its structures and practices had no intrinsic worth, but derived their value from their association with the Spirit-filled community. Initially the potential conflicts between Anabaptist and Spiritualist restitutionism were not apparent. The Grebel letters to Thomas Müntzer and the joint reforming venture of Kautz and Reublin in Strasbourg indicate that at first an alliance of Spiritualism and Anabaptism seemed a viable option. However, as the details of their respective visions of the restored church became clear, the structures and practices of the primitive church were divorced from the Spirit-filled community in eyes of the Spiritualists. Increasingly the "outward ceremonies" were viewed as stumbling blocks to greater spiritual understanding.

Like the Anabaptists, the Spiritualists derived their image of the true church from the Bible. In its pages they found the history of the Spirit-filled church through the ages. However, in contrast to the Anabaptists, who concentrated primarily on the New Testament to form their image of the true church, the Spiritualists tended to be more "flat-Bible" exegetes. Their different perspective is clear in the emphasis placed on the church of the prophets. This was a crucial element in the thought of Müntzer and it explains the translating activities of Denck and Hätzer. The longer view of the history of the "church" adopted by the Spiritualists, it appears, encouraged them to be more historically-minded initially than were their Anabaptist counterparts. In contrast to the relatively straight-forward Anabaptist appeal to New Testament practices and prescriptions, the Spiritualists were forced to argue from examples of the church of the Spirit through the ages and to sort through the parallels between the churches of those different ages. Likely Müntzer's application of the *ordo rerum* as an hermeneutical device to understand the lessons of history played an important role here. It was the criticism rather than the defence of New Testament restitutionism, then, that seems at first to have been the greater impetus to historical reflection and historical theorizing.

The elaboration of a comprehensive Spiritualist view of salvation history and the place of the apostolic church in it called forth a response from Anabaptist quarters. This interaction is most evident in the exchanges between Anabaptists, Spiritualizers and Spiritualists in Strasbourg at the beginning of the 1530s. However, the Strasbourg debates were only one episode, albeit a very important one, in a whole series of such exchanges. The writings of Bünderlin and Entfelder suggest that clashes in Moravia in the late 1520s had already fostered considerable reflection on salvation history and the history of the church. It is tempting to see as the source of the engagement with history in the Moravian conflicts the influence of Hubmaier, and for this reason we may have to qualify somewhat claims about the primacy of historical reflection among the Spiritualists. However, in the end, it was the Spiritualist Franck and the Spiritualizers Bünderlin and Entfelder who developed the most detailed historical schemes of the Radical Reformation. After the Strasbourg debates we see the steady elaboration of historical visions and historical arguments in Anabaptist traditions which continued to confront Spiritualist challenges. In part this continued challenge came from unresolved tensions between Spiritualist and Anabaptist elements from within the Anabaptist movements. In part it also came from the continued influence of Spiritualist traditions from outside Anabaptism. Arising largely as a defensive response to challenges to their communities and their practices, historical arguments and historical visions developed by the Hutterites and Mennonites became important confessional tools by the late sixteenth and seventeenth centuries. By reaching for the historical record in their attempts to clarify and legitimate group identity, the Anabaptist leaders were joining their counterparts in the Catholic and Protestant churches and entering Europe's confessional age.

The role of historical writing in the confessional strategies of the Hutterites and Mennonites also points out one of the great ironies of the Radical Reformation. As they fleshed out the details of their historical visions, Anabaptist authors drew increasingly on Sebastian Franck's *Chronica* as an important source for their historical knowledge. Often the material from the *Chronica* was marshalled to counter Spiritualist challenges to their congregations derived as well from Franck's writings. In other words, the thought of the great Reformation opponent of all sectarianism was appropriated to consolidate groups that history remembers as the Protestant sects. This suggests that not only the details of history, but also historical works themselves were treated as common property in the great battle over the Christian past, and it highlights once again the importance of "conversation" in the evolution of Radical Reformation historical visions.

BIBLIOGRAPHY

Primary Sources

Augustine of Hippo. *City of God*. Henry Bettenson, trans. David Knowles, ed. Harmondsworth: Penguin, 1972.

Baylor, Michael. ed. and trans. *Revelation and Revolution: Basic Writings of Thomas Müntzer*. Bethlehem, PA: Lehigh University Press, 1993.

Beck, Josef. ed. *Die Geschichtsbücher der Wiedertäufer in Oesterreich-Ungarn, 1526-1785*. Vienna, 1883; reprint ed. Nieuwkoop: B. De Graaf, 1967.

Braght, Thielemann J. van. *The Bloody Theater or Martyrs Mirror*. trans., Joseph F. Sohm. Scottdale, PA: Herald Press, 1950.

Bünderlin, Johannes. "Erklerung durch Vergleichung der Biblischen geschrifft, das der Wassertauf sampt andern eüsserlichen gebreuchen, in der Apostolischen kirchen geübt." in Köhler. fiche 1167-1168, number 246.

Bünderlin, Johannes. "The Reasons Why God Descended and Became Man in Christ, Through Whom, and How, He Atoned for and Restored Man's Fall and Man Himself Through the Messiah Whom He Sent." Claude R. Foster, Jr. and Wilhelm Jerosch, eds. and trans. *MQR* 42 (1968): 260-84.

The Chronicle of the Hutterian Brethren. the Hutterian Brethren, eds. and trans. Vol. 1. Rifton, NY: Plough Publishing House, 1987.

Hans Denck: Schriften. 3 vols. Baring, Georg and Fellmann, Walter. eds. *Quellen zur Geschichte der Täufer*, vol. 6. Gütersloh: C. Bertelsmann Verlag, 1955-1960.

Dyck, Cornelius J.; Keeney, William E.; and Beachy, Alvin J. eds. and trans. *The Writings of Dirk Philips, 1504-1568*. Scottdale, PA and Waterloo, ON: Herald Press, 1992.

Johann Eberlin von Günzburg, Ausgewählte Schriften, Enders, Ludwig. ed. Vol. 1. Halle: Max Niemeyer, 1896.

Ehrenpries, Andreas. "An Epistle to the Brotherly Community as the Highest Command of Love," in Robert Friedmann, ed., *Brotherly Community and the Highest Command of Love*. Rifton, NY: Plough Publishing House, 1978. 1-77.

Entfelder, Christian. "Von den Mannigfaltigen zerspaltungen im Glauben, die in diesen Jahren enstanden sind" in Laube 2: 934-83.

Entfelder, Christian. "Von Gottes vnnd Christi Jesu unnsers Herren erkandtnuß/ ain bedacht/ . . ." in Köhler. fiche 1343, number 3527.

Opus epistularum Des. Erasmi Roterodami. 11 vols. Allen, P.S.; Allen, H.M.; and Garrod, H.W. eds. Oxford: Clarendon Press, 1906-1958.

Desiderii Erasmi Roterdami opera omnia. Leclerc, Jean. ed. 10 vols. Leiden, 1703-1706; reprint ed. 1961-1962.

Erasmus of Rotterdam. *The Collected Works of Erasmus*. Toronto: University of Toronto Press, 1974 ff.

Fast, Heinold, ed. *Der linke Flügel der Reformation*. Bremen: Carl Schünemann Verlag, 1962.

Fast, Heinold. ed. *Quellen zur Geschichte der Täufer in der Schweiz*, Vol. 2: *Ostschweiz*. Zurich: Theologischer Verlag, 1973.

Franck, Sebastian. *Chronica, Zeitbuch unnd Geschichtsbibel*. Ulm, 1536; photoreprint ed., Darmstadt: Wissenschaftliche Buchgesellschaft, 1969.

Franck, Sebastian. *Sämtliche Werke*, Vol. 1: *Frühe Schriften*. Krauer, Peter Klaus. ed. Berlin: Peter Lang, 1993.

Friedmann, Robert. ed. *Glaubenszeugnisse oberdeutscher Taufgesinnter II. Quellen zur Geschichte der Täufer*. Vol. 12. Gütersloh: Gerd Mohn, 1967.

Furcha, Edward J. ed. and trans. *The Essential Carlstadt: Fifteen Tracts by Andreas Bodenstein (Carlstadt) from Karlstadt*. Scottdale, PA and Waterloo, ON: Herald Press, 1995.

Furcha, Edward J. with Battles, Ford Lewis. eds. and trans. *Selected Writings of Hans Denck*. Pittsburgh: Pickwick Press, 1975.

Harder, Leland. ed. *The Sources of Swiss Anabaptism: The Grebel Letters and Related Documents*. Scottdale, PA and Kitchener, ON: Herald Press, 1985.

Hasenberg, Kathleen E. trans. (with an introduction by Robert Friedmann). "A Notable Hutterite Document: Concerning True Surrender and Christian Community of Goods." *MQR* 31 (1957): 22-62.

Hillerbrand, Hans. "Ein Täuferbekenntnis aus dem 16. Jahrhundert." *ARG* 50 (1959): 40-50.

Hoffman, Melchior. "Auslegung der heimlichen Offenbarung des Apostels und Evangelisten Johhanes, Vorrede." in Laube 1: 492-500.

Hoffman, Melchior. "Weissagung aus der heiligen, göttlichen Schrift." in Laube 2: 910-33.

Hoffman, Melchior. "The Ordinance of God." *SAW*. 182-203.

Hubmaier, Balthasar. *Schriften*. Westin, Gunnar and Bergsten, Torsten. eds. *Quellen zur Geschichte der Täufer*, vol. 9. Gütersloh: Gütersloher Verlagshaus Gerd Mohn, 1962.

Hut, Hans. "Eine christliche Unterrichtung, wie göttliche Schrift in Übereinstimmung gebracht und beurteilt werden soll." in Laube 1:687-701.

Hut, Hans. "Ein Sendbrief Hans Huts, eines einst vornehmen Vorstehers im Wiedertäuferorden, widerlegt durch Urbanus Rhegius." in Laube 1:858-61.

Ulrich von Hutten, Opera. 7 vols. Böcking, Eduard. ed. Leipzig: B.G. Teubner, 1859-1869; reprint ed., Aalen and Osnabrück: Otto Zeller, 1963-1966.

Josephus, Flavius. *Works*, vol. 1: *Antiquities of the Jews*. William Whiston, trans. London: 1820.

Karlstadt, Andreas Bodenstein von. *Karlstadts Schriften aus den Jahren 1523-25*. 2 vols. Hertzsch, Erich. ed. Halle (Saale): Max Niemeyer Verlag, 1956-1957.

Klaassen, Walter. ed. and trans. *Anabaptism in Outline: Selected Primary Sources*. Scottdale, PA and Kitchener, ON: Herald Press, 1981.

Klaassen, Walter; Packull, Werner; and Rempel, John. trans. *Later Writings by Pilgram Marpeck and his Circle*, Vol. 1: *The Exposé, A Dialogue, and Marpeck's Response to Caspar Schwenckfeld*. Kitchener, ON: Pandora Press, 1999.

Klassen, William, Klaassen, Walter, eds and trans. *The Writings of Pilgram Marpeck*. Scottdale, PA and Kitchener, ON: Herald Press, 1978.

Köhler, Hans-Joachim; et al. *Early Modern Pamphlets: Sixteenth-Century German and Latin 1501-1530*. Leiden: IDC, 1980ff.

Krebs, Manfred; Rott, Hans Georg. eds. *Quellen zur Geschichte der Täufer*. Vol. 7: *Elsaß, 1. Teil: Stadt Straßburg 1522-1532*. Gütersloh: Gerd Mohn, 1959.

Laube, Adolf; Schneider, Annerose; and Weiß, Ulman. eds. *Flugschriften vom Bauernkrieg zum Täuferreich (1526-1535)*. 2 vols. Berlin: Akademie Verlag, 1992.

D. Martin Luthers Werke: Kritische Gesamtausgabe: Briefwechsel. 18 vols. Weimar: Böhlau, 1930-1985.

D. Martin Luthers Werke: Kritische Gesamtausgabe. 63 vols. Weimar: Böhlau, 1883-1983.

Marpeck, Pilgram. *Quellen und Forschungen zur Geschichte der oberdeutschen Taufgesinnten im 16. Jahrhundert: Pilgram Marpecks Antwort auf Kaspar Schwenckfelds Beurteilung des Buches der Bundesbezeugung von 1542*. Vienna & Leipzig: Carl Fromme, 1929.

Matheson, Peter. ed. and trans. *The Collected Works of Thomas Müntzer*. Edinburgh: T&T Clark, 1988.

Thomas Müntzer. Schriften und Briefe: Kritische Gesamtausgabe. Gütersloh: Gütersloher Verlagshaus Gerd Mohn, 1968.

Muralt, Leonhard von and Schmid, Walter. eds. *Quellen zur Geschichte der Täufer in der Schweiz*. Vol. 1: *Zurich*. Zurich: S. Hirzel Verlag, 1952.

Oecolampadius, Johannes. "Von Sacrament der Dancksagung (1526)." in Visser, Paul. ed. *The Anabaptist, Mennonite and Spiritualist Reformation*. Leiden: IDC, 1977 ff. # 53.

Oyer, John. ed and trans. "The Pfeddersheim Disputation, 1557." *MQR* 60 (1986): 304-51.

Philips, Dietrich. *Enchiridion or Handbook of the Christian Doctrine and Religion compiled (by the grace of God) from the Holy Scriptures for the benefit of all lovers of the Truth*. Kolb, A.B. trans. Berne: Light and Hope, 1958.

Philips, Dietrich. "The Church of God." *SAW*. 226-62.

Philips, Obbe. "A Confession." *SAW*. 204-25.

Pipkin, H. Wayne and Yoder, John Howard. eds. and trans. *Balthasar Hubmaier: Theologian of Anabaptism*. Scottdale, PA and Kitchener, ON: Herald Press, 1989.

Rideman, Peter. *Account of Our Religion, Doctrine and Faith Given by Peter Rideman of the Brothers Whom Men Call the Hutterians*. Rifton, NY: Plough Publishing House, 1970.

Die Schriften Bernhard Rothmanns. Stupperich, Robert. ed. Münster: Aschendorffsche Verlagsbuchhandlung, 1970.

Corpus Schwenckfeldianorum. 19 vols. Hatranft, Chester D.; Johnson, Elmer E.S.; and Schultz, Selina Gerhard; eds. Leipzig & Pennsburg, 1907-1961.

Sider, Ronald J., ed. and trans. *Karlstadt's Battle with Luther: Documents in a Liberal-Radical Debate*. Philadelphia: Fortress Press, 1978.

Stadler, Ulrich. "Cherished Instructions on Sin, Excommunication, and the Community of Goods." *SAW*. 272-84.

Stupperich, Robert, ed. *Melanchthons Werke in Auswahl*, vol. 1: *Reformatorische Schriften*. Gütersloh: C. Bertelsmann Verlag, 1951.

Valla, Lorenzo. *The Profession of the Religious and the principal arguments from The Falsely Believed and Forged Donation of Constantine*. Pugliese, Olga Zorzi. ed. and trans. Toronto: Centre for Reformation and Renaissance Studies, 1985.

Verduin, Leonard. trans. and Wenger, John C. ed. *The Complete Writings of Menno Simons c. 1496-1561*. Scottdale, PA: Herald Press, 1956.

Waite, Gary K. ed. and trans. *The Anabaptist Writings of David Joris*. Scottdale, PA and Waterloo, ON: Herald Press, 1994.

Williams, George H. and Mergal, Angel M. eds and trans. *Spiritualist and Anabaptist Writers: Documents Illustrative of the Radical Reformation*. Philadelphia: Westminster Press, 1957.

Wolkan, Rudolf. ed. *Geschicht-Buch der hutterischen Brüder*. Vienna: Carl Fromme, 1923; reprint ed., Cayley, AB: MacMillan Colony, 1974.

Yoder, John Howard. ed. and trans. *The Legacy of Michael Sattler*. Scottdale, PA: Herald Press, 1973.

Huldrych Zwingli sämtliche Werke. Egli, Emil; Finsler, Georg; Köhler, Walther; Farner, Oscar; Blanke, Fritz; von Muralt, Leonard; Künzli, Edwin; and Pfister, Rudolph. eds. Leipzig: Hensius, 1911-1935

Secondary Sources

Ahrens, Hans-Herbert. "Die religiosen, nationalen und sozialen Gedanken Johann Eberlins von Günzburg mit besonderer Berücksichtigung seiner anonymen Flugschriften." Phil. Diss., Hamburg, 1939.

Augustijn, Cornelis and Parmentier, Theo. "Sebastian Franck in den nördlichen Niederlanden 1550 bis 1600" in Müller, *Sebastian Frank*. 303-18.

Augustijn, Cornelis. *Erasmus: His Life, Works, and Influence*. J.C. Grayson, trans. Toronto: University of Toronto Press, 1991.

Backus, Irena. "Erasmus and the Spirituality of the Early Church" in Hilmar Pabel, ed. *Erasmus' Vision of the Church*. Kirksville, MO: Sixteenth Century Journal Publishers, 1995. 95-114.

Backus, Irena, ed. *The Reception of the Church Fathers in the West: From the Carolingians to the Maurists*. 2 vols. Leiden: E.J. Brill, 2001.

Backus, Irena. "Ulrich Zwingli, Martin Bucer and the Church Fathers" in Backus, ed. *Reception of the Church Fathers in the West*. 2: 627-60.

Backus, Irena. *Historical Method and Confessional Identity in the Era of the Reformation (1378-1615)*. Leiden and Boston: E.J. Brill, 2003.

Bailey, Richard. "The Sixteenth Century's Apocalyptic Heritage and Thomas Müntzer." *Mennonite Quarterly Review* 57 (1983): 27-44.

Bainton, Roland H. "Changing Ideas and Ideals in the 16th Century." *Journal of Modern History* 8 (1936): 417-43.

Bainton, Roland H. "The Left Wing of the Reformation." *Journal of Religion* 21 (1941): 124-34.

Bainton, Roland. *The Reformation of the Sixteenth Century*. Boston: Beacon Press, 1952.

Barge, Hermann. *Andreas Bodenstein von Karlstadt*, vol. 1: *Karlstadt und die Anfänge der Reformation*. Leipzig: Friedrich Brandstetter, 1905. Vol. 2: *Karlstadt als Vorkämpfer des laienchristlichen Puritanismus*. Leipzig: Friedrich Brandstetter, 1905.

Bauman, Clarence. *Gewaltlosigkeit im Täufertum: Eine Untersuchung zur theologischen Ethik des oberdeutschen Täufertums der Reformationszeit*. Leiden: E.J. Brill, 1968.

Bauman, Clarence. *The Spiritual Legacy of Hans Denck: Interpretation and Translation of Key Texts*. Leiden: E.J. Brill, 1991.

Baylor, Michael. "Thomas Müntzer's First Publication," *SCJ* 17 (1986): 451-58.

Baylor, Michael. "Theology and Politics in the Thought of Thomas Müntzer: The Case of the Elect," *ARG* 79 (1988): 81-102.

Beck, James. "The Anabaptists and the Jews: The Case of Hätzer, Denck and the Worms Prophets," *MQR* 75 (2001): 407-27.

Bejczy, István. *Erasmus and the Middle Ages: The Historical Consciousness of a Christian Humanist*. Leiden: E.J. Brill, 2001.

Bender, Harold S. "The Anabaptist Vision," *MQR* 18 (1944): 67-88.

Bender, Harold S. *Conrad Grebel c. 1498-1526: The Founder of the Swiss Brethren Sometimes Called Anabaptists*. Goshen, IN: Mennonite Historical Society, 1950.

Bender, Harold S. "The Zwickau Prophets, Thomas Müntzer and the Anabaptists," *MQR* 27 (1953): 3-16.

Bender, Harold S. "Pilgram Marpeck, Anabaptist Theologian and Civil Engineer," *MQR* 38 (1964): 231-65.

Bensing, Manfred. *Thomas Müntzer und der Thüringer Aufstand 1525*. Berlin: VEB Deutscher Verlag der Wissenschaften, 1966.

Bergsten, Torsten. *Balthasar Hubmaier: Anabaptist Theologian and Martyr*. Irwin J. Barnes and William R. Estep, trans. William R. Estep, ed. Valley Forge, PA: Judson Press, 1978.

Biesecker-Mast, Gerald. "Anabaptist Separation and Arguments Against the Sword in the Schleitheim *Brotherly Union*," *MQR* 74 (2000): 381-402.

Bietenholz, Peter. *History and Biography in the Work of Erasmus of Rotterdam*. Geneva: Librarie Droz, 1966.

Bietenholz, Peter. "How Sebastian Franck Taught Erasmus to Speak with his Radical Voice." *Bibliothèque d'Humanisme et Renaissance* 62 (2000): 233-48.

Blanke, Fritz. "Anabaptism and the Reformation" in Hershberger, ed., *Recovery of the Anabaptist Vision*. 57-68.

Blough, Neal. "Pilgram Marpeck, Martin Luther and the Humanity of Christ," *MQR* 61 (1987): 203-12.

Blough, Neal. *Christologie Anabaptiste: Pilgram Marpeck et l'humanite du Christ*. Geneva: Labor et Fides, 1984.

Blough, Neal. "Pilgram Marpeck and Caspar Schwenckfeld: The Strasbourg Years" in Jean-Georges Rott and Simon L. Verheus, eds. *Bibliotheca Dissidentium: Scripta et Studia #3*. Baden-Baden and Bouxwiller: Éditions Valentin Koerner, 1987. 371-80.

Blough, Neal. "*The Uncovering of the Babylonian Whore*: Confessionalization and Politics Seen from the Underside," *MQR* 75 (2001): 37-55.

Boeft, Jan den. "Erasmus and the Church Fathers" in Backus, ed. *Reception of the Church Fathers in the West* 2: 537-72.

Boyd, Stephen. "Anabaptism and Social Radicalism in Strasbourg, 1528-1532: Pilgram Marpeck on Christian Social Responsibility," *MQR* 63 (1989): 58-76.

Boyd, Stephen. *Pilgram Marpeck: His Life and Social Theology*. Durham, NC: Duke University Press, 1992.

Brady, Thomas A. Jr., Oberman, Heiko A., and Tracy, James D., eds., *Handbook of European History 1400-1600*, vol. 2: *Visions, Programs, and Outcomes*. Grand Rapids, MI: Wm B. Eerdmans, 1996.

Bräuer, Siegfried. "Thomas Müntzers Kirchenverständnis vor seiner Allstedter Zeit" in Bräuer and Junghans, eds., *Der Theologe Thomas Müntzer*. 100-28.

Bräuer, Siegfried and Junghans, Helmar, eds. *Der Theologe Thomas Müntzer: Untersuchungen zu seiner Entwicklung und Lehre*. Göttingen: Vandenhoeck and Ruprecht, 1989.

Bräuer, Siegfried. "Der Briefwechsel zwischen Andreas Bodenstein von Karlstadt und Thomas Müntzer" in Bubenheimer and Oehmig, eds. *Querdenker der Reformation*. 187-209.

Brecht, Martin. "Die Theologie Bernhard Rothmanns." *Jahrbuch für Westfälische Kirchengeschichte*. 78 (1985): 49-82.

Brendler, Gerhard. *Das Täuferreich zu Müntzer 1534/35*. Berlin: Deutscher Verlag der Wissenschaft, 1966.

Brendler, Gerhard. *Thomas Müntzer: Geist und Faust.* Berlin: VEB Deutscher Verlag der Wissenschaften, 1989.

Brunk, Gerald R., ed. *Menno Simons: A Reappraisal. Essays in Honor of Irvin B. Horst on the 450th Anniversary of the Fundamentboek.* Harrisonburg, VA: Eastern Mennonite College, 1992.

Bubenheimer, Ulrich. *Consonantia Theologiae et Iurisprudentiae: Andreas Bodenstein von Karlstadt als Theologe und Jurist zwischen Scholastik und Reformation.* Tübingen: J.C.B. Mohr [Paul Siebeck], 1977.

Bubenheimer, Ulrich. *Thomas Müntzer: Herkunft und Bildung.* Leiden: E.J. Brill, 1989.

Bubenheimer, Ulrich and Oehmig, Stefan, eds. *Querdenker der Reformation: Andreas Bodenstein von Karlstadt und seine frühe Wirkung.* Würzburg: Religion und Kultur Verlag, 2001.

Burschel, Peter. "Zur Geschichtstheologie der Täufer," *ARG* 95 (2004): 132-55.

Chudaska, Andrea. *Peter Riedemann: Konfessionsbildendes Täufertum im 16. Jahrhundert.* Gütersloh: Gütersloher Verlagshaus, 2003.

Clasen, Claus-Peter. "Nuernberg in the History of Anabaptism," *MQR* 37 (1965): 25-39.

Cohn, Norman. *The Pursuit of the Millenium.* (2nd ed.) New York: Harper Torchbooks, 1961.

Coutts, Alfred. *Hans Denck 1495-1527: Humanist and Heretic.* Edinburgh: Macniven and Wallace, 1927.

D'Amico, John F. "Beatus Rhenanus, Tertullian and the Reformation: A Humanist's Critique of Scholasticism," *ARG* 71 (1980): 37-63.

D'Amico, John F. "Ulrich von Hutten and Beatus Rhenanus as Medieval Historians and Religious Propagandists in the Early Reformation" in Paul Grendler, ed. *Roman and German Humanism, 1450-1550.* Aldershot: Variorum, 1993. XII: 1-33.

De Bakker, Willem. "Bernhard Rothmann: The Dialectics of Radicalization in Münster" in Goertz, ed. *Profiles of Radical Reformers.* 191-202.

De Bakker, Willem. "Bernhard Rothmann: Civic Reformer in Anabaptist Münster" in Horst, ed. *The Dutch Dissenters.* 105-16.

De Jung, Christoph. *Wahrheit und Häresie: Eine Untersuchung zur Geschichtsphilosophie bei Sebastian Franck.* Zurich: Samisdat, 1980.

De Jung, Christoph. "Sebastian Francks nachgelassene Bibliothek." *Zwingliana* 16 (1983-85): 315-37.

Demke, Christoph, ed. *Thomas Müntzer. Anfragen an Theologie und Kirche.* Berlin: Evangelische Verlagsanstalt, 1977.

Dempsey Douglass, E. Jane. *Justification in Late Medieval Preaching: A Study of John Geiler of Keisersberg.* 2nd ed. Leiden: E.J. Brill, 1989.

Deppermann, Klaus. "Melchior Hoffmans Weg von Luther zu den Täufern" in Goertz, ed. *Umstrittenes Täufertum.* 173-205.

Deppermann, Klaus. "Melchior Hoffman: Contradictions Between Lutheran Loyalty to Government and Apocalyptic Dreams" in Goertz, ed. *Profiles of Radical Reformers.* 178-90.

Deppermann, Klaus. *Melchior Hoffman: Social Unrest and Apocalyptic Visions in the Age of Reformation.* Trans by Malcolm Wren and ed. by Benjamin Drewery. Edinburg: T. and T. Clark, 1987.

Deppermann, Klaus. "Michael Sattler. Radikaler Reformator, Pazifist, Märtyrer," *MGBl* 47/48 (1990/91): 8-23.

Deppermann, Klaus. "Sebastian Francks Straßburger Aufenhalt" in Jan-Dirk Müller, ed. *Sebastian Frank (1499-1542).* 103-118.

Dickens, A.G. *Reformation and Society in Sixteenth-Century Europe*. London: Thames and Hudson, 1966.

Dickens, A.G. and Tonkin, John. *The Reformation in Historical Thought*. Oxford: Basil Blackwell, 1985.

Dipple, Geoffrey. "Humanists, Reformers and Anabaptists on Scholasticism and the Fall of the Church," *MQR* 68 (1994): 461-82.

Dipple, Geoffrey. "Uthred and the Friars: Apostolic Poverty and Clerical Dominion Between FitzRalph and Wyclif," *Traditio* 49 (1994): 235-58.

Dipple, Geoffrey. "Luther, Emser and the Development of Reformation Anticlericalism," *ARG* 87 (1996): 38-56.

Dipple, Geoffrey. *Antifraternalism and Anticlericalism in the German Reformation: Johann Eberlin von Günzburg and the Campaign Against the Friars*. Aldershot: Scolar Press, 1996.

Dipple, Geoffrey. "'Yet from time to time there were men who protested against these evils': Anabaptism and Medieval Heresy" in Gordon, ed. *Protestant History and Identity*. I: 123-37.

Dipple, Geoffrey. "Sebastian Franck in Strasbourg," *MQR* 73 (1999): 783-802.

Dipple, Geoffrey. Sebastian Franck and the Münster Anabaptist Kingdom." in Packull and Dipple, eds. 91-105.

Dipple, Geoffrey. "Pilgram Marpeck, the Spiritualizers and the Anabaptist View of Church History" in C. Arnold Snyder, ed. *Commoners and Community: Essays in Honour of Werner O. Packull*. Kitchener, ON: Pandora Press, 2002. 217-32.

Dismer, Rolf. "Geschichte, Glaube, Revolution: Zur Schriftauslegung Thomas Müntzers." PhD Diss. University of Hamburg, 1974.

Doornkaat Koolman, Jacobus ten. *Dirk Philips: Friend and Colleague of Menno Simons 1504-1568*. Trans by William Keeney, ed. by C. Arnold Snyder. Kitchener, ON: Pandora Press, 1998.

Driedger, Michael. *Obedient Heretics: Mennonite Identities in Lutheran Hamburg and Altona during the Confessional Age*. Aldershot: Ashgate, 2002.

Drummond, Andrew W. "Thomas Müntzer and the Fear of Man," *SCJ* 10 (1979): 63-71.

Drummond, Andrew W. "The Divine and Mortal Worlds of Thomas Müntzer," *ARG* 71 (1980): 99-112.

Dülmen, Richard van. *Reformation als Revolution: Soziale Bewegung und religiöser Radikalismus in der deutschen Reformation*. Munich: Deutscher Taschenbuch Verlag, 1977.

Dyck, Cornelius. "The Suffering Church in Anabaptism," *MQR* 59 (1985): 5-23.

Ecke, Karl. *Schwenckfeld, Luther und der Gedanke einer apostolischen Reformation*. Berlin: Verlag von Martin Warneck, 1911.

Elliger, Walter. *Thomas Müntzer: Leben und Werk*. Göttingen: Vandenhoeck and Ruprecht, 1976.

Elton, G.R. *Reformation Europe, 1517-1559*. London: Fontana, 1963.

Fast, Heinold. "Die Sonderstellung der Täufer in St. Gallen und Appenzell, *Zwingliana* 11 (1960): 223-40.

Fast, Heinold. "Hans Krüsis Büchlein über Glauben und Taufe: Ein Täuferdruck von 1525," *Zwingliana* 11 (1962): 457-75.

Fast, Heinold. "Hans Denck and Thomas Müntzer," *MQR* 45 (1971): 82-83.

Fast, Heinold. "Conrad Grebel: The Covenant on the Cross" in Goertz, ed. *Profiles of Radical Reformers*. 118-31.

Fast, Heinold. "Vom Amt des 'Lesers' zum Kompilator des sogenannten Kunstbuches. Auf den spuren Jörg Malers" in Fischer and Kobelt-Groch, eds. *Aussenseiter zwischen Mittelalter und Neuzeit*. 187-217.

Fischer, Norbert and Kobelt-Groch, Marion, eds. *Aussenseiter zwischen Mittelalter und Neuzeit: Festschrift für Hans-Jürgen Goertz zum 60. Geburtstag*. Leiden: E.J. Brill, 1997.

Fix, Andrew. "Mennonites and Collegiants in Holland, 1630-1700," *MQR* 64 (1990): 160-77.

Fix, Andrew C. *Prophecy and Reason: The Dutch Collegiants and the Early Enlightenment.* Princeton, NJ: Princeton University Press, 1991.

Fix, Andrew. "Radical Religion and the Age of Reason" in Andrew Fix and Susan Karant-Nunn, eds. *Germania Illustrata: Essays on Early Modern Germany Presented to Gerald Strauss*. Kirksville, MO: Sixteenth Century Journal Publishers, 1992. 35-55.

Foster, Claude R., Jr. "Hans Denck and Johann Buenderlin: A Comparative Study," *MQR* 49 (1965): 115-24.

Friedmann, Robert. "Eine dogmatische Hauptschrift der hutterischen Täufergemeinschaften in Mähren," *ARG* 28 (1931): 80-111, 207-41; 29 (1932): 1-17.

Friedmann, Robert. "The Oldest Church Discipline of the Anabaptists," *MQR* 49 (1955): 162-66.

Friedman, Robert. "A Hutterite Book of Medieval Origin," *MQR* 30 (1956): 65-71.

Friedmann, Robert. "Thomas Müntzer's Relation to Anabaptism," *MQR* 31 (1957): 75-87.

Friedmann, Robert. "The Philippite Brethren: A Chapter in Anabaptist History," *MQR* 32 (1958): 272-97.

Friedmann, Robert. *Hutterite Studies* (Essays by Robert Friedmann edited by Harold S. Bender.) Goshen, IN: Mennonite Historical Society, 1961.

Friedmann, Robert. "Jakob Hutter's Epistle Concerning the Schism in Moravia in 1533," *MQR* 38 (1964): 329-43.

Friedman, Robert. "Second Generation Anabaptism as Illustrated by the Walpot Era of the Hutterites," *MQR* 44 (1970): 390-93.

Friedmann, Robert. "Peter Riedemann: Early Anabaptist Leader," *MQR* 44 (1970): 5-44.

Friedmann, Robert. *The Theology of Anabaptism: An Interpretation*. Scottdale, PA and Kitchener, ON: Herald Press, 1973.

Friesen, Abraham. "Thomas Müntzer and the Old Testament," *MQR* 47 (1973): 5-19.

Friesen, Abraham and Goertz, Hans-Jürgen, eds. *Thomas Müntzer: Wege der Forschung.* Darmstadt: Wissenschaftliche Buchgesellschaft, 1978.

Friesen, Abraham. "Martin Cellarius: On the Borders of Heresy" in Goertz, ed. *Profiles of Radical Reformers*. 234-46.

Friesen, Abraham. "Thomas Müntzer and Martin Luther," *ARG* 79 (1988): 59-80.

Friesen, Abraham. "Menno and Münster: The Man and the Movement" in Brunk, ed. *Menno Simons: A Reappraisal.* 131-62.

Friesen, Abraham. *Thomas Muentzer, a Destroyer of the Godless*. Berkeley and Los Angeles: University of California Press, 1990.

Friesen, Abraham. *Erasmus, the Anabaptists, and the Great Commission.* Grand Rapids MI: William B. Eerdmans, 1998.

Gäbler, Ulrich. "Johannes Bünderlin" in Séguenny and Rott, eds. *Biblioteca Dissidentium*, vol. 3. Baden-Baden: Koerner, 1982. 9-42.

Garside, Charles Jr. "Ludwig Haetzer's Pamphlet Against Images: A Critical Study. *MQR* 34 (1960): 20-36.

Geiger, Gottfried. "Die reformatorischen Initia Johann Eberlins von Günzburg nach seinen Flugschriften" in Horst Rabe, Hans-Georg Molitor and Hans-Christoph Rublack, eds. *Festgabe für Ernst Walter Zeeden zum 60. Geburtstag am 14. Mai 1976.* Münster: Aschendorffsche Verlagsbuchhandlung, 1976. 178-201.

Gilmore, Myron P. "Fides et Eruditio: Erasmus and the Study of History" in *Humanists and Jurists: Six Studies in the Renaissance.* Cambridge, MA: Harvard University Press, 1963. 87-114.

Gockel, Matthias. "A Reformer's Dissent from Lutheranism: Reconsidering the Theology of Hans Denck (ca. 1500-1527)." *ARG* 91 (2000): 127-48.

Goertz, Hans-Jürgen. *Innere und äussere Ordnung in der Theologie Thomas Müntzers*. Leiden: E.J. Brill, 1967.

Goertz, Hans-Jürgen, ed. *Umstrittenes Täufertum 1525-1975: Neue Forschungen*. Gottingen: Vandenhoeck and Ruprecht, 1975.

Goertz, Hans-Jürgen, ed. *Profiles of Radical Reformers: Biographical Sketches from Thomas Müntzer to Paracelsus*. English Edition. Walter Klaassen, ed. Kitchener, ON: Herald Press, 1982.

Goertz, Hans-Jürgen. "Thomas Müntzer: Revolutionary in a Mystical Spirit" in Goertz, ed. *Profiles of Radical Reformers*. 29-44.

Goertz, Hans-Jürgen. "Zwischen Zweitracht und Eintracht. Zur Zweideutigkeit täuferischer und mennonitischer Bekenntnisse." *MGBl* 43 / 44 (1986 / 87): 16-46.

Goertz, Hans-Jürgen. "Zu Thomas Müntzers Geistverständnis" in Bräuer and Junghans, eds. *Der Theologe Thomas Müntzer*. 84-99.

Goertz, Hans-Jürgen. *Thomas Müntzer: Apocalyptic Mystic and Revolutionary*. Jocelyn Jaquiery, trans. Peter Matheson, ed. Edinburgh: T. & T. Clark, 1993.

Goertz, Hans-Jürgen. "Kleruskritik, Kirchenzucht und Sozialdisciplinierung in den täuferischen Bewegungen der frühen Neuzeit" in Heinz Schilling, ed. *Kirchenzucht und Sozialdisciplinierung im frühneuzeitlichen Europa*. Berlin: Duncker and Humblot, 1994. 183-98.

Goertz, Hans-Jürgen. "Zucht und Ordnung in nonkorfomistischer Manier. Kleruskritik, Kirchenzucht und Sozialdisciplinierung in der Bewegungen der Täufer" in *Antiklerikalismus und Reformation: Sozialgeschichtliche Untersuchungen*. Göttingen: Vandenhoeck und Ruprecht, 1995. 103-14.

Goertz, Hans-Jürgen. *The Anabaptists*. Trevor Johnson, trans. London: Routledge, 1996.

Goertz, Hans-Jürgen. "'A Common Future Conversation': A Revisionist Interpretation of the September 1524 Grebel Letters to Thomas Müntzer" in Packull and Dipple, eds. *Radical Reformation Studies*. 73-90.

Goeters, J.F. Gerhard. *Ludwig Hätzer (ca. 1500 bis 1529), Spiritualist und Antitrinitarier: Eine Randfigur der fruhen Täuferbewegung*. Gütersloh: C. Bertelsmann Verlag, 1957.

Goeters, J.F. Gerhard. "Zwinglis Werdegang als Erasmianer " in Martin Greschat and J.F.G. Goeters, eds. *Reformation und Humanismus. Robert Stupperich zum 65. Geburtstag*. Witten: Luther-Verlag, 1969. 255-71.

Gordon, Bruce, ed. *Protestant History and Identity in Sixteenth-Century Europe*. Vol. 1: *The Medieval Inheritance*. Vol. 2: *The Later Reformation*. Aldershot: Scolar Press, 1996.

Gordon, Bruce. "The Changing Face of Protestant History and Identity in the Sixteenth Century" in Gordon, ed. *Protestant History and Identity in Sixteenth Century Europe*. I: 1-22.

Gregory, Brad. "Prescribing and Describing Martyrdom: Menno's *Troestlijke Vermaninge* and *Het Offer des Heeren*." *MQR* 71 (1997): 603-13.

Gregory, Brad. *Salvation at Stake: Christian Martyrdom in Early Modern Europe*. Cambridge, MA: Harvard University Press, 1999.

Gritsch, Eric W. *Reformer Without a Church: Thomas Muentzer*. Philadelphia: Fortress Press, 1967.

Gritsch, Eric W. *Thomas Müntzer: A Tragedy of Errors*. Minneapolis: Fortress Press, 1989.

Gross, Leonard. "Dialogue Between a Hutterite and a Swiss Brother, 1573." *MQR* 44 (1970): 45-58.

Gross, Leonard. *The Golden Years of the Hutterites: The Witness and Thought of the Communal Moravian Anabaptists During the Walpot Era, 1565-1578*. Scottdale, PA and Kitchener, ON: Herald Press, 1980.

Gross, Leonard. "Jakob Hutter: A Christian Communist" in Goertz, ed. *Profiles of Radical Reformers*. 158-67.

Gross, Leonard. "Hans Schnell: Second Generation Anabaptist." *MQR* 68 (1994): 351-77.

Haas, Martin. "Der Weg der Täufer in die Absonderung" in Goertz, ed., *Umstrittenes Täufertum*. 50-78.

Haas, Martin. "Michael Sattler: On the Way to Anabaptist Separation" in Goertz, ed., *Profiles of Radical Reformers*. 132-43.

Hall, Thor. "Possibilities of Erasmian Influence on Denck and Hubmaier in Their Views on the Freedom of the Will." *MQR* 35 (1961): 149-70.

Harrison, Wes. *Andreas Ehrenpreis and Hutterite Faith and Practice*. Kitchener, ON: Pandora Press, 1997.

Hayden-Roy, Patrick. *The Inner Word and the Outer World: A Biography of Sebastian Franck*. New York: Peter Lang, 1994.

Headley, John M. *Luther's View of Church History*. New Haven and London: Yale University Press, 1963.

Heger, Günther. *Johann Eberlin von Günzburg und seine Vorstellungen über eine Reform in Reich und Kirche*. Berlin: Duncker und Humblot, 1985.

Hegler, Alfred. *Geist und Schrift bei Sebastian Franck: eine Studie zur Geschichte des Spiritualismus in der Reformationszeit*. Freiburg i.Br: J.C.B. Mohr, 1892.

Heimann, Franz. "The Hutterite Doctrines of Church and Common Life. A Study of Peter Reidemann's Confession of Faith of 1540." *MQR* 26 (1952): 22-47, 142-60.

Hendrix, Scott H. "In Quest of *Vera Ecclesia*: The Crisis of Late Medieval Ecclesiology." *Viator* 7 (1976): 347-78.

Hendrix, Scott H. *Luther and the Papacy: Stages in a Reformation Conflict*. Philadelphia: Fortress Press, 1981.

Hershberger, Guy, ed. *The Recovery of the Anabaptist Vision. A Sixtieth Anniversary Tribute to Harold S. Bender*. Scottdale, PA: Herald Press, 1957.

Hillerbrand, Hans. "An Early Anabaptist Treatise on the Christian and the State." *MQR* 32 (1958): 28-47.

Hillerbrand, Hans. *A Fellowship of Discontent*. New York: Harper and Row, 1967.

Hillerbrand, Hans. "Anabaptism and History." *MQR* 45 (1971): 107-22.

Hillerbrand, Hans, ed. *Radical Tendencies in the Reformation: Divergent Perspectives*. Kirksville, MO: Sixteenth Century Journal Publishers, 1988.

Hinrichs, Carl. *Luther und Müntzer: Ihre Auseinandersetzung über Obrigkeit und Widerstandsrecht*. Berlin: Walter de Gruyter and Co., 1952.

Holborn, Hajo. *Ulrich von Hutten*. Göttingen: Vandenhoeck and Rupprecht, 1968.

Holl, Karl. "Luther und die Schwärmer," *Gesammelte Aufsätze zur Kirchengeschichte*, vol. 1: *Luther*. Tübingen: J.C.B. Mohr [Paul Siebeck], 1927. 420-67.

Honemeyer, Karl. "Thomas Müntzers Allstedter Gottesdienst als Symbol und Bestandteil der Volksreformation" in Friesen and Goertz. *Thomas Müntzer: Wege der Forschung*. 213-26.

Horsch, John. "The Swiss Brethren in St. Gall and Appenzell." *MQR* 7 (1933): 205-26.

Horst, Irvin Buckwalter. "Menno Simons: The New Man in Community" in Goertz, ed. *Profiles of Radical Reformers*. 203-13.

Horst, Irvin Buckwalter, ed. *The Dutch Dissenters: A Critical Companion to Their History and Ideas*. Leiden: E.J. Brill, 1986.

Hsia, R. Po-Chia. *Social Discipline in the Reformation: Central Europe 1550-1750*. London and New York: Routledge, 1989.

Jensen, DeLamar. *Reformation Europe: Age of Reform and Revolution*. Toronto: D.C. Heath, 1992.

Jones, Rufus M. *Spiritual Reformers in the 16th and 17th Centuries*. Macmillan, 1914. Reprint edition. Boston: Beacon Press, 1959.

Josipovic, Mario and McNiel, William. "Thomas Müntzer as 'Disturber of the Godless:' A Reassessment of his Revolutionary Nature." *MQR* 70 (1996): 431-47.

Junghans, Helmar. "Thomas Müntzer als Wittenberger Theologe" in Bräuer and Junghans, eds., *Der Theologe Thomas Müntzer*. 258-82.

Keeney, William. "Dirk Philips' Life." *MQR* 32 (1958): 171-91.

Keeney, William. "The Writings of Dirk Philips." *MQR* 32 (1958): 298-306.

Keeney, William Echard. *The Development of Dutch Anabaptist Thought and Practice from 1539-1564*. Nieuwkoop: B. De Graaf, 1968.

Keller, Ludwig. *Ein Apostel der Wiedertäufer*. Leipzig: Verlag von S. Hirzel, 1882.

Kim, Kee Ryun. *Das Reich Gottes in der Theologie Thomas Müntzers* Frankfurt: Peter Lang, 1994.

Kintner, Philip. "Studies in the Historical Writings of Sebastian Franck (1499-1542)." PhD Diss. Yale University, 1957.

Kintner, Philip L. "Sebastian Franck and the Problem of History." Typescript.

Kirchhoff, Karl-Heinz. "Was There a Peaceful Anabaptist Congregation in Münster in 1534?" Elizabeth Bender, trans. *MQR* 44 (1970): 357-70.

Kirchhoff, Karl-Heinz. *Die Täufer in Münster 1534/35: Untersuchungen zum Umfang und zur Sozialstruktur der Bewegung*. Münster: Aschendorffsche Verlagsbuchhandlung, 1973.

Kirchhoff, Karl-Heinz. "Die Endzeiterwartung der Täufergemeinde zu Münster 1534/35." *Jahrbuch für Westfälische Kirchengeschichte* 78 (1985): 19-42.

Kittelson, James M. *Wolfgang Capito: From Humanist to Reformer*. Leiden: E.J. Brill, 1975.

Kiwiet, Jan J. *Pilgram Marbeck: Ein Führer der Täuferbewegung im süddeutschen Raum*. Kassel: J.G. Oncken Verlag, 1957.

Kiwiet, Jan. "The Life of Hans Denck." *MQR* 31 (1957): 227-59.

Kiwiet, Jan. "The Theology of Hans Denck." *MQR* 32 (1958): 3-27.

Klaassen, Walter. "Spiritualization in the Reformation." *MQR* 37 (1963): 67-77.

Klaassen, Walter. "Speaking in Simplicity: Balthasar Hubmaier." *MQR* 40 (1966): 139-47.

Klaassen, Walter. "Church Discipline and the Spirit of Pilgram Marpeck" in I.B. Horst, A.F. DeJong and D. Visser eds. *De Geest in het geding*. Alphen an den Rijn: H.D. Tjeenk Willink, 1978. 169-80.

Klaassen, Walter. "The Anabaptist Critique of Constantinian Christianity." *MQR* 55 (1981): 218-30.

Klaassen, Walter. "Eschatological Themes in Early Dutch Anabaptism" in Horst, ed. *The Dutch Dissenters*. 15-31.

Klaassen, Walter. "Investigation into the Authorship and Historical Background of the Anabaptist Tract *Aufdeckung der Babylonischen Hurn*." *MQR* 61 (1987): 251-61.

Klaassen, Walter. "Menno Simons Research 1837-1937, 1986-1990" in Brunck, ed. *Menno Simons: A Reappraisal*. 181-197.

Klaassen, Walter. *Living at the End of the Ages: Apocalyptic Expectation in the Radical Reformation*. Lanham, NY: University Press of America, 1992.

Klassen, Herbert. "The Life and Teachings of Hans Hut." *MQR* 33 (1959): 171-205, 267-304.

Klassen, William. "Pilgram Marpeck's Two Books of 1531." *MQR* 33 (1959): 18-30.

Klassen, William. "Was Hans Denck a Universalist?" *MQR* 39 (1965): 152-54.

Klassen, William. "The Relation of the Old and New Covenants in Pilgram Marpeck's Theology." *MQR* 40 (1966): 97-111.

Klassen, William. *Covenant and Community: The Life, Writings and Hermeneutics of Pilgram Marpeck*. Grand Rapids: Wm. B. Eerdmans, 1968.

Klassen, William. "The Limits of Political Authority as Seen by Pilgram Marpeck." *MQR* 56 (1982): 342-64.

Klassen, William. "Pilgram Marpeck: Liberty Without Coercion" in Goertz, ed. *Profiles of Radical Reformers*. 168-77.

Klötzer, Ralf. *Die Täuferherrschaft von Münster. Stadtreformation und Welterneurung*. Münster: Aschendorff, 1992.

Klötzer, Ralf. "Hoffnungen auf eine andere Wirklichkeit. Die Erwartungshorizonte in der Täuferstadt Münster 1534/1535" in Fischer and Kobelt-Groch, eds. *Aussenseiter zwischen Mittelalter und Neuzeit*. 153-169.

Koch, Ernst. "Das Sakramentsverständnis Thomas Müntzers" in Bräuer and Junghans, eds., *Der Theologe Thomas Müntzer*. 129-55.

Kolb, Robert. *For All the Saints: Changing Perceptions of Martyrdom and Sainthood in the Lutheran Reformation*. Macon, GA: Mercer University Press, 1987.

Kolb, Robert. "Philipp's Foes, but Followers Nonetheless: Late Humanism among the Gnesio-Lutherans" in Manfred P. Fleischer, ed. *The Harvest of Humanism in Central Europe: Essays in Honor of Lewis W. Spitz*. St. Lewis: Concordia Publishing House, 1992. 159-78.

Kommoß, Rudolf. *Sebastian Franck und Erasmus von Rotterdam*. Berlin, 1934; reprint ed., Nendeln/Lichtenstein: Kraus Reprint Ltd., 1967.

Koop, Karl. *Anabaptist-Mennonite Confessions of Faith: The Development of a Tradition*. Kitchener, ON: Pandora Press, 2004.

Kot, Stanislaw. "Polish Brethren and the Problem of Communism in the XVIth Century." *Transactions of the Unitarian Historical Society*, 11 (1956): 38-53.

Krahn, Cornelius. *Menno Simons (1494-1561). Ein Beitrag zur Geschichte und Theologie der Taufgesinnten*. Karlsruhe i.B.: Heinrich Schneider, 1936.

Krahn, Cornelius. "Menno Simons' Fundament-Boek of 1539-1540." *MQR* 13 (1939): 221-32.

Krahn, Cornelius. "Anabaptism and the Culture of the Netherlands" in Guy F. Herschberger, ed. *The Recovery of the Anabaptist Vision: A Sixtieth Anniversary Tribute to Harold S. Bender*. Scottdale, PA: Herald Press, 1957. 219-36.

Krahn, Cornelius. "Menno Simons' Concept of the Church" in Cornelius J. Dyck, ed. *A Legacy of Faith: A Sixtieth Anniversary Tribute to Cornelius Krahn*. Newton, KS: Faith and Life Press, 1962. 17-30.

Krahn, Cornelius. *Dutch Anabaptism: Origin, Spread, Life and Thought*. Scottdale, PA and Kitchener, ON: Herald Press, 1981.

Krajewski, Ekkehard. "The Theology of Felix Manz." *MQR* 36 (1962): 76-87.

Kreider, Alan F. "The Servant is not Greater than his Master: The Anabaptists and the Suffering Church." *MQR* 58 (1984): 5-29.

Kreider, Robert. "Anabaptism and Humanism: An Inquiry into the Relationship of Humanism to the Evangelical Anabaptists." *MQR* 26 (1952): 123-41.

Kuratsuka, Taira. "Gesamtgilde und Täufer: Der Radikalisierungsprozeß in der Reformation Münsters: Von der reformatorischen Bewegung zum Täuferreich 1533/34." *ARG* 76 (1985): 231-70.

Langer, Otto. "Inneres Wort und inwohnender Christus. Zum mystischen Spiritualismus Sebastian Francks und seinen Implikationen" in Müller, ed. *Sebastian Franck*. 55-69.

Leff, Gordon. "The Apostolic Ideal in Later Medieval Ecclesiology." *Journal of Theological Studies* n.s. 18 (1967): 58-82.

Leff, Gordon. "The Making of the Myth of a True Church in the Later Middle Ages." *The Journal of Medieval and Renaissance Studies*. 1 (1971): 1-15.

Liechty, Daniel. *Andreas Fischer and the Sabbatarian Anabaptists: An Early Reformation Episode in East Central Europe*. Scottdale, PA: Herald Press, 1988.

Lindberg, Carter, ed. and trans. "Karlstadt's *Dialogue* on the Lord's Supper." *MQR* 53 (1979): 35-77.

Littell, Franklin H. "The Anabaptist Doctrine of the Restitution of the True Church." *MQR* 24 (1950): 33-52.

Littell, Franklin H. "Spiritualizers, Anabaptists, and the Church." *MQR* 29 (1955): 34-43.

Littell, Franklin. *The Anabaptist View of the Church. A Study in the Origins of Sectarian Protestantism*. Boson: Starr King Press, 1958.

Littell, Franklin H. *The Origins of Sectarian Protestantism: A Study of the Anabaptist View of the Church*. New York: Macmillan, 1964.

Littell, Franklin H. "In Response to Hans Hillerbrand." *MQR* 45 (1971): 377-80.

Locher, Gottfried W. "Das Geschichtsbild Huldrych Zwinglis. *Theologische Zeitschrift* 9 (1953): 275-302.

Lohmain, Anne Marie. *Zur geistigen Entwicklung Thomas Müntzers*. Leipzig and Berlin: B.G. Tuebner, 1931; reprint ed. Hildesheim: Verlag Dr. H.A. Gerstenberg, 1972.

Looß, Sigrid and Matthias, Markus, eds. *Andreas Bodenstein von Karlstadt (1486-1541): Ein Theologe der frühen Reformation*. Lutherstadt Wittenberg: Drei Kastanien Verlag, 1998.

Looß, Sigrid. "Andreas Bodensteins von Karlstadt Haltung zum 'Aufruhr'" in Bubenheimer and Oehmig, eds. *Querdenker der Reformation*. 265- 76.

Lucke, Wilhelm. "Die Enstehung der '15 Bundesgenossen' des Johann Eberlin von Günzburg," Phil. Diss., Halle, 1902.

Maier, Paul L. *Caspar Schwenckfeld on the Person and Work of Christ: A Study of Schwenckfeldian Theology at its Core*. Assen: Van Gorcum, 1959.

Maron, Gottfried. *Individualismus und Gemeinschaft bei Caspar von Schwenckfeld: Seine Theologie, dargestellt mit besonderer Ausrichtung auf seinen Kirchenbegriff*. Stuttgart: Evangelisches Verlagswerk, 1961.

Maron, Gottfried. "Thomas Müntzer als Theologe des Gerichts" in Friesen and Goertz, eds. *Thomas Müntzer: Wege der Forschung*. 339-82.

Mau, Rudolf. "Müntzers Verständnis von der Bibel" in Demke, ed. *Thomas Müntzer. Anfragen an Theologie und Kirche*. 21-44.

Maurer, Justus. "Karlstadt und der Bauernkrieg" in Merklein, ed. *Andreas Bodenstein von Karlstadt, 1480-1541*. 95-106.

McLaughlin, R. Emmet. "Schwenckfeld and the Strasbourg Radicals." *MQR* 59 (1985): 268-78.

McLaughlin, R. Emmet. *Caspar Schwenckfeld, Reluctant Radical: His Life to 1540*. New Haven and London: Yale University Press, 1986.

McLaughlin, R. Emmet. "Sebastian Franck and Caspar Schwenckfeld: Two Spiritualist Viae" in Müller, ed. *Sebastian Franck*. 71-86.

McLaughlin, R. Emmet. "Reformation Spiritualism: Typology, Sources and Significance." Typescript.

McLaughlin, R. Emmet. "Spiritualismus." *Theologische Realenzyklopädie*. Vol. 31. Berlin: Walter de Gruyuter, 2000. 701-8.

McLaughlin, R. Emmet. "Apocalypticism and Thomas Müntzer," *ARG* 95 (2004): 98-131.

McNiel, Bill. "Andreas Von Karlstadt as a Humanist Theologian" in Packull and Dipple, eds. *Radical Reformation Studies*. 106-19.

McNiel, William. "Andreas von Karlstadt and Thomas Müntzer: Relatives in Theology and Reformation. PhD diss., Queen's University, 1999.

Meihuizen, H.W. "Spiritualistic Tendencies and Movements among the Dutch Mennonites of the 16th and 17th Centuries." *MQR* 27 (1953): 259-304.

Meihuizen, H.W. *Galenus Abrahamsz 1622-1706: Strijder voor een onbeperkte verdraagzaamheid en verdediger van het Doperse Spiritualisme.* Haarlem: H.D. Tjeenk Willink & Zoon N.V., 1954.

Meihuizen, H.W. "The Concept of Restitution in the Anabaptism of Northwestern Europe." *MQR* 44 (1970): 141-58.

Merklein, Wolfgang, ed. *Andreas Bodenstein von Karlstadt 1480-1541: Festschrift der Stadt Karlstadt zum Jubiläumsjahr 1980.* Karlstadt: Historischer Verein, 1980.

Moeller, Bernd. "The German Humanists and the Beginnings of the Reformation" in *Imperial Cities and the Reformation.* Ed. and trans. H.C. Erik Middlefort and Mark U. Edwards. Durham, NC: Labyrinth Press, 1982. 19-38.

Moger, J. Travis. "Pamphlets, Preaching and Politics: The Image Controversy in Reformation Wittenberg, Zürich and Strassburg." *MQR* 75 (2001): 325-54.

Muller, Frank. "Jacob Kautz" in André Séguenny and Jean Rott, eds. *Bibliotheca Dissidentium,* Vol. 17. Baden-Baden and Bauxwiller: Koerner, 1995. 7-31.

Müller, Jan-Dirk, ed. *Sebastian Franck (1499-1542).* Wiesbaden: Harrasowitz Verlag, 1993.

Müsing, Hans-Werner. "The Anabaptist Movement in Strasbourg from Early 1526 to July 1527." *MQR* 51 (1977): 91-126.

Nauert, Charles G. *Agrippa and the Crisis of Renaissance Thought.* Urbana: University of Illinois Press, 1965.

Nelson, Stephen F. and Rott Jean. "Strasbourg: The Anabaptist City in the Sixteenth Century." *MQR* 58 (1984): 230-40.

Neuser, Wilhelm H. *Die reformatorische Wende bei Zwingli.* Neukirchen: Neukirchener Verlag, 1977.

Nicoladoni, Alexander. *Johannes Bünderlin von Linz und die oberösterreichischen Taufergemeinden in den Jahren 1525-1531.* Berlin: R. Gaertners Verlagsbuchhandlung, 1893.

Nienkirchen, Charles. "Reviewing the Case for a Non-Separatist Ecclesiology in Early Swiss Anabaptism." *MQR* 55 (1982): 227-41.

Norelli, Enrico. "The Authority Attributed to the Early Church in the *Centuries of Magdeburg* and the *Ecclesiastical Annals* of Caesar Baronius" in Backus, ed. *Reception of the Church Fathers in the West.* 2: 745-74.

Overfield, James. *Humanism and Scholasticism in Late Medieval Germany.* Princeton: Princeton University Press, 1984.

Oyer, John. "Anabaptism in Central Germany." *MQR* 34 (1960): 219-48; 35 (1961): 5-37.

Ozment, Steven. *Mysticism and Dissent: Religious Ideology and Social Protest in the Sixteenth Century.* New Haven and London: Yale University Press, 1973.

Ozment, Steven. "Sebastian Franck: Critic of the 'New Scholastics,'" in Goertz, ed. *Profiles of Radical Reformers.* 226-33.

Packull, Werner. "Denck's Alleged Baptism by Hubmaier: Its Significance for the Origin of South German-Austrian Anabaptism." *MQR* 47 (1973): 327-38.

Packull, Werner. "Gottfried Seebass on Hans Hut: A Discussion." *MQR* 49 (1975): 57-67.

Packull, Werner. *Mysticism and the Early South German-Austrian Anabaptist Movement 1525-1531.* Scottdale, PA and Kitchener, ON: Herald Press, 1977.

Packull, Werner O. "Hans Denck: Fugitive From Dogmatism" in Goertz, ed. *Profiles of Radical Reformers.* 62-71.

Packull, Werner. "Melchior Hoffman - A Recanted Anabaptist in Schwäbisch Hall?" *MQR* 57 (1983): 83-111.

Packull, Werner. "A Reinterpretation of Melchior Hoffman's *Exposition* Against the Background of Spiritualist Franciscan Eschatology with Special Reference to Peter John Olivi" in Horst, ed. *Dutch Dissenters*. 32-65.

Packull, Werner. "Pilgram Marpeck: *Uncovering of the Babylonian Whore* and Other Anonymous Anabaptist Tracts." *MQR* 67 (1993): 351-55.

Packull, Werner. *Hutterite Beginnings: Communitarian Experiments During the Reformation*. Baltimore and London: Johns Hopkins University Press, 1995.

Packull, Werner. "Weite Wege von Mähreu nach Hessen. Die zweite Missionsreise Peter Riedemanns" in Fischer and Kobelt-Groch, eds. *Aussenseiter zwischen Mittelalter und Neuzeit*. 171-85.

Packull, Werner O. and Dipple, Geoffrey L., eds. *Radical Reformation Studies: Essays Presented to James M. Stayer*. Aldershot: Ashgate, 1999.

Packull, Werner. "The Origins of Peter Riedemann's *Account of Our Faith*." *SCJ* 30 (1999): 61-69.

Packull, Werner O. "Preliminary Report on Pilgram Marpeck's Sponsorship of Anabaptist *Flugschriften*." *MQR* 75 (2001): 75-88.

Packull, Werner O. "A Hutterite Account of Who's Who Among Anabaptist Founders. Or How Well Informed Were the Anabaptist Hutterites about their Beginnings." Typescript.

Pater, Calvin. *Karlstadt as the Father of the Baptist Movements: The Emergence of Lay Protestantism*. Toronto: University of Toronto Press, 1984.

Peachey, Paul. "The Modern Recovery of the Anabaptist Vision" in Herschberger, ed. *Recovery of the Anabaptist Vision*. 327-40.

Peters, Frank. "The Ban in the Writings of Menno Simons." *MQR* 29 (1955): 16-33.

Petersen, Rodney L. *Preaching in the Last Days: The Theme of "Two Witnesses" in the Sixteenth and Seventeenth Centuries*. Oxford: Oxford University Press, 1993.

Peuckert, Will-Erich. *Sebastian Franck: Ein Deutscher Sucher*. Munich: R. Piper and Co., 1943.

Pipkin, H. Wayne. "The Baptismal Theology of Balthasar Hubmaier." *MQR* 65 (1991): 34-53.

Pipkin, H. Wayne, ed. *Essays in Anabaptist Theology*. Elkhart, IN: Institute of Mennonite Studies, 1994.

Preus, James. *Carlstadt's Ordinaciones and Luther's Liberty: A Study of the Wittenberg Movement 1521-22*. Cambridge, MA: Harvard University Press, 1974.

Quiring, Horst. "The Anthropology of Pilgram Marpeck." *MQR* 9 (1935): 155-64.

Radlkofer, Max. *Johann Eberlin von Günzburg und sein Vetter Hans Jakob Wehe von Leipheim*. Nördlingen: Verlag der C.H. Beck'schen Buchhandlung, 1887.

Raeder, Siegfried. "Thomas Müntzer als Bibelubersetzer" in Bräuer and Junghans. eds. *Der Theologe Thomas Müntzer*. 221-57.

Rau, Susanne. *Städtische Geschichtsschreibung und Erinnerungskultur im Zeitalter der Reformation und Konfessionalisierung in Bremen, Hamburg und Köln*. Hamburg and Munich: Dölling and Galitz Verlag, 2002.

Reid, Darrel. "Luther, Müntzer and the Last Days: Eschatological Hope, Apocalyptic Expectations." *MQR* 68 (1995): 53-74.

Rich, Arthur. *Die Anfänge der Theologie Huldrych Zwinglis*. Zurich, 1949.

Roehrich, Gustave Guillaume. *Essay on the Life, Writings and Doctrine of the Anabaptist Hans Denck*. Original Diss.: Strasbourg, 1853. Trans by Claude R. Foster, William F. Bogart, Mildred M. Van Sice. Lanham, MD: University Press of America, 1983.

Rogge, Joachim. "Müntzers und Luthers Verständnis von der Reformation der Kirche" in Demke, ed. *Thomas Müntzer*. 7-19.

Roth, John D. "Harmonizing the Scriptures: Swiss Brethren Understandings of the relationship between the Old and New Testament during the last half of the sixteenth century" in Packull and Dipple, eds. *Radical Reformation Studies*. 35-52.

Rothkegel, Martin. "Die Nikolsburger Reformation 1526-1535: Vom Humanismus zum Sabbatarismus." ThD diss., Charles University Prague, 2000.

Rothkegel, Martin. "Die Nikolsburger Reformation 1526-1535." *MGB* 59 (2002): 181-86.

Rupp, Gordon. *Patterns of Reformation*. Philadelphia: Fortress Press, 1969.

Schantz, Douglas. "The Ecclesiological Focus of Dirk Philip's Hermeneutical Thought in 1559: a Contextual Study" in Pipkin, ed. *Essays in Anabaptist Theology*. 197-209.

Scheible, Heinz. *Die Entstehung der Magdeburger Zenturien: Ein Beitrag zur Geschichte der historographischen Methode*. Gütersloh: Gütersloher Verlagshaus Gerd Mohn, 1966.

Schilling, Heinz. "Confessional Europe" in Brady, Oberman and Tracy, eds. *Handbook of European History*. 2:641-81.

Schlachta, Astrid von. *Hutterische Konfession und Tradition (1578-1619): Etabliertes Leben zwischen Ordnung und Ambivalenz*. Mainz: Verlag Philipp von Zabern, 2003.

Schmid, Hans Dieter. *Täufertum und Obrigkeit in Nürnberg*. Nürnberg: Stadtarchiv, 1972.

Schrag, Dale. "Erasmian and Grebelian Pacifism: Consistency or Contradiction?" *MQR* 62 (1988): 431-54.

Schulze, Manfred. "Martin Luther and the Church Fathers" in Backus, ed. *The Reception of the Church Fathers in the West*. 2: 573-626.

Schwarz, Richard. *Die apokalyptische Theologie Thomas Müntzers und der Taboriten*. Tübingen: JCB Mohr, 1977.

Scott, Tom. "The 'Volksreformation' of Thomas Müntzer in Allstedt and Mühlhausen," *JEH* 34 (1983): 194-213.

Scott, Tom. *Thomas Müntzer: Theology and Revolution in the German Reformation*. New York: St. Martin's Press, 1989.

Seebass, Gottfried. "Das Zeichen der Erwälten: Zum Verständnis der Taufe bei Hans Hut" in Goertz, ed. *Umstrittenes Täufertum*. 138-64.

Seebass, Gottfried. "Hans Hut: The Suffering Avenger" in Goertz, ed. *Profiles of Radical Reformers*. 54-61.

Séguenny, André. "Christian Entfelder" in André Séquenny and Jean Rot, eds. *Bibliotheca Dissidentium: Répertoire des nonconformistes religieux de siezième et dix-septième siècles*. Vol. 1. Baden-Baden: Éditions Valentin Koerner. 1980. 37-48

Sider, Ronald J. *Andreas Bodenstein von Karlstadt: The Development of His Thought 1517-1525*. Leiden: E.J. Brill, 1974.

Sider, Ronald J. "Andreas Bodenstein von Karlstadt: Between Liberal and Radical" in Goertz, ed. *Profiles of Radical Reformers*. 45-53.

Snyder, C. Arnold. *The Life and Thought of Michael Sattler*. Scottdale, PA and Kitchener, ON: Herald Press, 1984.

Snyder, C. Arnold. "The Influence of the Schleitheim Articles on the Anabaptist Movement: An Historical Evaluation." *MQR* 63 (1989): 323-44.

Snyder, C. Arnold. "Beyond Polygenesis: Recovering the Unity and Diversity of Anabaptist Theology" in Pipkin, ed. *Essays in Anabaptist Theology*. 1-33.

Snyder, C. Arnold. *Anabaptist History and Theology: An Introduction*. Kitchener, ON: Pandora Press, 1995.

Snyder, C. Arnold. "The 'Perfection of Christ' reconsidered: the later Swiss Brethren and the Sword" in Packull and Dipple, eds. *Radical Reformation Studies*. 53-69.

Snyder, C. Arnold. "The (Not-So) Simple Confession of the Later Swiss Brethren. Part I: Manuscripts and Marpeckites in an Age of Print." *MQR* 73 (1999): 677-722.

Snyder, C. Arnold. "The (Not-So) Simple Confession of the Later Swiss Brethren. Part II: The Evolution of Separatist Anabaptism." *MQR* 74 (2000): 87-122.

Spitz, Lewis. "Luther's View of History: A Theological Use of the Past" in John W. Klotz, ed. *Light of Our World: Essays Commemorating the 150th Anniversary of Concordia Seminary*. St. Louis: Concordia Seminary, 1989. 139-54. Reprint ed., Lewis Spitz, *The Reformation: Education and History*. Aldershot: Variorum, 1997. VI: 139-54.

Sprunger, Mary S. "The Golden Age: Prosperity and the Martyr Tradition." *Mennonite Life* 45 (1990): 28-31.

Stadtwald, Kurt. *Roman Popes and German Patriots: Antipapalism in the Politics of the German Humanist Movement From Gregor Heimburg to Martin Luther*. Geneva: Librarie Droz, 1996.

Stayer, James. "The Münsterite Rationalization of Bernhard Rothman." *Journal of the History of Ideas* 28 (1967): 179-92.

Stayer, James M. "Melchior Hoffman and the Sword." *MQR* 45 (1971): 265-77.

Stayer, James. "Die Anfänge des schweizerischen Täufertums im reformierten Kongregationalismus" in Goertz, ed. *Umstrittenes Täufertum*. 19-49.

Stayer, James M. Packull, Werner O. and Deppermann, Klaus. "From Monogenesis to Polygenesis: The Historical Discussion of Anabaptist Origins." *MQR* 49 (1975): 83-121.

Stayer, James. *Anabaptists and the Sword*. 2nd ed. Lawrence, KS: Coronodo Press, 1976.

Stayer, James. "Reublin and Brötli, the Revolutionary Beginnings of Swiss Anabaptism" in Marc Lienhard, ed. *The Origins and Characteristics of Anabaptism*. The Hague: Martinus Nijhoff, 1977. 83-102.

Stayer, James M. "The Anabaptists" in Steven Ozment, ed. *Reformation Europe: A Guide to Research*. St. Louis: Center for Reformation Research, 1982. 135-59.

Stayer, James. "Wilhelm Reublin: A Picaresque Journey Through Early Anabaptism" in Goertz, ed. *Profiles of Radical Reformers*. 107-17.

Stayer, James. "Zwingli and the 'viri multi et excellentes': The Christian Renaissance's Repudiation of the *Neoterici* and the Beginnings of Reformed Protestantism" in E.J. Furcha and H.Wayne Pipkin, eds. *Prophet, Pastor, Protestant: The Work of Huldrych Zwingli after Five Hundred Years*. Allison Park, PA: Pickwick Publications, 1984. 137-54.

Stayer, James. "Davidite vs. Mennonite" in Horst, ed. *The Dutch Dissenters*. 143-59.

Stayer, James. "Was There a Klettgau Letter of 1530?" *MQR* 61 (1987): 75-76.

Stayer, James. "Christianity in One City: Anabaptist Münster, 1534-35" in Hillerbrand, ed. *Radical Tendencies in the Reformation*. 117-34.

Stayer, James. "Thomas Müntzer in 1989: A Review Article." *SCJ* 21 (1990): 655-70.

Stayer, James. *The German Peasants' War and Anabaptist Community of Goods*. Kingston and Montreal: McGill-Queen's University Press, 1991.

Stayer, James. "Saxon Radicalism and Swiss Anabaptism: The Return of the Repressed." *MQR* 67 (1993): 5-30.

Stayer, James M. "Sächsischer Radikalismus und Schweizer Täufertum: Die Wiederkehr des Verdrängten" in Günter Vogler, ed. *Wegscheiden der Reformation: Alternatives Denken vom 16. bis zum 18. Jahrhundert*. Weimar: Verlag Hermann Böhlaus Nachfolger, 1994. 151-78.

Stayer, James. "Reeling History Backwards: The Anabaptists as a Key to Understanding Thomas Müntzer More Conservatively." Meiji University International Exchange Programs Guest Lecture Series, No. 9, 1995. Center for International Programs, Meiji University, 1996.

Stayer, James M. "Review Essay: Anabaptist History and Theology." *MQR* 70 (1996): 473-82.

Stayer, James M. "Theologians of Revolution in the Peasants' War? The Cases of Balthasar Hubmaier and Thomas Müntzer." Typescript.

Stayer, James. "The Radical Reformation" in Brady, Oberman, Tracy, eds. *Handbook of European History*. 2: 249-82.

Stayer, James. "The Passing of the Radical Moment in the Radical Reformation." *MQR* 71 (1997): 147-52.

Stayer, James. "'Luther und die Schwärmer.' Karl Holl und das abenteuerliche Leben eines Textes" in Fischer and Kobelt-Groch, eds. *Aussenseiter zwischen Mittelalter und Neuzeit*. 269-88.

Stayer, James. "Unsichere Geschichte: Der Fall Münster (1534/35). Aktuelle Probleme der Forschung." *MGBl* 59 (2002): 63-78.

Steinmetz, David. *Reformers in the Wings*. Philadelphia: Fortress Press, 1971.

Strauss, Gerald. "The Course of German History: The Lutheran Interpretation" in *Enacting the Reformation in Germany: Essays on Institution and Reception*. Aldershot: Variorum, 1993. I: 665-86.

Strübind, Andrea. *Eifriger als Zwingli: Die frühe Täuferbewegung in der Schweiz*. Berlin: Duncker and Humblot, 2003.

Struder, Gerald C. "A History of *The Martyrs' Mirror*." *MQR* 22 (1948): 163-79.

Stupperich, Robert. "Sebastian Franck und das münsterische Täufertum" in Rudolf Vierhaus and Manfred Botzenhart, eds. *Dauer und Wandel der Geschichte. Festgabe für Kurt von Raumer zum 15 Dezember 1965*. Münster: Verlag Aschendorff, 1966. 144-62.

Swartzentruber, A. Orley. "The Piety and Theology of the Anabaptist Martyrs in Van Braght's *Martyrs' Mirror*." *MQR* 28 (1954): 5-26, 128-42.

Teufel, Eberhard. *"Landräumig." Sebastian Franck, ein Wanderer an Donau, Rhein und Neckar*. Neustadt an der Aisch: Verlag Degener and Co., 1954.

Toews, John. "Sebastian Franck: Friend and Critic of Early Anabaptism." PhD Diss., University of Minnesota, 1964.

Troeltsch, Ernst. *The Social Teachings of the Christian Churches*. 2 vols. Olive Wyon, trans. London: George Allen and Unwin, 1931.

Ullmann, Wolfgang. "Das Geschichtsverständnis Thomas Müntzers" in Demke, ed., *Thomas Müntzer-Anfragen an Theologie und Kirche*. 45-63.

Veen, Mirjam G.K. van. "Spiritualism in the Netherlands: From David Joris to Dirck Volckertsz Coornheert." *SCJ* 33 (2002): 129-50.

Verduin, Leonard. *The Reformers and Their Stepchildren*. Grand Rapids: Eerdmans, 1964.

Verheus, S.L. *Zeugnis und Gericht: Kirchengeschichtliche Betrachtungen bei Sebastian Franck und Matthias Flacius*. Nieuwkoop: B. De Graf, 1971.

Vice, Roy L. "Ehrenfried Kumpf, Karlstadt's Patron and Peasants' War Rebel." *ARG* 86 (1995): 153-74.

Vice, Roy L. "Valentin Ickelsamer's Odyssey from Rebellion to Quietism." *MQR* 69 (1995): 75-92.

Vogler, Günter. "The Anabaptist Kingdom of Münster in the Tension Between Anabaptism and the Imperial Policy" in Hillerbrand, ed. *Radical Tendencies in the Reformation*. 99-116.

Vogler, Günter. *Thomas Müntzer*. Berlin: Dietz Verlag, 1989.

Voogt, Gerrit. *Constraint on Trial: Dirck Volckertsz Coornheert and Religious Freedom*. Kirksville, MO: Truman State University Press, 2000.

Voolstra, Sjouke. "Themes in the Early Theology of Menno Simons" in Brunk, ed. *Menno Simons: A Reappraisal*. 37-55.

Vos, K. *Menno Simons, 1496-1561: Zijn Leven en Werken en Zijne Reformatorische Denkbeelden.* Leiden: E.J. Brill, 1914.

Waite, Gary K. *David Joris and Dutch Anabaptism 1524-1543.* Waterloo, ON: Wilfred Laurier University Press, 1990.

Weaver, J. Denny. "Discipleship Redefined: Four Sixteenth-Century Anabaptists." *MQR* 54 (1980): 255-79.

Weigelt, Horst. *Sebastian Franck und die lutherisches Reformation.* Gütersloh: Gerd Mohn, 1972.

Weigelt, Horst. "Caspar von Schwenkfeld: Proclaimer of the Middle Way" in Goertz, ed. *Profiles of Radical Reformers.* 214-25.

Weigelt, Horst. "Sebastian Franck und die lutherische Reformation. Die Reformation im Spiegel des Werkes Sebastian Francks," in Müller, ed. *Sebastian Franck.* 39-53.

Weis, Frederick Lewis. *The Life, Teachings and Works of Johannes Denck.* Pawtucket, RI, 1925.

Weis, Frederick Lewis. *The Life, Teachings and Work of Ludwig Hetzer 1500-1529.* Dorchester, MA: Underhill Press, 1930.

Wenger, John C. "The Theology of Pilgram Marpeck." *MQR* 12 (1938): 205-56.

Wenger, J.C. Trans. and ed. "A Letter from Wilhelm Reublin to Pilgram Marpeck, 1531." *MQR* 23 (1949): 67-75.

Williams, George H. *The Radical Reformation.* 1st ed. Philadelphia: Westminster Press, 1962.

Williams, George H. *The Radical Reformation.* 3rd ed. Kirksville, MO: Sixteenth Century Journal Publishers, 1992.

Williams, Glanmore. *Reformation Views of Church History.* Richmond, VA: John Knox Press, 1970.

Windhorst, Christof. *Täuferisches Taufverständnis: Balthasar Hubmaiers Lehre zwischen traditioneller und reformatorischer Theologie.* Leiden: E.J. Brill, 1976.

Windhorst, Christof. "Balthasar Hubmaier: Professor, Preacher, Politician" in Goertz, ed. *Profiles of Radical Reformers.* 144-57.

Wiswedel, W. "Oswald Glaidt von Jamnitz." *ZKG* 55 (1937): 550-64.

Wiswedel, Wilhelm. "Gabriel Ascherham und die nach ihm benannte Bewegung." *ARG* 34 (1937): 1-35, 235-62.

Wiswedel, Wilhelm and Friedmann, Robert. "The Anabaptists Answer Melanchthon." *MQR* 29 (1955): 212-31.

Wolgast, Eike. "Herrschaftsorganization und Herrschaftskrisen im Täuferreich von Münster 1534/35." *ARG* 67 (1976): 179-202.

Wolgast, Eike. "Die Obrigkeits - und Widerstandslehre Thomas Müntzers" in Bräuer and Junghans, eds. *Der Theologe Thomas Müntzer.* 195-22.

Wollgast, Siegfried. *Der deutsche Pantheismus im 16. Jahrhundert. Sebastian Franck und seine Wirkungen auf die Entwicklung der pantheistischen Philosophie in Deutschland.* Berlin: VEB, 1972.

Wollgast, Siegfried. "Zu Sebastian Francks philosophischen Auffassungen." *Daphnis: Zeitschrift für Mittlere Deutsche Literatur* 25 (2-3) (1996): 221-305.

Wray, Frank J. "History in the Eyes of the Sixteenth-Century Anabaptists." PhD diss, Yale University, 1954.

Wray, Frank J. "The Anabaptist Doctrine of the Restitution of the Church." *MQR* 28 (1954): 186-96.

Wray, Frank J. "The 'Vermanung' of 1542 and Rothmann's 'Bekenntnis.'" *ARG* 47 (1956): 243-51.

Wray, Frank J. "Bernhard Rothmann's Views on the Early Church" in Franklin H. Littell, ed. *Reformation Studies.* Richmond, 1962. 229-38.

Wulkau, Curt. "Das kirchliche Idea des Johann Eberlin von Günzburg." Ph.D. diss, Halle-Wittenberg, 1922.

Yoder, Jesse. "A Critical Study of the Debate between the Reformed and the Anabaptists, Held at Frankenthal, Germany in 1571." Ph.D. diss, Northwestern University, 1962.

Yoder, Jesse. "The Frankenthal Debate with the Anabaptists in 1571: Procedure, Participants." *MQR* 36 (1962): 14-35.

Yoder, Jesse. "The Frankenthal Disputation: Part II." *MQR* 36 (1962): 116-46.

Yoder, John Howard. "Balthasar Hubmaier and the Beginnings of Swiss Anabaptism." *MQR* 33 (1959): 5-17.

Yoder, John Howard. "The Hermeneutics of the Anabaptists." *MQR* 41 (1967): 291-308.

Yoder, John Howard. "Anabaptism and History: Restitution and the Possibility of Renewal" in Goertz, ed. *Umstrittenes Täufertum.* 244-58.

Yoder, John Howard. *Anabaptism and Reformation in Switzerland: An Historical and Theological Analysis of the Dialogues Between Anabaptists and Reformers.* David Karl Stassen and C. Arnold Snyder trans. C. Arnold Snyder ed. Kitchener, ON: Pandora Press, 2004.

Zeeden, Ernst Walter. *Die Entstehung der Konfessionen: Grundlagen und Formen der Konfessionsbildung im Zeitalter der Glaubenskämpfe.* Munich and Vienna: R. Oldenbourg, 1965.

Zeman, Jarold K. *The Anabaptists and the Czech Brethren in Moravia 1526-1628: A Study of Origins and Contacts.* The Hague and Paris: Mouton, 1969.

Zijlstra, Samme. "Menno Simons and David Joris." *MQR* 62 (1988): 249-56.

Zijlstra, S. *Om de Ware Gemeente en de Oude Gronden: Geschiedenis van de Dopersen in de Nederlanden 1531-1675.* Hilversum and Leevwarden: Uitgeverij Verloren and Fryske Akademy, 2000.

Zijlstra, Samme. "Anabaptists, Spiritualists and the Reformed Church in East Frisia." *MQR* 75 (2001): 57-73.

Zimmermann, Wilhelm. *Der große deutsche Bauernkrieg.* Berlin: Dietz Verlag, 1953.

Zorzin, Alejandro. "Karlstadts 'Dialogus vom Tauff der Kinder' in einem anonymen Wormser Druck aus dem Jahr 1527: Ein Beitrag zur Karlstadt Bibliographie." *ARG* 79 (1988): 27-58.

Zorzin, Alejandro. *Karlstadt als Flugschriftenautor.* Göttingen: Vandenhoeck and Ruprecht, 1990.

INDEX

A

B

C

D

E

F

G

H

I

J

K

L

M

N

O

P

Q

R

S

T

U

V

W

Y

Z